Best Compliments

A TALE OF TWO REVOLTS

Best wishes

A TALE OF TWO REVOLTS

INDIA'S MUTINY AND
THE AMERICAN CIVIL WAR

Rajmohan Gandhi

HAUS
LONDON

First published in Great Britain in 2011 by

HAUS PUBLISHING Ltd
70 Cadogan Place, London SW1X 9AH

First published in India in
Viking by Penguin Books India 2009

Copyright © Rajmohan Gandhi 2009, 2011

Typeset in Sabon by SÜRYA, New Delhi

Printed in Great Britain by CPI Antony Rowe
Chippenham and Eastbourne

ISBN 978 1 906598 85 3

A CIP catalogue record for this book is available from the British Library

Photographs 1, 2, 3, 5, 8, 9, 10, 11, 12 and 13 courtesy
Nehru Memorial Museum and Library, New Delhi

Visit our website
www.hauspublishing.com

To dearest Ramu
(1937–2007)

CONTENTS

PREFACE

As new novels, histories, films, commemorations and fresh archival digs testify, the two revolts featured in this book continue to command lay and scholarly interest a century and a half after they were enacted on opposite ends of our world. In a passing remark in *Revenge & Reconciliation*, my 1999 study of two strands in Indian history, I expressed surprise that nobody had taken a joint view of 'two events that took place on opposite sides of the globe at virtually the same time—the American Civil War . . . and the Indian Rebellion'.

Since no one else took the hint, I decided to do it myself. The result is a story of two revolts, three countries (India, America and England), one century (the nineteenth), and one epoch (the Victorian, although Abraham Lincoln shines uniquely in it). The cast of characters is large and includes several who became famous in varying degrees; others who I hope will stay at least in some memories; and a few who were giants in intellect or spirit, or both.

Two dramas were being enacted, at about the same time, on two far-apart stages. Were the characters in one aware of the other drama? Were they interested in the other drama? Were they influenced by it? Did they comment on it? Looking at the other drama, did they cheer one set of actors as against another set? And if they did, why? Were there common features in the two?

I wanted to bring both dramas to one stage. The two casts did not have to merge with one another, but they could follow one another in sequential acts and scenes. And perhaps for a scene or two, both casts could be on stage together. In short, while others continued their digging into the history of 1857 in India or of the

American Civil War for a new archaeology, I realized I could offer a new choreography.

The two insurrections were independent and separate events. Yet, I nursed a curiosity about the information Americans had or did not have on the 1857 Revolt and its suppression, and about the interest they took in it. Likewise, I was keen to know what leading Indians of the time heard about the American Civil War, and what they thought about it. I also had the desire to see how India's future was shaped by the two events, even though one of them occurred very far from our shores. I decided to investigate this by following the lives of five inhabitants of India who were young (at least relatively) when the rebellion and the Civil War occurred, and who went on to influence India during and after their lifetime—Sayyid Ahmed Khan, Ishwarchandra Vidyasagar, Jotiba Phule, Allan Octavian Hume, and Bankimchandra Chatterjee, listed here in the order of their birth.

Apart from anything else, therefore, this book examines how these five reacted to the two revolts and looks also, if only briefly, at the rest of their lives. I do not claim that these five 'represent' their times in a truer way than others. But they are all fascinating characters and each of them wrestled with a changing order. Yet, retaining a focus on these five was not so easy, for they competed with scores of other interesting characters who showed up. However, these five emerge as people forming a bridge towards our times.

Actually, there are two bridges (as well as two revolts) in this book. One joins 'then' with 'now'; the other joins 'here' with 'there'. One links nineteenth-century India with India today, the other links the India of the 1850s–60s with the America of that time. Connecting America 'then' with today's America, or a similar exercise with respect to Britain, was beyond my scope.

I was clear on the entry point for my tale—William Howard Russell of *The Times* of London, who witnessed both conflicts, as well as some earlier and later ones. Though the title was not used in his reports from the front lines, Russell was perhaps the world's first 'war correspondent'. As far as I know, Russell did not actually meet any of the five Indians I have listed—though Vidyasagar (thirty-eight years old at the time) and Bankim (then twenty) were undoubtedly in Calcutta when Russell arrived there to cover the rebellion. Likewise, a forty-one-year-old Sayyid Ahmed was very much in the neighbourhood when Russell went to Rohilkhand and Delhi to witness the end of the rising. Allan Octavian Hume, directly involved in coping with the rebellion, and later a founder of the Indian National Congress, was a twenty-nine-year-old district officer in Etawah in 1858 when, in nearby Kanpur, Russell tried to ascertain the truth in the reports of atrocities in that city by the rebellion's leaders.

As for Jotiba Phule, he was an active forty-nine-year-old in Pune, when in 1875–76, a decade after the end of the American Civil War, Russell again journeyed to India and visited the Marathi country, this time accompanying the Prince of Wales. Thus a thread that weaves the different stories of this book together is the life, or perhaps I should say the voice, of a travelling Irish newspaperman. But there are other threads too.

As I read for this project, hoping that Russell would help unify its themes, it became obvious that I had to broaden its scope. For, on reaching the year 1854 on my journey (along with Russell) to the 1857 rebellion, I ran into a twenty-eight-year-old Russian officer, Leo Tolstoy, then fighting and also critiquing the 1854 Crimean War even as Russell (eight years older than Tolstoy) was reporting that war from the opposite (British) side. Could I leave out of my inquiry the Russian novelist and sage who later impacted not only the world but India in particular with his sharp views on violence and war?

I also had to ask whether I could merely brush past Karl Marx (two years older than Russell), whose analysis of the then ongoing 1857 rebellion, written week by week in London and published in the *New York Tribune*, offered almost the only challenge to the uniform American summing-up of the rebellion as an eruption of oriental barbarism? At the present time, a larger number of believing Marxists live in India than perhaps in any other country, but even if this were not the case, Marx's scrutiny of 1857 and of British imperialism demanded a place in this study. So both Tolstoy and Marx are part of this tale.

No one can compress, in any 'fair' or 'representative' manner, a century into a volume or even a series of volumes; and no two persons will select the same 'representatives'. I did not attempt to locate 'true' representatives, Indian or non-Indian, of the nineteenth century. But on the path towards understanding aspects of the two revolts, I bumped into remarkable Indian and non-Indian inhabitants of that century and could not resist an urge to interrogate them.

Today we do not study a country in isolation. Our understanding, we know, remains limited and even becomes misleading if another country is not brought in for a comparison. What is true of the present may also be true of the past. Our understanding of the 1857 Revolt can only be enhanced and clarified by a study of the American Civil War. The opposite is also true and studying the two together may enable us to recognize the global spirit of the times when they occurred.

Also, the rapidly growing USA-India relationship of our day can do with an awareness of older connections, which are likely to interest the increasing number of Indians studying, working, or living in the USA, as well as Americans involved today with India. Then there are those, an expanding number, who through parents or grandparents are linked to both America and India. Being Indian as well as American by culture and blood, they should know the histories of both lands. For them, this book may serve as an introduction.

I must thank Zack Poppel, graduate student of history at the University of Illinois at Urbana-Champaign, for the valuable research assistance that he provided, which was made possible by the Arnold O. Beckman Award obtained by me at the university. I thank the university for this award, for the amazing range of material in its libraries, and for its stimulating atmosphere.

Five American scholars—I will name them in alphabetical order— have been of particular help with this project. Dr Bryon Andreasen, research historian at the Abraham Lincoln Presidential Library and Museum in Springfield, Illinois, was generous with his time in unearthing information about India in 1857–58, a time when Lincoln lived in Springfield. Professor Orville Vernon Burton of the University of Illinois helped greatly through his landmark work, *The Age of Lincoln*, published in 2008. Also of the University of Illinois, Professor James Hurt almost magically produced for me the essay about Lincoln and India written in

1927 by the poet Vachel Lindsay. And professors Fred Jaher and Blair Kling (again from the University of Illinois) took the trouble of reading the entire manuscript and made extremely useful suggestions. Professor Kling's 1977 work, *The Blue Mutiny*, and his ideas on a common background for the two revolts have been of real help to me. For these contributions, and for their encouragement of this book, I offer all five my best thanks. I am grateful too to Dr Rini Bhattacharya Mehta, also of the University of Illinois, for her helpful perspectives on nineteenth-century Bengal, and to Justice P.B. Sawant, former chairman of the Press Council of India, for the material he lent me on nineteenth-century Maharashtra.

I should also thank the libraries I worked in or borrowed from and their helpful personnel. This study would have been impossible without the remarkable South Asia collections of the University of Illinois Library, and I have benefited also from Kolkata's Asiatic Society, National Library and the Raj Bhavan library.

Others will judge whether the perspective of this volume is fresh or useful. Its stories are in any case irresistible, which is the chief reason for retelling them. I hope they have not suffered undue damage while passing through my hands.

May 2009   RAJMOHAN GANDHI

CHAPTER 1

BRITANNIA RULES
THE WAVES

INDIA, ENGLAND AND AMERICA, 1850–57

Tell the India-England-America story any which way, the Irish will get into it, which may be no bad thing. We will start *this* India-England-America story in England in the year 1850, when William Howard Russell, an Irishman uncertain about his Catholicism, but instinctively sympathetic towards the underdog, was a talented thirty-year-old reporter with *The Times* of London, covering (among other things) parliamentary speeches from the Press Gallery. The Press Gallery was where some years earlier Charles Dickens (1812–70) too had sat, taking down shorthand notes. Samuel Johnson had also apprenticed in this gallery in the previous century. In 1832, Dickens (with whom Russell would form a friendship) had observed the passage of the Reform Act, which did away with some but not all of the 'rotten' parliamentary seats bought for cash; the Act also extended voting rights, enabling one out of five British men (but no woman) to vote.

At the same time, in 1850, another man with Irish connections, Henry John Temple, better known as Lord Palmerston, was the sixty-six-year-old foreign minister ('foreign secretary', to use the official designation) of the United Kingdom. A hereditary owner of lands in Ireland, and also in England, Palmerston was a passionately patriotic Englishman. One of his British biographers admiringly described him as 'the living embodiment of John Bull, the man who would truckle to no foreigner, who believed his own countrymen to be the salt of the earth, who would "stand no nonsense"'.[1]

Kind in his own mind to Irish peasants, but viewed differently by them, Palmerston had been a UK minister off and on from 1809 onwards; yet in 1850 he was on the verge of losing his position. Many members of Parliament were upset that Palmerston had threatened Greece with warships merely because Athens had not responded promptly to the demands of a British citizen called Don Pacifico, who did not enjoy a high reputation in any case. Confronted by a motion of censure, Palmerston stood up in the House of Commons on 25 June 1850 and fought for his political life. He ended with these words:

> As the Roman, in days of old, held himself free from indignity when he could say, 'Civis Romanus Sum' ('I am a Roman citizen'), so also a British subject in whatever land he may be, shall feel confident that the watchful eye and the strong arm of England will protect him against injustice and wrong.[2]

We learn that 'Palmerston resumed his seat amidst loud and prolonged cheering' by the MPs.[3] Their minds changed, Palmerston survived. He went on to become Prime Minister, not once but twice. He was the Prime Minister when 1857 occurred in India, and again, at the age of seventy-seven, when the American Civil War occurred. Both conflicts would be covered for The Times by William Howard Russell.

'What is the purpose,' Palmerston had asked in that 1850 speech, 'for which in time of peace we keep ships of war in foreign stations?'[4] The 'gunboat diplomacy' that Palmerston practised is a phrase that remains in use in the twenty-first century. Another oft-quoted aphorism of international politics is also from Palmerston: 'Nations have no permanent friends or allies, they only have permanent interests.'

In 1850, England appeared to be the world's foremost political and economic power. France seemed unable to recover from Napoleon's defeats (1814–15). Germany and Italy were yet to emerge as unified nations, while Austria and Russia were finding it difficult to control their subjects, and the Turkish empire was in decline. Continental Europe had been ravaged by recent wars, but not England, which, however, had fought a war with America on the latter's soil. That 1812–15 war had ended in a draw, yet England had preserved its hegemony over Canada and inflicted damage on the USA, even though American independence was reiterated by the war. Later, in 1826, Australia was formally claimed by the UK. In the 1840s, after crushing the Sikhs (the last of their Indian opponents), the British had added all of the Punjab, the Northwest Frontier, and Sindh to their Indian conquests.

By 1850, therefore, the entire Indian subcontinent belonged to the British, apart from territories acquired in Africa, the Middle East, and the Caribbean. England had reached 'the peak of her power, prestige and wealth'.[5] The British people were more than pleased with a leader like Palmerston, whose 'gamesome mien and cocksure expression were endearingly familiar to them' from cartoons.[6] (Newspapers did not as yet print photographs.) Palmerston's jocose personality, robust good health, and ability to gallop on a horse for many miles (automobiles would appear only four decades later) seemed just the characteristics that a John Bull should have. They fitted one leading a nation that enjoyed leading the world. The British people also loved their Queen Victoria, who (like the Irish journalist Russell) was thirty years old in 1850. When she became queen, she had been only seventeen.

In 1851, six million people, about a third of the British population, visited the Great Exhibition in a new imposing structure called the Crystal Palace in London's Hyde Park. Here they saw a triumphant display of British arms, manufactures and global influence. The force behind the exhibition was Prince Albert, Victoria's German-born consort. Albert and the five-foot-high queen did not like the tall Palmerston. It seems, in fact, that no British sovereign ever 'regarded a minister of the Crown with more intense dislike than Victoria did Lord Palmerston at the summit of his career as Foreign Secretary'.[7] Palmerston's style was deemed undignified by Victoria and Albert, who also disapproved of the foreign secretary's policies in Europe. While the royal couple welcomed the effort to unify Europe's Germans (an endeavour destined to attain success in 1871), Palmerston opposed it.

The British people loved Victoria but shared Palmerston's outlook, which no doubt is why 'for more than fifty years [he] was a minister of the Crown, for ten Prime Minister, [and] for sixteen Foreign Secretary'.[8]

~

William Howard Russell did not have any advantages of birth, but he possessed what before long would be called 'Victorian virtues'— the ability for concentrated hard work, dedication to the job at hand, respect for the truth, and moral courage, all of which added up to 'self-help'. Yet, he differed remarkably from his contemporaries in two ways. One, though he would see lots of it, Russell did not like war. Two, he viewed the imperialist expansion of Britain in the nineteenth century not as proof of superiority (whether of race or religion), but as an expression of greed and arrogance. Russell derived this perspective from his Irish roots, but also from an awareness from his knowledge of history that empires that rise also fall.

When, after an education at Dublin's Trinity College, Russell joined *The Times* in 1841, he was only twenty-one. The editor, John Thadeus Delane, who joined the paper in the same year after an Oxford education, was twenty-three. Russell's biographer, Alan Hankinson, calls Delane, who remained editor for thirty-six years, '. . . arguably the best editor any British newspaper has ever had— quick in apprehension, generally sound in judgment, the centre of a network of highly-placed informants, shrewd in choosing men and adept in handling them, totally dedicated to the paper'.[9]

The paper was owned by John Walter, but the editor had to manage its finances as well, which in the 1840s were in a precarious state. Yet, because of fearless reporting, *The Times* was known as 'The Thunderer' and had the largest circulation and the greatest prestige in the UK—indeed in the world.

Russell was required to bring news to *The Times* before other newspapers or the government could get it. In addition to Parliament, Russell covered Irish events (including a potato famine) and other occurrences. With his ability to quickly write up enormously long, detailed and yet lively accounts of trials and other happenings, including the 1851 opening of the Crystal

Palace, Russell satisfied Delane and Walter at *The Times* and enthralled its readers. He had also joined one of London's famous colleges of law, the Middle Temple, and was called to the Bar in 1850. By this time he was married and his wife Mary had given birth to two children. In religion, Russell 'settled down to a tolerant Anglicanism, going to church if not too inconvenient, presided over morning family prayers, and felt slightly guilty while playing cards on the Sabbath.'

'A loving if largely absentee husband,' he was convivial and had a fund of stories plus a ready wit. Willing to offer a song in a pleasing baritone voice, he was capable also of drinking to excess. Along with a bias for the underdog, Russell harboured (like some other Irish) an interest in aristocracy and celebrity. Hankinson calls Russell 'a Conservative open to new liberal ideas, grateful for the hierarchical society that provided order' and 'even more grateful' for living in 'a land where ideas could be freely exchanged'.[10]

People with whom he exchanged ideas and friendship (in places in London like the Garrick Club and the Fielding Club) included Dickens and another literary lion, William Makepeace Thackeray (1811–63). Max Müller (1823–1900), the German Sanskritist and one of the earliest scholars of eastern religions, was also among Russell's good friends. Russell had run into Müller on a ship from France to England in 1846—the German was travelling to study in the library of the East India Company. (Launched in 1600, the East India Company had governed India on behalf of the Crown from 1773.) Müller, who soon established himself in Oxford, became Russell's friend for life. The Irishman's ties with Dickens and Thackeray would also last till their deaths.

Karl Marx, 1818–83. Another German who moved to London at about this time was Karl Marx. There is no suggestion that Russell met him there, but since we will encounter Marx later on, let us take in some facts about him.

Though descending from a line of rabbis, Marx's father had become a Lutheran Christian in order to be allowed to practise law. Karl Marx was born in 1818 in the town of Trier and was educated in Bonn and Berlin. At the age of seventeen, he penned lines (in Latin originally) that suggested a religious faith as well as a wish to make a mark on the world:

> If [a man] works only for himself, he may perhaps become a famous man of learning, a great sage, an excellent poet, but he can never be a perfect, truly great man.
>
> History calls those men the greatest who have ennobled themselves by working for the common good . . . religion itself teaches us that the ideal being whom all strive to copy sacrificed himself for the sake of mankind . . . and who would dare to set at nought such judgments?
>
> If . . . we can most of all work for mankind, no burdens can bow us down, because they are sacrifices for the benefit of all; then we shall experience no petty, limited, selfish joy, but our happiness will belong to millions . . . and over our ashes will be shed the hot tears of noble people.[11]

For unknown reasons, the young author of these striking words seems to have acted callously towards his siblings and parents. But literature interested him (Shakespeare in particular). He also wrote, and thought, and was captured by the idea that progress comes from clash. By the late 1830s, a twenty-year-old Marx had become a radical writer, poet and activist. Though he earned a Berlin doctorate in 1841, opposition to his activities forced him to move from place to place in Europe. In Paris, in 1844, he established a lifelong friendship and collaboration with another German with similar views, but in possession, unlike Marx, of some funds—Friedrich Engels. By this time, Marx was married— despite opposition by the bride's family—to Jenny von Westphalen, the beautiful daughter of a Prussian baron.

Marx, who at seventeen had written of the positive influence of religious faith, said when he was twenty-five that it was an empty 'sigh of the oppressed creature'. Though religion seemed to give 'a heart' to 'a heartless world', its promises were illusory. It was no more than an 'opium of the people', he wrote in 1843.[12] In 1845, after Marx had defended (in a radical German paper published in Paris) an attempt to assassinate Frederick Wilhelm IV, the King of Prussia, he was ordered to leave Paris. Based now in Brussels, Marx collaborated with Engels to produce, in 1848, *The Communist Manifesto*, which declared in its opening sentence, 'A spectre is haunting Europe, the spectre of Communism,' and a few sentences later, 'The history of all hitherto existing society is the history of class struggles.'

That year Marx was back in Paris to witness an insurrection, which, however, was crushed. Forced to move out again, Marx first went to Cologne, where a radical newspaper started by him was suppressed, and then, via Paris, to London. Arriving in London in May 1849, Marx lived and wrote there for the rest of his life, supported by the Manchester-based Engels, and was largely ignored by the British police.

~

If Russell did not meet Marx in London, there is no indication either that he met two well-known Indian visitors to England in the 1830s and 1840s—the reformer, educator and polymath, Rammohan Roy (1772–1833) and the entrepreneur, Dwarkanath Tagore (1794–1846), better known later as the grandfather of Rabindranath Tagore.

India's titular Mughal king, Akbar Shah II, had paid for Roy's 1831 journey to England and given him the title of 'Raja' (prince). Two years later, after Roy had met royalty and other eminent British, and, among other things, pleaded for an increase in the pension that Akbar Shah II was receiving from the British, the visitor from India—widely accepted as a founder of modern Indian thought—died in Bristol. Tagore, who visited England twice on business in the 1840s, was received by Victoria herself.

INDIA IN 1850

He was a man of unsurpassed vigour. He bowed to no one, nor could he tolerate any form of disrespect or abuse. He always did as he saw fit; it was entirely unlike him to follow someone else's whim. . . . He firmly believed that it was better to die than become the servant of another. He was completely free of desire and as such, never had to bow to anyone.[13]

This description of his paternal grandfather by the Bengali educator/ reformer Ishwarchandra Vidyasagar (1820–91) identified values that Vidyasagar thought were paramount. These were also traits that observers would perceive in Vidyasagar. Thirty years old in

1850 (and therefore of the same age as Russell and Victoria), Vidyasagar was 'a short, dark-skinned person with deep-set eyes, firm lips and a high forehead'.[14] Born into a poor family of Brahmin pandits in a village called Birsimha (or Birsingha), more than 40 miles west of Calcutta, he rose to become professor of literature at Calcutta's Sanskrit College in December 1850. The British had opened the College in 1826 to equip young Hindus with traditional as well as modern knowledge in the belief that its students would go on to educate their country. The College was also where Vidyasagar himself had studied for twelve years. In January 1851, he became its principal.

Apart from a few Vaidyas (today seen as high-caste Hindus, but then termed Shudras), only Brahmins could attend the Sanskrit College. All its students and teachers were male. A similar institution for Muslim scholarship, the Calcutta Madrassah, had been started much earlier, in 1781, within a few years of British rule over Bengal. Thanks to voluntary rather than official efforts, Calcutta's Hindu College, forerunner of today's Presidency College, opened in 1817. Despite its name, it was more 'secular' and 'modern' than the Sanskrit College. In its founding, a role was played by Rammohan Roy, the man who later died in Bristol in 1833.

Vidyasagar and the novelist/magistrate Bankimchandra Chatterjee (1838–94) were two of Roy's intellectual successors, but, as we shall see, not quite his followers. In 1850, Bankim was only a twelve-year-old student in the English school of a Mr Tidd in the town of Midnapore in Bengal, where Bankim's father was posted as a deputy collector, then a high office for an Indian. A Bengali Brahmin like Vidyasagar (and Roy), Bankim had been married the previous year, at the age of eleven, to Mohini Devi, who was five years old. Marriage around that age was the norm; consummation occurred later. A brilliant student, Bankim had already won a major school prize by the time he was twelve, and in two years his poems would start appearing in a journal.

As with Bankim, Vidyasagar's precocity too had been noticed early in his village school. As a result, at the age of eight he was made to walk with his father the forty-plus miles to Calcutta, where he was expected to find his fortune. The final 19 miles on this three-day journey were paved with macadam. As the boy

Vidyasagar walked this stretch, he learnt Roman numerals from the milestones the British had laid.

With its bustle and its abundance of English merchants, and despite the squalor of North Town, where the natives crowded themselves, Calcutta promised future richness. However, protective of his Brahmin heritage, Vidyasagar's father would not send his boy to an English school in Calcutta. On the other hand, a *Sanskrit* College, even if British-run, seemed safe. For twelve years, the boy lived in difficult and insanitary conditions in Calcutta, cooking for himself and studying at the Sanskrit College.

When at twenty he completed his studies there, he was given the name by which he is known to this day, 'Vidyasagar' or ocean of learning. Otherwise, his surname would have been Bandyopadhyay, or Banerjee, as the English (and many Indians) agreed to simplify it, even as a consensus emerged on Chatterjee or Chatterji for Bankim's last name, Chattopadhyay, and Mukherjee for Mukhopadhyay.

But for titles given to him, Rammohan Roy too would have been a Banerjee. He had disliked the creation of Sanskrit College. A foe of idolatry and of practices like suttee, but questioning also the Christian doctrine of the Trinity, Roy preferred a break with tradition. In 1828 he founded the Brahmo Samaj, or the Society of Believers in the One True God. Though he had served the East India Company for a few years, Roy possessed an independent mind open to, but also scrutinizing of, new ideas. What had occurred in that mind was not a replacement of old Oriental beliefs by new Western ones, but a thought-through blending of the two.

The Madrassah-educated Roy, who was proficient in Sanskrit, Farsi, Arabic, Bengali and English, had played a crucial part in the abolition in India in 1829 of sati or suttee, the practice of widows willingly or unwillingly burning themselves to death on their husbands' funeral pyres. That 1829 law, passed when Lord William Bentinck was the Governor General, was an Indo-British innovation. Its British supporters, official and missionary, were chary of provoking social unrest, and without Roy's insistence they would not have thought of defying a religious custom through a law.

Roy welcomed the advent of the British in India, of which a key milestone was the 1757 Battle of Plassey, when the East India Company's soldiers, led by Robert Clive (who invited charges of 'chicanery, deceit and venality'[15]), defeated Sirajuddaula, the nawab who had ruled Bengal under the remote aegis of the Delhi-based Mughal emperor. Eight years later (in 1765), British firepower forced the Mughal ruler to 'give' to the British—to the East India Company, to be more precise—this large eastern province, inclusive of today's Bangladesh and modern India's states of West Bengal, Assam, Bihar and Orissa.

Within five years of British rule over Bengal, a great famine brought death, suffering and crime on an enormous scale. Roy was born two years after that devastation and faced its impact as he was growing up. This famine would provide a sombre context for some of Bankim's future novels, and its memory was a factor in the almost desperate drive of Bengalis like Vidyasagar's father to give their sons a chance to prosper.

We may quickly note some other milestones in the Bengal-Britain story. In 1793, Lord Cornwallis, a new Governor General who had been an army general in America (where he lost a crucial 1781 battle in the Revolutionary War), instituted a 'Permanent Settlement' of the lands of Bengal. By this measure (later extended to some other areas), intermediaries who had collected land taxes on behalf of the Mughal government, and later for the British, became owners of the lands on which they had gathered revenue. Required under the Settlement to pay a fixed fee to the government, the new landlords were left free to collect rents indiscriminately from peasant-farmers who had now become their tenants.

Intended to make the land marketable, but also to divert Indian money to land, thereby freeing all trade in movables for the British, the Permanent Settlement created a new class of rich Indian landlords. Most happened to be high-caste Hindus. The East India Company, meanwhile, monopolized the production and sale of opium, salt and tobacco.

William Jones (1746–94) and William Carey (1761–1834) should also be remembered here. The founder of the Asiatic Society of Bengal, Jones was an Orientalist convinced of the excellence of the ancient Hindu mind. He did not refute fellow-Britons who thought the Hindus of *his* time to be 'degenerate and abased', yet Jones was certain that 'in some early age' the Hindus 'were splendid in arts and arms, happy in government, wise in legislation and eminent in various knowledge . . .'[16]

Because missionaries could so easily get in the way of its business in India, the Company was wary of encouraging them. But in 1813, domestic pressure in Britain forced through official approval for missionary work in India. Even before 1813, several British missionaries were active in (and from) the Danish enclave of Serampore, 12 miles north of Calcutta. The Baptist evangelist, William Carey, was one of them. Because of his expertise in Bengali (and Sanskrit), in 1801 Carey was made professor of Bengali in Calcutta's College of Fort William, started the previous year to train young Britons joining the East India Company. Here, recruits were expected to fathom India's languages and cultures and learn, as well, the skills of governance.

This Fort William College complemented the East India Company's Haileybury College in England (in Hertford, north of London), which from 1805 to 1858 prepared British youths of sixteen to eighteen (usually nominated by the Company's directors) for work as the Company's 'writers' or clerks in India and elsewhere overseas. This ability to hand out appointments to the gentry's younger sons (who usually had no lands or titles in their future) gave the Company enormous political and economic influence in Britain.

In 1801, the dedicated Carey brought out a European-style grammar of the Bengali language in Calcutta. Edited by him, Bengali versions of the epics Mahabharata and Ramayana appeared in 1802. A Sanskrit grammar text written by him came out in 1806, and a Bengali–English dictionary was published in 1815.[17] Edward Said would contend in the twentieth century that by standardizing and restructuring its languages, men like Carey sought to control the Orient,[18] and we know that Rammohan Roy carried on vigorous disputations with men like Carey.

Yet, as we marked earlier, Roy welcomed the British presence in India. This he did not because they had ended Muslim rule over Bengal (a reason for some others to welcome British rule). In fact, Roy valued Islam, having taken 'to heart the Islamic emphasis on the unity of God and the equality of human beings', which his scholarship in Persian and Arabic had uncovered.[19] The reason for Roy's thankfulness was that the British had opened doors and windows for Indians.

Edward Said would charge that despite their professed focus, Orientalists like Jones and Carey were actually (if not openly) more interested in the West than in the East. Roy's criticism was the exact opposite. He thought they were caught up too greatly with the Orient. Wherever the truth lies, it is indisputable that men like Carey laid out stepping stones for Vidyasagar, Bankim and many others. Interaction with Europeans like Carey helped kindle the intellectual and social sparks of what would be called the Bengal Renaissance.

We may note here that William Jones was one of the eminent figures portrayed in a book translated into Bengali by Vidyasagar in 1849, called *Exemplary and Instructive Biography*, authored by the brothers William and Robert Chambers. Others who featured in the book, which Vidyasagar called *Jivancharit*, included Copernicus, Galileo and Newton.[20] Through such role models (none of them Indian), Vidyasagar wished to promote knowledge among Bengalis and steel in their character.[21]

Meanwhile, in 1813, the East India Company had been required by Parliament to spend 'not less than a lakh of rupees' a year for public education in India. This was not a huge sum, but it provoked sharp competition between British Orientalists demanding support for Sanskrit and Arabic schools in India, and Anglicists pressing for a focus on the teaching of English. The dispute was settled in 1835 by the oft-quoted Minute on Education, endorsed by Governor General Bentinck, in which Thomas Babington Macaulay, then the education member of the Governor General's council, laid down that the British goal in India was to 'form a class who may be interpreters between us and the millions whom we govern, a class of persons Indian in blood and colour, but English in tastes, in opinions, in morals and in intellect,' while adding a judgement that 'a single shelf of a good European library was worth the whole native literature of India and Arabia'.

~

By 1850, after the Sikhs were defeated in the Punjab, British rule encompassed all of the Indian subcontinent. Ultimate authority was held in London and divided between the directors of the East India Company and the British Cabinet. In India, the Calcutta-based Governor General was in charge.

From Calcutta, the Governor General directly governed the large Bengal Presidency and supervised the governors heading the other two (and equally large) presidencies—Bombay (which included much of today's Maharashtra, Madhya Pradesh and Gujarat in India, and all of Pakistan's Sindh province), and Madras (which included much of today's Tamil Nadu, Andhra Pradesh, Karnataka and Kerala)—as also the chiefs of other provinces, including the Punjab and what was known as the North Western Provinces (the western half of today's Uttar Pradesh, and not to be confused with a later creation, the Northwest Frontier Province).

In addition, the Governor General was guide and master to Indian princes possessing numerous chunks of territory, many of them large. In 1850, the Governor General of India and the governor of Bengal was James Broun-Ramsay, the Marquess of Dalhousie (1812–60). Prior to being appointed (at the age of thirty-six) to the top British post in India, he had served in the British Cabinet, including as president of the Board of Trade. Now, he governed British India's extensive presidencies and provinces, where, under him, white officials controlled cities and the countryside. Plus, he controlled the fate of the rajas and nawabs ruling over India's numerous 'native' pockets. Unshakeably convinced (like Macaulay) of Indian inferiority[22] and having resolved to consolidate and extend direct rule by the British, Dalhousie annexed the Punjab in 1849.

He was also implementing the 'doctrine of lapse', which enabled the British to take over any princely state that in the Governor General's judgement lacked a suitable male heir. Under this doctrine, the states of Satara, Jaitpur and Sambalpur were absorbed into British India in 1849, Jhansi and Nagpur would be in 1853, and Oudh (or Avadh) was annexed in 1856.

Since India had been conquered portion by portion, subjugation was, by 1850, an old story in places like Madras, Bombay and Calcutta, a fairly recent occurrence in places such as Poona (taken in 1817) and Delhi (captured in 1803), and a fresh event in Sindh, the Punjab and the Frontier territory close to Afghanistan.

13

Everywhere, humiliation was the twin of subjugation, but that was not the whole picture.

For the British had also brought some quite dazzling things—new institutions (including colleges like the Hindu College and the Sanskrit College, and new kinds of hospitals, schools and law courts), new technology (including the printing press, macadamized roads, and steamships; railways and the telegraph would start in India, thanks to Dalhousie, in 1853), new laws (including the 1829 Abolition of Suttee Act), and newspapers. While the *Englishman*, a daily, cautioned India's Britons against overeagerness in spreading Christianity, the *Friend of India*, a weekly published from Serampore, thought that it was for preaching Christ that Providence had brought British rule to India.

One of Britain's reforming measures in India was an 1843 ban on slavery, which had existed in some pockets under both Hindu and Muslim masters. Slavery in India was linked to caste hierarchies or to debt, and (unlike in the western hemisphere) Indian slaves and their masters generally looked alike, although there were also some instances of Africans kept as slaves in India. Despite the ban, de facto slavery continued, usually in the form of serfdom, for slaves lacked mobility and were often unaware of the ban.[23]

Calcutta in 1850, and Ishwarchandra Vidyasagar (1820–91). Originating in the seventeenth century, the city of Calcutta had a population in 1850 of less than 300,000, including about 4,000 British, who lived and worked close to the Hooghly River, and 650 Armenians (who had settled in the Calcutta area well before the British). The Governor General lived in a magnificent Government House built in the first few years of the nineteenth century. An older great mansion, Belvedere, had housed Governors General before the new palace was built, including Warren Hastings, who served from 1773 to 1785 as the Company's first Governor General of India.

In 1850, the Mint (built in 1829), the General Post Office on the Strand, the Town Hall (built in 1811), the Asiatic Society building on Park Street (1808), and St Paul's Cathedral (1847) were some of the other imposing buildings in the southern part of Calcutta, which became known as 'the city of palaces'. Printing presses were spreading fast in the city, providing employment to some of the many who made their way to British India's capital, dreaming of an escape from poverty. Vidyasagar, who wrote his first book in 1842 and three other books before the end of 1850, acquired (in partnership with a Sanskrit College professor) a press of his own in 1847, which would print his and others' works.

In 1841, within weeks of completing his studies at Sanskrit College, the twenty-year-old Vidyasagar had been made 'head pandit' in the Bengali department of Calcutta's College of Fort William. Three years later, the Governor General, Lord Hardinge, had a long talk at Fort William with Vidyasagar, who was but twenty-four at the time. From Fort William College, where he held a significant but subordinate post, Vidyasagar moved up to lead the Sanskrit College. As Bankim's father (and others) had done, and as Bankim himself would before long do, Vidyasagar had joined an enterprise run by the subjugating British.

Vidyasagar was proud of his Brahmin, Bengali and Indian roots. True, he had read Shakespeare, established a printing press, and written petitions to the government, but, as the missionary J.C. Marshman had found out, 'a man's being able to read Milton, Shakespeare, or understand Dr Johnson' did not necessarily 'make him less susceptible to the honour of being a Brahmin'.[24] Vidyasagar identified independence, responsibility and 'devoted effort' as the qualities that individual Brahmins (and others) needed to pursue in the promising yet humiliating times that the British had opened up. A strategy of betterment—of one's situation and that of others—would help overcome humiliation.

Unlike most fellow Brahmins and most fellow Hindus, Vidyasagar was not inclined to pray before idols. Rammohan, on his part, had directly opposed idol worship and asked people to pray to the One Formless God. Vidyasagar did not join Roy's Brahmo Samaj, though he was close to some of its leaders. Neither did he turn to Christianity, even though he collaborated on projects with more than one Christian. And although Calcutta contained a number of Muslims, Vidyasagar did not probe Islamic perspectives the way Rammohan, with his knowledge of Persian and Arabic, had done. Vidyasagar kept his distance too from the Derozians, the freethinking followers of Henry Louis Derozio, a brilliant young Eurasian who taught at Hindu College and opened windows in scores of able minds before dying in 1831 at the age of twenty-two.

Though Vidyasagar's response to the changing world around him was practical rather than theological, it was also a profoundly moral response, shaped by the poverty of his childhood and youth. As his notion of self-control extended to a refusal to speak about his own feelings, we discover them only when he writes of others, for example, in his account of the time when his father Thakurdas had tried his luck in Calcutta, well before Vidyasagar was born. The account describes Thakurdas's attempt to sell his only utensils (a brass plate and a brass water pot) to scrape together a few paisa for food, and his 'wandering the streets of North Calcutta (the so-called Native Town, sometimes also called Black Town) weak and helpless with hunger, only to be saved from starvation by a compassionate widow who offered him some parched rice and yoghurt'—a gesture, Vidyasagar tells us, that 'could never have come from a man!'[25]

The moral spring inside Vidyasagar made him work for the right of Hindu widows to remarry, and against the right of Hindu males to have multiple wives, which produced more widows, especially when old men died after marrying young wives. Thanks to that spring, people would find Vidyasagar taking a cripple off the street to his home, or buying *luchi*s and curd for a poor Muslim, or risking cholera or malaria by nursing afflicted colleagues.[26] In partial deference to his Brahmin tradition, Vidyasagar kept a tuft of hair at the back of an otherwise shaved head, yet people said that 'it was immaterial' to him 'whether the person needing [his] help was a Muslim or a Christian' or bore another label.[27] That moral spring also made Vidyasagar the agent of an educational revolution. Not only did he train teachers and scholars in the Sanskrit College, he wrote (and printed) a series of school-books that took Bengali as a written language to hundreds of thousands of homes.

In a plan that Vidyasagar outlined in 1850, the Sanskrit College was to become not only 'a seat of pure and profound Sanskrit learning' but also 'a nursery of improved vernacular literature, and of teachers thoroughly qualified to disseminate that literature amongst the masses of their fellow-countrymen.'[28] The goal was to be achieved by *reducing* class time given to Sanskrit, *increasing* the teaching of Bengali, and making English a *compulsory* subject. As he saw it, 'an enlightened Bengali literature' would emerge only if students had access both to 'European sources' and to Sanskrit.[29] Moreover, by familiarizing students with critical analyses in Western writings, he felt the teaching of English would enable students to also examine 'errors' in Hindu thinking.[30]

Through the twelve school-books and readers he wrote, and the thousands of students whom his college trained, Vidyasagar's vision was realized. One of the school books, *Varnaparichay*, is in print to this day and available in most Calcutta book-stalls. Rabindranath Tagore would say in times to come that reading the simple, rhythmic prose of *Varnaparichay* as a child was what 'called forth his own love of the Bengali language'.[31]

Whether or not Vidyasagar was the first person to introduce the comma, the semicolon and other punctuation marks into Bengali writing (as has been claimed by some), his hands brought life to an inert language,[32] and he is said to have laid the foundation stone of modern Bengali prose.[33] Even in 1854, an admirer (a 'missionary with a profound knowledge of Bengal') could assert that Vidyasagar had 'made the Sanskrit College a royal academy for Bengali' and used 'the noble Sanskrit' not for 'Brahminical enthralment' but as 'the lever for giving dignity to the language of the masses.'[34]

And in 1850, a year after Drinkwater Bethune had established the Calcutta Female School, India's first public school for girls, Vidyasagar was made the honorary secretary of that school. However, we should also mark the conclusion of the American scholar Brian Hatcher, who has researched Vidyasagar's pedagogical and moral/religious thinking, that the 'devoted effort' underlined by Vidyasagar as a critical value was drawn by him from his Brahmin/Hindu tradition.[35] The norm also happened to be very close to, if not identical with, the key Victorian notion of self-help.

Whether or not there can be a fair-and-concise label for Vidyasagar in terms of religious belief ('reformist Hindu', 'Christianized Hindu', 'agnostic', or whatever), we must mark a limitation in the practical implications of his belief system. We know that Vidyasagar wanted 'the education of the highest classes on a comprehensive scale'. He thought that 'by educating one boy in a proper style, the government does more towards the real education of the people than by teaching a hundred children mere reading, writing and a little of arithmetic.'[36] In practice, this meant a lack of enthusiasm for schooling children not 'of the highest classes', which of course meant 'not of the highest castes'.

Despite opposition from orthodoxy, Vidyasagar successfully persuaded the Sanskrit College authorities to take in a few Kayasth students (a few Vaidya students were already being admitted), but that still left out the bulk of the Hindu community. This exclusion, as well as Vidyasagar's scepticism about education for the masses, should be recognized, but we should be careful before blaming an individual for a failing belonging to his times. The scepticism about education for the masses was fully shared by British officials in India—at this time, only a few Christian missionaries seemed involved in taking education to (some of) the low-born, who comprised India's majority.

Delhi in 1850, and Sayyid Ahmed Khan (1817–98). With a population of about 160,000, Delhi in 1850 was a good deal more Indian—in architecture, culture and education—than Calcutta. Though the British had captured the city in 1803 (easily overcoming Shah Alam II, the weak occupant of the Mughal throne, as well as the Maratha soldiers who controlled the ruler), its great edifices were still almost all of Asian design, with many possessing historic and also lasting grandeur—the Qutub Minar, Humayun's Tomb, the Red Fort, the Jama Masjid, the Old Fort, and many more. Two of these great structures, the Jama Masjid and the Red Fort (both built by Shahjahan, the Mughal who reigned from 1628 to 1658 and who was also the driving force behind the Taj Mahal in Agra), lay within the city walls, which extended 7 miles in circuit and contained seven gates.

Following its capture, one of Delhi's Muslim scholars, Shah Abdul Aziz, had declared that India had turned from a land of God into a land of war. However, the Mughal throne survived, if only in name, and a descendant of Babur continued to sit on it. In 1806, Shah Alam II was succeeded by Akbar Shah II (1806–37), who was followed in 1837 by the poet-emperor, Bahadur Shah II, better known as Bahadur Shah Zafar.

Though little more than a pensioner of the East India Company, Zafar, seventy-five years old in 1850, was addressed as 'His Majesty' by the Company's officers, whose chief in Delhi, Sir Thomas Metcalfe, carried the title of resident. Metcalfe, who served as resident from 1831 onwards, was answerable to Dalhousie, the Calcutta-based Governor General, and also to the governor of the North Western Provinces (NWP), who was headquartered in Agra, about 150 miles south of Delhi. However, in Delhi Metcalfe was the Briton on the spot, the man-in-charge.

Posted near the Red Fort, a contingent of British guards underlined the Company's hegemony, but for the sake of form the British agreed that in protocol the emperor would outrank the Governor General and that the resident would approach him with folded hands. In practice, however, Zafar had to plead for small favours from Metcalfe, who for his own residence had built an enormous mansion called Metcalfe House on the slopes beyond the city's northern gate (Kashmiri Gate), and for his office another large building called Ludlow Castle, which was closer to the Fort but still outside the city walls. Before Thomas, his brother Charles had been the resident, and Thomas's son, Theo, was one of Delhi's principal magistrates, with executive and judicial powers.

Well before Zafar had acceded to the throne, the East India Company ceased to strike its rupees in the name of the Mughal emperor (a privilege the Company had earlier sought and obtained), and it was Dalhousie's intention to ease Zafar (or at any rate Zafar's heir) out of the magnificent Red Fort, and thus bring appearances closer to reality. Moreover, the Governor General had rejected Zafar's request that his choice among sixteen sons, Jawan Bakht (only nine in 1850 and born to his favourite wife Zinat Mahal), be recognized as heir apparent.

Conscious of a lofty heritage that stood out on every horizon in Delhi, but daily made aware of his inferiority vis-à-vis the city's British officers (not to mention their superiors in Agra and Calcutta), Zafar found refuge from humiliation in composing poetry or in presiding at recitations by other poets. In fact, the old king was himself an accomplished poet (in Urdu, Persian, Punjabi and Braj) and also a calligrapher, a patron of gardening and painting, and a serious Sufi.

Packed into sections of the Fort, numerous relatives of the emperor and of his wives lived in squalor that mocked their royal connections. And Zafar himself remembered with bitter sadness that Dalhousie and Metcalfe were able to control his life because his Mughal forebears, yielding at first to entreaties and later to pressure, had provided warrants of authority with which the East India Company established first a toehold, then a foothold and eventually its mastery over India. 'Here is the place,' William Howard Russell would recall in 1858, referring to the Red Fort, 'from which came the haughty ukases that gave to a few trembling humble traders the right to hold lands in India' if the British traders offered 'service and submission'.[37]

The atmosphere of Zafar's court was eclectic. The king went oftener to Sufi shrines than to mosques, practised Shia rites as much as Sunni ones, objected to the slaughter of cows, and took part in Hindu festivals by spraying colours during Holi and attended the Ram Lila at Dussehra, and bestowed presents on his Hindu functionaries. Not very far from the Fort was Delhi College, which emerged in the 1820s and combined the activities of a pre-existing madrasa with new departments that taught English, astronomy and mathematics along European lines. The initiative and financing of Delhi College was also a joint affair, with the East India Company and Muslim aristocrats both contributing. A European was its principal.

However, most of Delhi's leading Muslims continued to live in a world where scholarship was sought in traditional ways. Elite youngsters learned grammar (for Arabic, Persian and Urdu), rhetoric, astronomy and philosophy in madrasas or from private tutors. The Mughal capital was nonetheless the hub of a lively (and in some ways mixed) intellectual and cultural style, including in music (vocal and instrumental), art and poetry. Linked to this hub was a mixed-race community that had grown in Delhi following the presence for decades of several Europeans (not just the British) around the Mughal throne. One of them, Colonel James Skinner (his father was a Scot and mother a Rajput), built the large St James's Church near Kashmiri Gate.

And printing presses had recently arrived, resulting in the publication of periodicals in Urdu and English, including one in

Urdu on behalf of the palace. A European called George Wagentreiber, whose wife Elizabeth was Skinner's daughter, edited the *Delhi Gazette*, which was read by the British and the mixed-race (or 'Anglo-Indian') community.

One of Metcalfe's predecessors as resident in Delhi, General Sir David Ochterlony, had taken several Indian wives and concubines. Born in 1758 in Boston of a Scots father and an American mother, Ochterlony arrived in India as a nineteen-year-old in 1777, helped in the 1803 capture of Delhi, and played a major role in the Company's 1814–16 war with Nepal that ended, interestingly enough, in an Anglo-Nepalese alliance and opportunities for the Company to enlist Nepal's Gurkhas as soldiers. Ochterlony served for six years as resident in Delhi before his death in 1825.

There were not too many Britons in Delhi. Many more lived in Agra, the NWP capital, and in Meerut (also in the NWP, 45 miles north-east of Delhi), where numerous British officers and soldiers of the Bengal army were based. As at other stations in India, Delhi's Britons, most of them hard-working, were acutely conscious of hierarchies within their small white world. An occasional drama or concert, or a race of dogs or a game of cricket, enlivened their existence. Almost all of them found the heat trying, and almost all had several Indian servants.

Hierarchies in Delhi's Indian world were sharper, if anything, and more complex. People were graded up and down by caste (and by class), and separated by both caste and religion. Many walked to their work in the city from villages ringing it, and trudged back at night. Inside Delhi, which was half-Hindu and half-Muslim, Muslims outnumbered and outranked Hindus in the enfeebled court, but in the bazaars, Hindu traders outnumbered Muslim traders and were generally richer. Hindus were also more willing than Muslims to go to British-run schools or work for the East India Company.

Since British gunboats and steamships were hidden a thousand miles or more beyond Delhi's horizons—off Calcutta, or in Bombay or Madras—while Mughal buildings and the emperor's court stood very close, it was possible for some Indians in Delhi to picture British rule as temporary. Others took a different view. Having worked for the East India Company in Calcutta and also in Iran and Burma, an elite Muslim called Khwaja Farid, for instance, realized that the British were in India to stay. As Khwaja Farid had good British contacts, Akbar Shah II had made him First Minister, responsible for balancing the royal household budget. It was under Farid's eye and in his large *haveli* that his maternal grandson Sayyid Ahmed Khan, born in 1817, was raised.

Farid and his daughter Aziz-al-Nisa taught Sayyid Ahmed and his siblings to avoid the company of working-class children and to turn up 'immaculately clean' for the post-dinner lesson in Persian, Urdu or mathematics that Farid gave. Aziz-al-Nisa's husband, Mir Muttaqi, was a bit of a mystic and less involved in the children's education, but it was from him that Sayyid Ahmed inherited the Sayyid connection, establishing him and his siblings as descendants of Prophet Muhammad.

The big-built Sayyid Ahmed (who enjoyed wrestling) and his older brother, Sayyid Muhammad, also learnt Arabic and oriental medicine from private tutors. Despite his assessment of British power, Farid did not arrange English-language lessons for the talented boys. Nor were they sent to Delhi College, which in spite of its mixed auspices was seen as a British institution whose usefulness could not be openly conceded by self-respecting members of the Mughal court.

Sayyid Muhammad, the older brother, bought a printing press and started an Urdu journal, *Sayyad-ul-Akhbar* in 1837,[38] and in 1839, after Khwaja Farid and Mir Muttaqi were both dead and royal stipends had ceased, a twenty-two-year-old Sayyid Ahmed (only three years older than William Russell in England and Vidyasagar in Calcutta) joined the judicial service of the East India Company as a munsif or sub-judge, working successively in Agra, Mainpuri and Fatehpur Sikri, all in the NWP.

Sayyid Ahmed also wrote tract after tract in brilliant Urdu, mostly on historical subjects. When he was twenty-five (in 1842), the new emperor, Zafar, bestowed honorifics on Sayyid Ahmed. Prefixes given in an earlier era to a lord of the Mughal court were now conferred on a young salaried munsif of the East India Company. In 1847, Sayyid Ahmed (now thirty years old) published one of his major studies, *Athar As-Sanadid*, a survey of Delhi's monuments. He had joined the Delhi Archaeological Society that

Metcalfe had started. Offering a chronology of Delhi's rulers, Sayyid Ahmed began, interestingly enough, with Hindu kings. Later, in 1855, he published a new edition of *Ain-i-Akbari*, the sixteenth-century work of Emperor Akbar's minister, Abul Fazl. Wanting to present a figure that the nineteenth century could esteem, Sayyid Ahmed chose the broad-minded Akbar over the narrowly focussed Aurangzeb, who had died in 1707. Sayyid Ahmed also admired Rammohan Roy. As a boy in 1830, he saw Roy when, prior to his voyage to England, the Persian-speaking founder of the Brahmo Samaj visited Delhi and called on the Mughal king. By 1850, Sayyid Ahmed was a proud and gifted Muslim and Indian, willing under necessity to work for an alien Company that had humbled his courtly forebears and his king, but seeking compensation by studying a prouder past to which his forebears were linked.

Etawah and Allan Octavian Hume (1829–1912). Also working at this time for the East India Company in the NWP (part, let us repeat, of today's UP) was a Scotsman called Allan Octavian Hume. Twelve years younger than Sayyid Ahmed, Hume had come to India in 1849 as a twenty-year-old and joined the Company's Bengal Civil Service in the town of Etawah, about 75 miles east of Agra, as a police officer.

Allan's father Joseph, hailing from Montrose (from 'that hardy sea-faring race which peoples the north-east coast of Scotland'[39], as Allan Hume's colleague and biographer, Wedderburn, would say), had also worked for the East India Company. During his successful Indian stint, which began in 1796, Joseph Hume learnt a couple of Indian languages, played the middleman between Company officers and Indian princes, and also put by enough money to buy a British parliamentary seat. For thirty years, Joseph Hume led the Radical Party in Parliament, where, apart from speaking on Indian affairs, he strove to extend the suffrage, institute the ballot, and ban flogging in the army.

As a thirteen-year-old, his son Allan wanted to join the Royal Navy and served briefly in the Mediterranean. His interest was captured also by the political campaigns in the 1840s of Richard Cobden (1804–65) and John Bright (1811–89) against the 'Corn laws'—British duties on imports of wheat. But India and the East

India Company were stronger pulls. Allan joined the Haileybury College in Hertford, and though he studied medicine and surgery as well, in 1849 he was posted to Etawah as a member of the Bengal Civil Service.

In the pages to come, and amidst the storms they cover, we will keep an eye on the lives of Russell, Vidyasagar, Bankim, Sayyid Ahmed and Allan Hume, and a few others who will presently emerge. We will try, as far as possible, to keep these lives in our minds, recognizing from time to time how close or far apart they are in space, and remembering also their difference in years. Of the five so far named, Sayyid Ahmed is the oldest, having been born in 1817, and Bankim (b. 1838) the youngest. Russell, who will get close in space to all of them, is three years younger than Sayyid Ahmed, as is Vidyasagar.

Bombay, Poona, and Jotiba Phule (1826–90). Different from both eastern and northern India, western India in 1850 contained two prominent yet culturally contrasting locations. One was Europeanized Bombay, a coastal island (once owned by Portugal) that was part of the dowry received by the British monarch, Charles II, when he married the Portuguese princess, Catherine, in 1661. The other was Poona, 130 miles south-east of Bombay, the capital for a hundred years (until their 1817 ouster by the British) of the Brahmin Peshwas.

Being an island (a group of islands, to be precise), British Bombay was secure. Its great natural harbour attracted trade. Construction projects, including works that 'joined' Bombay's several islands, drew people to what once was an almost empty space. By the end of the eighteenth century, Bombay had about 90,000 people, including Parsis, Jews, Marathi-speakers, Hindu and Muslim Gujaratis, and speakers of Telugu. Industry, including shipbuilding, grew.

Still, British Bombay developed more slowly than British Calcutta. In 1850, the Victoria Terminus, Flora Fountain, the High Court building and the University Tower had not yet been thought of. The city had some old Portuguese churches, an Anglican church built in 1718, and the new 'Afghan' Church, built in 1843 to commemorate British soldiers who had died in Afghanistan. Yet, most impressive perhaps was the Asiatic Society Building, which served also as the Town Hall. Completed in 1835, it featured an enormous portico with eight Doric columns, reached by thirty grand steps.

The Asiatic Society had been given an original fourteenth-century manuscript of Dante Alighieri's *Divine Comedy* by Mountstuart Elphinstone (1779–1859), who had joined the East India Company in 1796. Serving from 1811 as the British resident at the court in Poona of the Peshwa ruler, Bajirao II, Elphinstone played a part in battles that ousted Bajiraro. In 1819, he began his eight years as the governor of Bombay.

The Peshwas. Starting first as ministers in the Maratha kingdom established in the seventeenth century by the singular Shivaji (1627–80), a chieftain from a peasant caste, the Peshwas had assumed direct and hereditary rule in 1713. Where Shivaji's had been a popular Hindu kingdom supported by the peasantry and the 'lower' castes, administered by a talented elite (mostly Brahmins and Kayasths), and served by Muslims as well as Hindus, Peshwa rule had in effect become Brahmin rule, and the rule especially of Brahmins of a particular subgroup, the Chitpavans.

There were periods when Maratha[40] armies, often steered from Poona by the Peshwas, but led at times by chieftains from peasant castes, reached as far as Lahore in the north and Bengal in the east and eyed the throne in Delhi, which had been continuously weakening following the death in 1707 of Aurangzeb. Strategic and military skill was displayed by more than one Peshwa. Yet, scholars have painted an appalling picture of life in Poona shortly before the British took it over.

It is said that the last Peshwa, Bajirao II (1776–1851), 'lavishly fed about forty thousand pauperised ... Brahmins who flattered him as their lord. In times of famine the government ... helped only the Brahmins. The noise created by the serving of meals to countless Brahmin beggars and the chant of their mantras filled the Poona skies.' Peasants were 'inhumanly harassed'. If taxes were not paid (usually because a famine had left peasants penniless), 'boiling oil from the frying pan was poured' on the peasants or 'heavy stones were mercilessly placed on backs.' Floggings were common. Women committed suicide. According to one scholar, 'Poona had become a den of ignorance and immorality, vice and disease.'[41] The British were therefore thanked for ending Peshwa rule in and around Poona in the Marathi-speaking region (or Maharashtra), even as, six decades earlier, they were thanked in Bengal for ending Sirajuddaula's 'cruel and lecherous' rule.[42]

In part because he had earlier allied with them against neighbouring Indian princes, Bajirao II received a handsome, if conditional, deal from the British. He would retain the 'Maharaja' title (though not the 'Peshwa' one) and get an annual pension of a hundred thousand pounds for the rest of his life; but he would have to move all the way to a village called Bithur near Cawnpore (now Kanpur) in the NWP, and never return to Poona. His family, retainers and followers, totalling about 1,200 people, accompanied Bajirao to north India in 1818. The British did not expect the forty-two-year-old Bajirao, credited with a 'feeble constitution' and 'debauched habits',[43] to live for long, but he did not die until 1851. In Bithur, he became known for charity and an interest in classical music.

~

Twenty-four years old in 1850, Joti (or Jotiba) Phule was the son of Govind Phule, who grew flowers and fruit on a plot of land outside Poona and sold his produce in a shop in the city. The Phules belonged to the Mali-kunbi community, placed at the 'lower' end of Maharashtra's peasant or 'middle' castes who had welcomed the exit of Bajirao II. Govind had taken the unusual step of sending Joti, when the boy was five or six, to a school opened by the British in Poona—unusual because schooling, whether indigenous or modern, was supposed to be only for Brahmins, and certainly not for a Mali child.

Even so, Govind enrolled his boy in a school in Poona's Budhwar Wada, started in 1832 by a Mr Stevenson, but later run by the government—and before long withdrew Joti from it. He had been successfully pressurized. Two men then intervened: a teacher of Urdu and Persian called Gaffar Beg Munshi, who was a Muslim, and a Briton, perhaps a missionary, known to us only as Legit. Noticing Joti's ability, the two urged Govind to send the boy to the Scottish Mission school that had opened in Poona.[44]

In 1841, when Joti was fourteen or fifteen, he was enrolled here.

A biography of Phule (by Dhananjay Keer) states that in this school, where he spent six years and became proficient in English as well as Marathi, Joti's mind was captured not only by stories about Shivaji, but also by accounts of George Washington and by Thomas Paine's *Rights of Man*.[45] This makes Joti's boyhood unusual for another reason—usually in the 1840s, India's schoolchildren learnt about British rather than American heroes. A classmate close to Joti was a Brahmin boy, Sadashiv Govande, who had studied with Joti in the previous school as well. Along with Sadashiv and a couple of other boys, Joti embraced, while in the Scottish Mission school, the idea of One God and of a morality valid for all—doing good to others and avoiding harming others. The missionaries had played a role in the youths' thinking, but there is no evidence that Joti, who at this time was in his late teens, became a Christian or was invited to become one.

Keer relates two episodes from Joti's time in the Scottish Mission school. In one, Joti is pushed out of a wedding procession because of his 'low' birth. Since an unnamed Brahmin friend was the groom, Joti had joined the procession, but, on being recognized as a non-Brahmin, he was shouted at for 'defiling' the ceremony and ordered to leave. In the other episode, Joti has a scrap with two arrogant British soldiers he has somehow bumped into.[46]

In a future work, *Gulamgiri* ('Slavery'), Phule would say that in the 1840s—in his late teens—he wanted to drive the British out of India. The thought was sown in his mind, he says, by Brahmins 'in the privacy of their hearths'. They spoke of how, if they were united, Indians of different castes could 'compete with the Americans, the French and the Russians'. Evidently these Brahmins quoted Paine and other 'celebrated authors' to Phule.

It was exciting talk. Warning Joti against Christian missionaries who sought 'a fraternal relationship with the Shudras', the unnamed Brahmins for a while 'misled' and 'misguided' him, Phule writes.[47] He even learnt swordplay and fencing in order to fight the British one day. 'But,' adds Phule, 'when [he] reflected long and deeply ... the true meaning of the motivated propaganda of these "enlightened" Brahmins dawned' on him,[48] and he abandoned the fancy.

The wedding procession incident had set his emotions on fire and he sharply disagreed with his father's advice, which was to (a) recognize Brahmin superiority, (b) stomach the insult, and (c) be thankful that he was not thrashed. Yet, his humiliation was not simple to avenge. He needed to control his feelings, wait, and figure out a practical reply.

In August 1848, a year after he had graduated from the Scottish Mission school, Joti knew what at least part of the reply should be, for that year, in an unprecedented initiative, he started a school for girls in the home of a well-wisher in Poona. In the following three years, he started a few more schools in different parts of Poona. Some of these schools had both boys and girls; at least one took in children from the 'low' and 'untouchable' castes; and one, possibly his first, was for girls from Brahmin and other 'high' or 'middle' castes. The precise chronology of these schools is hard to pin down. While Phule's *Gulamgiri*, published in 1873 and containing some autobiographical references, indicates that the school for 'upper caste' girls came before the rest, his biographer Dhanajay Keer, writing in 1964, mentions the one for girls from the 'low' castes as Phule's first school.

Recognizing that 'the low castes, Mahars, Mangs, Chambhars, etc., composing a great part of my countrymen', were 'sunk deep in ignorance and misery', he had responded (Phule would later write) to an inner prompting 'to better their conditions through means of education'.[49] He had been inspired by what a Miss Farrar was doing for the education of girls in Ahmednagar (about 120 miles north-east of Poona), where Joti had gone to visit Sadashiv Govande, now in a government job.

By setting up a school for girls, whether from the 'highest' or the 'lowest' classes, Joti Phule had done what neither Vidyasagar (who was six years older) nor Sayyid Ahmed (nine years older), or any other Indian for that matter, had done so far. A few schools for girls indeed existed here and there, including in Poona, but they were run by missionaries. An American mission had started two or three such schools around Poona in 1840, and the Scottish Mission too ran a girls' school there.

Yet, twenty-two-year-old Joti Phule from the Mali caste was the very first Indian to start a school for girls anywhere in India. He was supported in this initiative by his wife Savitri (who belonged to the same caste). Joti had been married to her when he was about fourteen years of age, and she had been taught reading and writing by Joti, and also by his Brahmin friend, Sadashiv, who sent books for her from Ahmednagar. Phule would later claim that by the time of that decisive visit to Miss Farrar's schools in Ahmednagar, he had already realized that 'the root of education' lay in how mothers addressed 'the disposition of children between their second and third years'.[50] Hence the necessity for girls' schools.

Foes screamed 'Outrage!' when the Phules taught low-caste children, and Joti's father Govind succumbed to the social pressure. Joti and Savitri were ordered to leave the family home that had given them meals and shelter while they spent all their time and energy in running the school or in persuading parents to send their girls to the school. Now all that time and energy had to go into earning a living. In five or six months, the school was closed. As he would recall in 1853,

> Having, however, by my teaching the low castes become odious to my caste-men, my father at last drove me out of his house and left me to shift for myself in the best way I could. So the school was . . . closed, and I was compelled to engage in business to gain a livelihood.[51]

But only for the time being. For Joti (like Vidyasagar in Calcutta) possessed business acumen as well. He was able, through trade and contract work, to better his circumstances. Within months, his school reopened in a room arranged by his friend Sadashiv in Poona's Peth Joona Ganj locality. Clothes and also 'special' drinking water—which was bought by Joti, for public cisterns and wells were off limits to these 'low-caste' or outcaste children— were supplied to pupils. British officers like Major Candy, who headed Poona's Sanskrit College (begun in 1821 and open only to Brahmin boys), supported the school with books. When the number of pupils increased, Phule hired a larger place owned by a Muslim in the same area.

And on 3 July 1851, a school for children from humble backgrounds opened in the home of Annasaheb Chiplunkar, an affluent and forward-looking Brahmin, in Poona's Budhwar Peth quarter. It had a three-man managing committee headed by Phule. Working without remuneration, Savitri Phule taught as a schoolmistress. In September, another girls' school was started at Rasta Peth, and in March the next year, a third school was opened in Vetal Peth.

If some of Poona's Brahmins backed Phule, others were livid. The idea of a woman, Joti's wife, helping in the teaching felt even more scandalous than 'untouchables' being taught. One not eligible to learn was daring to teach! Savitri Phule was stopped in the street, abused, and sometimes sprayed with dirt and stones. According to Keer, she would calmly reply: 'God forgive and bless you. I am doing my duty.'[52]

The British, whether in Poona or Bombay, were more than impressed. Issues of the *Bombay Guardian* from 1851 to 1854 contain a series of articles about Phule's new schools and the roles he and his wife were playing. Open British recognition of Phule's work helped its survival and restrained his enemies, yet no major shift in educational policy in favour of 'low' castes took place. Despite the unpopularity they had incurred as a result of the excesses of Bajirao II, Brahmins remained influential elites whom the British chose not to confront. Without Brahmin intermediaries, the British could not, in practical terms, rule over Maharashtra. Also, since Brahmin rule was what the British had displaced in Maharashtra, Brahmins were their most likely future foes. It made sense not to provoke them too much.

Like Vidyasagar, Phule championed vernacular education. In 1849, his backing proved crucial in diverting a portion of government funds set aside for supporting Sanskrit writings to prizes for books in Marathi, whether translated or original. Though an important Brahmin, Gopalrao Deshmukh, had led the bid on behalf of the vernacular, an angry street reaction by Brahmins in defence of a 'Sanskrit only' policy threatened to torpedo it. But when Phule enlisted 'two hundred strong men from the Mahar-Mang locality' who escorted 'the lovers of Marathi', the threat collapsed.[53]

It is striking that 'untouchables' rather than his own peasant caste are the people that Phule naturally and successfully turned to. A rebel, it would seem, against all domination—of 'low' castes by 'higher' castes, women by men, 'untouchables' by 'low' castes, of Indians by the British—Phule made allies beyond his own group, the Mali-kunbis.

AMERICA IN 1850

American expansion, Abraham Lincoln, and slavery. In 1850, American whites were concentrated along the eastern coast of the USA, but many were alert to the potential both of the West Coast and of the vast tracts between the Atlantic and the Pacific. America's major cities (north to south) were Boston, New York, Philadelphia, Washington, Richmond, Charleston and New Orleans. Chicago, which contained a much smaller population, was seen as a western city.

Though a number of Americans had opposed the 1846–48 war with Mexico that brought Texas, California, Nevada, and Utah into the USA, this westward expansion was generally accepted by Americans as their country's 'manifest destiny'—of an almost visible certainty that the USA would annex or settle new areas. Thus, the universalist thinker Ralph Waldo Emerson (1803–82) said that while he rejected war 'as a means of achieving America's destiny', he realized that 'most of the great results of history are brought about by discreditable means.'

However, Abraham Lincoln (1809–65), a member of the US House of Representatives during the 1846–48 war, thought that 'greed and mendacity' on the American side had drawn Mexico into that war. He shared the suspicion that a desire for new territories for slavery was part of the motivation.[54] The most direct foe of this war was Henry David Thoreau (1817–62), who showed his opposition by refusing to pay taxes and was jailed as a result. Another product of the incident was Thoreau's essay, *Civil Disobedience*, which would encourage Gandhi half a century later.

Like Emerson a student of Hindu thought, Thoreau wrote in his 1848 diaries of the 'sublimity' of Oriental conceptions.[55] Such a statement risked sneers in America but not danger, for while the founders of modern America had generally satisfied their spiritual thirst at the fount of Christianity, they had also consciously provided against the establishment of any state religion. As for

Emerson, he cited the Gita, wrote a poem called 'Brahma', and corresponded with Max Müller across the Atlantic on Hindu texts.

Thomas Jefferson (1743–1826), author of the Declaration of Independence and the third President of the USA, thought that as important as the Declaration was the first American law (passed in Virginia) that guaranteed religious freedom. According to James Madison, who served from 1809 to 1817 as the fourth President, that law was meant to include, in 'the mantle of its protection, the Jew and the Gentile, the Christian and the Mahometan, the Hindoo and infidel of every denomination'.[56]

Reflecting also (in Walden Pond in Concord, Massachusetts) on the export of ice from Concord all the way to India, Thoreau added:

> While I incredulous read the vast cosmogonal philosophy of Ancient India—in modern New England[,] the Brahmen's Stoic descendant still sits in his native temples and cools his parched lips with the ice of my Walden well . . . By the miracle of commerce we . . . cool our lips at the same well.[57]

Also celebrating native Americans, or 'Indians' as they were called (and at times are still called), Thoreau had opposed wars and expulsion drives aimed at them, which other Americans saw as divinely ordained or unavoidable. Thoreau also opposed the enslavement of blacks. 'It was said,' Winston Churchill would note in the twentieth century, 'that both these races (the Red and the Black) were downtrodden by White ascendancy as truly as animals are mastered, used, or exterminated by mankind.'[58]

A twenty-three-year-old Abraham (or Abe) Lincoln was a recruit in the Black Hawk War of 1832, in which an Illinois militia fought the 'Indians'. Lincoln did not see much action in this exercise, but Indians had figured in his family history. In 1786, his grandfather, also called Abraham Lincoln, had been killed by attacking Indians while planting corn in the state of Kentucky. One of the attackers had his sword raised to also kill the slaughtered man's eight-year-old son, Thomas, when Thomas's older brother Mordecai, fifteen at the time, shot the Indian dead. Twenty-three years later, the surviving Thomas would sire Abe Lincoln.

From Kentucky, a hinterland state on the southern side of the

North-South border and the first state west of the Allegheny mountains to be settled by pioneering whites, the Lincolns moved north, first to Indiana and then to Illinois. In 1850, forty-one-year-old Abraham Lincoln, having completed a single term in the US Congress, exchanged his political career (which had started in 1834 as a Whig member of the General Assembly of Illinois state) for a law practice in Springfield, the Illinois capital.

Raised in rough circumstances in Kentucky and troubled by illness and ill luck (including a young son's death in 1850), Lincoln, always an acute observer of real life around him, had become a successful lawyer, debater and raconteur. Also, he had soaked up basic texts such as the Bible, Shakespeare's plays and poems, the 1776 Declaration of Independence and the 1788 American Constitution.

The Whig Party that Lincoln had joined favoured a protective tariff as an economic measure and also because it underscored America's national identity—a tariff proved that America was separate from Europe and, equally important, a single nation. The Democratic Party, on the other hand, wanted free trade, which had strong advocates in the agricultural South. There, and also in the new territories that were settled as America moved westward, 'Liberty' was the favourite watchword, though it was clear that only whites could enjoy it.

In the North—in cities like Philadelphia, New York and Boston, where business and manufacturing were rapidly growing—'Union' was stressed as much as 'Liberty', and in a famous utterance in 1830, the Whig leader from Massachusetts, Daniel Webster, had declared in the Senate that 'Liberty *and* Union' were inseparable sentiments. Though the speech was made in Washington, it stirred a twenty-one-year-old Lincoln who had newly arrived in the state of Illinois.

In the debates over liberty, Union and tariffs, both the North and the South sought to win the newly emerging West. Would North and West align against the South, or would the South and West align against the North? An unspoken yet crucial element in the debate was slavery, over which northern and southern states were sharply divided. In the South, where slavery was widespread, the 'peculiar institution', as it was euphemistically called, was viewed as one of two crucial foundations for the economy—the other being cotton, the universally demanded fibre that slaves picked in the South's fields. Christianity, it was claimed, permitted slavery.

Some decades earlier, during America's Revolutionary War against Britain, prominent southerners had voiced reservations against slavery, but economics stilled the disquiet. Only with the work of slaves, it seemed, could the South's plantations produce the increasing quantities of cotton sought in Britain, France and elsewhere in Europe. The 'necessity' for slavery made it consistent with Christianity. Indeed, of the South's four million slaves in the 1850s, over 660,000 were owned by ministers and other prominent Christians.[59]

However, importing slaves into the USA had been banned in 1808, about two hundred years after the first slaves had been brought to North America; in 1833, England had banned slavery in all its colonies. While slaves continued to be illegally brought into the USA, many more were born into slavery in the American South and raised, sold, kept and worked as slaves.

In the 1850s, the South had about six million whites, nearly 350,000 of whom owned slaves. While forty thousand whites controlled plantations requiring more than twenty field hands (generally slaves), the South's politics was run by three or four thousand leading slave-owners. A great many other whites were yeomen farmers owning few or no slaves, and there was a class also of 'mean' whites owning little land or wealth who were 'capable of being formed into an army'.[60]

Rebelling against enslavement, an African-American called Nat Turner and seventy-five followers had killed about fifty whites in Virginia in 1831. Turner and his associates were executed, and about a hundred innocent slaves also lost their lives in reprisals. Some slaves ran away to Mexico for freedom, or to uncontrolled parts of Florida, where native Americans provided shelter to fugitives. Their refusal to hand over fugitive slaves was a cause of a war in the 1830s and 1840s against Seminole Indians, whose chief had married a runaway slave. The Seminoles' resistance to being pushed westward across the Mississippi into what later became Oklahoma was another cause of that war.

Nat Turner's revolt and other similar bids aroused anxieties that were stoked by slavery's proponents, who asserted that if slaves were freed, neither the white man's life nor the white woman's honour would be safe.[61] Slavery and the South had become synonyms, but southerners underlined the decline in wealth that coincided with the end of slavery in British colonies in the Caribbean, and they offered a defence that would find some future sympathy from Winston Churchill:

> There was a grace and ease about the life of the white men in the South that was lacking in the bustling North .... Vast numbers of black men, caught upon the west coast of Africa, had been transported like cattle across the Atlantic to be the property of their purchasers. They had toiled and multiplied. The bulk had become accustomed to their state of life, which, though odious to Christian civilization, was physically less harsh than African barbarism. The average Negro slave, like the medieval serf, was protected by his market value, actual and procreative, as well as by the rising standards of society, from the more senseless and brutal forms of ill-usage.[62]

Churchill's suggestion that slaves were not ill-treated beyond a limit because they were valuable, and also because standards of treating inferiors were improving, echoed the arguments of southern whites in the America of the 1850s. Churchill would add:

> The slave-owning aristocracy in much of the South felt a class-superiority to the business, manufacturing, and financial society of the North. The Puritan stock of the North regarded the elegant gentry of the South with ... wrath and censure ... [In the southern view] the Yankees[63] were jealous of a style and distinction to which vulgar commercialism could never attain.[64]

Much of Lincoln's own state, Illinois, though located (like Indiana and Kentucky) in 'the West' of the USA of his time, was 'southern' in culture and prejudice, and Lincoln himself possessed his share of the latter. A yeoman southerner by birth and upbringing, Lincoln valued, like many in the South, reputation or honour, which depended, among other things, on a person's response to triumph or adversity, not on one's wealth. Also, he did not think that a black was a white's equal in intelligence or should equal the white socially, and he was opposed to interracial marriage. But he thought that slavery was sinful and had to end.

Early sights of enslaved men chained together in boats on the Mississippi and Ohio Rivers had tormented Abraham Lincoln. His father Thomas had reacted similarly to enslavement scenes in Virginia and Kentucky, and in fact it was to get away from slavery that the Lincoln family had moved to Indiana and then to Illinois. They were by no means the only southerners uncomfortable with slavery. While a majority welcomed it, quite a few even in the 'deep' South (in the states of Alabama, Mississippi, Louisiana, Georgia, and South Carolina) responded with dislike, as did many more in the 'upper' South (Virginia, North Carolina, Tennessee, and Arkansas) and the 'border' states (Kentucky, Missouri, Maryland, and Delaware). Not surprisingly, a 'southern' state's location—whether it lay in the lower or the upper South, or along the 'border' with the North—mattered.

How could slavery end? Lincoln seems early on to have discerned a possible path towards that outcome. While the American Constitution not only did not ban slavery, but seemed even to provide room for it, the Declaration of Independence, America's founding document, had taken another line, for it said,

> We hold these truths to be self-evident, that all men are created equal, that they are endowed by their Creator with certain unalienable Rights, that among these are Life, Liberty and the pursuit of Happiness . . .

Since it was not stated or implied anywhere that African-Americans were to be excepted from the category of 'all men', the words made the abolition of slavery a manifest American duty whenever abolition became politically and practically possible. One way of preparing the public mind for ending slavery was to point out that in America's story the Union had preceded the Constitution.

This legal view was designed to knock down the southern claim that a 'compact' between the North and the South had created the Constitution, which then created the Union. Having in the past chosen to join, the South could in the future decide to secede. In contrast, Lincoln (and some others in the North) held that the Declaration of Independence, which came twelve years before the Constitution, was 'the sovereign act of a single people'.[65]

'White' America grew on the East Coast, but knew it would expand westward. The first independent Congress of the United States laid down that a new territory could acquire statehood and a share in American governance once it gained a requisite population. As a state, it could send delegates to the federal House of Representatives—their number depending on the state's population—and, irrespective of population size, two delegates to the federal Senate, like every other state in the Union.

This meant that if a new territory became a slave state, it could influence America as a whole in favour of slavery. 'Abolitionists', as they were called, hated an 1850 Compromise in the US Congress between the North and the South over slavery in the new states. While this Compromise ensured that California (where the historic Gold Rush began in 1848) would not permit slavery, and produced a new 'free' state of Maine (carved out of Massachusetts), it accepted Texas and the territory of Missouri as slave states. Moreover, the Compromise also required all US citizens, including those living in the North, to assist in the return of runaway slaves.

Unlike Thoreau and many others opposed to slavery, Lincoln went along with this Fugitive Slave Law, as it was called. Some in the North burnt copies of the Law, but Lincoln acquiesced in it. In the years between the 1850 Compromise and the 1861 start of the Civil War, the North grew in industrial power and population while the South's economy, based on plantations and agriculture, remained stagnant. The result was the South's defeat in the Civil War that was to follow.

We do not know if Lincoln foresaw this, but he certainly thought that time was needed to assemble an attack on slavery. Also, he seemed to feel that 'one can remain opposed to slavery while making temporary concessions to the South in order to keep the nation together',[66] and he hated the possibility of a war over the issue. Lincoln would not forget that even the Revolution that overthrew British rule and brought America to birth had been a cruel affair. He wrote that 'it breathed forth famine, swam in blood, and rode on fire; and long, long after, the orphan's cry and the widow's wail continued to break the sad silence that ensued.'[67]

Less disapproving of war in general and born into a tradition of slave-owning was Robert E. Lee of Virginia, whose father had been a governor of the southern state. Two years older than Lincoln, Lee was a star cadet at the United Sates Military Academy at West Point in the state of New York, which he joined as an eighteen-year-old in 1825. Entering the Corps of Engineers, Lee distinguished himself in the 1846–48 Mexican War. In 1852, he became the head of the West Point academy. Notwithstanding his background, Lee seems to have conceded that slavery was 'a moral and political evil in any country'.[68]

In 1850, even while developing fast, America was a largely rural country with a total population of twenty-three million, which was three times the 1815 figure. Large numbers of Irish, Germans, Scandinavians and Britons had recently come in. The North's big cities were New York (with 515,000 people), Baltimore (168,000), Boston (136,000), and Philadelphia (121,000). Chicago, in Lincoln's Illinois, had only 29,000 inhabitants. The South's major towns were led by the port city of New Orleans (in Louisiana), which had a population of 116,000, followed by Charleston on South Carolina's Atlantic coast, with 42,000, and Richmond in Virginia with 27,000. About 40,000 people lived in Washington, the nation's capital, where stately buildings stood next to vacant spaces, and where housing was generally flimsy.

A quarter of New York's residents in 1850 were Irish, most of them new immigrants. The *Tribune*, founded in 1841 by Horace Greeley and also edited by him, was the city's most respected newspaper. A foe of alcoholism, tobacco, prostitution, the Mexican War and slavery (and a supporter of vegetarianism), Greeley attacked the Fugitive Slave Law. He also hired talented writers. The paper's chief rival, the *Herald*, started in 1835 by a Scottish immigrant, James Gordon Bennett, attacked abolitionists like Greeley, publicized crime, and in 1850 sold about 20,000 copies a day, compared with the *Tribune*'s circulation of around 16,000.

The America-Britain-India triangle. For about a hundred years, from the 1680s (when the East India Company acquired footholds on India's coastline) until the 1780s (when British rule was overthrown in the United States), some persons of British origin had found employment in both India and America.

We saw earlier that Lord Cornwallis, the Governor General responsible for the 'Permanent Settlement' in Bengal, had previously served in America as a general on the losing British side. Another well-known instance is that of Elihu Yale, governor from 1687 to 1692 of Fort St George, the East India Company's base in Madras. Profits made in India by Yale, who had Welsh origins, helped found the University of Yale in New Haven, Connecticut. We also saw earlier that David Ochterlony, born in 1758 in Boston to a Scots father and an American mother, came as a nineteen-year-old to India, where he rose to high office and also took several native wives and concubines. Carrying Indian, British and American blood, Ochterlony's descendants were part of the mixed-race community, mentioned earlier, that grew around the humbled Mughal court.

Recent research has disclosed that Indians began entering the USA as early as 1624, i.e., within a generation of European settlers arriving there. They were brought as indentured workers or slaves by Europeans from ports in Bengal, Madras, Pondicherry, Malabar, Bombay and Goa. Over the next two centuries, several hundred Indians may have landed in America in this manner. Most converted to Christianity, took Western names, and married African-American or mixed-race women.[69]

For about eight decades from 1780 to 1860, American trade with India took place mostly through the ports of Boston and Salem in Massachusetts, rather than through New York or Philadelphia. At first, in the latter part of the eighteenth century, finished textiles of cotton and silk were the principal imports from India. Later, as Britain and America rapidly industrialized and India's cottage-based textile industry was knocked out, sailing ships from America that took ice (among other things) to India, brought back indigo and hides. Sailing from Boston, the clipper *Tuscany* first took ice to India in 1833. Carried in insulated holds and exported by a Boston merchant, Frederic Tudor, ice was brought to the ports of Calcutta, Madras and Bombay.[70]

From 1812 onwards, a ship from America to India was apt to carry a missionary or two as well. Dying within weeks of arriving in India in 1812 with her husband Samuel Newell, nineteen-year-old Harriet Newell was described in the American press as the country's first woman martyr in the missionary field; and John Scudder of New Jersey, who sailed for India and Ceylon in 1819, would be remembered as America's first medical missionary to the region.

Ships returning from India also brought linseed (for its oil, used in manufacturing paint and varnish) and jute, increasingly the material used for baling cotton and bagging corn. In the late eighteenth and very early nineteenth century, trade with India amounted to an impressive 5 per cent of America's foreign trade (a peak figure fated to fall with time). Mariners and merchants brought back shawls, images and stories from India. '[E]specially in coastal cities and towns, India—its products, its civilization, its religions—touched the imaginations of countless Americans.'[71] Several Americans became serious students of India's history and religions, and of British rule in India. While British studies on India were the principal resource for American scholars, the latter were capable of reading between the lines.

Embracing all religions equally, the poet Walt Whitman (1819–1892), who grew up in New York, would write a verse called 'A Passage to India' when the Suez Canal opened. Boston's relationship to India, and to Calcutta in particular, was however stronger than New York's. It would be reflected in the phrase 'Boston Brahmins', used to describe elite Bostonians descending from early British immigrants and marrying within their 'caste'.

Though America and Britain were now rivals, and had fought a war with each other in 1812–15, they were also cousins with much in common. American clippers took cotton to Liverpool and other British ports and returned with a variety of manufactured products. Economically, at any rate, America still had a colony's relationship with the 'mother' country, to some extent resembling India's link with Britain; and the British were inclined to feel superior to their American cousins.

Persons with the means journeyed in both directions across the Atlantic, out of nostalgia or curiosity or for inspiration. Others read works written across the water. In the late 1840s, the historical writings of Thomas Babington Macaulay, who had returned from India to the UK in 1838, became very popular in America.

In 1842, a thirty-year-old Charles Dickens was feted on his first American tour, but the writings emerging from it, *American Notes* and the novel *Martin Chuzzlewit*, contained remarks that shocked and wounded Americans. Viewing America through a prism of resentment at its secession from England, and disapproving of the casualness Americans showed and the equality they assumed, Dickens attacked American manners. He compared the US Congress unfavourably with London's Parliament, even while admitting that Parliament's proceedings had often sent him to sleep in the Press Gallery. While the American spirit had reminded others of Cincinnatus, who in old age was willing to put his hand to the plough, Dickens seemed to think that the American Cincinnatus put his big feet on the tablecloth. His assessment was wholly at odds with what had been offered ten years earlier in *Democracy in America* by the Frenchman, Alexis de Tocqueville, who had also made a journey across America.

Like Tocqueville, Dickens wanted to taste and test America's large experiment in democracy. At the end of a visit that took in much of the country (except the South, which he avoided because of its slavery), Dickens suspected that the future *might* belong to America. Yet, he spotted—in addition to a disagreeable familiarity— a willingness to condone brutal violence, and callousness towards the 'Indians', blacks and Irish, and felt that these odds were hard to surmount. One winter night, after carefully mounting precarious stairs in a large house on a squalid New York street, he enters a space where 'the bare beams and rafters meet overhead, and calm night looks down through the crevices in the roof'. Adds Dickens:

> Open the door of one of these cramped hutches full of sleeping negroes. They have a charcoal fire within; there is a smell of singeing clothes, or flesh, so close they gather round the brazier; and vapours issue forth that blind and suffocate. From every corner, as you glance about you in these dark retreats, some figure crawls half-awakened ... Where dogs would howl to lie, women, and men, and boys slink off to sleep, forcing the dislodged rats to move away in quest of better lodgings.[72]

Similar British scenes too had been painted by Dickens, but Americans did not appreciate such depictions of their country. In particular, condemnation by Britons of American slavery annoyed many Americans, especially in the South, and in 1840 a southern senator, John C. Calhoun of South Carolina, responded with a countercharge. The East India Company, Calhoun declared, was keeping 'the whole of Hindostan' as 'one magnificent plantation' and exercising a power over its Indian 'slaves' that was 'far more unlimited and despotic than that of any southern planter over his slaves'.[73]

Also in 1840, another pro-slavery American, E.W. Stoughton, wrote mockingly of Britain as a 'Christian, slavery-hating nation' that coerced Indians to grow poppies for producing opium.[74] Men like Calhoun and Stoughton were suggesting that empire was worse than slavery. On the other hand, abolitionists in both America and Britain hoped that exports of Indian cotton under the empire's umbrella would reduce Europe's dependence on cotton from the American South.

BRITAIN, 1850–57

In London in November 1852, William Howard Russell covered the heraldic state funeral of England's most respected son, the Duke of Wellington, who had died at the age of eighty-three. More than half a century earlier, in 1799, Arthur Wellesley, as the Duke was then known, had defeated Tipu Sultan in Seringapatam, thereby ending the strongest resistance in southern India to British rule; in 1815, in his most famous triumph, he had overcome Napoleon at Waterloo.

Before the Duke's death, Russell (in his words) had often 'stopped in the street and taken off my hat as the well-known figure of the Duke ... [riding] from the Horse Guards to the House of Lords; the thin form in the plain blue frock coat, with white stock and buckle showing above the neck, and white duck trousers strapped over the boots which bore his name. Never ... did he omit to raise his right hand to the brim of his hat as a return to the salutations of the people.'[75]

To paint a scene with words was Russell's style and also his task—as noted earlier, *The Times* did not as yet print photos. Albert, the Prince Consort, had designed the Wellington funeral. Russell captured it for posterity. After walking with thousands, observing larger numbers massed along London's streets, and witnessing the service held at St Paul's Cathedral, Russell wrote out 16,000 words that appeared in the paper in the morning in more than seven unbroken columns of small type. This is how he described the procession:

> It was full, it was strong, but it was not rapid. As the boom of the guns, fired to mark the progress of the funeral car, reached the ears of the vast mass that filled the streets, there was a movement as though the multitude had become a living entity, with every muscle vibrating, as though it formed a great python. ... A million and a half of people beheld and participated in the ceremonial ... On no occasion in modern times has such a concourse of people been gathered together. ... [The funeral] finally closed its course at the lofty threshold of the metropolitan cathedral, the centre of London, now engaged by a new tie to the affections of the country by having deposited under its dome the ashes of England's greatest son.'[76]

This Russell-recorded ceremonial of 18 November 1852 seemed to be another confirmation, close on the heels of the Great Exhibition, of England's primacy in the world.

The Crimean War. Soon this assessment was put to a test. At first, the issue was the right to the keys to Jerusalem's ancient shrines: should the Orthodox Church, protected by Russia, have the right, or should the Roman Catholic Church, supported by France, hold the keys? The Sultan of Turkey, whose empire included the Holy Land as well as portions of Europe, found it impossible to decide in favour of either Russia or France. After a while, the Russians lost patience and moved in militarily.

Was the Czar, seen as tyrannical by many Britons, going to change the balance of power in Europe? The British Prime Minister, Lord Aberdeen, was reluctant to be pushed into a war, and *The Times* backed his caution, but an elemental restiveness forced Aberdeen's hand—restiveness that for forty years 'a generation brought up on tales of victories over Napoleon I and bubbling with confidence had been denied any military expression of its strength'.[77]

When in November 1853 the Russian fleet knocked out the Turkish Black Sea Fleet in the port of Sinope, feeling in Britain was inflamed. Reversing its opinion, *The Times* called for war on Russia, and Aberdeen realized he would lose the premiership if he did not yield to the popular mood. In February 1854, when war was anticipated but not declared, editor Delane asked Russell to go to the eastern Mediterranean to cover the expected conflict. It was sure to be brief, said Delane. Russell would be given handsome allowances, and his wife and children (four by now) would join him for part of what was foreseen as primarily an excursion. (Among the few Britons opposing the Crimean War, and military adventurism and armament-building in general, was John Bright, who with Richard Cobden had led a successful agitation in the 1830s and 1840s against duties on imports of wheat.) Dickens and Thackeray attended a farewell party given for Russell, who went via France to Malta, where British troops awaited instructions. On 26 March, the French declared war on Russia; the next day, the British did likewise.

But the world's leading power was unprepared for the ensuing war in the Crimea. Though the British army was 'fine-looking' and 'brilliantly dressed' in red jackets, its generals were too old and their methods outdated.[78] The rule of wearing the full uniform irrespective of the weather did not help. Command was reserved for the wealthy (who bought positions), and the seniority rule kept the high command in elderly hands. Supplies were slow to reach the front and often shoddy when they did. Water was scarce, the food for soldiers and horses bad, and medical attention flawed.

Worst of all, commanders made blunders, none more infamous than the Charge of the Light Brigade in Balaklava on 25 October 1894. Later generations would recite Tennyson's verse about the 'disaster', as Russell would call it in the opening sentence of his report, but that immediate account was as powerful as poetry, or as a motion picture of the future:

> At ten minutes past eleven our Light Cavalry Brigade advanced . . .
> As they rushed towards the front, the Russians opened on them from the guns in the redoubt on the right, with volleys of musketry and rifles. Thy swept proudly past, glittering in the morning sun in all the pride and splendour of war. We could scarcely believe the evidence of our senses! Surely that handful of men are not going to charge an army in position? Alas! it was but too true . . . They advanced in two lines, quickening their pace as they closed towards the enemy.

A more fearful spectacle was never witnessed than by those who, without the power to aid, beheld their heroic countrymen rushing to the arms of death. At the distance of 1200 yards the whole line of the enemy belched forth, from thirty iron mouths, a flood of smoke and flame, through which hissed the deadly balls. Their flight was marked by instant gaps in our ranks, by dead men and horses, by steeds flying wounded or rider-less across the plain . . .

With diminished ranks, thinned by those thirty guns, which the Russians had laid with the most deadly accuracy, with a halo of flashing steel above their heads, and with a cheer that was many a noble fellow's death-cry, they flew into the smoke of the batteries, but ere they were lost from view the plain was strewn with their bodies and the carcasses of horses . . . At thirty-five minutes past eleven not a single British soldier, except the dead and dying, was left in front of those bloody Muscovite guns.[79]

Written on 25 October, Russell's 'Letter' from the front travelled by land and sea to London and was only published on 14 November. Day after day, Russell rivetingly conveyed what he was witnessing. 'What can any novelist write,' Thackeray asked a friend, 'so interesting as our own correspondent?'[80] In private letters to Delane, Russell also conveyed deep concern, saying that troop morale was dangerously low. When the influential editor passed on Russell's private comments to his contacts in the Cabinet and Parliament, the result was a conclusion that the Aberdeen government had to go. A resolution questioning the government's handling of the war was passed by 305 votes to 148, and Aberdeen resigned.

Visiting the Crimea a few months later, the Duke of Newcastle, who had been Aberdeen's war secretary, told Russell, 'It was you who turned out the government.'[81] The man who had replaced Aberdeen as Prime Minister was none other than Lord Palmerston, over seventy years old at this juncture, 'but still possessed of considerable bellicose energy'.[82]

At the end of December 1855, after spending twenty-two months on the Crimean War, Russell returned home. The war ended in April 1856. No side had conducted it ably, and many reputations were damaged, but Russell had found recognition and fame. This was above all because his uncensored reporting had forced Britain to shed its lethargy and send essential supplies to its army. He obtained his facts from ordinary soldiers who spoke openly to Russell, which they did thanks to his cordial personality. Twenty years later, recalling his Crimean reporting, he would write in a diary: 'I don't think but for my Irish nature I could have got along so well.'[83]

Willing also to admit mistakes in his assessments, Russell had built trust in his readers and in fact won 'a formidable following'.[84] He was criticized, however, for providing details in his public dispatches that the Russians, had they been competent, could have used against British positions. Fortunately for the British, the Russians proved incapable of taking advantage. Russell's own line on the question, articulated in one of his dispatches, was that, 'Although it may be dangerous to communicate facts likely to be of service to the Russians, it is certainly hazardous to conceal the truth from the British people.'[85]

Albert, the Prince Consort, was infuriated by Russell's reporting of British failures and wrote to a friend during the war that 'Mr Russell ought to be turned out of the camp.' But Victoria recorded in her journal the view of an army officer (who had praised Russell's reporting to the Queen) that 'certain things ought to be made known, else they would not be remedied.'[86]

After the war, Dublin's Trinity College made its former student an honorary Doctor of Literature. Russell was lauded in other ways too. Overcoming his fear of public speaking, he lectured up and down Britain on his war experiences. But the freedom from censorship that had given Russell and *The Times* an unprecedented voice during the Crimean War would not remain unfettered much longer.

Leo Tolstoy, 1828–1910. It was not a freedom that Turkish, French or Russian correspondents enjoyed, as Leo Tolstoy, among others, had found out. When, during the Crimean War, he wrote *Sevastopol in December 1854*, *Sevastopol in May 1855*, and *Sevastopol in August 1855*, Tolstoy, just into his late twenties, was a sub lieutenant of artillery on the Russian side. Born into an aristocratic, landowning family in Russia, Tolstoy had fought courageously at the front, but writing too was pulling him, as well as a wish to portray the war candidly. He sent his piece to the censor, as he had to, and had difficulty recognizing what came back.

Nonetheless, his powerfully graphic Sevastopol accounts, the second of which questioned the popular view of war as a romantic and purely patriotic exercise, established young Tolstoy's literary reputation in Russia. When he wrote the first account, he had just arrived at the front. '[His] enthusiasm was intact; he was afloat on a tide of heroism. As yet he could see in the defenders of Sebastopol neither ambition nor vanity, nor any unworthy feeling. For him the war was a sublime epic.'[87]

In the second account, however, Tolstoy recorded the self-love and vanity he saw around him: 'As there were many men, so also were there many forms of vanity ... Vanity, vanity, everywhere vanity, even at the door of the tomb!' He added: 'The literature of our century [is] nothing but the interminable history of snobs and egotists.'

The observer in the Tolstoy of the Crimean War missed no detail. Two pages describe 'all that passed in the mind of [an] unhappy man during the second following upon the fall of the shell, while the fuse was hissing towards explosion' and then another whole page deals with 'all that passed before him after it exploded, when he was killed on the spot by a fragment which struck him full in the chest'.

He also saw what others did not. As Romain Rolland would later put it, Tolstoy's 'clear, disillusioned gaze' in Sevastopol 'plumbs to the depths the hearts of his companions in arms; in them, as in himself, he reads pride, fear, and the comedy of those who continue to play at life though rubbing shoulders with death. Fear ... is stripped of its veils and shown in all its nakedness.'[88]

Forgetting the patriotism of his first narrative, Tolstoy curses what he now sees as an impious war, and wonders why soldiers on both sides, most of them Christians professing a 'great law of love and of sacrifice', do not, upon realizing what they have done, 'fall upon their knees repentant, before Him who in giving them life set within the heart of each, together with the fear of death, the love of the good and the beautiful'.[89]

There is no evidence that Russell knew of Tolstoy at this point, but we know that unlike many Britons of the time, Russell refused to think of Russians as uncouth or inferior. In the summer of 1856, he went to Russia to cover the coronation in Moscow of a new Czar, Alexander II, and then travelled all the way to revisit his 'old haunts' in the Crimea.

His 13,000-word account of the coronation of 7 September 1856, written that very evening, was another triumph. An editorial that appeared along with the report, no doubt authored by a much-impressed Delane, said:

> In all his 60 million subjects, in his hundred races, and his names of terror—in that devoted band of servants that stand round the throne of the Czar, he had not on that day a more useful and effective friend than the skilful Irishman who was recording for all the world, on tablets more enduring than brass or stone, the greatness of his power, the magnificence of his Court, the loyalty of his subjects, the devotion of his church, and the simple, natural affection of his family . . .[90]

Possessing more than skill, Russell also informed the British public that 'the English church in Moscow had not been closed even at the height of the Crimean War, even though the Russians found the congregation praying for the Queen's victory over all her enemies.'[91]

The future would know of Tolstoy as a powerful dissenter from the chauvinism that marked the nineteenth century, but in these pages we will find Russell's voice also at times supporting the dissenters. Before he proceeded to Russia for the coronation, Russell had been invited to breakfast with the Prime Minister at Palmerston's house in Piccadilly. After the other guests left, the old Premier asked Russell to stay. The two talked for forty or so minutes about the British army and its generals. Though Russell was asked a few questions, Palmerston did much of the talking, among other things defending the British policy of voluntary enlistment as against the French practice of conscription. 'I went away with the feeling,' Russell would recall, 'that I had cut rather a poor figure . . . for Lord Palmerston seemed to know more about our Army than I did.'[92]

INDIA, 1850–57

But did the Prime Minister know enough about his army in India, where Lord Dalhousie remained Governor General until 1856? Actually, there were four British armies in India. One, the smallest, comprised the (purely British) Queen's Regiment that served directly under the Crown. The other three were the East India Company's Bengal, Bombay and Madras armies that had been raised from the seventeenth century onwards.

In 1856, there were about 40,000 whites and 250,000 Indians in these armies, roughly six Indians to one Briton—a change from an earlier three-to-one ratio. The Indians were mostly sepoys (infantrymen) or sowars (cavalrymen), and the lowest ranking British officer was senior to the highest ranking Indian officer; but British trust in the sepoys and sowars was the norm. Fifty years earlier, in an incident in 1806, sepoys in the Madras army had indeed revolted in Vellore in the Tamil country, rallying in the name of Tipu Sultan (1750–99), whom the British had vanquished seven years previously, but that rebellion had been crushed and forgotten.

Deployed all across northern, central and eastern India—from Peshawar and Karachi to Calcutta and further east—the Bengal army obtained a great many of its Indian recruits in Avadh or, as the British spelt it, Oudh or Oude, a large kingdom west of Bihar and east of the North Western Provinces that from 1722 had detached itself from a declining Mughal empire. From the 1760s onwards, Avadh had acknowledged the Company's supremacy, allowing a Company resident to base himself in its grand capital, Lucknow, along with a band of British troops, who were paid for by Avadh. And in 1801, Avadh had given up half of its territory to the British. On a chunk of this surrendered land, close to the border of truncated Avadh, the British developed Cawnpore (now Kanpur) as a military and trading town.

Now, in the 1850s, Avadh was providing the Bengal army with most of its Indian soldiers. A fourth of these were Muslim. High-caste Hindus (mainly Brahmins plus a percentage of Rajputs) formed the bulk of the remaining three quarters, though some Sikhs, Gurkhas and lower-caste Hindus were beginning to enter the ranks. Swallowing high-caste scruples against crossing the seas, Indian units of the Bengal army had served for Britain in China in 1840–42, in Burma in 1852, in the Crimea in 1854, and in Persia in 1856. Hindus and Muslims had fought side by side in harsh and dangerous conditions and formed bonds. In Britain's failed campaigns in Afghanistan in 1839–42, the Bengal army had paid much of the price. And it was the Bengal army that in the 1840s had helped Britain annex Sindh and finally overcome the Sikhs controlling the Punjab.

That offensive into the Punjab (directed by Dalhousie) had been preceded by an 1837 treaty between Avadh and the Company that included a British promise not to annex the kingdom.

However, not content with Avadh's supply of Hindu and Muslim soldiers (about 50,000 in 1856) and its role as a buffer state, and despite the treaty, Dalhousie annexed the kingdom in 1856. The king, Wajid Ali Shah, Dalhousie alleged, was unfit to rule. Wajid Ali Shah was indeed dissolute, peculiar and old. But the charge was only a pretext for Dalhousie's plan of Britain's westward expansion across India, which matched America's expansion, also westward, in the 1840s.

To Dalhousie, it was Britain's manifest destiny to replace decadent Indian customs and worthless Indian institutions with efficient (and also, of course, profitable) white rule. Then, perhaps, India would make up for the loss of America. Britain's position as the centre of the world would be underscored, and America and India would have to be content with frontier status.

Edwin Blood, a nineteen-year-old from Newburyport, Massachusetts, who had sailed to Calcutta in 1854 for a job as a supercargo's clerk and to experience the Orient, felt certain of Dalhousie's 'genius'. Blood wrote in his journal that India had 'become a field of glory to Dalhousie'.[93] Applying his 'doctrine of lapse' and rejecting adopted heirs, Dalhousie had taken over Satara in 1848, Jhansi in 1853, and Nagpur in 1854. (The doctrine could not apply to Avadh, where biological heirs clearly existed, but that was of no account to the Governor General.)

When her husband Gangadhar Rao, the Brahmin ruler of Jhansi, died in 1853, his widow-queen, the young and beautiful Lakshmibai (née Tambe) pleaded for the recognition of a son adopted just before the ruler's death as the heir, and of herself as regent. Dalhousie turned down both requests. Two years earlier, after the death in Bithur (15 miles north of Kanpur) of Bajirao II, the Governor General had similarly turned down the pleas of the last Peshwa's adopted son, Dhondoo Pant (or Nana Sahib, as he was formally called), for the pension, titles and honours that Bajirao had received.

Nana Sahib had asked for most if not all of his adoptive father's pension, the 'Maharaja' title if not the 'Peshwa' one, and a gun salute of the sort that Bajirao and other Indian princes were receiving from the East India Company. Though each nursed the rejection, both Lakshmibai and Nana Sahib (their palaces about 150 miles apart) kept up cordial relations with British officials, hoping to earn better terms.

While the queen-widow's popularity and 'the force and charm of her personality' were noticed by the British,[94] the thirty-three-year-old Nana Sahib's hospitality in Bithur and his skill at billiards were also appreciated by visiting Britons who called him 'the Maharaja' (though Dalhousie refused to do so), even though Nana Sahib spoke very little English. From his adoptive father, Nana Sahib had inherited a palace, retainers, horses, elephants and other assets, and he had the backing of a few of the late Peshwa's advisers who had accompanied Bajirao II from Poona to Bithur. Hoping that Dalhousie might be overruled, Nana Sahib sent an emissary, Azimullah Khan, in 1854 to London, where he stayed for many months.

Apparently raised in humble circumstances (his mother had worked as an ayah), Azimullah had done well in a British school in Cawnpore and found employment as a secretary with two British brigadiers. Accused of corruption by the second of these and dismissed, Azimullah entered Nana Sahib's service and won his complete confidence.[95] In London he presented himself as an Indian prince. Failing, however, in his mission, Azimullah returned to Bithur in 1855, but not before stopping in Constantinople en route.

There, at Missirie's Hotel, who should meet him but William Howard Russell, then covering the Crimean War. Four years later, Russell would record in his diary that at Missirie's he had run several times into Azimullah, 'a handsome slim young man of dark-olive complexion, dressed in an Oriental costume which was new to me, and covered with rings and finery'. Speaking both French and English, Azimullah boasted to Russell of his success with women in London. News of a Russian gain at the expense of the British and the French seemed to excite Azimullah, who then also managed to get to the war front at Balaklava.

Here, Russell looked after Azimullah and his horse and answered some of the curious visitor's questions before going off to a mess dinner with British soldiers. When late at night Russell returned, he found that his camp bed was occupied, with Azimullah asleep in it, and also that his stores had been 'freely enjoyed' by the visitor. 'In the morning,' Russell would write, Azimullah 'was up and off, ere I was awake,' but in a note that he left Azimullah 'beg[ged]' to thank Russell 'most truly for his kind attentions'.[96]

Later, Russell would be told that Azimullah had thought the French army's morale in the Crimea to be stronger than the British army's, and that soon after Azimullah's return to India (before the annexation of Avadh), he and Nana Sahib—bitter at the 'irrevocable determination of the authorities' to reject Nana Sahib's request—spent a good deal of time in Lucknow, the Avadh capital, and 'exhibited considerable insolence and hauteur towards the Europeans they met'.[97]

Avadh's annexation was Dalhousie's last major act as Governor General. Not every Englishman cheered it. One who did not was W.H. Sleeman, who had been the resident in Avadh from 1849 to 1854. While clear about the kingdom's problems, Sleeman told Dalhousie of his fear 'that annexation would lead to mutiny in the Bengal Army, for Oudh was "the great nursery of the sepoys"'.[98] Dalhousie dismissed the warning, since in the British mind there existed, at this time, a reassuring picture:

> You might see the sepoy, watchful and tender as a woman, beside the sick-bed of the English officer, or playing with the pale-faced children [in] his captain's bungalow. There was not an Englishwoman in the country who did not feel measureless security in the thought that a guard of sepoys watched her house or who would not have travelled, under such an escort, across the whole length and breadth of the land.[99]

This picture was not entirely false. While the average sepoy was not comfortable in the thick red coat and the heavy headgear that were prescribed, he commanded prestige in his village, and his monthly pay of seven rupees, though much lower than that of a white soldier, was decent enough. He felt loyal to the Company and to his white officer, who often took a personal interest in his sepoys.

But the picture was incomplete, for when angry the officer swore at the sepoy, calling him 'nigger' or '*suar*' (swine), and at times struck him. Moreover, the sepoy—who inside his uniform was only an Avadh peasant—felt loyalty also to his caste fraternity where major matters were jointly settled and communication was swift, as was ex-communication. He felt some loyalty too towards Wajid Ali Shah, the Avadh king, and to the Hindu or Muslim *talukdar* or baron who was the intermediary between Avadh's peasants and the king.

Effete as he was, Wajid Ali Shah had not oppressed the castes or communities joining the Bengal army. His removal (unlike the removal in Poona, forty years earlier, of Bajirao II, and also unlike the 1849 removal of Sikh rule from the Punjab) brought no relief to the peasantry. Employed hitherto in the king's police or as retainers or servants for the king's nobles and officials, many villagers, in fact, lost their jobs as the king's establishment shrank. These villagers, many of them closely related to the Bengal army's sepoys, sang dirges and followed the departing king all the way—about 55 miles—from Lucknow to Kanpur, the British headquarters on the edge of what now had become the 'former' kingdom of Avadh.

Annexation was followed by regulations that hit Avadh's talukdars, who thus far had enjoyed an independent right in their territory to a share of the peasants' produce. Most of these talukdars, who controlled law and order through their own militias, were Muslims or high-caste Hindu Rajputs. Set on 'modernization'—on curtailing the influence of these traditional barons and creating a direct relationship between British tax gatherers and the village community or the village proprietor—Dalhousie assumed that Avadh's peasants, including the sepoys, would hail the new land policy.

They did not. Though vastly poorer than the talukdars, the sepoys often belonged to their talukdar's caste, unless (as was true of a large number) they were Brahmins, which made them the highest-born anyway. Refusing to see themselves as beneficiaries of the new land policy, Avadh's peasant-sepoys were bewildered, if not shaken, by the attack on traditional arrangements. Under those arrangements, the talukdar was expected to take care of the peasant in return for the latter's labour, loyalty, and willingness to take up arms on the lord's behalf. Fear and force often entered the relationship, yet a web of obligations and duties tied the talukdar and the peasant-sepoy to each other.

Well below these sepoy-peasants, socially and economically, were the more numerous low castes and untouchables who had no link to the land except as ill-paid day (or night) labourers. These unfortunates inhabited worlds that were far from, and yet dominated by, the well-knit network of which the talukdar was the head and the sepoy-peasant (whether Brahmin, Rajput or Muslim) a loyal if inferior beneficiary. The ability to look down upon these unfortunates was an important source of the sepoy's prestige, as important as the Bengal army's uniform and pay. In fact, a high-caste junior officer often commanded greater influence in his regiment than a white officer sporting a much higher military rank.[100]

Resisting the supposed appeal of the new land policy, the Avadh sepoy was also nursing several grievances. One was the entry of 'lower' castes into the Bengal army, which had brought up tricky questions of sepoys from 'high' and 'low' castes eating, cooking, and bathing together. Equally difficult, if not more so, had been the question of joining British campaigns overseas, for Hindus were not supposed to cross the sea. Another grievance was the loss, following the absorption into British India of the Punjab and Sindh, of the 'external' allowance for serving in those places. Again, though only a few Sikhs had joined the Bengal army, the Avadh sepoy disliked their entry, even as Sikhs remembered that it was the Avadh sepoy—the Sikhs called him 'Hindustani' or 'Poorbia' ('easterner')—who had filled the ranks of the Bengal army that overcame the Sikhs in the 1840s.

Joined to these grievances was a lessening of the sepoys' awe of

British soldiers and officers in India, who in the 1840s had suffered heavy losses and reverses, if not defeats, in Afghanistan and the Punjab.[101]

~

The sepoys' edginess did not greatly bother Lord Dalhousie as he neared his departure from India. A 'man of firm, decided views and of masterful disposition'[102] who commanded one hundred elephants in his train when crossing the Ganges,[103] Dalhousie could count several accomplishments.

The Bengal Presidency, hitherto run directly by the Governor General, was given a governor of its own under Dalhousie's rule. More importantly, the telegraph was brought to India; the postal system was taken across the whole land; roads, canals, and bridges were built or extended; the first railway service (21 miles from Bombay to Thane) was launched; and plans were carried forward to open three universities, in Calcutta, Bombay and Madras.

In 1856, Dalhousie was succeeded as Governor General in Calcutta by Charles John Canning, whose father had died as Prime Minister. Like Dalhousie, the forty-four-year-old Canning too had served in the British government before coming out to India.

Meanwhile, Ishwarchandra Vidyasagar (who was thirty-six in 1856) had continued writing (and printing) his Bengali schoolbooks. He had also intensified his campaigns on behalf of the Hindu widow. Shunned as a temptress and an omen of ill luck, ordered to shave her head and remain hidden, burdened with heavy work, denied tasty food, frequently starved, and prohibited from marrying again, the Hindu widow had sympathizers but needed a champion.

In 1855, Vidyasagar demanded a law to permit Hindu widows to remarry. 'In this country,' he wrote, 'men-folk are devoid of kindness, justice, a sense of good and evil . . . Let women be never again born in such an accursed land.'[104] His insistence worked. Despite strong objections from numerous Hindus (36,763 signed a petition opposing widow remarriage, compared with 987 signatures in its favour[105]) and urgings for caution from a section of India's British, the Hindu Widows' Remarriage Act was passed in 1856. Though 'the act was only permissive', it seems to have 'offended the vast majority of orthodox Hindus all over India'.[106]

In December of that year, the new law was used for legitimizing the marriage of one of Vidyasagar's colleagues at Sanskrit College, Shreeshchandra Vidyaratna, with a widow. Later, one of Vidyasagar's sons would also marry a widow. What Rammohan Roy had been to suttee abolition, Vidyasagar became to widow remarriage. Whether or not others in the Calcutta of his day matched his intellect, none (Benoy Ghose points out) equalled Vidyasagar in 'conviction and courage'.[107]

Eighteen years old in 1856, the precocious Bankim published his first volume of poetry that year, which was also when he joined what used to be Calcutta's Hindu College as a law student. To announce that its doors were open to all, it had been renamed Presidency College in 1855. In 1857, Bankim joined the new Calcutta University. In the following year, he and a person named Jadunath Basu would become the university's first two graduates.

Delhi, 1856. The annexation of Avadh perturbed Zafar, the eighty-one-year-old king in Delhi. Anything could now happen to *his* pensions, perks and preferences. Though the oldest of his living sons, Mirza Fakhru, who to Zafar's horror had been confabulating with the British resident for several years and whom the British wished to see as his successor (if there had to be one), died in 1856, the emperor was again firmly told that young (and, as Zafar knew, unruly) Jawan Bakht would not be accepted as his heir.

When Thomas Metcalfe, resident from 1835 in Delhi, died in 1853, seemingly of poison, the British had suspected a palace hand in the incident, possibly that of Jawan Bakht's mother Zinat, but there was no proof. In any case, Simon Fraser, who followed Metcalfe as resident, was as keen as his predecessor to clip the emperor's prestige and in fact to see Mughal kingship end with Zafar, a goal fully shared by the new Governor General, Lord Canning. Not to recognize an heir apparent was one way to achieve the goal.

One person immediately affected by the annexation of Avadh was Zafar's poet laureate from 1854, Mirza Asadullah Khan, better known as Ghalib (1796–1869). Later to be called the finest Urdu poet, perhaps, of his or any other time, Ghalib had for years lagged behind another poet, Muhammad Ibrahim Zauq (1789–1854), in royal recognition and popular acclaim, and he had always been short of money. A pension from Avadh had eased Ghalib's situation. With annexation, that dried up. Though older than Sayyid Ahmed Khan by twenty years, Ghalib was friends with the writer and sub-judge. Both had been raised in Delhi's courtly culture. In assessing the British advent, the older man was more detached and more positive than Sayyid Ahmed, who through his studies clung to the Mughal past.

On a visit to Calcutta, Ghalib had seen steamships and other products of European technology, and he was impressed also by British trade and diplomacy. When, in 1855, Sayyid Ahmed sent Ghalib his edition of *Ain-i-Akbari*, and solicited a review of this record of Akbar's reign, the poet asked the younger man to live in the present:

> You waste your time.
> Put aside the *Ain*, and parley with me;
> Open thine eyes, and examine the Englishmen,
> Their style, their manner, their trade and their art.[108]

Yet, parleying with the British was not easy even for Ghalib. Invited to apply for the post of professor of Persian at Delhi College (getting the job would solve his financial problems), Ghalib arrived at the gate in a palanquin and waited for the college secretary, a Mr Thomason, to welcome him—Mughal etiquette required a dignitary like Ghalib to be escorted into a place by the host. When it was explained to Ghalib that while the British would receive him thus when, for example, he attended a reception by the resident, the present case, when Ghalib was a candidate for employment, was different, the poet chose to go back. He had realized, said Ghalib, that the new position would reduce, not increase, the dignity to which he was accustomed.[109]

Something else troubled people in Delhi in the 1850s: a spurt in missionary activity. Quite a few Britons in India (and in Britain) seemed convinced that it was to bring India to Christianity that Providence had enabled Britain to conquer India. Thus Herbert Edwardes, the commissioner of Peshawar, said that God had given the Empire to the British because 'England had made the greatest effort to preserve the Christian religion in its purest apostolic form.'[110]

Should representatives of the world's greatest power remain nervous while talking of Christianity to Indians? And how right was the old policy of keeping British rule separate from Christianity?

A few civil and military officers spoke of Christianity's virtues to Indian subordinates. In a well-publicized ceremony in Delhi's St James's Church in July 1852, Padre Midgeley John Jennings baptized (evidently on their request) two prominent Hindus of Delhi: a doctor, Chaman Lal, whose help was often sought by King Zafar, and Chaman Lal's friend, Master Ramchandra, a gifted mathematics lecturer at Delhi College. Jennings lodged with Captain Douglas, commandant of the palace's British guards, in the commandant's rooms above the Lahori Gate to the Fort's west. He was therefore seen in the city as an integral part of the British set-up. After the ceremony, Jennings, an advocate for a bolder missionary attempt, wrote to the Society for the Propagation of the Gospel in London that 'never was a field riper for missionary efforts'.[111]

But many of Delhi's Hindus and Muslims suddenly felt insecure. Jennings himself noted that, drawn by the event, a large 'Hindu population' had 'assembled around the Church'.[112] The curious Hindu crowd was disturbed, not enthusiastic. Parents (Hindu and Muslim) removed children from Delhi College. Many ulama cautioned the faithful against missionary and British intentions, which were seen as one and the same. They also criticized Zafar's 'excessive' tolerance. The king had inherited and encouraged an eclectic culture where people of diverse or even mixed beliefs, and of mixed races, felt at ease. Now, from more than one side, purity in religious practice and in race was being demanded. If you were different, you were also wrong, and possibly an enemy. Later in 1856, some Hindus in Delhi (and elsewhere) interpreted the Hindu Widows' Remarriage Act, for which Vidyasagar had pressed, as another attack on Hinduism.

Etawah, 1856. In Etawah, situated between Agra and Kanpur, twenty-six-year-old Allan Octavian Hume had in 1856 become the acting collector, or district chief. Three years earlier, he had married an Englishwoman in India, Mary Anne Grindall.

Hume's hobby was studying birds, and he had collected numerous specimens. As an officer, he had made education his priority.

Pestering provincial bosses in Agra, Hume extracted permission to start free elementary schools that were supported by landed proprietors. Speaking to them in Hindustani, the language of the area, Hume persuaded the zamindars to pay a cess that was sufficient to start thrity-two village schools in April 1856. By January 1857, 181 schools (each with a teacher) had been established in the district, with a total of 5,186 pupils, including two girls. Of the 181 teachers, eight were paid Rs 6 per month, thirty were paid Rs 5, and 134 received Rs 4 monthly. Hume thought that 'many of them for the pay they receive [were] very able men'.[113]

In August 1856, a central English and vernacular school was opened in Etawah town. By January 1857, there were 104 students here, and three scholarships were instituted for Etawah's students in the Agra College, one paid for by Hume himself.[114] His commitment had influenced, and in some ways created, a larger Etawah community.

Poona, 1856. In Poona, Jotiba Phule was enlisting steady support for his schools for girls and 'untouchables' from a few Hindu traders, four Brahmin teachers, white missionaries and British officials. A formal recognition of his unusual role occurred in November 1852 at a gathering of Poona's Indian and British elite in the Peshwa's old palace. At this ceremony, chaired by Major Candy, the head of Poona's Sanskrit College, twenty-six-year-old Jotiba Phule was presented with a pair of shawls. Horror at a Shudra being honoured in the Peshwa's house was on the whole muted. Criticism became more vocal later when it transpired that Phule's schools were receiving a portion of monies originally earmarked for prizes for Brahmins.

In 1853, Phule was an interested spectator in a bitter dispute over opening the Sanskrit College to all castes of Hindus. Poona's Brahmins were sharply divided, not in the least in opposing columns in two Marathi journals, *Dnyanaprakash* and *Dnyanodaya*. One side alleged that in Calcutta broadening had led to Hindus being taught the Bible. Untrue, replied *Dnyanodaya*. The question was resolved in favour of broadening, but scholarships remained restricted to Brahmins.

Sadly, Phule was obliged at this time to withdraw himself from the schools he had started. 'Differences of opinion' had 'led to a rift' with Brahmin colleagues on the schools' governing bodies. In *Gulamgiri*, Phule would claim that it was 'when I began to explain to the students in my schools the deceits and frauds [in some ancient texts] . . . subtle differences of opinion sprang up between me and my [Brahmin] colleagues'.[115]

Opposition to Phule became extreme in 1855 when he wrote a play, *Tritiya Ratna*, that portrayed a farmer's family facing first a self-aggrandizing Brahmin priest and then a Christian missionary. The play concluded with the suggestion that acquiring knowledge was better than worshipping idols. At this, according to Keer, Phule's biographer, 'hot heads among the reactionaries planned to put an end to Jotirao's life.' They allegedly hired two 'low-caste' men who, armed with swords, entered Phule's home in the dead of night. But the two did not strike Phule. It is stated that they were won over by the bearing of Phule and his wife and went on to become his lieutenants. Asked later about the attempt on his life, Phule is reported to have said, 'They did not know what they were doing.'[116]

An 'untouchable' girl of fourteen studying in one of Jotiba's schools wrote (apparently in 1855) a forceful essay on Maharashtra's Mahars (traditionally removers of carcasses and cleaners of cremation grounds) and Mangs (traditionally involved in making ropes and baskets). Evidently a Mang, the young writer is not named in the book by Keer that quotes her, but other sources suggest that her name was Muktabai. Says the essay:

> Formerly we were buried alive in the foundations of buildings. We were not allowed to pass by the talimkhana (school). If any man was found to do so, his head was cut off playfully. We were not allowed to read and write . . . God has bestowed on us the rule of the British and our grievances are redressed. Nobody harasses us now. Nobody hangs us. Nobody buries us alive . . . We can now . . . put on cloth around our body . . .[117]

AMERICA, 1850–57

From June 1851 to April the following year, *National Era*, an abolitionist weekly published in the American capital, printed forty-one instalments of the story of Eliza, a young slave woman, her family and their owners. To catch runaways, even in states that had banned slavery, and to punish those helping runaways was the purpose of the Fugitive Slave Law of the previous year. Stung by the Act, Harriet Beecher Stowe, born in Connecticut and living in Maine, both states where slavery had been outlawed, had written the *National Era* account, which portrayed reality in fictionalized form.

Stowe's *Uncle Tom's Cabin* was published as a book in March 1852. (Dickens's novels in England also first appeared as newspaper instalments.) In the novel, young Eliza finds freedom for herself and her boy by fleeing to Canada. Her joy seems identical to the relief that Muktabai, the Mang girl, expressed half a world away, at about the same time.

It was an emotion experienced by about a thousand slaves who escaped every year during the 1850s from the American South into the North, Canada and Mexico.[118] Uncle Tom, the novel's black slave who cares for his masters but refuses, despite beatings, to tell on runaways, and Simon Legree, the spiteful slave trader, also represented real people. Within months, in America and in England, hundreds of thousands of copies of *Uncle Tom's Cabin* were printed and sold. America's shame had been exposed. Many were stirred, others enraged.

Not talking about slavery, keeping the balance between slave and free states, and focusing on economic expansion were three ways in which America had thus far 'dealt' with the issue. The economy had boomed in the early 1850s. Rail lines and roadways had greatly expanded. Both the North and the South shared in the growth, and seemed to tolerate each other.

Uncle Tom's Cabin broke the unspoken agreement. (A well-known story states that when Lincoln met Harriet Beecher Stowe after the Civil War had commenced, he said, 'So this is the little lady who started the big war.') A couple of years after *Uncle Tom's Cabin* came out, the US Congress agreed that two new northern territories emerging from recent expansion, Kansas and Nebraska, could decide for themselves whether to permit slavery or not. This seemed a violation of the 1850 compromise (hated by abolitionists yet condoned by Lincoln) that confined slavery to specified states.

A key initiator of the Kansas-Nebraska Act was Stephen Douglas, a forty-one-year-old Senator from Illinois and like Lincoln a lawyer practising in Springfield. Belonging to the Democratic Party, four years younger than Lincoln, and as short as Lincoln was tall, Douglas was called the 'Little Giant'. He justified the new measure in the name of popular sovereignty, but Lincoln called the justification 'a mere deceitful pretence for the benefit of slavery'.[119] As feelings hardened on both sides, and as slavery proponents tried to influence the future of Kansas by settling there, the Republican Party was formed in the North, with resistance to the advance of slavery as its chief plank. Among the many joining the new party was Lincoln, now forty-five years old.

By permitting the expansion of slavery, America, he said, was undermining the 'liberal' cause 'throughout the world'. 'No man,' Lincoln added, 'is good enough to govern another man, without the other's consent.'[120] Yet not only did Lincoln not see interracial socializing as a realistic goal, he supported the voluntary deportation of blacks to Africa. He thought that the blacks' voluntary departure would free American soil of the stigma of slavery and simultaneously restore 'a captive people to their long-lost fatherland'.[121]

The scheme was wholly impracticable. For one thing, America's blacks did not wish to go back to Africa. For another, southern whites did not wish to free slaves for deportation—no amount of land or bank stock or money could match the prestige of a 'darkling trudging at your heels'.[122] Finally, slavery's opponents in the North did not wish to pay for the travel of any blacks willing and able to leave for Africa.

Certain that 'King Cotton' was supreme, some southerners dared the North to force the South to secede. And as immigration into America continued to grow (including of many Catholics, which aroused unease in the mostly Protestant white population), some slavery defenders declared that not just abolitionists, but foreigners and Catholics too were threatening American stability. Lincoln expressed his private reaction in a letter in August 1855:

> As a nation, we began by declaring that 'all men are created equal'. We now practically read it, 'all men are created equal, except Negroes' . . . [Before long, it would] read, 'all men are created equal, except Negroes, and foreigners, and Catholics'.[123]

In May 1856, a Congressman from South Carolina, Preston Brooks, marched up to the seat in the Senate chamber of Massachusetts' Charles Sumner, who two days earlier had harangued the Senate against slavery's spread, and whipped Sumner numerous times with a cane until the victim lay bleeding on the Senate floor. In Brooks's view, Sumner had crossed the line by implying in his Senate speech that slavery had a dark sexual side as well.

Mass meetings across the South declared Brooks a hero who had avenged Sumner's attack on southern honour. To show that he was ready to pay a price for what he had done, Brooks resigned from his seat, only to be re-elected with a large majority. By this time, five pro-slavery settlers had been killed on Pottawatomie Creek in Kansas. Angered by the burning of an anti-slavery settlement in Lawrence, Kansas, provoked also by Brooks's assault on Sumner, and aided by some of his sons, John Brown, a fifty-one-year-old white farmer and tanner, had led the assault.

Brown felt that God had commanded him to kill for the sake of freedom and equality. But the five victims on the creek had not been involved either with the burning in Lawrence or with the attack on Sumner. Moreover, mutilation and decapitation marked the murders. The South was enraged and all of America was shocked, yet Brown's career as a daring and violent abolitionist would continue for three more years. While acknowledging that Brown 'agreed with us in thinking slavery wrong', Lincoln would not approve of his violence.[124]

At the end of 1856, a Republican bid for the American presidency failed (some in the South had threatened secession if the Republican candidate won), and March 1857 saw a remarkable pronouncement by the US Supreme Court. A black slave called Dred Scott, born somewhere in Virginia and owned by a Mrs Emerson of the state of Missouri (where slavery was permitted), sought freedom from the courts on the ground that while moving across the country with his owners, he had spent a total of seven years in Illinois and Wisconsin, areas where slavery was disallowed. The case reached the Supreme Court, which deliberated upon it in February 1857.

Not only did the Supreme Court reject Scott's plea by a seven to two majority; its majority opinion, written by the eighty-year-old Chief Justice, Roger Taney, declared that no black person, whether free or slave, whether born in America or Africa, could be an American citizen or sue in an American court, and also that a slave was but property, 'bought and sold and treated as an ordinary article of merchandise'.

The Supreme Court went on to hold that since they took away the right to property, acts preventing slavery's extension (such as the Missouri Compromise) were unconstitutional. The new American President, James Buchanan of the Democratic Party, concurred with the opinion penned by Chief Justice Taney. Buchanan was, in fact, 'secretly communicating with the Supreme Court' before the opinion was made public.[125]

In New York, Horace Greeley's *Tribune* (to which Karl Marx was sending pieces from London from 1852) called the judgment 'wicked and false' (11 March 1857). Offering his reaction in Springfield, Illinois, Abraham Lincoln began with a Biblical sentence, 'A house divided against itself cannot stand,' and followed up with a stark prognosis:

> I believe this government cannot endure permanently half slave and half free. I do not expect the Union to be dissolved—I do not expect the house to fall—but I do expect it will cease to be divided. It will become all one thing, or all the other. Either the opponents of slavery will arrest the further spread of it, and place it where the public mind shall rest in the belief that it is in the course of ultimate extinction; or its advocates will push it forward, till it shall become alike lawful in all the States, old as well as new—North as well as South.

Senator Douglas did not object to the Dred Scott judgment. Any state opposing slavery, he argued, could prevent its extension by refusing to provide police protection to slave-owners. 'Popular sovereignty' would either allow or prevent slavery. Privately, however, Douglas was certain that American democracy was, in his words, 'made by white men, on the white basis, for the benefit of white men and their posterity for ever'.[126] Since only white males had the vote, popular sovereignty meant white sovereignty.

While aiming for the presidency, and therefore seeking support from whites in the South and the North, Douglas was also a participant in America's economic expansion. He managed to alienate the South's businessmen by championing a transcontinental railroad from Chicago to the west coast. These businessmen had sunk capital in an alternative, more southern, railroad which would start either at Memphis (in Tennessee) or New Orleans (in Louisiana) and cross Texas before reaching the West Coast.

We may note also the prediction at this time of the black abolitionist and writer, Frederick Douglass. Born in 1818 in Maryland to a slave mother and serving his masters as a boy, Douglass had slipped away when he was twenty to Philadelphia and New York, where he became a voice against slavery. Refusing to be unnerved by the Supreme Court's verdict on Dred Scott, Douglass said in May 1857:

> [W]e, the abolitionists and coloured people, should meet this decision, unlooked for and monstrous as it appears, in a cheerful spirit. This very attempt to blot out forever the hopes of an enslaved people may be one necessary link in the chain of events preparatory to the downfall and complete overthrow of the whole slave system.

Added Douglass:

> Those who profess to favour freedom and yet deprecate agitation are men who want crops without ploughing up the ground. They want rain without thunder and lightning. They want the ocean without the awful roar of its many waters.[127]

With other Americans, however, pro-slavery sentiment remained strong and was at times defended by pointing to British doings in India. In 1857 an American called Joseph Stiles advised Britons speaking out against slavery to hold their peace upon that subject and 'review [Britain's] own conduct in India' and also 'her treatment of China'.[128] Another American, a merchant called George Francis Train who had made a journey to India, wrote of Dalhousie's annexation of Avadh as an example that could justify American attempts to obtain new lands for slavery in the Caribbean.[129]

LONDON, 1857

About the time that the US Supreme Court was deliberating on Dred Scott's petition, in London, the old Prime Minister, Lord Palmerston, faced a censure motion because of a small vessel off the Chinese coast called the *Arrow*. Owned by a Chinese man called Hsiao Cheng but flying a British flag (a practice permitted by China-based British officials to foster trade between England and China), the *Arrow* was caught in flagrant piracy by Chinese seamen employed by Canton's viceroy, Yeh Ming-Chen. All its crew, twelve Chinese and a man from Northern Ireland, were arrested.

Ruling Hong Kong as governor, Sir John Bowring was also in charge of all British affairs in China, whose emperor was in no position to prevent the presence, enforced by the East India Company's warships, of many British and other Europeans in several Chinese ports. Alleging that the British flag had been insulted, Bowring demanded that Yeh release all the arrested and make an apology.

In response, the white man and nine Chinese were released by Yeh, but the action was deemed wholly insufficient by Bowring, who also dismissed a discovery that the *Arrow*'s registration as a British vessel had in fact expired three weeks before it engaged in piracy. Following orders from Bowring, much of Canton, including Yeh's palace, was bombarded by British gunboats. There were inflammatory statements by Yeh and retaliatory burnings of British factories in Canton.

It took weeks for news of these events to reach London and the British government. We do not have Russell's reactions, but in an editorial *The Times* described Yeh as 'one of the greatest monsters that ever disgraced humanity',[130] and Lord Palmerston defended the man on the spot, Bowring. Convinced, however, that action against a non-British pirate vessel did not justify what had followed, Richard Cobden moved a censure motion against Palmerston. Several stalwarts supported Cobden's motion, including three future prime ministers, Gladstone, Disraeli and Peel. 'Hobbl[ing] into the House on two sticks' because he was 'suffering from a severe attack of gout,'[131] Palmerston replied:

> The issue is between Sir John Bowring and Yeh. ... Sir John Bowring is essentially a man of the people ... What is this other man who has been made the subject of panegyric ...? What is the character of this Yeh? He is one of the most savage barbarians that ever disgraced a nation ... In the contest between these two men,

it is most extraordinary that partiality should turn rather towards this barbarian than towards the British representative.

The whole of Cobden's speech, Palmerston added, had been pervaded with 'an anti-English feeling, an abnegation of all those ties which bind men to their country and to their fellow-countrymen ... which I should hardly have expected from the lips of any member of this House'.

In the House of Commons, Cobden's motion was carried by a small majority (263 to 247) and the government fell, but among the British public Palmerston had stoked the desired emotion, a fervour that was at once national, racial and imperial, and even perhaps religious. In the new election, the sole issue, as presented by Palmerston, was the 'insolent barbarian' who had 'violated the British flag' and 'offered rewards for the murder of British subjects in that part of China'.[132]

Palmerston returned to office with the biggest majority seen in Britain for a quarter-century. Cobden lost his seat. In June, a rejuvenated Palmerston was noticed 'astride a fine spirited horse riding in the Queen's train from Windsor to Ascot and back'. After a few days, however, 'that serenity was shattered,' Palmerston's biographer would later write, 'when with the suddenness of a tropical storm the news of the Indian Mutiny broke over the country.'[133]

CHAPTER 2

GALLOPING FURY

INDIA, 1857

Writing in 1868 about *War and Peace*, his newly published novel on a war fought some decades earlier between Russia and Napoleon's France, Leo Tolstoy would say:

> Studying so tragic an epoch, so rich in the importance of its events, so near to our own time, and regarding which so many varied traditions survive, I arrived at the evident fact that the causes of historical events when they take place cannot be grasped by our intelligence.
>
> To say (which seems to everyone so simple) that the causes of the events of 1812 lay in Napoleon's domineering disposition and the patriotic firmness of the Emperor Alexander I is as meaningless as to say that the causes of the fall of the Roman Empire were that a certain barbarian led his people westward and a certain Roman emperor ruled his state badly, or that an immense hill that was being levelled toppled over because the last labourer struck it with his spade.[1]

Even though the 1857 Revolt did not occur 'so near to our own time', 'many varied traditions' have endured regarding that tragic period which too was 'rich in the importance of its events' and which also has seemed to defy a crisp and concise explanation. However, almost all accounts of the Revolt published that year or the next begin with the same incident.

THEATRES OF REVOLT

In the middle of January 1857, an unidentified low-caste lascar (sailor) in a military station near Calcutta requested a Brahmin sepoy (also not named) of the Bengal army to share some water from his *lota* or jug. Saying 'I don't know your *jaati*,' the Brahmin declined, whereupon the rebuffed lascar is said to have rejoined, 'You will soon lose your caste, as ere long you will have to bite cartridges covered with the fat of pigs and cows.'[2]

The low-caste lascar was referring to cartridges for a new rifle developed by James P. Lee at England's Enfield arsenal and therefore called the Lee-Enfield or Enfield rifle. These cardboard cartridges contained greased powder-and-shot, and soldiers had to use their teeth to tear open the wrapping.

At first, British officers who heard of the alarm expressed by both Hindu and Muslim sepoys denied that the fat either of cows (sacred to Hindus) or of pigs (anathema to Muslims and also to Brahmins, who felt polluted by the taste of any animal) was present in the cartridges for the Enfield rifle. Afterwards, the officers said that if the sepoys so wished, they could buy oil and wax from the bazaar and prepare cartridges themselves.

A later inquiry would reveal that prohibited fats were indeed present in the first cartridge batches, but not in subsequent ones.[3] Yet in January and February 1857 these facts were not established. In the wake of the annexation of Avadh and of misgivings regarding the religious intentions of India's British rulers, stories of a plan to pollute the sepoys out of their religion travelled faster than British denials. The sepoys' jaati or caste networks not only ensured that the reports spread fast and far; they also made dissent from a joint front almost impossible.

Suddenly, a hopeless dilemma appeared to face the sepoys. If, obeying their British superiors, they bit the cartridges, they would reject their blood and their faith. Yet, under army discipline, disobedience would invite death. The sepoys did not know where to go for advice—their trust in British officers had abruptly vanished and they did not seem to have Indian counsellors. Distance from all cartridges, including old ones for older rifles, was their first response, and stealthy defiance the next.

In early February of that year, the British noticed that the telegraph office in Barrackpore (16 miles from Calcutta's Fort William) had been burnt down. On 11 February, General Hearsey, head of the Bengal army in the Presidency, made a sombre assessment: 'We are dwelling on a mine ready for explosion.'[4] But like the sepoys the general too did not know what to do. Enforcing obedience was as risky as permitting disobedience, for in early 1857 the Bengal Presidency possessed only a small number of white soldiers—many were stationed in the Punjab while others were in Burma or on their way back from an Anglo-Persian war.

Moreover, while the Governor General, Lord Canning, was in Calcutta to take final decisions, another man who could not be bypassed, General Anson, the Bengal army's commander-in-chief, was far away in Simla, a hill station amidst the Himalayan mountains of northern India that had been 'discovered' around the time of Britain's successful wars against the Sikhs.

The end of February onwards, British officers in different parts of north India noticed—with curiosity and anxiety—that villagers were quietly sending a few chapatis to each adjacent village. 'In an incredibly small space of time', almost all of the NWP had received and sent chapatis.[5] What mysterious message these travelling chapatis carried would never be uncovered, but activity aimed at the British was taking place, coinciding with the hundredth anniversary of an event that, many agreed, started British rule over India—Robert Clive's 1757 victory at Plassey over Sirajuddaula.

Intriguingly, this activity was taking place far from Calcutta, from where the British ran India, and closer to Delhi, where, as we saw earlier, British rule seemed less solid. Though apparently lacking leaders to guide them, the disaffected sepoys had instinctively grasped the significance of India's pre-British capital.

Even so, the 1857 Revolt's first shots were fired in eastern India. During an open parade in Barrackpore on 29 March, an Avadh sepoy of the 34th Light Infantry, Mangal Pandey, fired at two Britons, missing both, and then rushed at them with his drawn sword. Both Britons were wounded, but only one of the sepoys on parade went to their rescue. Orders to fire at Pandey were ignored by the rest. 'He is a Brahmin and no one will shoot at him,' a white officer was told. A couple of sepoys even struck the officers

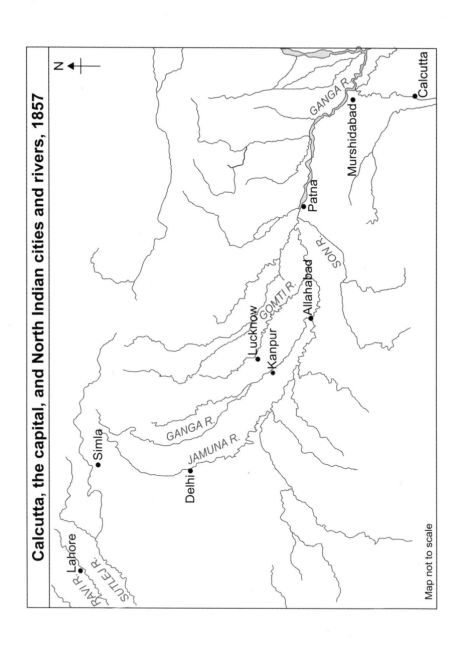

Calcutta, the capital, and North Indian cities and rivers, 1857

N

RAVI R.
Lahore
SUTLEJ R.

Simla

Delhi

JAMUNA R.

GANGA R.

Lucknow
GOMTI R.
Kanpur

Allahabad

SON R.

Patna

GANGA R.

Murshidabad

Calcutta

Map not to scale

who had been attacked. 'It is for our religion,' Pandey shouted. 'From biting these cartridges we shall become infidels.'

In the end, Pandey was overpowered, tried, and, in April, executed.[6] On 31 March, another disobedient regiment, the 19th Light Infantry, was disarmed and disbanded in Berhampore, 120 miles from Calcutta, in the presence of European troops, and on 6 May, the 34th was similarly disbanded in Barrackpore.

On 2 April, after it was found that Colonel S.G. Wheler, the commanding officer of the 34th Light Infantry, had openly advocated Christianity before his sepoys, the *Englishman* criticized his ways and said that if the Government did not 'act promptly and decisively', there was 'no saying how far the mischief may spread'.[7] But the *Friend of India* argued that Wheler's conduct was 'simply the logical consequence of religious liberty', which army officers should not be deprived of.[8]

When the execution of Pandey was announced as a warning at army stations across northern India, sepoys murmured and hissed. Mangal Pandey had gone beyond refusing to bite cartridges, he had tried to kill; but agitated sepoys concluded that he had died for resisting pollution.

Pandey's death was followed by a series of fires in the Bengal army's stores, offices and bungalows across northern India—in the Punjab, the NWP, and elsewhere. Troubled local commanders pondered disbanding and disarming their companies, but since in most places sepoys outnumbered white soldiers, discretion seemed the better part of valour. Moreover, British officers could not, as a rule, imagine *their* sepoys rebelling. 'Every officer argued, and sincerely believed that whatever other sipahis [sepoys] might do, the men of his regiment would remain true.'[9]

Meerut. Ironically enough, the storm burst in the only NWP station where white soldiers outnumbered native sepoys—in Meerut, 45 miles north-east of Delhi. Writing weeks or even months later for the October 1857 number of London's *Quarterly Review*, a British writer, Thomas Frost, was still fuming at what happened and did not happen in Meerut on 10 May:

Eighty-five men of the 3rd Bengal Light Cavalry out of a company of ninety had openly refused to use the cartridges, and, sentenced to imprisonment, for [periods] varying from six to ten years, were now in irons in the jail of Meerut. The sullenness and disaffection of their comrades were visibly increased, and incendiary fires, enough it might be supposed to have put the European force on the alert, were nightly occurring.

On Sunday, the 10th of May, the morning services of the church had been attended as usual by the European men and officers, and many were again preparing for evening prayer; when suddenly a signal was given that the Native troops were in open mutiny. Colonel Finnis of the 11th Bengal Native infantry, a fine soldier, beloved and respected by all, immediately rode to the parade and commenced haranguing his men.

They seemed moved by his address, but at that moment a shot from the ranks of the 20th, who had now just arrived on the ground, struck his horse; and that shot decided the fate of the day. Another and another followed, and he fell riddled with balls—the first victim, out of hundreds, of the infatuated confidence of the officers in the loyalty of their native men.

But the frenzy of rebellion had not yet reached its height, and the sepoys of the 11th, with a lingering feeling of regard, allowed their officers to escape with their lives. The reign of mercy was but short. The 3rd Light Cavalry, who had meanwhile ridden to the jail, and by the aid of a native smith had knocked off their comrades' irons, returned bringing in their rear upwards of a thousand other prisoners maddened with their unexpected liberty.

English ladies were abroad driving about in their carriages, civilians in their buggies, ayahs with the children were taking their evening stroll, when the yells and shots of the mutineers suddenly burst upon them. In a moment, the barracks and the thatched bungalows were fired, and each officer as he made his appearance was shot down at his door. And now ensued a scene of indiscriminate violence, the particulars of which we forbear to repeat.[10]

That night the sound of galloping hoofs was heard in Meerut by a British lieutenant who also heard a shout, 'Quick, brothers, quick! Delhi! Delhi!' Sowars of the 3rd Cavalry, most but not all of them Muslims, were on their way to Delhi, where they hoped to secure the blessing of Bahadur Shah Zafar, the poet-king of Hindustan reduced to pleading for favours from the East India Company, but a king nonetheless, and a descendant of Babur, Akbar and Shahjahan.

But the horsemen were not pursued. Meerut was still British-run, but reeling under the day's assaults, its British force was unable or unwilling to give chase. Adds Frost:

> No station in India was so well supplied with European soldiers. They considerably outnumbered the Native troops. In other places it might be good policy for fear to wear the cloak of moderation; but here the real power was with the British force . . .
> Melancholy it is to read the account of the delays, the purposeless wanderings, the aimless firings into woods and thickets, of the English soldiers on that eventful night, when, hearing that the body of mutineers had set off for Delhi, they blindly affected to pursue them.[11]

Delhi. Soon after dawn on 11 May, sowars of the 3rd Cavalry, who had galloped all night under the light of the moon, crossed the Jamuna on a bridge of boats, passed the gates of the Red Fort, approached King Zafar's balcony, and called out to him. They wanted the king to bless and, in fact, lead their defiance. If Zafar agreed, the East India Company would be turned into a rebelling entity and the panting sepoys into loyal soldiers of India's king. If this ploy showed a brilliant political sense, the sowars were also well informed. They knew that at that time Delhi, while accommodating several companies of the Bengal army's Indian sepoys and a large supply of its heavy artillery, contained hardly any white officers or soldiers.

It contained, of course, its British civilians—the resident, Simon Fraser, magistrates, including Theo Metcalfe, and scores of other officials and non-officials, and their families, including Padre Jennings, who lived with Captain Douglas, commandant of the palace guard, above Lahori Gate, at the western end of Chandni Chowk, Delhi's great shopping street that extended westward from the Red Fort.

Annoyed by the sowars' noise but sensing something major afoot, the eighty-two-year-old king summoned his First Minister, Hakim Ahsanullah Khan, and also Captain Douglas, for consultation. When the sowars shouted up their message to him, Zafar pleaded his age and played for time. He also secretly asked a messenger to ride a camel to Agra and inform Colvin—who as the NWP governor was the most important British functionary in the region—that the Bengal army's sowars were pressurizing him.

The clamour from below the king's balcony grew louder, and more sepoys and sowars arrived from Meerut to make the same demand. Saying to the men from Meerut that they were disturbing the palace's ladies, Douglas left to close the several gates to the city. By this time, however, hundreds of additional sepoys, with Hindus now outnumbering Muslims, had poured in from Meerut, igniting an anti-British fury that raced across Delhi, knowing neither limits nor mercy.

Within a few hours—before ten in the morning—Captain Douglas, Padre Jennings, Jennings's beautiful daughter Annie, her friend Miss Clifford, the resident, Simon Fraser, Fraser's deputy, Thomas Collins, the head of Delhi Bank on Chandni Chowk, Beresford, the head of the telegraph office, Charles Todd, and almost all other whites in the city, including women and children and all twenty-three members of Collins's extended family, were slaughtered.

The killers included sepoys and sowars from Meerut, Delhi-based sepoys, palace employees, and city ruffians who joined in the frenzy. Wounds real and imagined had been swiftly and barbarously avenged. Leading the death squads were the men from the Bengal army who claimed they were killing for the sake of Hinduism and Islam, and who seemed also to be telling themselves that to kill was the only way to avoid being killed.

Fraser, a senior magistrate called John Ross Hutchinson, Captain Douglas, Padre Jennings, the Padre's daughter (who had been recently engaged) and her friend were all cut down at Lahori Gate after they had made a stand. Their plea that the women be taken to the king's zenana was rejected.

Almost all of Delhi's brown Christians were also murdered. When, on hearing a tumult on the street, the popular physician Dr Chaman Lal emerged from his hospital in Daryaganj to see what the matter was, others pointed him out as a Christian. A sowar pinned the doctor down and asked if he was in fact a Christian. When Chaman Lal answered 'Yes' he was instantly shot to death. His clinic was also destroyed. So was Delhi College.

Aided by accident or by ingenious helpers (usually a sweeper, dhobi or bhishti, or another low-caste person), a few Europeans, Eurasians and Indian Christians escaped, including Theo Metcalfe, who, like Fraser and Douglas, had resisted the attackers. Unlike them, he had been left alone by his assailants after a large brick knocked him down near Ajmeri Gate. After falling into a ditch, Metcalfe had fainted. When he opened his eyes, the attackers had gone but his horse was still nearby. While riding off, he was noticed by the *thanedar* of Paharganj police station, a man called Muinuddin Hussain Khan, who hid Metcalfe, clothed him in Indian dress, and helped him escape.

Also among the survivors was Master Ramchandra, the mathematics teacher at Delhi College who had converted to Christianity along with Chaman Lal. Most survivors ended up in Karnal in the Punjab, 90 miles north of Delhi, or in Meerut, which the British still controlled. George Wagentreiber, publisher of the *Delhi Gazette*, and his mixed-race wife Elizabeth, who were among the lucky ones, found shelter in Panipat, half-way from Delhi to Karnal.

Punjab. Before dying or escaping, Delhi's Britons managed to do two crucial things. An Englishman blew up one of the two magazines in the city storing the Bengal army's weapons and ammunition—the deafening explosion was heard by Zafar, by everyone else in Delhi, and even by many outside Delhi. And an escaping Eurasian assistant in the telegraph office called William Brendish tapped out in Morse code a terse message to Ambala in the Punjab. Sowars from Meerut, the telegram stated, were burning houses and killing Britons in Delhi.

From Ambala, the telegram was relayed to Lahore, the Punjab capital, to Peshawar, the Pashtun city that had come to the British after the defeat of the Sikhs, and to Simla, where General George Anson, the Bengal army's C-in-C, was recuperating. The telegram not only alerted British commanders who proceeded to disarm the many companies of the Bengal army stationed in the Punjab and the Frontier (administratively part of the Punjab at this time), it triggered a successful move to enlist a large number of Punjabis (mostly Sikh but also many Muslims) and Pathans in new British-run regiments that would seek to retake Delhi. A parallel move to enlist Gurkha troops was also mounted.

Sikh chieftains, including those who had bitterly fought the British in the 1840s, were enlisted one by one by the Punjab's chief commissioner, John Lawrence, an Irish Protestant officer of the Company who had served in the province from 1849. The manner in which the Punjab had been ruled—by John Lawrence, his older brother Henry, now the chief commissioner of recently annexed Avadh but previously governor of eastern Punjab, and other British officers—had impressed the Punjab's peasantry, Sikh as well as Muslim, who retained unpleasant memories of extortions by warring Sikh factions just prior to British rule. Approached by John Lawrence in May and June 1857, each Sikh chieftain contributed a levy of soldiers. 'The fiercer spirits were everywhere enrolled, and the very class most likely to create disturbance [in the Punjab] was drained off to serve'[12] in what would be called the Delhi Field Force (DFF).

The Bengal army's sepoys in their various stations in the Punjab were ordered to disarm. This could have invited an instant mutiny, but the orders were backed by superior weapons, and most sepoys sullenly obeyed. Many tried to run to their kinsmen in Delhi, but the British effectively, if brutally, exploited the Sikhs' dislike for the 'Poorbias' or the 'Hindustanis', which stemmed from the sepoys' role on the British side during the 1840s.

Sikhs in the Punjab countryside were offered fifty rupees for every 'Hindustani' they captured, dead or alive. As a British civilian would observe, 'The smothered spirit of a martial people was kindled into a flame; escape for a deserter was hopeless, for every village became to him a hornet of nests.'[13] The Sikhs' memory of the deaths of their Gurus at Mughal hands was also used to mobilize them against a Mughal standard. Many Punjabi Muslims too were willing to enlist on the British side. They preferred stability to an uncertain Mughal revival or judged that the British would win.

Despite Britain's earlier wars with the Afghans, Lawrence was willing to summon reinforcements for the DFF all the way from Peshawar, thus leaving the frontier city unguarded, and trusting in a pact he had made with Dost Muhammad Khan, the Afghan ruler. However, disobedience was ferociously deterred. In the space of three days, forty sepoys from the 55th regiment were blown from cannons in Peshawar.[14]

London. The telegraph installed by Dalhousie had aided the British within India, but the Arabian Sea and other waters prevented communication by wire between India and London. Telegrams were forwarded from Bombay by ship to Suez, from there by train via Cairo to Alexandria, and then again by ship to England. Therefore it was only in June that England heard of Meerut and Delhi, 'with the suddenness of a tropical storm'. In fact, the initial reporting of the Revolt in *The Times* of London consisted only of a response to a comment in the French press that India was revolting against British rule.[15]

The immediate reaction of Palmerston, the Prime Minister, was to suspect Russia. His second reaction was to refuse to take the news seriously. That 'a rabble of native troops could defeat a British army was to him an impossible thought'.[16] This haughtiness was risky, but it seemed to steady his ministry at a difficult time. Refusing to doubt the eventual result, Palmerston declined with thanks offers of help from friends in Europe, including one from King Leopold of Belgium.

'I am of the opinion,' the premier said in a letter to Albert, the Prince Consort, 'that we ought to win this Innings against the Sepoys off our own Bat.'[17] Yet, when more grim news came, Palmerston was ready 'to strip the country of its defenders', gambling that the Russians would not take advantage of Britain's vulnerability.[18]

Canning's Calcutta too was not always easy for the British in Meerut, Agra or Simla to reach. Telegraph lines often went down. At times the sepoys managed to cut them. At its core, therefore, the British response to the Revolt was a reply not of leaders in London or Calcutta, but of the men on the spot—individual officers at each site of rebellion.

Delhi. Old Zafar, to return to him and to 11 May, vacillated for a few hours during which he heard of some of the Delhi killings, asked that the surviving Christians be brought to the fort, and asked also for shrouds for burying Fraser, Douglas and the Jenningses. A few Christians were brought in, and cloth for shrouds as well, but angry sepoys who had established themselves in the fort tore up the shrouds that were being prepared.

By the afternoon, Zafar succumbed. Placing his hand on their heads, he blessed an array of rebels one by one. Around midnight, he authorized the firing of a twenty-one-gun salute to announce that Hindustan finally had its own legitimate ruler again. Later, Zafar would claim that he had yielded under duress, but there is evidence that he was pleased to fill the Mughal throne once more with more than titular authority, and pleased too that the plans to terminate his dynasty—hatched by the Company's Governors General in Calcutta, governors in Agra, and residents in Delhi— had been defeated by the Company's own sepoys.

But Zafar's happiness was crossed by disgust, frustration and helplessness. In their intoxication at defeating and killing the British, the sepoys were rude to him. Also, while the new army that had defected to him—its ranks growing with sepoys who entered Delhi after mutinying elsewhere in northern India—had no clear commanders, the king had no money to maintain it. And the now anarchic city of Delhi had no administration to replace the British one, which meant that its merchants, shopkeepers and other well-off citizens were at the mercy of looters.

The king's helplessness was underscored when British women and children who had taken refuge in the Red Fort, apparently numbering a score or more, were massacred. Zafar's pleas for their lives were ignored, but they might have survived had he put them in his harem.[19]

The Britons who had seen Delhi being taken over by the rebels had hoped for rescuing expeditions from Meerut or the Punjab. In the last week of May, a force led by Brigadier Archdale Wilson did set forth from Meerut. At Hindan, 12 miles from Delhi, Wilson's men encountered fierce resistance from a rebel force that, on its part, had hoped to proceed all the way in the opposite direction to Meerut. Though after a hard fight the battle of Hindan was won by the British, Wilson abandoned the idea of continuing towards Delhi. The foe was stronger than expected, and Wilson felt he needed a larger attacking force.

This force, under the leadership of General George Anson, the C-in-C, was to comprise units from Simla in the hills, from Ambala, which lay at the foot of these hills, and from elsewhere in the Punjab. Unwilling at first to accept what had happened,

Anson tried nonetheless to assemble the Delhi Field Force, which however did not move from Ambala towards Delhi until the night of 24 May. Defections and difficulty in finding bullocks, camels and elephants to carry stores and equipment slowed its advance. Then cholera struck and felled many, with Anson himself succumbing to the disease on 27 May in Karnal.

It was only on 8 June that the DFF, now led by General Henry Barnard and joined the previous day by Wilson's force from Hindan, reached the city's northern outskirts. After a furious fight, it occupied vital positions on the Ridge overlooking the city. These positions—about a mile and a half from city walls—included a large house that a man called Hindu Rao had built twenty years earlier, the Flagstaff Tower, and Metcalfe House. Possessing artillery and guns of many kinds, the DFF men on the Ridge included Britons, Sikhs, Punjabi Muslims, Pathans and Gurkhas.

In Karnal, Barnard's force had been joined by Theo Metcalfe, the twenty-nine-year-old magistrate who had escaped from Delhi. He was eager to aid the DFF with his intimate knowledge of Delhi's streets, and to return to the house his father had built. As Barnard's men pressed on towards the city's outskirts, Theo Metcalfe's rage—he was 'maddened with revenge'[20]—led to the death of several innocent Indians. Theo contributed to the 'bitter feeling that prevailed generally in the British camp' against the 'Pandies', as the rebels were called, after Mangal Pandey, for 'their treachery, black ingratitude, and cruelty', to quote George Dodd's words written in 1858.[21]

By this time, the British had suffered major setbacks in the Avadh capital, Lucknow, and in Kanpur (Cawnpore), 55 miles to Lucknow's south-west. On 30 May, rebelling sepoys had forced Henry Lawrence, Avadh's chief commissioner, and all the Europeans of Lucknow, as well as 700 Indians loyal to the British, to retreat inside a few buildings and face a siege that the population of Lucknow seemed to support. A week later, Kanpur mutinied and an attack was launched on hundreds of Europeans, many of them old or ill, who were huddled inside a so-called Entrenchment that seemed easy to breach. At the head of Kanpur's rebels was none other than Nana Sahib of nearby Bithur, whose efforts to secure for himself the Maharaja title and the pension of his deceased father, the former Peshwa Bajirao II, had come to naught.

The news of these reverses travelled to the DFF who were camped on the Ridge overlooking Delhi and to the rebels gathering in the city under the Mughal banner, disheartening the former and cheering the latter. Commanded by twenty-nine-year-old Mirza Mughal, Zafar's fifth son, the rebels had tried on 8 June to halt the DFF's advance and prevent the occupation of the Ridge, but were forced to abandon the slopes and retreat into the city. Though the DFF suffered casualties (fifty-one killed, 133 wounded, and about fifty horses killed), rebel losses were much higher.

For a little over three months, from 8 June to 14 September, the British on the Ridge watched the city, sent spies into Delhi, defended their rear against rebel forays and their front against rebel assaults, and planned an eventual assault of their own. They were being reinforced too from the Punjab and the Frontier with more officers and men, European as well as native, but also with heavy batteries for breaching Delhi's thick walls. These additions, organized by John Lawrence, Punjab's chief commissioner, were however slow in coming.

For much of this time, there was more shelling from Delhi onto the Ridge than in the opposite direction. Many Bengal army guns and a large store of ammunition had fallen into rebel hands, and these hands too were multiplying. On 2 July, the British watched helplessly from their distant positions as five more regiments of mutinying sepoys marched, bands playing, into the city, carrying heavy guns with them.

Both the city and the Ridge faced shortages, sickness and death. For the people of Delhi, worse than the British presence on the Ridge was the disorder in the countryside around the city. Armed robbers dominated the roads and supplies ceased to flow into the city, where angry complaints mounted from sepoys receiving little or no pay, and from merchants forcibly deprived of their goods by the sepoys.

Zafar's wives and sons competed for influence, including over the sepoys, but eventually the king gave charge of his army to Sikandar Bakht Khan, who had joined from Bareilly. General Bakht Khan, as he was soon called, restored a modicum of order, but his unconcern for Hindu sensibilities created problems for Zafar, who was obliged to clip Bakht Khan's powers and enlarge those of Mirza Mughal, to whose influence Zafar's favourite wife Zinat seemed reconciled even as she continued to espouse the succession claims of her son, Jawan Bakht, who was sixteen in 1857.

From the start an enthusiastic supporter of the rebels, Mirza Mughal seemed able to carry both Muslims and Hindus with him and to bring some order to the city. Hindu-Muslim tensions had flared up in the third week of May after a maulvi charged in the Jama Masjid that Hindus were helping the British. Following Hindu protests, Zafar insisted that while a holy war was being waged against the English, he had 'forbidden it against the Hindus'.[22] Tensions rose again in July, when Hindu sepoys murdered five Muslim butchers after accusing them of cow slaughter. Clear that a Delhi divided by religion would slip from his hands, Zafar reinforced the ban on cow slaughter.

A letter in Zafar's name addressed to all the princes of India sought support for the Revolt on the ground that India's different faiths were under attack. Mirza Mughal was thought to be the man behind this circular letter, which denounced, among other things, the law against sati. Whether distant princes like the Maharaja of Kashmir or the Nizam in Hyderabad or the Gaekwad of Baroda actually received the letter is not known. None of them, and none of the principal Rajput or Maratha chiefs, joined the Revolt.

The poet Ghalib was among the witnesses of the change in Delhi. Later, he would pen verses on the rude murder of gentle ladies in the city and also on the terrible reprisals which the British would mete out. In May and June 1857, however, Ghalib and people like him, no matter where their sympathies lay, lived in complete uncertainty. Although the British were contending with the rebels for Delhi, few in the city could predict the winner.

Also living in Delhi were the relatives of forty-year-old Sayyid Ahmed Khan, who was assisting the Company's governance in the town and district of Bijnor, which lay to the north-east of Meerut (which was to Delhi's north-east).

Bijnor. The region of Rohilkhand (the British spelt it Rohilcund), where Bijnor was located, got its name from long dominance by

Muslim Rohillas of Pashtun origin, who in pre-British times had lived in an uneasy relationship both with the Sunni Mughals of Delhi/Agra and with the Lucknow-based Shia rulers of Avadh, to which Rohilkhand had belonged until 1801.

Rohilla chiefs in towns like Bareilly, Moradabad, Bijnor and Najibabad had ruled over a peasantry that was mainly Hindu, but numerous Hindu landlords and merchants also commanded influence in the district. After the advent of British, both Muslim nawabs and Hindu landlords continued to function in Rohilkhand (and elsewhere in the NWP), but the nawabs' political influence was clipped. Also, British revenue policies in the NWP seemed to strengthen a village community or a village proprietor vis-à-vis a talukdar or *jagirdar* who enjoyed rights over numerous villages and who was often, but not always, a Muslim.

After the Meerut and Delhi events, mutinies spread quickly across Rohilkhand. On 31 May, its two biggest towns, Bareilly and Moradabad, fell to rebels led by Khan Bahadur Khan, grandson of an eighteenth-century Rohilla hero. We may mark too that Bakht Khan, the soldier Zafar selected for leading the rebel army in Delhi, was a Rohilla.

Zafar's blessing had given the rebellion crucial prestige across north India, but its rapid spread also revealed that in addition to impressing many Indians with its features, British rule had engendered shame as well, which the rebellion had replaced with pride. Cruelty from the Indian side was only one part of the Revolt's story.

Seizing his opportunity, Mahmud Khan, the Rohilla nawab of Najibabad, set himself up as the chief of Bijnor district and an ally of Khan Bahadur Khan. The story of Mahmud Khan's rise and fall comes to us from Sayyid Khan, the Company's sub-judge or *sadr amin* in Bijnor. Being one of the very few detailed accounts by Indians of what happened around them in 1857, Sayyid Ahmed Khan's record of Bijnor during the Revolt is almost unique. To be sure, it is a very pro-British report written by one in their employ immediately after the restoration of British rule—its even-handedness and accuracy of detail are thus open to challenge. But while assessing the account we should also remember what we have previously noticed—the writer's pride in his Mughal past, his continuing regard for Delhi's enfeebled royal court, and his disagreement with Ghalib, who had held that the British, not the Mughals, merited research.

Sayyid Ahmed's history of Bijnor during the Revolt is detailed enough to give us sixty-two names of British and Indian employees of the district administration, led by the collector and district magistrate, Alexander Shakespeare, the joint magistrate, George Palmer, the judge, John Wilson, and the surgeon, Dr Knight. He lists the five *tahsildar*s, all of whom are Muslims; an Indian doctor (a Bengali Hindu called Tara Chunder Sen); an Indian clerk (another Bengali Hindu, Babu Kali Charan) among five clerks or 'writers', the other four being British; and others working in the district's treasury, police and jails, or as school inspectors. While Sayyid Ahmed was the sub-judge, another Indian, Muhammad Rahmat Khan, was deputy collector and thus senior to Sayyid Ahmed. But it is clear from this and other accounts that forty-year-old Sayyid Ahmed was the team's crucial member, the chief link between the administration and the people of Bijnor, including, as we will see, the leaders of the rebellion.

On 12 May (Sayyid Khan relates) Bijnor first heard of what had happened in Meerut two days earlier. On 17 May, Currie, the postal superintendent, was robbed in the district. On 6 June, after three weeks of suspense, a confident Mahmud Khan left his base in Najibabad in eastern Bijnor and arrived 'with a party of his comrade Pathans' in Bijnor town, which bordered Meerut district. 'The hearts of our old servants,' Sayyid Ahmed continues, 'were all fixed on Mahmud Khan. There can be no doubt that they were all siding with him and paying court to him.' After meeting Mahmud Khan and his supporters, Sayyid Ahmed realized, and his British superiors agreed, that if the white officers and their families did not leave the town at once, 'we would be left without even a pro-English mouse to escort them to asylum across the river Ganges'.[23]

'At the time,' Sayyid Ahmed would write, 'there was no way out except to hand over the district to ... Mahmud Khan.' Collector Shakespeare, according to Sayyid Ahmed, met the nawab and told him, 'I am going; I turn over the district to you. Administer it well. Make use of our clerks and look after them.' According to Sayyid Ahmed's account, 'Mahmud Khan then asked for a letter' recording what the collector had said. Sayyid Ahmed wrote out the letter, which Shakespeare signed:

> Since the administration is, in fact, entrusted to you for as long as the Government may wish, you must administer it well and must also effectively protect the personal properties of the Collector and the Joint Magistrate that are in the residence, and all the property, effects, and government offices. Dated June 7, 1857.[24]

Escorted to the river boundary by some of Mahmud Khan's men, all the white officers and staff and their families left that day, making for Meerut or the Himalayan foothills, which were still under British control. However, Sayyid Ahmed and Muhammad Rahmat, the deputy collector, remained in Bijnor.

Sayyid Ahmed's account does not speak of the impact on Bijnor of the British reverses in Lucknow and Kanpur at the end of May and in early June, or of the killings in Kanpur at the end of June and in early July (which we will soon look at), though it once mentions Nana Sahib (referred to as 'Nana Rao Dhandu Pant Maratha'). But we must assume that news arriving from Lucknow and Kanpur, and from Delhi, influenced Bijnor's mood and the bets its people were laying.

According to Sayyid Ahmed, on 17 June Mahmud Khan asked him for an oath of allegiance, offering in exchange 'an estate of your choice'.

> At first I was very frightened about what to say in reply. After an interval of thought, I became convinced that a straightforward and honest statement was always for the best. I stated humbly: 'Nawab Sahib! I can certainly take an oath that I will be your well-wisher and that I will not be ill-disposed toward you. However, I cannot join with you if you aim to seize more land or fight against the English.' I said: 'By God! . . . The authority of the English officers will never go . . . Except for the English authorities, no one else can rule in Hindustan.'[25]

Whether or not we accept this as a literally accurate account, there is enough evidence to show that in June Sayyid Ahmed pluckily negotiated the safe passage of Bijnor's Britons and that in August—when British triumph was by no means obvious—he left to rejoin his British colleagues. In the intervening two months, while Sayyid Ahmed and Muhammad Rahmat evidently remained indoors, fearing for their lives, there were violent clashes for control between Mahmud Khan's Pathans and bands mobilized by the district's Hindu merchants and landlords, who held sway in pockets of the district. Temples and mosques were damaged, lives were lost, property was looted.

On 6 August, three influential men based in the Hindu stronghold of Haldaur (Maharaj Singh of Haldaur; and Bijnor's Nain Singh and Jodh Singh, who were camped in Haldaur because of intimidation by Mahmud Khan) brought a force of about 4,000 armed peasants into Bijnor town and routed Mahmud Khan's soldiers. A surprised Mahmud Khan was forced to flee to Najibabad, Bijnor's Muslims lost lives and property, and there was general looting.

Sayyid Ahmed Khan was pleased with Mahmud Khan's defeat and may well have contributed to it with advice or encouragement offered to the Hindus. But he was not pleased with the destruction of files that he had carefully kept and sorted:

> The by now excited villagers next attacked the Cutcherry [court building], to loot the English reference books and the volumes of survey maps. They looted whatever could be looted. After thatching had been thrown inside, the Collectorate and Criminal Courts were set alight; miscellaneous bundles from other rooms were taken out one after another to be thrown on this burning fire. The roof of some burning rooms of the Cutcherry fell in. The neat offices of the Criminal Court, the Collectorate, the Sadr Amini, and the Registrar of Deeds, all of whose files had just been arranged alphabetically, were thus turned into ashes.[26]

It now seemed inevitable that Mahmud Khan would return to Bijnor and punish Sayyid Ahmed and Muhammad Rahmat. On 12 August, the two escaped to Haldaur, which however had become hostile to all Muslims after a 'Muhammadi flag', as Sayyid Ahmed calls it, was raised in Najibabad. At the end of August, a massacre of Muslims in Haldaur forced Sayyid Ahmed and Muhammad Rahmat to flee stealthily to Meerut. In that British-controlled city, Judge John Wilson, Sayyid Ahmed's immediate boss, called on the sub-judge, who was 'ill and in much pain', and thanked him. We must infer that the plucky Sayyid Ahmed was blessed with luck as well, and also that he employed some skilful diplomacy.

Etawah. Following the events of May 1857, rebels were ascendant over much of today's Uttar Pradesh, in some places for days, elsewhere for weeks, and in some areas for months or even longer. The only major towns that remained more or less continuously under British control were Agra, Meerut (after the shock of 10 May), and Benares.

Etawah town, from where twenty-eight-year-old Allan Octavian Hume ran Etawah district and looked after the scores of schools he had set up and fostered, was situated almost exactly halfway, going south-east, from Agra to Kanpur. In May 1857, Etawah district had an area of 1,693 square miles, a population of 722,000, and an annual revenue of 136,500 pounds. 'Crime was decreasing, revenue flowing easily, the Great Canal spreading fertility through an ever-widening area, the railroad fast ripening. The community seemed happy and contented.'[27]

On 13 May, three days after the Meerut eruption, a small party of rebel sepoys appeared in Etawah. They were all captured or shot dead. On 18 and 19 May, another band of fugitives from the 3rd Cavalry regiment appeared in Jaswantnagar, 10 miles from Etawah town, and set themselves up in a Hindu temple there. Rushing in a buggy to Jaswantnagar, Hume and two others, an Englishman and an Indian, killed some of the armed fugitives, evicted the rest, and returned to Etawah.

But news of the rebellion in Kanpur, less than a hundred miles away, ignited a mutiny in Etawah town. Though Hume managed to send all European women and children from Etawah to the safety of Agra Fort (an escort of British males and Indian sentries loyal to Hume accompanied them), his own survival was in doubt. For some days, he stayed on in the town, protected by Hindu and Muslim friends, but on 17 June he too had to escape to Agra. Later he would write:

> Can I forget the brave friends and followers who in those dark days of danger and distress stood by me, protected me, and fought for and beside me in 1857—aye, and in too many cases sealed with their lifeblood the record of their friendship and fidelity? NEVER![28]

From Agra Fort, Hume kept up secret communications with his Indian contacts in Etawah; and on 5 July he helped defend a British position in Agra that came under rebel attack.

Kanpur. Though part of the NWP, this commercial town on the south-western bank of the Ganga lay far from Agra, the provincial capital. And though only 55 miles from Lucknow, Kanpur was firmly separated by the river from the Avadh capital. It was its own support, as was Lucknow.

Flowing past Bijnor and Kanpur, the Ganga was joined in Allahabad (120 miles east of Kanpur) by the Jamuna, after the latter first watered Delhi and then Agra. In the British mind, a fort in Allahabad that Akbar had built in the sixteenth century, and the city of Allahabad, were both utterly critical. The Allahabad Fort 'constituted the armed gate through which alone' any help from Calcutta, about 500 miles east of Allahabad, could in case of need reach Kanpur or Lucknow.[29]

Cities like Allahabad, Lucknow and Kanpur were geographically divided between their European half and the rest, a segregation that William Howard Russell would soon describe:

> There is no common street ... and the one knows nothing of the other. *Here* are broad roads, lined on each side with trees and walls, or with park-like grounds, inside which you can catch glimpses of gaily-painted one-storied villas, of brick, covered with cement, decorated with Corinthian colonnades, porticoes, and broad verandahs—each in its own wide park, with gardens in front, orchards, and out-offices. *There* are narrow, tortuous, unpaved lanes, hemmed in by tottering, haggard, miserable houses, close and high, and packed as close as they can stand (and only for that they would fall), swarming with a hungry-eyed population.[30]

As the British saw it, Kanpur and Lucknow were situated in 'the weak middle' of northern India, between the two strong ends of Calcutta and the Punjab. When the news of Meerut and Delhi reached him, Canning thought that the British in the Punjab could both recapture Delhi *and* protect Lucknow and Kanpur. An offer from British civilians in Calcutta to enlist and fight in 'the weak middle' was therefore turned down.

However, the slowness with which the DFF was assembling

changed the Governor General's mind. London being many weeks away, Canning sent a letter on 29 May to Singapore, addressed to Lord Elgin, who was proceeding to China as the British envoy, and requested the diversion to India of troops assigned to China. Said Canning:

> In the valley of the Ganges between Calcutta and Agra for a length of 750 miles there are barely one thousand European soldiers whilst there are several . . . stations of importance . . . held by native troops alone. If mutinous rebellion raised its head at any of these spots the Government of India is literally without any force to put it down.[31]

Elgin saw the letter on his arrival in Singapore on 3 June. As a result, the China-bound troopship *Simoon*, which reached Singapore on 19 June with 700 men of the 5th Fusiliers, was directed to proceed to Calcutta instead.

Canning also summoned two senior soldiers who were in India but far from Calcutta—the Bombay-based general, Henry Havelock, who was sixty-two, and the Madras-based Scotsman, Colonel James Neill, forty-seven, who had fought in the Crimean War. Neill reached Allahabad with the 1st Madras Fusiliers on 9 June and found that though Allahabad Fort had been ingeniously saved (thanks in part to a Sikh unit), rebels had killed and looted in Allahabad city, to which he and his column had to give attention. Havelock, who left Bombay by boat, reached Calcutta via Ceylon on 17 June. At the end of June, he reached Allahabad and his column, which included the 78th Highlanders, joined Neill's.

Conditions were worse than rough by this time for the British in Kanpur, who were led by a sixty-seven-year-old major general, Sir Hugh Massy Wheeler, and also for Lucknow's Britons, led by Chief Commissioner Henry Lawrence.

Wheeler had spent fifty-four years in India. His spouse (some chroniclers call her an 'unofficial' wife) was an Indian. Those in his care in Kanpur included relatives of many of the soldiers posted in Lucknow, numerous British invalids, and his own family. After the Meerut and Delhi events, he had asked the city's British and Eurasian communities to be ready to move to army barracks to the east of the city, about a mile from the river, which would be critical to access Allahabad.

Consisting of two main buildings (one with a *pukka* and the other with a thatched roof) and a few outhouses, the barracks area was surrounded by a trench and a four-foot-high mud wall. Inmates would call it the Entrenchment. Apart from its British soldiers and their families, Kanpur also contained (in a total population of around 60,000) a few British civilians and businessmen, headed by the collector, a man called Hillersdon, and several Eurasians. While the city had many prosperous Indian merchants, the area's most eminent Indian lived outside the city, in Bithur.

Described by one Englishman who knew him as an 'excessively uninteresting person',[32] Nana Sahib, who was in his mid-thirties, was clearly influential, possessing not only a palace but numerous supporters, horses, elephants and firearms—plus the prestige of the Peshwas, which still mattered in some circles. In 1856 and early 1857, he showed his resentment towards the British, who had consistently rejected his requests, by 'shutting himself up in his palace at Bithoor' and discontinuing his hospitality to British visitors.[33] We saw previously that the British in Lucknow had perceived 'insolence' and 'hauteur' in Nana Sahib and his associate Azimullah Khan, when (in 1856), they together spent a good deal of time in the Avadh capital.

But no doubt Nana Sahib himself was looked at with hauteur. Visiting Kanpur in February 1858—after the city's killings, revenge killings, battles and destruction—William Howard Russell tried to imagine 'what was once this station of Cawnpore' and came up with these scenes:

> The solemn etiquette, the visits to the Brigadier and the General, the invitations to dinner, the white kid-gloves, the balls, the liveries, the millinery anxieties of the ladies, the ices, and champagne, and supper, the golden-robed Nana Sahib moving about amid haughty stares and ill-concealed dislike. 'What the deuce does the General ask that nigger here for?'[34]

To return to 1856, both Henry Lawrence and Avadh's financial commissioner, Martin Gubbins, were troubled by the vibes given off by Nana Sahib and Azimullah and said so to Wheeler in Kanpur. Later, it would also be recalled that—'on the pretence of a pilgrimage to the hills'—Nana Sahib and Azimullah were reported to have visited (possibly in early 1857) 'the military stations all along the main trunk-road' from Kanpur to Ambala, presumably including Meerut. In this report, it was suggested that befriending Gurkha soldiers was part of their plan.[35]

But Wheeler was unwilling to share the suspicion, in part, it would be suggested, because his wife was of the same caste as Nana Sahib, but also because Hillersdon, the Kanpur collector, seemed to trust him. 'Between [Hillersdon] and Nana Sahib there had been considerable official intercourse, and the Englishman had been pleased by [Nana Sahib's] friendly and courteous manner and conversation.'[36] When the news of Meerut reached Kanpur, Nana Sahib seems, in fact, to have offered to shelter Hillersdon's wife and family in his palace in Bithur 'where, he assured [Hillersdon], they would be safe against any possible outburst' from Kanpur-based sepoys.[37]

The offer was not taken up but later, on 22 May, when Nana Sahib turned up at Kanpur with two guns and 300 men from Bithur and indicated that he would defend the British, Hillersdon and Wheeler chose to trust him. '[B]eing Mahrattas,' Wheeler observed, referring to Nana Sahib's men, 'they are not likely to coalesce with others.'[38]

By now, Wheeler had received information that the 2nd Light Cavalry intended to revolt. Ordering a wholesale move of Europeans and Eurasians to the barracks, Wheeler also asked Nana Sahib to take charge of the treasury in Nawabganj on the city's outskirts.

Alternately friendly and sullen towards the British, the man viewed by Kanpur's Britons as influential if undistinguished saw in May 1857 a promising build-up of circumstances. If with his help the British defeated the rebels, he would earn from the Company more than he had begged for. And if the rebels won with his support, the Peshwas would be back in business, with himself on a throne. The latter was the outcome he preferred, but, like a great many others in northern India at this time, Nana Sahib did not know who would win.

Sepoys impatient to go to Zafar's aid in Delhi forced Nana Sahib's hand. On 5 June, all four of the Bengal army's Indian regiments in Kanpur—the 2nd Light Cavalry and the 1st, 53rd and

56th regiments of the Native Infantry—revolted. That day, or according to other sources, the previous day, a sepoy deputation called on Nana Sahib and apparently said to him, 'Maharaja, a kingdom awaits you if you join our enterprise but death if you side with our enemies.' Nana Sahib reportedly replied,

> What do I have to do with the British? . . . I only pretended to help them. At heart I am their mortal enemy . . . I am altogether yours.[39]

The sepoys demanded that Nana Sahib 'place his hand on his head and take an oath'. He did as asked and was proclaimed their leader. The 2nd Light Cavalry made for the treasury, where Nana Sahib's men helped them to the cash. With Nana Sahib at their head, the four regiments took off for Delhi, a distance of about 270 miles.

By this time, Kanpur had already seen some looting and in addition to the treasury, the magazine with its store of guns and ammunition too had gone into rebel hands, but Wheeler and other Britons in Kanpur, while shaken by the revolt and Nana Sahib's support of it, felt relieved by the departure of the sepoys. However, British relief was short-lived, for the regiments and Nana Sahib were soon back in Kanpur; they had not gone 5 miles when, at Kalyanpur, they made an about-turn at dawn on 6 June.

That day, by beat of drums, Nana Sahib was declared to be the Peshwa. His enemies at Bithur, led by the late Peshwa's widows, were disposed of. The widows' agent Goredhun and his family were killed, as also the servants of another agent, Chimnaji Appa.[40] The next day, Wheeler received a message from Nana Sahib that the Entrenchment would be attacked.

We do not know for certain whether the initiative to return to Kanpur was Nana Sahib's or Azimullah's or that of forty-three-year-old Ramchandra Panduranga, better known as Tatya Tope, son of a close adviser to Bajirao II, who later emerged as the ablest military leader on the rebel side. What seems clear is that while he acknowledged the Mughal king's supremacy, Nana Sahib preferred a Hindu chieftaincy in the Kanpur-Bithur area over service in the Delhi court of the old Muslim king.[41]

In 1859, after eventual defeat, Nana Sahib would claim in a letter to the British that he had 'joined the rebels from helplessness', which is what Tatya Tope would also say in April 1859, after his capture and shortly before he was hanged. According to Tope's statement, the sepoys 'surrounded us and imprisoned the Nana and myself'.[42] Nana Sahib was never captured or interrogated, and all the whys and whens of his story will never be fully known. After 6 June 1857, British opinion in and around Kanpur was that Nana Sahib, 'this wolf in sheep's clothing', had 'planned to deceive the English from the beginning'.[43] It would be claimed that 'the outward demeanour of the Nana Sahib was never more suave than it was just before the outbreak. He was the adviser, and the trusted adviser, of the civil authorities.'[44]

Another view was that while the sepoys may have compelled Nana Sahib to proceed towards Delhi, he and his close advisers convinced the sepoys to return to Kanpur. According to Malleson, Nana Sahib 'and his agents' were employed throughout the night of 5 June in persuading the sepoys marching to Delhi 'that their work was but half done so long as one English person remained alive' in Kanpur. After the British in Kanpur were exterminated, 'we will march to Dehli—I first of all at your head'.

The Entrenchment, a mile or so south of the Ganga, contained about 450 men, 330 women and children, and six guns. On 31 May and on 1 and 2 June, they were joined by another 115 men who had been sent westward, via Allahabad, by Canning. The newcomers brought word that larger reinforcements were on the way. Thereupon, Wheeler sent fifty of the newcomers to Lucknow to aid Lawrence, who on 22 May had sent eighty-four men to Kanpur from his limited supply.

On the other side, a rebel subedar, Tika Singh, was made a general and commander-in-chief. Guns from the magazine captured by the rebels daily shelled the Entrenchment, which was besieged as well.

All through the first day's bombardment the shrieks of the women and children were 'terrific', but after that ordeal of initiation 'they never uttered a sound except when groaning from the horrible mutilations they had to endure'.[45]

Supplies of water, food and medicines quickly ran low, and the heat was fierce. Dozens of deaths occurred everyday, through sickness and shells. By the time the siege ended, the British side had tipped 250 bodies into a well. Among the dead were women and children, Collector Hillersdon and his wife, and Lieutenant Godfrey Wheeler, his father's 'favourite darling son', who was 'sitting on a sofa, recovering from a wound while one of his two sisters fanned his face, when a round-shot came hurtling over the mud wall and knocked his head clean off'.[46]

But rebel attempts to shatter or burn the Entrenchment failed— the four-foot-high mud walls withstood a lot of shelling, and constant British fire discouraged the rebels from charging the low walls and scaling them.

Thanks to British agents (white, brown or mixed) who slipped out, a few messages were exchanged between the Lucknow and Kanpur camps. In one of these messages, Lawrence assured Wheeler that Havelock was on his way to Kanpur and also to Lucknow, and urged the general not to make any deal with Nana Sahib.[47] But before this cautionary word could be received, a deal was indeed struck.

On 25 June, after eighteen days and nights of continuous shelling, a European or Eurasian woman who was a prisoner of the rebels (either old Mrs Greenway, whose European family owned a large business in Kanpur, or Mrs Jacobi, a much younger Eurasian woman, depending on which of two conflicting accounts is true) arrived at the Entrenchment in a palanquin, bearing an offer from Nana Sahib set down in the well-recognized handwriting of Azimullah: 'All those who are in no way connected with the acts of Lord Dalhousie, and are willing to lay down their arms, shall receive a safe passage to Allahabad.'

Dalhousie, of course, was the Governor General who had rejected Nana Sahib's pleas, enforced the doctrine of lapse and annexed Avadh.

Old Wheeler was unwilling to accept the offer, but exhausted younger colleagues prevailed upon him, pointing out that in three days the Entrenchment would be entirely without food, and arguing that the chance to save the women and children was worth taking. 'Had there been no women or children,' one of the younger men, Mowbray Thomson, would later claim, 'we should have made a dash for Allahabad rather than thought of surrender.'[48]

Later that day (25 June), Wheeler proposed 'honourable

surrender' of the 'shattered barracks and free exit under arms, with sixty rounds of ammunition per man', carriages for the women and children, and boats 'furnished with flour' to take the party to Allahabad. The next day, he was informed that Nana Sahib had accepted the terms. A man called Todd who had taught English to Nana Sahib was sent to obtain his signature on the treaty of surrender. Returning with the signature, Todd reported that he had been 'kindly' received by his former pupil.

Satichaura and Bibighar. Though tainted by surrender, the prospect of departure for Allahabad, set for the morning of 27 June, brought joy to the Entrenchment. The dal-chapati ration for the evening meal on 26 June was doubled, and apart from a single accidental shot from the British, which invited a rebel volley in return, the inmates experienced their first quiet night in three weeks.

In the morning, a few elephants, palanquins, and carts arrived to take the Britons to Satichaura Ghat on the Ganga. The old, infirm and limbless among them, and these were numerous, felt grateful to Nana Sahib for this thoughtfulness. Others walked to the river.

Both sides of the path were lined by large crowds excited by a momentous event: the peaceful departure with their families of a British force, thought invincible until the other day, but now worn down by an alliance between a prince born in Maharashtra and sepoys who shared the language and culture of the area around Kanpur. As the British party trudged to the river bank, a few sepoys came up to offer respectful farewells to those who had been masters until they had become enemies, and to their wives, or to their widows. Touching words were exchanged.

At Satichaura Ghat on the river, boats were ready, and crew too had been provided. Half or more of the British had stepped inside the boats (including, according to some reports, Wheeler and his wife), and two or three boats had begun to move, when a bugle note sounded from a temple on the bank. At this, the boatmen jumped off the boats and waded to the shore, but not before they had placed burning charcoal in the thatches of most boats.

Fires started in many of them. A few of the British shot at the escaping boatmen, missing most of them, but by this time, fifteen or sixteen rebel troopers had opened carbines from close range on the people attempting to embark. Some of the British tried to push their boats and a few succeeded, but found rebels on both banks firing 'from ambush in which they were concealed'. Also in action were 'four nine-pounders, carefully masked and pointed to the boats'. Boats that did move were targeted from both banks and also from boats in the water. Many Britons were felled at or near the boats before these could move; persons who tried to make it back to the shore were gunned or cut down. According to some versions, Wheeler and his wife were cut down near a boat.[49]

Tatya Tope was the man in charge at Satichaura, operating, it was claimed, from the room from where the bugle note came.[50] Though not present at the ghat, Nana Sahib was keeping track from quarters nearby and giving orders.

In implementation of these orders, all survivors, including those who had not yet reached the boats, were arrested. While all the men were shot dead right away, the women and children, about 170 in all, were first taken to a place called Savada House, and then to another house called Bibighar, once built by a British officer for his Indian mistress, but later used as a military depot. About forty other women and children were already confined in Bibighar, survivors from a party of European refugees from Fatehgarh who had entered Kanpur a few days after 6 June. All males in that party had been killed, apparently on Nana Sahib's orders.

Less than fifty yards from Bibighar was the hotel that Nana Sahib had made his Kanpur quarters. On 15 July—by when news had come that Havelock and Neill were approaching with their columns—Nana Sahib evidently ordered the killing of all the women and children imprisoned in Bibighar. The sepoys refused, it seems, to shoot at them, and the women of Nana Sahib's household threatened to jump from their upper-storey windows if the hostages were killed.

But butchers and others willing were found, and the long and tiring task of killing around 200 people with swords was duly completed by dawn on 16 June, though a few of the still-living were also dumped, along with dead bodies, into a well. The British would later cite 'a credible report' that Nana Sahib, having 'ordered a nautch', had passed the 'evening with singing and dancing'.[51]

In April 1859, both Tatya Tope, who was about to be hanged in central India, and Nana Sahib, who sent a letter while a fugitive in Nepal, would claim that the Satichaura killings were not ordered by them. According to Tope's statement, he arranged forty boats for the British to proceed to Allahabad, but the rebels 'commenced a massacre' and 'set the boats on fire'. Nana Sahib's letter, addressed to 'the Queen, Parliament, the Court of Directors, the Governor General, and all officers civil and military', spoke of the women and children he had hoped to save and accused '*your* sepoys' (emphasis added) and so-called '*budmashes*' for the Satichaura and the Bibighar killings.[52]

Notwithstanding the similarity in these explanations offered from far-apart places, they have to be rejected, for the events they seek to explain were immediately followed by fierce fights in and around Kanpur in which the prince and his associate, Tatya Tope, worked in complete unison with the sepoys against the British arriving from the east.

Moreover, by 25 July 1857 the British were in possession of documents establishing Nana Sahib's direct role in the Satichaura killings, including an instruction from him for killings to be arranged from the Avadh bank of the Ganga, because (as he put it) at the Kanpur shore, his administration was committed to letting the British go to Allahabad.[53]

Before long, the British would also learn that a council had met in Kanpur and decided that the best way of getting the British out of the Entrenchment was to offer safe passage 'down the river and then kill them'. Nana Sahib, General Tika Singh, Azimullah and a maulvi called Liakat Ali were among those who participated in the planning session.[54] The stratagem had received a boost from an assessment elicited from a Eurasian spy in Indian garb who was arrested after he had slipped out of the Entrenchment.

This man, W.J. Shepherd, one of only five from the Entrenchment who would survive past July 1857, was asked by a man 'having the appearance of authority' on the rebel side whether or not the British would accept an offer of safe departure. He could not 'exactly tell', Shepherd replied, not suspecting the questioner's intent, but he added that 'the females were certainly anxious to get away by any means' and that 'for their sakes' an offer 'made in a satisfactory manner' was likely to be accepted.[55]

On 1 July, right on the heels of Satichaura, Nana Sahib got himself crowned as the Peshwa. Kanpur and Bithur were illuminated and a proclamation informed the population that 'by the bounty of the glorious Almighty' and 'the enemy-destroying fortune of the Emperor' in Delhi, Kanpur had 'been conquered', the Christians 'sent to hell', and both Hinduism and Islam 'confirmed'.[56] Nana Sahib, ever conscious of the traditional turf of the Peshwas, claimed in the proclamation that the Christians of 'Poona, Satara and other places' too had been 'destroyed', which however was not true of either Poona or Satara (60 miles south of Poona).[57]

This jubilant coronation was hardly the response of a 'helpless' man submitting to unruly sepoys. It was the fulfilment of a dream nursed for years and achieved by a betrayal that was as daring as it was heartless. Nana Sahib himself would have called the betrayal a compulsion of new circumstances and the only way to survive.

The 'undistinguished' and oft-brooding Nana Sahib had more to him than what the British saw. His belief in his importance, which, to his annoyance, the British refused to echo, was not an attractive quality, but faith in his future helped Nana Sahib at critical moments. As Bajirao II's adopted heir, he believed in his destiny, and this belief rallied support. He also had, we will find, a sharp nose for an approaching enemy and the skill to elude that enemy, which was aided by spies and by an understanding of northern India's terrain. He possessed too the political sense to accept the umbrella of Delhi's Mughal king, and a self-respect that hated the idea of foreigners ruling India.

According to one speculative view, 'Nanasahib and Azimulla Khan [may have] played a leading part' in organizing the entire rebellion.[58] We know from Russell that Azimullah had discerned British military weaknesses on his visit to the Crimean front. Did Nana Sahib and Azimullah sow seeds of rebellion in the different stations in North India they visited before the Revolt? Yet, if ending British rule was their aim, why didn't either of them leave any record, at least towards the end of their lives, to suggest that? Why, on the contrary, did Nana Sahib leave evidence to show that in 1857 he was coerced by the sepoys?

Only questions, not answers, are possible at this distance of time. What we know is that Nana Sahib could think internationally, at times seeking aid from Britain's rivals (just as some of his Peshwa forebears had done), even while trying to placate Britons who could help or harm him, and even if his expectations were often grandiose. We have, too, the story of his reported bid to enlist Gurkha backing.

Also, he was supported on and off the battlefield by persons loyal to the Peshwa cause, of whom the most notable was Tatya Tope. Then, though he was caught out at times, he had the dexterity, at every ugly incident, to leave behind hints that could absolve him of a leading role, or suggest that on his part he was helpless, or that he had tried to save women and children. What Nana Sahib did not have was a strong sense of right and wrong, or of the sanctity of human life.

For many, the events of 1857 compressed human dilemmas into tough tight moments, yet there were those who resolved the dilemmas in favour of sparing lives. Earlier, we saw Bijnor's rebelling nawab, Mahmud Khan, assisting the safe passage of the district's Europeans before assuming control, and Etawah's Indians helping Allan Hume and other Britons to reach Agra. This happened in several other places too.

Because of their numbers, Kanpur's Britons presented a tougher challenge, but there is no evidence that Nana Sahib gave any thought to their possible survival, even when those Britons included children and women, or people who had sat at his dining table at Bithur, or called him 'Maharaja', or tutored him, or an old general who had won the respect of many sepoys and was partial to speakers of Nana Sahib's own language, Marathi. Nana Sahib's focus on his own future—above all a throne and a title, but also survival at all costs—seemed to require every beat of his heart.

~

Later there would be reports, never confirmed, of a young white or Eurasian woman abducted at Satichaura by sepoys and surviving,

or killing abductors before killing herself, or marrying a sepoy—
or of more than one such woman. A daughter of Wheeler was
mentioned in this connection, but none of the stories was ever
corroborated.

Rape, more heinous than murder in Victorian Britain, was
alleged in some stories in the British press, but there was never any
proof or even a specific charge of rape. Since it was deemed
polluting to the perpetrator, the rape of a foreign woman was
something the sepoys had to abhor or, if it ever occurred, conceal.

On 27 June, more than a dozen of the Satichaura Britons fought
for hours for their lives—shooting, dodging, rowing and swimming
away—but in the end, only four survived: Mowbray Williams,
who would provide a detailed account of the Entrenchment and of
Satichaura, Delafosse, Murphy and Sullivan. A landlord in Murar
Mau on the Avadh side of the river, Digvijaya Singh, sheltered the
four despite Avadh's dominant anti-British sentiment. After two
weeks, they joined Havelock's column on its march to Kanpur.

It was not until 20 July that Canning in Calcutta learnt of
Bibighar. Much earlier, on 19 June (before Satichaura had occurred),
he had acknowledged the reality that 'in Rohilcund' and in 'the
Doab' (the region between the Ganga and the Jamuna)—'from
Delhi to Cawnpore and Allahabad'—'the country is . . . in rebellion
against us . . .'[59]

Canning's hopes rested on the columns of Havelock and Neill
that were trying to make their way to Kanpur and Lucknow.
These columns faced extreme heat, cholera, a sullen populace that
was reluctant to provide animals for moving the columns' heavy
guns and stores, and, at several places, a tough enemy. A Havelock–
Neill rivalry did not help, and the populace was horrified by the
punishment meted out by the advancing columns to real and
imagined rebel supporters.

In certain villages around Allahabad, apparently marked out by
Neill for complete slaughter for their alleged role in the rebellion,
his men did not spare 'the aged, women and children'. Many were
simply 'burnt to death'.[60] This happened before the middle of June,
and though no evidence seems to be available it has been speculated
that news of the torching of living people might have reached
Kanpur before the killings of Satichaura and perhaps contributed
to the apparent condoning of the massacre by many in the city.[61]

Hoping to stop the British before they could reach his fiefdom, Nana Sahib positioned substantial forces in Fatehpur, 40 miles east of Kanpur and 75 miles west of Allahabad, but was forced to retreat after heavy losses. He made fresh stands at Aong, Pandu Nadi (only hours before orders for the Bibighar killings were given), and finally, just outside Kanpur. In the last battle, Nana Sahib's men fought 'every inch of the ground' and fired with a 'precision and determination' that Havelock felt obliged to record.[62]

After his coronation, Nana Sahib had drawn up a fanciful list of territories he expected to control, including every space between Kashmir in the north and Ratnagiri in Maharashtra, and between Calcutta and Bombay, along with revenues that each province would provide. Evidently, the Peshwa also looked forward, documents suggest, to 'tributes from Kings, Princes and Rajahs', including rulers in China, Persia and Afghanistan—and the Queen of England. He planned to take good care of top appointees, and thought that his Prime Minister should receive a monthly salary of Rs 100,000, and other senior officials between Rs 25,000 and Rs 10,000; but a sepoy was to be paid not more than seven rupees, and a chaprasi six.[63]

On 17 July, however, only sixteen days after the coronation, Havelock reached Kanpur and Nana Sahib fled to Bithur. Fearful of retribution, many citizens too left the city, which Neill entered on 20 July. Crossing the river and getting to Lucknow was the task assigned to Havelock; Kanpur was left to Neill.

Neill's reaction to the floor in Bibighar, covered with blood and other objects, is widely known. Saying that he could not control his feelings after seeing ladies' and children's slippers, petticoats, straw hats and prayer books covered with blood, and expressing a resolve to 'punish with the most savage ferocity' the people he would deem responsible, Neill ordered that

> Every stain of . . . innocent blood shall be cleared up and wiped out, previous to their execution, by such miscreants as may be hereafter apprehended, who took an active part in the mutiny . . . The task will be made as revolting . . . as possible, and the Provost-Marshall will use the lash in forcing anyone objecting to complete his task. After properly cleaning up his portion, the culprit is to be immediately hanged [at the] gallows . . . erected close at hand.[64]

In compliance with this order, the culprit was required, before being hanged, to go down on his knees and lick clean a square foot of the floor covered with dried blood, 'which would be previously moistened with water by natives of the lowest caste'.[65] Neill also decided (he wrote in his diary) that 'all the Brahmins will be buried, all the Mahommedans burned.'[66] As total a humiliation as possible was the aim.

Bibighar's horror ranks high in the ugly story of humanity's offences, yet we must ask if everyone would have reacted to it the way Neill did. And we must remember too the scene, but forty days earlier, of villagers near Allahabad being burnt alive under the auspices of the judge of Bibighar. Enforced for three months, his order in Kanpur produced the hanging and humiliation of perhaps hundreds of Indians, including many 'who had no direct connection with the murders'.[67] Yet, though others might have responded differently, Neill was not alone.

> Private Metcalfe of the 32nd said that the Highlanders knelt down on being taken into the building and 'took a Highland oath that for everyone of our poor creatures who were thus slain, 100 of the enemy should bite the dust, and I need not add that they kept their vow'.[68]

~

Relieving their besieged compatriots at Lucknow's Residency was another vow the British in Kanpur had taken, but it was not going to be easy. In their capital and around it, Avadh's population opposed the British, and taking his force and guns across the 700-yard width of a swiftly flowing Ganga was a challenge for Havelock.

Moreover, Nana Sahib still had his defeated forces around Kanpur, and these were being encouraged by at least four other groups in northern India. Avadh rebels across the river constituted the strongest of these. Next were the Rohillas, just west of Avadh, under Khan Bahadur Khan, the nawab of Bareilly. Fighters gathered east of Allahabad under Kunwar Singh, a remarkable eighty-year-old landlord hailing from Jagdishpur in today's western Bihar, made up the third group. The fourth, south of the Jamuna, consisted of rebels who had deserted British stations in that region or the ranks of pro-British Indian princes, of whom the Maharaja of Gwalior was one.

Havelock and Neill had reimposed British authority over a narrow strip of land from Allahabad in the east to Kanpur in the west, and between the Ganga to the north and the Jamuna to the south. In addition, the British continued to control Benares, Agra Fort, Meerut, and most of the Himalayan hill stations. The rest of north India, east of the Punjab, was either in rebel hands or under no one, and by now, seventy of the Bengal army's eighty-four Indian regiments had revolted.

In some places, the news that Company Raj had been replaced with native rule may even have led (according to a report in an 1858 article in an American journal) to more land being cultivated. Also, 'a large majority' of chiefs in the vicinity around Delhi 'led their followers to the support of the king of Delhi'. When the English 'march[ed] through the country, they could obtain no information concerning the movements of the enemy from the natives, although these were perfectly conversant with their position'.[69]

For every rebel with a gun, there were several others in support— men and women who passed messages, cooked, carried or served food, fetched water, looked after horses, stored ammunition, or performed other tasks. Of logistics on the British side, we have descriptions, including some vivid ones; the Indian effort has to be entirely imagined.

Significantly, the popular mind had shifted its focus from the biting of cartridges to the white man's rule. Policemen newly recruited by the Company in Avadh were heard saying, '*Kala kala admee sab eiyk hyn*' (All dark-skinned men are one).[70] Now it was 'a struggle for mastery' and no longer merely 'a question of mistrust or discontent'.[71]

Though lacking anything like a unified command, rebels in their different locations grasped the meaning of Havelock's and Neill's presence in Kanpur, and of the British bid regarding Lucknow. If Havelock and Neill could be defeated, the British would be eliminated from north India and pushed away into Punjab in the west and Calcutta in the east. On the other hand, Havelock relieving the British in Lucknow, only 55 miles north of Kanpur, could start a process of British recovery.

For three weeks between 25 July and 16 August, there were fierce fights on the terrain between Kanpur and Lucknow, with one battle quickly following another. Twice, on 25 July and again on 13 August, Havelock managed to cross the Ganga and advance a few miles north. He won a couple of battles each time, inflicted heavy losses and captured large guns. Aware, however, of many more foes gathered ahead and of his own losses, he retreated more than once. And each time Havelock moved out of Kanpur, Neill's force there was put on the defensive. Other rebels attacked Havelock's advancing column from the flanks.

At Mangalwar, 6 miles north of the river, a messenger who had sneaked out of the Lucknow Residency met up with Havelock (on 25 July), bringing maps of the city and notes written in Greek. But Avadh's strongly anti-British villagers gave Havelock little cooperation, while Avadh's rebel forces offered tough resistance. Many of his men were laid low by cholera, heat and rebel fire. On 16 August, after Havelock, now back in Kanpur, had led another successful attack on Bithur, where Nana Sahib's forces had once more collected, the British general admitted that the rebels 'fought obstinately . . . even against my powerful artillery-fire'.[72]

But reinforcements could be seen on the horizon. On 13 August, three days before Havelock's latest battle in Bithur, General Sir Colin Campbell had landed in Calcutta to take command of all British forces in India. Lord Palmerston had spoken to him in London on 11 July and Campbell, who had performed with distinction in the Crimea, sailed for India the next day. Also recalled to India at this time, fresh from military successes in an Anglo-Persian war, was General Sir James Outram, previously an officer of the Company in Avadh.

A civil as well as an army officer, Outram was named the head of all British forces between Calcutta and Kanpur on 18 August, and simultaneously, the new chief commissioner of Avadh, succeeding Henry Lawrence, who had died in July in the Lucknow Residency after being hit by a rebel shell. While Campbell remained in Calcutta, Outram arrived in Allahabad on 1 September, to be joined there three days later by 600 new British soldiers who had journeyed by steamer from Calcutta.

On 15 September, Outram, Havelock and Neill met in Kanpur

to plan a fresh expedition to Lucknow, with Outram offering, despite his seniority, to serve under Havelock, who had become a hero to his Highlanders and to other British units.

Lucknow. Its palaces were newer, more 'European' in design, and more ornate than Delhi's Mughal structures, and dance and music had made Lucknow's culture less austere than Delhi's. In 1857, the thriving city had a population of around 600,000, which was thrice that of Delhi.

The British had thought it 'the finest city in India' and one that 'beat Delhi into fits'.[73] The Residency, where most Europeans lived, comprised a cluster of buildings, including a church and a hospital, on relatively high ground to the north of the city, on the south-western bank of the Gomti. The new Kaisarbagh Palace, built in 1850 by Wajid Ali Shah, Avadh's deposed ruler (now a prisoner in Calcutta), and the older palace, Chhatar Manzil, lay to the Residency's south. Further away were the Dilkusha Bagh and Sikandar Bagh Palaces, while the Alambagh Palace stood on the city's outskirts, in the direction of Kanpur.

Hazrat Mahal, one of the wives of the deposed ruler, became a rallying point for the rebellion. Her ten-year-old son, Birjis Qadr, was crowned king to succeed his father, and proclamations in the boy's name called for Hindu-Muslim unity and for the killing of Europeans and Christians. Zeal in aid of these Shia royalty of Avadh was worked up by a fiery Sunni maulvi called Ahmadullah from Faizabad, located 80 miles east of Lucknow, and communication was maintained with Nana Sahib's forces to the south. Solid backing was provided by a league of Avadh's talukdars, Hindu and Muslim, all hurt by the Company's post-annexation land policies. Each talukdar brought a personal army to Lucknow to strengthen the rebels. One of them was Beni Madho Singh, whose son had married the granddaughter of the man promoting disaffection east of Allahabad, Kunwar Singh. Whether Shia, Sunni or Hindu, Avadh's rebels freely acknowledged the suzerainty of Delhi's Sunni Mughal; it made sense to confront a European empire with the prestige of an older Asian empire.

The siege of Lucknow's British began on 1 July, following the defeat of Henry Lawrence, the Avadh chief commissioner, in battles against the city's rebelling sepoys. Able to speak Hindustani,

Lawrence had earlier tried, when the news of Meerut and Delhi reached him, to persuade Lucknow's elites to come together to forestall defiance in the city, but Lucknow-based sepoys mutinied on 30 May and quickly attracted popular support.

Though failing with words and guns, Lawrence had also worked with walls, preparing his Britons in the Residency area—'an irregular quadrangle a few hundred yards square'[74]—for a long siege. Buildings outside the compound were abandoned and some were blown up. Quantities of *atta*, dal, firewood and sand, enough for the survival of a thousand people for at least six months, were procured, and cattle and sheep were stocked for meat.

Each house or building within the compound was turned into a fortress with three lines of defence: a mud wall close to the house, beyond that a trench, and stockades as the outer barrier. Defenders were allotted to each building. Grain was stored in the church, and gunpowder as well as money (British and Indian) buried in the ground. All walls facing the city were strengthened with masonry and provided with loopholes for rifles. Batteries with 24-pounders and 9-pounders were positioned. All in all, the picture was very different from that of the Kanpur Entrenchment.

During its siege, about 3,000 people lived in different buildings in the Residency, including around 1,000 European and 700 native combatants, and around 600 European women and children. Those enforcing the siege, about 6,000 in number, included rebel sepoys and fresh Avadh recruits.

Led by Raja Jai Lal Singh, a Hindu who had been an important official in Wajid Ali's administration, the rebels too had strong guns, excellent marksmen who fired from buildings close to the Residency, and others who were able to hack their way under the Residency's ground and explode mines.

On 2 July, a shell exploded in Lawrence's room. As he lay dying, he mumbled words for his tombstone: 'Here lies Henry Lawrence who tried to do his duty. May the Lord have mercy on his soul.'[75] 'A hurried prayer was repeated amid the booming of the enemy's cannon, and a few spadefuls of earth speedily covered [his] mortal remains.'[76]

Deaths were a daily occurrence in the Residency, before long from disease as well as from rebel cannons and musketry. George Dodd would write:

It was a cruel vexation to the garrison to see and feel how much they were suffering through the skilful gunnery which the British had taught to the miscreants now in the insurgent army. The enemy's artillerymen displayed great rapidity, ingenuity, and perseverance, in planting batteries in positions totally unlooked for; some even on house-tops, and others in spots where the garrison could not respond to their fire.[77]

Among the rebel marksmen acknowledged by the British was an African servant in the ex-ruler's household 'who used his musket with deadly effect from Johannes' house'.[78] Lawrence was blamed for not having had the foresight to demolish this 'Johannes' house' (which however was later brought down by a bold British sortie), and also for having spared religious buildings from which firing was taking place. 'If Sir Henry Lawrence had been a sterner soldier, if he had not been influenced by such considerate feelings for the opinions and prejudices of others, the British would have lost fewer lives than they did in Lucknow.'[79]

Brigadier John Inglis, accepted as the camp commander after Lawrence's death, 'sent off letters and messages to Cawnpore and Allahabad; but none reached their destination, the messengers being all intercepted on the way. He did not know how his missives fared; he only knew that no aid, no intelligence, reached him, and so measured his resources with an anxious heart.'[80]

Desertions depleted the Residency's Indian contingent, and deaths rose. One day, a soldier was 'shot dead by a cannon ball in the very centre room of the hospital'. Every day and night, thousands of rebels fired shells, balls, and bullets from nearby buildings. The stench from dead animals became unbearable. Desperate men and women bought cigars, chocolates, beer, or brandy at fancy prices from fellow inmates.

On 23 July, however, 'a gleam of joy shot through the garrison; a messenger, amid imminent peril, had been to Cawnpore, and brought back news of Havelock's victories in the Doab.'

Inglis immediately sent him off again, with an urgent request to the gallant general to advance with his column to Lucknow as quickly as possible. The English residents began to count the days that must elapse before Havelock could arrive—a hopeful thing at the time, but bitterly disappointing afterwards; for they knew not how or why it was that succour did not arrive.[81]

But on the night of 22 September, a sepoy pensioner called Angad Tewari, who had been sent from the camp by Inglis 'with a letter he concealed in a quill in his rectum, came rushing through the lines, fired on by rebel sentries' with 'exciting news to impart'.[82] Havelock was on his way.

The next day, the Residency heard a distant but promising boom. Led by Havelock, Outram and Neill, a British column that crossed the Ganga four days earlier had reached Alambagh, 3 miles from the Residency, and Havelock wanted the Residency to know. Three more days of battle followed. Finally, on the night of 25 September, after bitter street-fighting in Lucknow in which Neill was killed by a rebel who 'fired a rifle held at arm's length',[83] Havelock led his column into the Residency through its Bailie Guard gate. Their entry was heralded by the sound of Highlander pipes.

> Great was the shout with which they were welcomed, and warm the grasp with which Inglis thanked his deliverers.[84]

The event would become a—if not *the*—classic story of Empire and also of the supposed clash between a heroic West and a cruel Orient. Followed and featured by the American press, it elicited a poem that would be prescribed in American schools for decades— 'Pipes at Lucknow' written by John Greenleaf Whittier (1807–92), the American Quaker poet and forceful advocate of the abolition of slavery:

> Sweet sounds the ancient pibroch
> O'er mountain, loch, and glade;
> But the sweetest of all music
> The pipes at Lucknow played ...
>
> Hushed the wounded man his groaning;
> Hushed the wife her little ones;
> Alone they heard the drum-roll
> And the roar of Sepoy guns.
> But to sounds of home and childhood
> The Highland ear was true;
> As her mother's cradle-crooning
> The mountain pipes she knew ...

Round the silver domes of Lucknow.
Moslem mosque and Pagan shrine,
Breathed the air to Britons dearest,
The air of Auld Lang Syne.

Familiar with Lucknow's layout, Outram had helped Havelock take the least predictable path through the city to the Residency. Even so, 119 officers and men were killed on 25 September on the British side, seventy-seven were missing and presumed killed, and 339 wounded—a loss that day of over 500 men. Rebel deaths were even more numerous. The Residency's losses during the eighty-seven-day siege included 550 combatant deaths, 230 sepoy desertions, and scores of other deaths, including of women.

Though it brought relief and reinforcement to the Residency, the Havelock column was too weak to conquer Lucknow city or to carry the Residency's inmates to safety elsewhere. The city's population sympathized with the rebels, and the Avadh country around Lucknow was still in rebel hands. But the Residency area under British occupation was now a little larger (incoming soldiers had seized, and also looted and vandalized, a few buildings close to the Residency), and the British also possessed Alambagh, 3 miles away.

Asserting that he was the new Avadh chief commissioner but controlling only a few acres of the province, Outram hoped for the arrival of another British force even as he, Havelock and Inglis took up the task of defending their positions in Lucknow.

Calcutta. Eastern India, we saw earlier, had been largely denuded of British soldiers. On 29 March, the Revolt's opening shots were fired by Mangal Pandey in Barrackpore, 16 miles from Calcutta. Unrest had followed the hanging of Pandey in April (in Barrackpore) and the disbandment, on 31 March and 6 May, respectively, of the Bengal-based 19th and 34th regiments. Why then did eastern India generally, and Calcutta in particular, escape the Revolt?

The presence in the city of a large number of Europeans—merchants, clerks, civil servants, policemen, doctors, lawyers, journalists, churchmen, and others, many of them armed—contributed to Calcutta's exemption from rebellion. Also, Calcutta was where reinforcements for the British landed by sea—from

Madras or Bombay and from places beyond. Even if the land was Indian, the sea seemed British.

Living in the Bengali hinterland, a large number of British indigo planters, all of them armed, were an additional force against rebellion. These indigo planters of eastern India, and other Britons running tea plantations in eastern and southern India, comprised the 'settler' part of India's British population. As indigo was hard to cultivate and losing value, Indian farmers were generally reluctant to sow indigo. Often they were coerced to do so by British planters, which led to strife. For this reason, and also because the East India Company did not really like independent Britons settling in India, Company officers and indigo planters had at times quarrelled with each other; but in face of a common threat faced by all Europeans, the disputes were put aside.

British confidence in Bengal had also been strengthened by the successful (though by no means easy) suppression between 1855 and 1857 of revolts by Santhal tribesmen in the forest districts of western Bengal. The Santhals had revolted at first against (Indian) moneylenders and landowners, and then against British planters and officials.[85]

Inside Calcutta, the British enjoyed the support of the population's influential Indians. Formed in 1851 by prominent Bengali landowners, including Debendranath Tagore, son of Dwarkanath and father of Rabindranath, 'to secure improvements in the local administration of the country', the British Indian Association was horrified by the Revolt. By the end of May, Indians with status or wealth came together at different meetings in Calcutta to 'sympathise with the Government ... and to offer assistance if required'.[86] Calcutta's British press reported but also lampooned the offer from 'black baboos' such as 'punchy old Toolsee Doss' and 'flat, flabby Ramdhone Ghose'.[87] Neither energy nor sincerity was ascribed to the apparently pro-British, partially westernized Calcutta native referred to by whites and Indians as the 'Bengali babu'.

Recalling an earlier address of fealty to the Bombay governor, composed largely by Parsis in western India, George Dodd would say in 1859, 'It was not more adulatory, not more filled with enthusiastic professions of loyalty, than many addresses presented to Viscount Canning in Bengal; but it more nearly corresponded with the conduct of those who signed it.'[88]

Yet, the anti-rebel feeling of Calcutta's Indian elites was real. Their pride lay in the Bengal Renaissance that interaction with Britons had helped sprout, and their enthusiasm in the British Indian Association's quasi-political activities. Rebellion would kill the dream of Bengal as the cradle of a modern India. However, Calcutta's Britons did not seem to trust these Indian elites for when 'news arrived from Havelock and Neill that all the Europeans at Cawnpore had been murdered', the city's British community became 'almost wild with excitement, rage, and terror' and dreaded a 'diabolical plot' in their city.[89]

The Kanpur news coincided with an incident involving an Allahabad regiment. After a British paper in Calcutta had carried a report of disaffection in the regiment, the colonel sent by post 'a very prompt denial' and expressed his 'fullest reliance' on his men. The paper carried the denial—and next to it a telegraphed report of the regiment's mutiny and the killing of the colonel.[90]

Stocking up on arms as news of the Revolt reached them, Calcutta's Britons demanded a probe into arms held by the natives. After a 'strict inquiry', Wauchope, Calcutta's commissioner of police, found that the sale of weapons had been 'very large during three months, but that nearly all the purchases had been made by Europeans, . . . that hardly a house in Calcutta, inhabited by Christians, was without one or more muskets or pistols', and also that there was 'no proof' of 'any considerable purchases of arms by the native population of Calcutta'.[91]

In fact, as we have already noted, 'the Indians of Calcutta . . . had little sympathy with the outbreak.'[92] The British had kept order in their city for a hundred years, and, while often outraged by white ridicule, elite Indians liked their opportunities in British India. They preferred the British devil they knew to the rebel—the uneducated sepoy—they had only heard about. Moreover, word was trickling in of assaults in Kanpur on Bengalis working there for the Company.

Even so, George Dodd would record, 'the European community at Calcutta violently hated the natives generally, and violently opposed Viscount Canning personally.' The Europeans believed that 'every mutineer who had taken up arms or quitted his ranks should be put to death; that every native, not a soldier, who aided the mutineers, should in like manner be put to death; that in every village in which a European lad been murdered, a telegraph wire cut, or a dak stolen, a swift tribunal should exercise summary justice; . . . and that vengeance, burning vengeance, was the only adequate measure to deal out to all who had offended.'[93]

Calcutta's Europeans were angered also by Canning's order of 13 June that restricted the freedom of journalists. Aimed at preventing native news-sheets from inflaming public opinion, the measure did not—it could not—exempt the European press from its purview.

In Calcutta and elsewhere in India, there were numerous Indian-owned news-sheets in 1857, but 'the copies printed of each [were] exceedingly limited.' Yet, the British were aware that each of 'the miserably written and badly lithographed little sheets of news' drew 'its group of men seated round a fluent reader, and listening to the contents; one single copy sufficed for a whole regiment of sepoys; and it [would later be recalled that] during a year or two before the Revolt, the sepoys listened with unwonted eagerness to the reading of articles grossly vituperative of the government.'[94]

Fuming at curbs on their writing and dreading rebellion in Calcutta, its Europeans demanded martial law. Rejecting the demand, Canning alienated the city's British afresh with a policy he announced at the end of July. Having learnt of the burning of villages in Allahabad, he issued orders against 'the indiscriminate hanging, not only of persons of all shades of guilt, but of those whose guilt was at the least very doubtful, and the general burning and plunder of villages, whereby the innocent as well as the guilty, without regard to age or sex, were indiscriminately punished, and in some instances sacrificed'.[95]

He was tauntingly called 'Clemency' Canning as a result, and the Queen was petitioned for his recall. She supported Canning, who had written to her of his 'shame' that 'not one [European] in ten seems to think that the hanging and shooting of forty thousand or fifty thousand men can be otherwise than practicable and right.'[96] To Lord Granville, the leader of the House of Lords, Canning wrote:

As long as I have breath in my body, I will pursue no other policy than that which I have been following—Not Only for the reason of expediency & policy above stated, but because it is immutably just. I will not govern in anger. Justice, and that as stern and inflexible as law and might can make it, I will deal out. But I will never allow an angry & undiscriminating act or word to proceed from the government of India as long as I am responsible for it.[97]

After the revolt was suppressed, a maker of sweets in north Calcutta called Paraney Moira prepared a special sweetmeat in honour of Lady Canning, the Governor General's wife. According to Sumanta Banerjee, writing in 1989, 'the sweetmeat is still popular as "ledi-keni" in Bengali homes.'[98] A researcher of folk culture in nineteenth-century Calcutta, Banerjee adds:

A popular song current in Calcutta in those days appeared to be more favourably disposed towards the ... [beret-wearing, pipe-playing] Scottish Highlander troops who arrived in Calcutta on their way to suppress the rebellion: *White men have come from Europe/ They wear jackets over their heads/ The earth is trembling under their footsteps/ Tantia Topi's pride will be humbled now/ Delhi will be re-conquered with ease/ Nana Sahib will get caught.*

On the other hand, Sumanta Banerjee found that the Rani of Jhansi, one of the Revolt's prominent characters and someone we will be looking at in this narrative, was a popular figure with Calcutta's folk painters, who sketched her as 'a courageous woman on horseback'.[99] Also, we know of three Calcutta papers that printed pieces in support of the Revolt and faced prosecution for doing so—*Samachar Sudhabarsan*, published in Bengali and edited by Shyamsundar Sen, and two that came out in Persian, *Sultan-ul-Akhbar* and *Durbin*.[100]

Vidyasagar and Bankim. While there is no evidence of any direct comment on the Revolt at this time by Vidyasagar or Bankim, Subal Chandra Mitra, who wrote Vidyasagar's biography within a decade of his death, observes:

The residents of Calcutta, both natives and European, passed anxious days and nights. No one dared leave his house for fear of life. European soldiers were posted to guard the city day and night.

Reinforcements were brought in from other places, and the Sanskrit College building was requested to quarter them.

There was no time to lose, and Vidyasagar made over the building to the Military without previously obtaining permission of his superiors. The College had to be closed for a few days. Subsequently when Vidyasagar wrote to Mr Young [the director of public instruction and Vidyasagar's boss] asking for his permission to hold the college somewhere else, the Director called for an explanation as to why he had . . . made over the premises to the Military without his permission. Vidyasagar said that he had done it for the safety of the state and that he had no self-interest in it.[101]

In 1858, a twenty-year-old Bankim and another man would be announced as Calcutta University's first-ever graduates. Decades later, Bankim, who occupied a judicial position in British-run Bengal and wrote several historical novels, would regret that he had not written one about Lakshmibai, the queen of Jhansi. According to Bhabatosh Chatterjee, editor of a notable Bankim volume, this is what Bankim said to a friend, Srishchandra Majumdar:

In this country, the women alone are human . . . You may refer to some great European women, but none is greater than the Rani of Jhansi. In the political field no other heroic woman is her equal. The English commander who encountered her in the field of action said, 'In the East, she is the only person who is truly male.'[102]

In another work (published in 1934), Srishchandra Majumdar is quoted as follows:

[Bankim] was all along conscious of the restrictions imposed on his freedom of opinion by the conditions of service under the Government. He wanted to write a novel depicting the character of the Rani of Jhansi but he gave up that idea for fear of incurring the displeasure of the Government.[103]

Anandamath, the novel about the 1770s that Bankim would publish in 1882, offers internal evidence of the Revolt's impact on him. A sentence in the novel, 'I see you will be blown one day from the cannon's mouth by the sepoys,'[104] could only be written by a student of the Revolt, even though in this *Anandamath* image, the sepoys would fire the cannon instead of being exploded at its mouth. Again, one of the novel's heroines, Shanti, a brave fighter who is a skilled rider as well, would remind anyone of the Rani of Jhansi.

We can thus infer that in 1857, this brilliant nineteen-year-old, interested as much in history and politics as in literature, closely followed the Revolt through the English and Bengali press of the day, and through remarks made around him by Indians and Britons. We can also surmise that he was stung by the lampooning of Bengali babus. But we have no direct knowledge of what he said or felt in 1857 about the Revolt.

What Vidyasagar, who was thirty-seven in 1857, thought of the Revolt is also not known to us, apart from inferences drawn from the episode of the Sanskrit College building. The law permitting the remarriage of Hindu widows for which he had campaigned, and which was seen as having helped fuel the rebellion, was now a year old. He continued as principal of the Sanskrit College and, in addition, worked as inspector of schools for portions of the Presidency. From what we know of Vidyasagar's life, we can assume that the Revolt would have troubled him, but he seems to have left no record of his response to it.

To go on record with a response was hard for Indian intellectuals like Vidyasagar and young Bankim. Expressing support for the rebellion would have invited punishment and was probably not their wish in any case. But supporting calls for vengefully suppressing it was also unpleasant, the more so in the light of European derision of Indian sympathy.

Silent on the Revolt, Vidyasagar continued to create more schools and also to mobilize opinion against polygamy. Also silent on the rebellion, young Bankim, who had published his first volume of poetry the previous year, pursued his law studies as well as a BA course in the newly-established Calcutta University, while also absorbing scenes and incidents for novels he knew he would soon write.

Harish Chunder Mukherjee and the Hindoo Patriot. There is, however, an interesting record of a contemporary Bengali voice on the Revolt, that of Harish Chunder Mukherjee, the Brahmin editor and owner of an English-language Calcutta weekly, the *Hindoo Patriot*, launched in the early 1850s.

Thirty-three in 1857, Mukherjee was employed by the Company as an assistant military auditor for a monthly salary of 400 rupees, an impressive amount for an Indian of the time. While working thus for the British, Mukherjee—a 'Derozian' of some sort, though only seven when Henry Derozio died, and a supporter of the British Indian Association—offered clear and independent opinions in his journal.

These views were offered every Thursday throughout 1857 and they merit our interest because they reveal the changing mood as well as some enduring opinions of at least one important segment of Calcutta's Hindu elite. Most of the quotes that follow have been taken from *Selections from English Periodicals of 19th-Century Bengal*, Volume 4, edited by Benoy Ghose.

On 2 April 1857, after the Barrackpore incident but before Meerut and Delhi had occurred, the *Hindoo Patriot* called the rebels 'murderers' but also said that a cause of the unrest was that native regiments had been 'denuded of their best (British) officers'. It was glad, the paper added, that 'inferior orders of caste' like 'the Chamars and the Dhomes' had been kept out of the Bengal army (Ghose, 19–20). Four weeks later, the paper wrote that it was 'absolutely necessary to increase the strength of the European forces in India' and that 'the strength of the sepoy army must be reduced' (46–47).

Referring to the sepoys' refusal in Barrackpore to go to the defence of British superiors when the latter were attacked, the *HP* added that the refusal showed that European commissioned officers of the Bengal army 'have utterly lost their prestige' (51). Two weeks later, on 14 May, the *HP* stoutly defended Bengalis against criticisms printed in a British-owned paper, the *Bengal Hurkaru*, which had advanced the thesis (this was before news of Meerut and Delhi had reached Calcutta) that successful but effeminate Bengalis, not Britons, were the real target of the wrath of the Avadh sepoys, who were 'stern and simple sons of war' (52–4).

Said the *HP* in response, 'The Hindoostanee sepoys . . . may envy the rise of Bengallees to power. [But the Bengallee is not despised.] The Bengallee is in the eyes of the Hindoostanee the Baboo par excellence.' The paper added, 'It seems to be an inevitable consequence of British rule in India that the Bengallees and the Parsees should outstrip the rest of their Indian fellow-subjects in civilization, knowledge and political progress. Their capacity is greater, their mental superiority is superior . . .' (52–54).

The paper went on to say that thanks to the 'Zemindary system' bequeathed by the Permanent Settlement, members of 'the class which own hereditary property' had multiplied in Bengal. The result was that whereas in the NWP British officials dominated the Indian landowner, Bengali landowners were unafraid of the British official (53).

After the news of Meerut and Delhi reached Calcutta, the *HP* recommended (on 21 May) death for 'every native soldier who has had a hand in that appalling outrage and who was not compelled to join it by the intimidation of his comrades' (60). Referring to British fears of mutiny in Calcutta, the paper wrote of 'the utter and known impossibility of [the rebels] obtaining either help or refuge' in the city (63).

Significantly, this 21 May article recognized that what was occurring was 'no longer a mutiny but a rebellion' (63), that there were 'grievances inseparable from subjection to a foreign rule', and that there was a wide though unjustified belief that the British 'want to convert Indians to Christianity'. 'Women and children talk of it', the paper said, while also expressing satisfaction that Governor General Canning had categorically disavowed any goal of conversion.

In another remarkable comment, this 21 May article noted that 'the mutineers have hastened towards the ancient capital of the country where resides the remnant of the former dynasty to which are turned in times of political commotion the eyes of all Indian political legitimists'.[105] In the heart of the Empire's headquarters—at a critical point of the Revolt—Mukherjee, an employee of the British, was acknowledging the potency of the Delhi throne, and the pull it exercised over *all* Indians, Hindus as well as Muslims.

A week later, the paper predicted an imminent recapture of Delhi (which however would not take place until September) and spoke of Lucknow as a city that sheltered 'the largest amount of reckless vagabondage to be found in any Indian town'. On 4 June, the *HP* said that the rebels were 'as brutal and unprincipled a body of ruffians as ever disgraced a uniform or stained the bright polish of a soldier's sword with the blood of murder' (80).

Indirectly criticizing British hotheads in Calcutta for spreading rumours of alleged disloyalty among Bengalis, the paper wrote: 'The Bengallees never aspired to the glory of leading armies to battle or the martyrdom of the forlorn hope ... A strong and versatile intellect enables them to think deeply and to think foresightedly ... They are aware that the British rule is the best suited to their quiet and intellectual tastes.' In due course, the Bengalis 'will rise yet further in the scale of equality with their foreign rulers and divide with them the honour and the responsibility of administering the affairs of the largest and the most well-established empire in Asia' (80).

A week later, on 11 June, the *HP* contested a British opinion that Hindus would not entertain an attachment to Queen Victoria. When Hindus showed a 'deep' and 'warm' feeling towards Akbar and his successors, why would they not show it towards Victoria? Young Bengal would in fact be 'the interpreter between his rulers and his countrymen' (91).

July saw a letter to the editor, signed only as 'C', which foreshadowed an important long-term sequel of the Revolt—an increase in Hindu-Muslim mistrust. We do not know who 'C' was—he seems to have been a Hindu anxious to dispel British suspicions regarding Calcutta's Hindus, and anxious also to warn Hindus against any return of Muslim rule. 'C' wrote on 2 July:

> Oppressed and trodden long by the relentless and inhumane Mahomedans [who are] unsoftened by the influence of sober reason, unillumined by the enlightened views of modern times but hardened into cruelty by avarice and rapacity, the marks of a diseased mind— and enjoying all the prosperity ever experienced by the country within the memory say of six generations, the natives [i.e., the Hindus] never wish, nor is [there] necessity, for new masters, [or] for a fate wholly precarious and uncertain (108).

Once the news of Kanpur reached Calcutta, the *HP* (on 9 July), referring to Nana Sahib, wrote of 'treachery so base, so vile, and so appalling' (109). 'The conflict of Asian stationaryism with an advancing civilization was inevitable,' the paper added, 'when the two were brought so closely together' (115). In September, commenting on British excesses in Allahabad, the *HP* thought that 'the work of retribution was carried a little too far' (165). Also in September, the paper published a list of Bengalis who had escaped from rebel-controlled places in central India.

Delhi. With sweepers and other workmen drafted for fortifying the city walls, sanitation had collapsed in the Mughal capital. Dead animals blocked its streets and sepoys bullied its shopkeepers. However, to the surprise of the British positioned at the Ridge with their Delhi Field Force, disorder inside the city did not seem to affect morale at the walls. The British heard of a verse that Zafar was said to have composed in Delhi: 'Those who vanquished rods of iron had been defeated by a single [greased] cartridge.'[106]

The Ridge was constantly shelled and frequently raided. Sickness added to British difficulties, and failing hope made the British heart sicker—reinforcements expected from the Punjab were not showing up. While some targets, including the Red Fort, were shelled from the Ridge from time to time, the DFF's guns were too weak to batter down the city walls, and its numbers too small for assaulting and holding the city.

Also demoralizing were changes in command. Anson's death on 27 May was followed by that of his successor, General Barnard, on 5 July, who also died of cholera. The man taking over, General Reed, was old and in fact an invalid. On 17 July, Reed retired and the command went to Archdale Wilson, who had brought the force from Meerut.

The gloomy news of the Satichaura incident had reached Delhi by now, and word of Bibighar followed. Though this was accompanied by reports of the advances of Havelock and Neill, Wilson thought he would be forced to postpone the bid for Delhi and pursue other objectives.

Meanwhile, the passion for revenge was rising. After his escape from Delhi, George Wagentreiber, the *Delhi Gazette* publisher, began publishing his paper in Lahore under a new name, the *Delhi Gazette Extra*. 'Week after week', he 'called hysterically for the complete destruction' of Delhi. In the 22 July issue, he demanded a 'massacre' that would 'sink' Delhi into 'the silence of the dead within its walls'.[107]

Wagentreiber would have hurrahed what Frederic Cooper, deputy commissioner of Amritsar district, did on 1 August. After chasing and capturing 303 out of 400 or more Hindustani sepoys who had escaped the previous day from Lahore jail, Cooper had them shot in batches of ten in Ajnala, which was not far from Lahore or Amritsar. When 237 bodies had been dumped into a deep dry well, Cooper ordered his Sikh and Muslim police to produce the remaining sixty-six prisoners for execution. Only twenty-one could be brought out of the small room where they had been packed together; the rest had died of suffocation. In a subsequent book, Cooper spoke of his pride that as 'a single Anglo-Saxon supported by a section of Asiatics' he had 'coldly presid[ed] over so memorable an execution'.[108]

Fear too had played a part in the Ajnala tragedy and, in fact, in many of the 1857 killings. After rising in revolt, the sepoys felt they had to kill in order to survive; and the British dealing with rebelling sepoys thought the same.

On 8 August, a thirty-four-year-old brigadier, John Nicholson, trudged up the Ridge outside Delhi and announced that 1,100 European and 1,500 Indian soldiers from the Punjab were on their way. They arrived on 14 August.

Nicholson's reputation—of being a man with a massive chest, strong limbs and an arrogant air—had preceded him at the Ridge. It was John Lawrence in Lahore who had summoned him from the Frontier, where, earlier, Nicholson had awed warlike tribesmen. On his way to Delhi, the young brigadier had annihilated more than one rebel unit.

Nicholson was welcomed as a hero by the Ridge's Britons, many of whom shared his opposition to 'simply hanging' those who had killed European women and children in Delhi; in his view, such men had to be 'flayed alive, impaled or burnt'.[109] Arriving from the Punjab two months earlier, another young officer asking for toughness and retribution, Lieutenant William Hodson, had taken charge of intelligence.

But it was not until early September, when a siege-train that Lawrence had assembled arrived from the Punjab, that assaulting Delhi was considered by Wilson and his staff. Including 'about thirty heavy pieces of artillery—guns, howitzers and mortars of large calibre', the siege-train had been delayed because even in the

Punjab the public was slow in providing men for escorting the guns or animals (elephants, camels, oxen and horses) for pulling the guns and for carrying food, fodder and stores.[110]

By early September 1857, 9,866 European and native soldiers, plus an unknown number of 'unarmed and undisciplined pioneers' had collected on the Ridge, apart from about 3,000 who were sick or wounded. Rebel strength in the city was estimated at more than 4,000 cavalry and 12,000 infantry, plus a large number of jihadis. On 12 September, word reached the Ridge that Bakht Khan was planning to mount a huge assault upon it, with old King Zafar himself at its head, and that the rebels, well aware of the arrival of the siege-train, hoped to overwhelm the British by force of numbers before the big guns tore open the city walls. Conflicting with this report was a message for a settlement, apparently sent by Hakim Ahsanullah Khan, the king's physician.

But by this time the British had put their plan into action. From 7 September, in spite of the shelling and firing, batteries were constructed close to the city's walls; 11 September saw a ferocious cannonade that felled portions of the walls; and on 14 September, four separate columns launched into Delhi, breaching its northern and western walls between Kashmiri Gate and Lahori Gate.

The rebels fought back with fury. Occupying every height and foothold at or near the walls, they rained shells, bullets and masonry on the soldiers who tried to blast or climb their way in. Simultaneously, the rebels tried to close every new breach with sand and stone. The resistance seemed to surprise the British. Leading an assaulting column at Lahori Gate, Nicholson turned around to urge his men to press on. At that precise moment, he was shot in the back. While 'slowly dying in his tent', he heard that Wilson was wondering about recalling the columns. 'Thank God,' Nicholson evidently cried out, 'I have strength yet to shoot that man, if necessary.'[111]

But Wilson did not call his forces back. The assaults continued amidst the hail of shells and bullets, through or over broken walls, past the dead and dying of both sides, and into the streets of Delhi. There, the British and their native companions (Sikh, Gurkha, Pathan and Punjabi Muslim) were met by the rebels' field artillery, and by bullets aimed from rooftops and windows. However, 'sapping forward from house to house' and backed by superior firepower, the incoming soldiers advanced along several streets, losing as well as killing many on the way.

Theo Metcalfe, who knew Delhi, guided a column into Chandni Chowk, while others reached Kashmiri Gate, Subzi Mandi and the Idgah. On 14 September, the attackers lost eight officers and 265 men, including 103 natives; their wounded included fifty-two officers and 822 men, of whom 310 were natives. The defenders lost a great many more, as did the city's civilian population.

Residents fled southwards through Delhi Gate or to the north past Kashmiri Gate or north-east, crossing the Jamuna by the bridge of boats that had earlier been taken by the British forces. Fighting inside the city continued for several days. On 19 September, an attacking party reached the Red Fort gate, blew it in and entered the palace.

> The enormous building was found to be deserted by all but a few fanatics and numerous wounded sepoys. Thus at length was the great city of Delhi re-conquered by its former masters; thus again did the Feringhee become paramount over the Mogul.[112]

More than 4,000 British and supporting Indians died between the end of May and 20 September, but Delhi was now under the rule of General Archdale Wilson, who ensconced himself in the Diwan-i-Khas, the palace's principal state room. Wilson asked young Hodson, the intelligence chief now made a captain, to somehow find the king and the princes. Since it was considered 'desirable to have the King's person in safe custody'[113]—it is not quite clear who among the British decided or communicated this—Hodson was allowed, he would later claim, to promise Zafar his life if he surrendered.

By bribing and threatening his contacts, Hodson discovered that the king and many in his family had fled southwards (via Ajmeri Gate) to the mausoleum of his ancestor, Humayun. Built close to the tomb of Nizamuddin Auliya, the thirteenth-century Sufi saint, Humayun's mausoleum was the nearest thing to a sanctuary for Zafar. Hodson went there on 21 September with a cavalry detachment.

Four months had changed everything. An aged king before

whom the Governor General was required to bow, the king whom the sepoys, repudiating their allegiance to the British, had held aloft as Hindustan's sovereign ruler and Akbar's worthy descendant, now lay crouched in a cavern near Humayun's tomb. From there he sought the young captain's understanding, with his favourite wife Zinat apparently playing a negotiating role. Promising King Zafar, his wife Zinat and their son Jawan Bakht their lives, Hodson took them into custody.

Riding back into the city with the royals in palanquins, Hodson entered the city through Lahori Gate where the British officer on duty reportedly asked him, 'Who have you there?' 'Only the king of Delhi,' Hodson replied, before taking his captives via Chandni Chowk to the Red Fort, where they were imprisoned in their own palace.[114] Evidently not pleased to learn that the king was alive, Wilson would later dispute Hodson's assertion that the general had authorized the captain to promise Zafar his life.

The next day, Hodson returned to Humayun's mausoleum with one hundred cavalry. Paid informers had told him that three princes who had acted as military commanders in Delhi—Mirza Mughal, Mirza Khizr Sultan, and Mirza Abu Bakr—were hiding there. After surrendering, the three were being taken to the city when, during a stop en route at what would become known as the Khooni Darwaza or the Gate of Blood (south of Delhi Gate on a road now named after Bahadur Shah Zafar), Hodson himself shot the three dead.

Did Wilson's displeasure that Zafar was alive prompt him to do this? But Hodson was not merely hoping to please a boss. He was exultant. To his family he wrote:

> Today, more fortunate still, I have seized and destroyed the King's two sons and a grandson (the famous, or rather infamous, Abu Bukt), the villains who ordered the massacre of our women and children, and stood by and witnessed the foul barbarity; their bodies are now lying on the spot where those of the unfortunate ladies were exposed. I am very tired but very much satisfied with my day's work.[115]

One of Hodson's associates, MacDowell, would write that the Sikhs in Hodson's party 'shouted with delight' at the execution of the Mughal princes.[116] To them, it was overdue retribution for the

1675 beheading in Delhi of Guru Tegh Bahadur, ordered by an earlier Mughal, Aurangzeb.

The flamboyance in Hodson's deed may have been exceptional, but in Delhi in September 1857 bloodlust was not. Lawless, instant execution was the pattern, and vengeance the watchword. Wilson had ordered that anyone caught with a weapon was to be killed, not taken prisoner, but the empty-handed were not spared either. Incoming soldiers—white and brown—and some British civilians too killed almost everyone in sight. A British official wrote at the time:

> All the city people found within the walls when our troops entered were bayoneted on the spot; and the number was considerable, as you may suppose when I tell you that in some houses forty or fifty persons were hiding. These were not mutineers but residents of the city, who trusted to our well-known mild rule for pardon. I am glad to say they were disappointed.[117]

An order from Wilson to let go of women and children was not always obeyed. An assistant commissioner of Gurgaon called Clifford, whose sister had been killed in Delhi in May, would claim to a friend that 'he had put to death all he had come across, not excepting women and children'.[118]

Referring to Wilson's instruction to 'make no prisoners but put all armed rebels to death', George Dodd would write:

> This was attended to; but something more was done, something darker and less justifiable. It is not customary for soldiers to stab wounded and sick men in an enemy's army; but such was done at Delhi. The sense of hatred towards the mutinous sepoys was so intense, the recollection of the atrocities at Cawnpore was so vivid, that vengeance took place of every other feeling. The troops did that which they would have scorned to do against the Russians in the Crimean war—they bayoneted men no longer capable of resistance ... [M]any a dark-skinned inhabitant of Delhi fell under the bayonet.[119]

Citing 'private information' possibly gleaned from royal archives but providing no other details, Cecil Woodham-Smith, one of Queen Victoria's biographers, states the following as a fact: 'In one episode outside the walls of the fort, 400 mutineers were hanged simultaneously, while British officers seated beneath sipped whiskies and sodas and regimental bands played.'[120]

Having returned now to Delhi, Master Ramchandra, the mathematics lecturer and Christian convert who had escaped on 11 May, found that his Christianity was of no help. He was thrashed again and again by British soldiers and officers. 'I am a Christian, sir,' he would cry. 'You are black as jet,' was one reply he received, followed by additional blows.[121]

Thrilled by the reconquest of Delhi, which was recorded in a formal announcement from Calcutta, even 'Clemency' Canning seemed to welcome vengeance:

> In the name of outraged humanity, in memory of innocent blood ruthlessly shed, and in acknowledgment of the first signal vengeance inflicted upon the foulest treason, the Governor General-in-council records his gratitude to Major General Wilson and the brave army of Delhi.[122]

Within a few days of Hodson's deed, twenty-one other Mughal princes were hanged. The Mughal dynasty had been blown away and Zafar's seed were being crushed, but these were not purely British achievements. The Revolt had contributed to them.

One interesting descendant, Firoz Shah (a grandson of Zafar), was however alive and moving between Avadh and the Rohilla country. When the Revolt erupted, he was not in Delhi but, according to one report, in Mecca on Haj. On 29 September 1857, Wagentreiber's *Delhi Gazette* published the text of a proclamation made by Firoz Shah in Azamgarh (north-east of Allahabad, and once part of Avadh). Speaking of the British as infidels who tyrannized Muslims and Hindus, but also of British policies that had hurt Indians of all kinds, the proclamation alleged that landowners were overtaxed, qualified Indians had been kept out of civil and military positions, and cheap British imports had killed the business of artisans.[123]

Erroneously linked, at the time, to Zafar, Firoz Shah's Azamgarh proclamation made points noticeably absent in the Revolt's typical manifestoes, which focussed almost exclusively on the alleged danger to religion under British rule.

Every house and shop in Delhi was ransacked by drunken British soldiers and their native associates. Looting continued for weeks. Colonel Henry Pelham Burn, appointed as Delhi's military governor, complained that 'several parties under European Commissioned officers' were 'searching for plunder within the city' and that 'even the Sabbath brings no rest to either plunderer or plundered'.[124] Burn, who 'took residence in Chandni Chowk in the house of Kutubuddin Sowdager',[125] reported on 24 October that 'loss of property from plunder by our soldiers or from its wanton destruction is estimated at the large sum of two crores of rupees.'[126]

Since not every suspect had been killed the way the three princes had been, a 'special commission' tried 3,306 suspects of whom 2,025 were convicted and 392 hanged. And because the Muslim nobility had lived in them, all houses between the Red Fort and the Jama Masjid were razed to the ground.

However, in his home in Ballimaran, the poet Ghalib survived, though a mentally ill brother of his was shot dead by a British soldier. A Muslim hakim of the pro-British Sikh ruler of Patiala lived in the same Ballimaran *mohalla*, and Patiala soldiers protecting the hakim from killings of vengeance (and intoxication) saved Ghalib as well, though little food or water was left in his house.

We saw earlier that Ghalib had admired British skill and art. After the Revolt, he was infuriated by the sepoys' bullying of Delhi's citizens, but the post-14 September destruction of Delhi shattered him, producing a line that would be quoted again and again: 'The dust of Delhi thirsts for Muslim blood.'

If some Sikhs saved Ghalib, other Sikhs had killed an uncle and a cousin of Sayyid Ahmed Khan, as the latter found out when he rushed to Delhi from Meerut as soon as he heard that the British had retaken the city. His uncle's house was right next to his own, where his mother had been living. She survived by hiding in a room outside the haveli where her syce (horse attendant) lived. She had been eating horse grain, but when Ahmed Khan found her, she had not had any water to drink for three days.

'Why have you come here?' the mother shouted. 'Everyone is being killed. You will be killed also.' Somehow fetching a jug of water for her, Sayyid Ahmed ran into an old female servant of his mother's who was also intensely thirsty. Though she insisted that his mother's need was greater, Sayyid Ahmed made the servant woman drink water, but she did not survive. Within a month, his mother too died in Meerut, where Sayyid Ahmed had taken her.

The city of Delhi had emptied—those who survived had fled. One of them was the Rohilla chief of Zafar's defeated army, Bakht Khan, who headed towards Lucknow.

AN OVERVIEW

Occurring at about the same time—between the middle and end of September 1857—Wilson's retaking of Delhi and Havelock's reinforcement of the Lucknow Residency damaged rebel morale even as it restored British spirits. The Mughal canopy lay in shreds on the ground, while a British general occupied the Red Fort. And there were about 20,000 more British soldiers in India than when the Revolt began. But the uprising was far from over. To Delhi's north-east, the Rohillas were defiant. The bulk of Avadh remained hostile and in Lucknow, the Residency and Alambagh remained vulnerable to attack. Nana Sahib and his supporters still roamed between Rohilkhand and Avadh.

Meanwhile, in Jhansi, to the south of Agra, a young Brahmin princess called Lakshmibai was 'managing the District for the British government', not because of a British wish to delegate power, but because rebels in Jhansi, who in June had killed sixty-odd Britons and Eurasians in the town, accepted her rule.[127] Tatya Tope and Nana Sahib were both in contact with her.

Before picking up these particular strands of the Revolt, we can look at a few general features. Though a majority of north India's Muslims and high-caste Hindus sympathized with the rebels, many of the lower castes, alienated by the scruples and disdain of the higher castes, did not. In Bengal, even the Hindu high castes did not back the sepoys, while in the Punjab, Sikhs and Muslims dissociated from the Revolt or supported the British. Most importantly for the British, the Bombay and Madras armies largely ignored the passions flowing from the Bengal army's sepoys.

Places such as Gwalior, Bhopal, Indore and Mhow saw disturbances, but the Maratha rulers of Gwalior and Indore remained loyal to the British, which helped preserve British hegemony over most of central India. In Rajasthan and Gujarat, a few chieftains upset by the doctrine of lapse tried to raise the flag of rebellion, but, being within easy reach of Bombay and its British troops, they were quickly put down.

Despite Nana Sahib's bid to recall Peshwa glories, the region of Maharashtra ignored the Revolt. Further south, the Nizam of Hyderabad, advised by Salar Jung, his Prime Minister, stayed firm in his alliance with the British. The Madras army remained quite loyal; a few rebelling Hindustanis in its cavalry were easily overcome.

British willingness to match, in reprisals, the horrors of Meerut, Delhi, Kanpur and elsewhere was another feature of the Revolt. Men deemed guilty were blown off cannons (including in the Northwest Frontier in May, and in Kanpur, under Havelock's orders, in July); men suspected of rebellion were strung up on trees (near Allahabad and elsewhere during the marches of Havelock and Neill); dark skin became a capital offence (including in Delhi); for being in the way, some women and children were slaughtered (in Delhi).

There were merciful exceptions on both sides. In some cases, friendly sepoys had 'protected their officers from harm, knocking down the muskets of others who would have shot them, or fetching carriages in which they could escape.'[128] One European officer would relate:

> Three sepoys caught hold of me, and said they would try and save me. They threw off my hat, tore off my trousers ... and covered me with my horsecloth ... Putting me between two, the third walked in front ... We got through all the sentries and crossed the river.[129]

Britons were willing to acknowledge uncompromising defiance when they saw it, whether during the rebels' defence of Delhi or on other occasions. A trooper called Potiphar recorded the demeanour of a sepoy of the 10th Native Infantry who was condemned to hang in Kanpur:

> The man of the 10th before being hung spoke to the crowd, which was immense of both natives and Europeans. He made use of the words that he was satisfied to die and we need not think that we were going to beat the sepoys because they would yet beat us. [He was] then swung into eternity.[130]

Cool courage left its mark. A Briton named F.A.V. Thurburn would write of the hanging, witnessed by him, of a native officer he knew. The Indian called out to Thurburn and asked to be remembered to the adjutant. Then, 'springing from the platform', he 'launched himself into eternity with the greatest nonchalance and coolness'.[131]

Letters and diary entries preserved the memory of many of 1857's British victims. As a result, we can picture them in their helplessness and humanness. It is less easy to do that with the Indians who fell in 1857. Near ones did not—perhaps could not—leave a record of how the Indians perished, or when, or where. In most cases, even their names are not given.

It is from the odd British letter or diary that we can picture Indian victims of 1857. Referring to the practice of blowing rebels from cannons, a Major North would record the destruction he witnessed of 'two sepoys captured in Oudh':

> They were both extremely fine men in the flower of their age, tall, athletic, graceful, with finely moulded limbs—almost resembling antique statues in bronze.[132]

Apparently the sepoys were generally 'of more imposing physique than the European soldiers'. Since there was never a shortage of Indian recruits, 'commanding officers were able to choose only the strongest, tallest and most presentable-looking men.'[133]

A young British lieutenant—a future earl and field marshal—left a vignette of Indian sorrow, indicating that families were involved in what was occurring. Frederick Roberts, who forty-two years later would lead British forces in the Second Boer War in South Africa, wrote in a letter:

> I came on three women watching the dead bodies of their husbands, none of them Sepoys I believe. It was such a sad sight, however, that I felt quite unhappy.[134]

From a scene like this the imagination has to construct scenes of sad farewells, anxious inquiries, the receipt of numbing news, explanations to a young wife, a little child or an aged parent, the search for a body ... And imagination alone has to suggest the inner life of even the protagonists on the Indian side. We may know (in some cases, and again mostly from British sources) when these leaders attacked or retreated, but not what they said or felt or how they got on with one another, let alone what passed between them and their families.

Poona. The former seat of the Peshwas chose not to be excited by the news from the north. Peasant castes as well as Brahmins continued to contrast the stability of British rule with memories of the wilfulness of the last Peshwa, Nana Sahib's father. Though nostalgic about aspects of Peshwa rule, Poona's Brahmins saw the British as the winning side in any conflict with rebelling Indians and hesitated to cheer Nana Sahib or his allies.

Jotiba Phule, on his part, openly 'breathed a sigh of relief when the revolt led by Nanasahib was suppressed'. Earlier, 'an agonizing fear had seized his mind'—success for Nana Sahib and his allies, he thought, would restore Brahmin rule in Maharashtra.[135] Phule felt that 'Brahmin malcontents' had 'engineered the Revolt'.[136] Yet, the Revolt seemed to say to him that the British would not be a permanent presence in India. Phule hoped that non-Brahmins would strengthen themselves vis-à-vis the Brahmins before the British left. What he wrote in an 1873 book probably also describes his thinking in 1857:

> [T]he English are but brief and transitory visitors to this ancient land of ours. They are here today and gone tomorrow! ... Therefore, true wisdom dictates that all of us Shudras should try to emancipate ourselves from the hereditary thraldom of the Brahmins with the utmost haste, and that too during the English rule in our country.

Added Phule, using the common pejorative 'Bhat' for a Brahmin:

> It was through Providential dispensation that the Revolt engineered by Bhat Nana (Peshwa) and his henchmen was put down by the brave English rulers.[137]

Assailed by fear, the British in Poona (and elsewhere in India) refused to recognize differences in Indian reactions to the Revolt. To them, Poona's passivity concealed hostility, and they were unwilling to trust even one like Phule. As he would later recall:

> Many erstwhile genuine English friends of mine grew indifferent to me and began to show signs of displeasure at meeting me. Since then I gave up visiting their homes.[138]

Lucknow again. In November, a substantial column from Delhi led by General Hope Grant and an even larger force that the commander-in-chief, General Sir Colin Campbell, had put together in Calcutta sought jointly to relieve the British communities that remained under siege and constant shelling in Lucknow—in the Residency and in Alambagh.

But the territory they marched through was dangerous, and the sixty-five-year-old Campbell was almost captured by rebels before he reached Kanpur on 3 November to lead the second British expedition into Lucknow. Grant's force of 3,500 crossed the Ganga at Kanpur ahead of Campbell's, but waited at Bantara, south of Alambagh, where they were joined on 9 November by Campbell and his men.

Campbell, who had left a body of troops in Kanpur for the city's defence, planned an attack on Lucknow from its south-eastern suburbs. Rebel strongholds en route to the Residency included the Dilkusha Palace and gardens, the Martiniere (a school built for British and Eurasian boys), the Sikandar Bagh Palace and gardens, Shah Najaf (the mausoleum for the first Avadh king), Moti Mahal and Kaisarbagh. Campbell hoped to take them one by one. After his artillery had cannonaded a stronghold, the infantry would storm it.

On 14 November, the British moved from Alambagh with batteries and a 4,000-strong attacking force, but the rebels offered tough resistance. The fiercest fighting took place on 16 November, at Sikandar Bagh and in Shah Najaf. At least 2,000 rebels perished in Sikandar Bagh alone, and sixteen Victoria Crosses were awarded that day to British soldiers, the highest number ever for a single day of combat.

But revenge and inhumanity were joined to bravery. Lieutenant Cubitt of the 5th Fusiliers would write: 'There were hundreds of sepoys dead and dying . . . While there I saw 64 collected, drawn up and bayoneted with yells of "Cawnpore". God forgive us . . .' Another participant, a Lieutenant Fairweather, would write:

> You may think me a savage, but I gloated over the sights of this charnel house. Who did not who saw the slaughter at Cawnpore? Among the corpses were those of several women . . . I saw the body of a woman . . . and by her a dead baby also shot with two bullet

wounds in it. The poor mother had tied the wounds round with a rag. McQueen (of the 27ᵗʰ Native Infantry) told me that he had seen a Highlander bayonet another woman.[139]

While Campbell and Hope Grant were moving westward towards the Residency, Havelock's forces harassed the rebels from the Residency area. On the night of 17 November, after 112 British had been killed and 345 wounded, Campbell, Hope Grant, Havelock, Outram and Inglis met one another. Outram and Havelock 'rushed out of [their] "prison" to greet Sir Colin'. After a six-month siege, Lucknow's Britons had found relief.[140]

Yet, the British triumph was far from complete and the Residency far from being secure. Kaisarbagh was still full of rebels, and thousands of other armed rebels continued to pose a threat to the British of Lucknow.

Campbell's solution, by no means risk-free, was to organize a migration to Kanpur of the sick, the wounded, the women and the children. In a parallel move, he abandoned the Residency altogether, and Alambagh, which had stronger defences, was made the new British sanctuary. There, Outram and 4,000 British men, most of them soldiers, entrenched themselves, while, on 27 November, a great procession wound its way from the Residency to Kanpur.

Defended by heavy guns and a large body of troops, a convoy of camels, ox carts and horse carts safely carried all vulnerable British—women, children and the infirm—and their Indian servants and belongings to the Ganga, and across it, to Kanpur. But by this time the British had taken a big hit: on 23 November, Havelock had suddenly died in the Dilkusha, from dysentery.

The *Hindoo Patriot*'s views. After Delhi was recaptured, Calcutta's *Hindoo Patriot* wrote admiringly (12 November 1857) of the British victory over heat and superior numbers, and added, referring to rebel misdeeds, 'The slayers of women and the murderers of children have ... two enemies, the human enemies whose desperation they have roused and the divine enemy whose laws they have outraged.'[141]

Alleging that England's newspapers, including *The Times* and the *Economist*, and the British press in India had urged the white soldier to 'revenge his country' on 'the people of India, in the bazaars of India', the 17 December issue of the *HP* praised Disraeli and Gladstone for their pleas against revenge (from Benoy Ghose's *Selections*, 219).

At the end of the year, the *HP*, in its 31 December issue, offered its assessment of the Revolt's consequences. One, Indian and Hindu prestige had fallen. 'For the time, every sentiment of goodwill and respect that foreigners entertained for us is in a state of annihilation.' Indians had become 'objects of the bitterest hostility' from the English people. Two, 'our path of social progress is completely barred'. The paper predicted that the law to restrain polygamy, for which Vidyasagar had pressed, would now face big hurdles. 'Abominations' like polygamy 'have gained a long lease of existence' (225). Even so, the *HP* expressed faith in the future: '[T]he year 1857, commemorated in characters of blood and fire, is probably destined to usher in an era of unexampled progress and happiness for a tenth of the human race' (226). Evidently the paper hoped that all sides would absorb the lessons that blood and fire had spelt out.

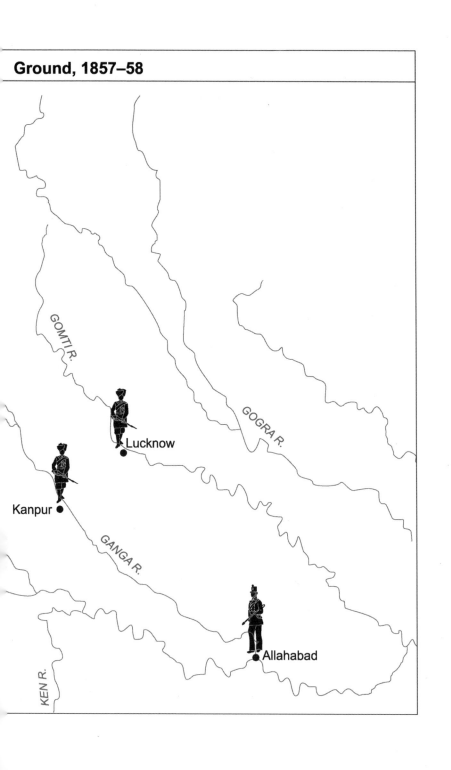

Ground, 1857–58

GOMTI R.

GOGRA R.

Lucknow

Kanpur

GANGA R.

KEN R.

Allahabad

CHAPTER 3

'HALF-DEVIL AND HALF-CHILD'
ENGLAND, AMERICA AND INDIA, 1857–59

We noted earlier that when word of Meerut and Delhi first reached England (26 June 1857), everyone, including Lord Palmerston, the Prime Minister, was stunned. It was the last thing that the world's strongest and most industrialized country ruling over the largest empire known to history had expected.

If at first Palmerston refused to take the news seriously, *The Times*, a considerable power in the land, was no different. On 4 July it ridiculed French newspapers for suggesting a serious revolt in India and pointed out that while France had been obliged to vacate several countries, Britain had added to its empire. Nor, to begin with, was great concern shown by the British public, which seemed more curious about ups and downs in domestic politics and the fate of Palmerston, who had several challengers.

As more bad news came in—there was about a six-week gap between an Indian event and knowledge of it in Britain—the public began looking for those who could be blamed: the East India Company, its system of patronage, and its mistakes in selecting officers for India; the general in Meerut who failed to order a chase of the sowars galloping towards Delhi; those who had permitted Delhi to be left without a garrison of British soldiers; and so forth.

When the role of greased cartridges was confirmed, reactions in Britain became sharply divided. Had the British in India been insensitive, annoying the natives? Or was the opposite true—was the rebellion a result of the Company's mistaken resistance towards missionaries who might have helped the natives to respond rationally and like civilized beings?

But in August, when excited voices in Britain spoke of Satichaura and Bibighar and of numerous killings elsewhere in India, and declared also that British women had been raped and mutilated before being killed, and children sliced before mothers or roasted on bayonets, the Guilty Object revealed itself. It was none other than Oriental Man himself, and his base nature.

Only a few heard, and fewer believed, other voices that pointed out that the killings, including of women and children, had been summary, and that the tales of rape or torture before murder were unsubstantiated. It seems that Palmerston, for one, never allowed himself to reject the stories of pre-murder atrocities.[1] Reprisal, vengeance, and subduing the savage Oriental became popular cries. In an unforgettable remark, Charles Dickens (who would persist, as far as America was concerned, in his opposition to slavery) wrote on 4 October 1857:

> I wish I were commander-in-chief in India ... I should do my utmost to exterminate the Race upon whom the stain of the late cruelties rested.[2]

Word that Canning 'had offered amnesty to mutineers not directly involved in the killings' had sparked off Dickens's remark.[3]

Once grimmer news came from India, Palmerston sent out soldiers and hoped that the Russians would not hit a Britain weakened in Europe.[4] In July, as we saw, he asked Colin Campbell to proceed to India as commander-in-chief; and over the rest of the year, much as he disliked Canning 'unilaterally assuming authority and diverting troops that were bound for China',[5] he sent reinforcements to Indian sea ports: Calcutta, Madras, Bombay and Karachi.

One of the few Britons unwilling to accept the atrocities stories, and someone who recognized the scale of the Indian rebellion, was a future Prime Minister, the fifty-four-year-old Conservative and protectionist politician, Benjamin Disraeli. At the end of July, he asked in the House of Commons:

> Does the disturbance in India indicate a military mutiny, or is it a national revolt? Is the conduct of the troops the consequence of a sudden impulse, or is it the result of an organized conspiracy?[6]

Disraeli, who was one of Palmerston's rivals, also criticized the liberties taken with India's traditional customs. 'The rise and fall of empires [were] not,' in his view, 'the affairs of greased cartridges.'[7] Arguing that larger issues were involved, including the risk from efforts to proselytize in India, Disraeli demanded the replacement of Company rule with Crown rule. The last demand was widely echoed, but the rest of Disraeli's speech went against popular sentiment. In a cartoon in *Punch* that emphasized his Jewish (and therefore Eastern) ancestry, Disraeli was called 'd'Israeli' and his face was sketched with supposedly Semitic features.

After an initial inclination to defend the East India Company, Palmerston accepted in September that Company rule needed to end. The people of Britain would no longer agree, he realized, to 'vesting the choice of the Governors of India' in the holders of East India Company stocks.[8]

In July and August, before the news of Satichaura and Bibighar hit Britain, a common reaction was to blame India's Muslims (including King Zafar) and Muslim fanaticism. 'The Hindoo', on the other hand, was seen as 'a tractable animal when he is managed with intelligence'. Remarking thus on 18 July, the *Spectator* added that India's rebels were 'half-children in understanding'.[9] But the news of Nana Sahib's turnabout and of his association with Satichaura and Bibighar provided an opportunity to focus also on the supposed immorality of Hinduism.[10]

On 22 August, *Punch* ran a full page cartoon, 'The British Lion's Vengeance on the Bengal Tiger', showing the lion of England jumping on the Indian tiger to avenge the killing of a defenceless white woman and child, whose bodies were also depicted. In dailies and weeklies, British soldiers were presented in heroic or stoic poses, and Indians as wild-eyed in attack or chaotic in retreat. Sermons in churches and articles in the press portrayed the challenge that Britain and Christianity faced from Islamic fanaticism and Hindu idolatry. Some, however, seeking to understand the Revolt in a deeper sense and a broader context, proposed a national day of prayer, fasting and reflection.

On 28 September, the newspapers announced that Queen Victoria had indeed declared Wednesday 7 October to be a national 'fast day' when, in her words, 'both we and our people may humble ourselves before Almighty God in order to obtain pardon for our sins.'[11] *The Times* too asked for a 'national self-examination'. On 7 October, many in Britain thought about the Revolt in India, or read or heard about it. Uncertainty hovered over the Empire's future—London had not yet heard that Delhi was back in British hands. Of the hundreds of sermons delivered across Britain that day, the most influential, perhaps, was given by a young Reformed Baptist preacher, Charles Haddon Spurgeon.

Described in the future as a 'prince of preachers', Spurgeon, only twenty-four in 1857, spoke in the Empire's grandest hall, the Crystal Palace—the imperial space that we have marked before—where 23,654 people heard him, constituting, as *The Times* would assert the next day, 'the largest audience that has assembled in modern times to listen to the exhortations of a minister of the gospel'.[12] Supported by resonating texts and ardent prayer, the points that Spurgeon made would stay in the British and indeed the Western mind for a long time. They were as follows:[13]

One, India's rebels were not 'patriots . . . delivering an oppressed country'. Their revolt was 'not the revolt of a nation'. Indeed, 'if India had revolted, history might perhaps have taught us that she had patriots in her midst.' But that was not the case, Spurgeon said.

Two, the rebels were 'our subjects'. The 'Sepoys had voluntarily given themselves up to our dominion, they had themselves taken oaths of fealty to Her Majesty and their officers.'

Three, their crimes were unspeakable. 'This tongue will not venture to utter what they have dared to do. Ye would rise from your seats and hiss me [away] from the pulpit which I now occupy, if I should but dare to hint at the crimes which have been done [by] them, not in secret, but in the very streets of their cities.'

Four, while the gallows were 'a fearful chastisement', executing the rebelling Sepoys was 'a horrible necessity'. British soldiers in

India should 'remember that they are not warriors merely, but executioners'.

Finally, said Spurgeon, 'we'—that is, the British—'are a sinful nation' too, 'governors' and people alike. He enumerated Britain's chief sins, as he saw them. For a start, India's British rulers 'never ought to have tolerated the religion of the Hindoos at all'. That religion condoned 'bestiality, infanticide, and murder'. Within Britain too, immorality was widespread. 'It is a most fearful thing that those who are honest and moral cannot walk the streets, without being insulted by sin in the robes of the harlot.' Moreover, many Britons were 'down-trodden' and paid 'far below their value to their masters'. Merchants were untrustworthy, and many a worker stole for personal purposes the time he was paid for.

After the sermon (the Spurgeon Archive informs us), nearly £700 were raised for the Indian Relief Fund, of which £25 was given by Florence Nightingale, whose service in the not-so-old Crimean War had made her famous.

The news of the Revolt, the 7 October sermons, and press comments before and after the 'fast day' persuaded the British mind that Indians—Hindus as well as Muslims—were like children when they were not like animals. What was valid for Europeans or Christians could not work with Indians or people like them. No doubt Christianity urged forgiveness, but not necessarily vis-à-vis Indians or people like them. With such people, vengeance was a Christian response. In 1899, Rudyard Kipling would ask the West to

Take up the White Man's burden—
Send forth the best ye breed—
Go bind your sons to exile
To serve your captives' need;
To wait in heavy harness,
On fluttered folk and wild—
Your new-caught, sullen peoples,
Half-devil and half-child.

But the 'half-devil half-child' image was held for a century or more before Kipling composed the line, and the India of 1857 seemed to validate it. We should mark, too (with Don Randall), that what was occurring with the fast day's reflections was the use of Indian events to understand where Britain stood, rather than what was happening in India.[14]

A few of those reflecting said that idolatry existed in Britain as well; a minister, Julius Lloyd, pointed out that 'Covetousness' and 'Licentiousness' were forms of idolatry. Like India, Lloyd noted, England too had its 'castes and classes'.[15] Recalling Christ's prayer in front of his persecutors—'Father, forgive them for they know not what they do'—another preacher, Reverend Stowell, added that India's sepoy rebels 'know not what they do',[16] implying that they were indeed human.

These, however, were rare and passing observations. In the main, the England of 1857 assumed British nobility and Indian baseness. Even when fast day sermons asked the British to amend their ways and repent, the goal was to deserve an outcome that God evidently had already determined—the triumph of Christianity and the British (the two were seen as synonymous) over India and its flawed faiths. Yet, the nationwide discussion sparked by the fast day left an interesting impact. The Empire was now defined in moral rather than commercial, political or military terms. As Randall puts it, 'It is not finally imperial interests but Christian faith and morality that oblige England to oppose Indian insurgency.'[17] This left scope for a future arithmetic of morality that could require England to do something very different, even to vacate India—if, for example, led by 'patriots in her midst', India as a nation were to revolt.

Marx and Engels. Comments on the Revolt in India sent from England by Karl Marx and Friedrich Engels were published, thanks to Horace Greeley's openness, in an American newspaper, the *New York Daily Tribune*, in 1857 and 1858. These views dissented sharply from the general British opinion.

In his 'Letter from England' carried by the *Tribune* on 15 July (but sent shortly after the news of Meerut and Delhi had reached England), Marx noted that by organizing native regiments the British had unwittingly created 'the first general centre of resistance which the Indian people was ever possessed of'. The fact that Hindus and Muslims had worked jointly, 'renouncing their mutual antipathies', also interested Marx, who however mistakenly suggested that 'the revolt of the Bengal army' was 'intimately connected with the Persian and Chinese wars'.

In a piece published in the *Tribune* on 18 August, Marx thought it possible that 'the Bombay and Madras armies' would consider 'openly joining' the Revolt. If many in Britain tended to underestimate rebel strength, Marx overestimated it. Referring to the British bid to re-enter Delhi, Marx wrote (*Tribune*, 29 August), 'In our opinion the next mail is likely to impart the news of the retreat of the English army.' About a month later, on 16 September, the *Tribune* carried a sardonic comment by Marx:

> The outrages committed by the revolted Sepoys in India are indeed appalling, hideous, ineffable—such as one is prepared to meet only in wars of insurrection, of nationalities, of races, and above all of religion; in one word, such as respectable England used to applaud when perpetrated by the Vendeans on the "Blues," by the Spanish guerrillas on the infidel Frenchmen, by Serbians on their German and Hungarian neighbors, by Croats on Viennese rebels, by Cavaignac's Garde Mobile or Bonaparte's Decembrists on the sons and daughters of proletarian France.

An article published the next day (17 September) quoted 'official Blue Books ... laid before the House of Commons' to show instances of torture by the British in India, who, in Marx's words, were 'by no means such mild and spotless benefactors of the Indian people as they would have the world believe'. However, admiration for Havelock's march towards Kanpur and Lucknow was disclosed in a letter that Engels wrote to Marx on 24 September:

> Havelock's troops have worked wonders. 126 miles in 8 days including 6 to 8 engagements in that climate and at this time of year is truly superhuman.[18]

In spite of this information, Marx did not expect the British in Lucknow to survive. This is what he wrote in the *Tribune* of 13 October 1857:

> As for Lucknow, the most gloomy previsions inspired by the recent mails are now confirmed. Havelock has again been forced to fall back on Cawnpore; there is no possibility of relief from the allied

Nepaulese force; and we must now expect to hear of the capture of the place by starvation, and the massacre of its brave defenders with their wives and children.

As we know, but Marx then did not, Havelock by this time had managed (on 25 September) to reinforce, though not evacuate, the British of Lucknow. Later, when the news of Campbell's successful recovery of the besieged Britons reached London, Engels felt let down by the rebels of Avadh and reacted in angry language:

> In fact, men who, partly drilled under European officers and provided plentifully with artillery, have never yet been able to overcome a single miserable inclosure defended by Europeans—such men are, militarily speaking, no better than savages, and a victory over them cannot add much to the glory of any army, however great the odds may be in favor of the natives (*Tribune*, 30 January 1858).

The qualification ('militarily speaking') could not hide the assumption even in Engels of a low level of civilization among Indians. We may note, too, that four years before the Revolt, Marx had qualified a sharp criticism of British policies in India with the following remark (*Tribune*, 5 August 1853):

> England has to fulfil a double mission in India, one destructive, the other regenerating—the annihilation of old Asiatic society, and laying the material foundations of Western society in Asia.[19]

Victoria. Possessing an understanding that was not in large supply in the Britain of 1857, the queen defended Duleep Singh, a nineteen-year-old Sikh prince living in exile in England from 1853, against the charge of not condemning the Revolt. Victoria told the foreign secretary, Lord Clarendon, who had raised the question with her, that a young Indian prince barred from his ancestral throne and compelled to live in Britain should not be expected to denounce Indians.[20]

Duleep Singh's silence was a small matter, but when two French newspapers, *Courrier de Paris* and *Univers*, suggested that Nana Sahib was not as evil as he was made out to be, and that Neill's deeds in Kanpur were darker, a British journal, the *Athenaeum*, expressed outrage, shortly after the fast day.[21]

From early November, when London learnt that Wilson, Hodson and company had finally taken Delhi, the mood relaxed. It seemed that the Empire was going to be preserved after all. Stories of how Hodson had dealt with the Mughal princes did touch off some unease, but his action was explained away as a by-product of an irresistible law of progress that required Asia's decrepit monarchies to yield before British prowess. It was assumed that those who swaggeringly execute a decree of that law are heroes and cannot be criminals. Palmerston's reaction to the recapture of Delhi was to ask that Delhi's largest mosque, the Jama Masjid, be razed to the ground, a suggestion that Governor General Canning successfully resisted.[22]

Russell. India's increased salience and the fact that portions of it continued in rebel hands convinced editor Delane that *The Times* should send Russell there for a year. He would be reimbursed all his expenses in India, Russell was told, and over the year his family in London would be given 600 pounds. In addition, the paper would buy, and hold for the family, bonds worth 500 pounds. It did not take Russell long to agree to these terms.

Lord Granville, the leader of the House of Lords, gave Russell a letter of introduction to Canning in which the Governor General was asked to be 'tolerably open and decently civil' to Russell. While Granville was sure that Russell would be fair in his reporting, Lord Clarendon, the foreign secretary, thought that Russell would not mind damaging the British position if that strengthened the image, established in Crimea, of a candid and critical war reporter.[23]

The thirty-eight-year-old correspondent, however, found it hard to leave London. Among other things, his wife Mary was unwell. Not telling the children that he was going away, on 26 December, he sailed for India. He crossed the Channel, took a train to Marseilles, boats from there to Malta and Egypt's Alexandria, and trains from Alexandria to Cairo and Suez. From Suez he sailed, via Aden, Ceylon and Madras, to Calcutta. Thousands, including soldiers, had made that kind of voyage, but they did not all know how to record it. Nor did they have Russell's sense of history.

～

AMERICAN REACTIONS TO THE 1857 REVOLT

Before accompanying Russell to India, we will look at reactions to the Revolt in different parts of the USA. In 1857, domestic issues that eventually led to the Civil War dominated American newspapers, which, following the discovery of the telegraph and the new steam-driven rotary press, had greatly expanded in the 1840s and 1850s. However, India's Revolt was prominently featured and discussed. Indeed, an article in a Presbyterian journal published in Philadelphia asserted that 'the year 1857 will be henceforth known as the year of the Sepoy Revolt.'[24]

While proud of having overthrown British rule in the previous century and still, in varying degrees, Anglophobic, Americans sympathized with the British—white Anglo-Saxon Christians like them—rather than with India's rebels, and were fascinated by the distant war. They looked forward to ships from Europe that brought the latest news from India.

To begin with, James Gordon Bennett, editor of the *New York Herald*, seemed willing to hear the rebels' case. On 15 July, his paper wrote of 'generations of elaborate oppression' that had made Indians 'almost helpless' and of 'the poor Hindus' who had been 'trampled by the British, their lands seized, their daughters ... ravished, their sons ... made servants ...' Blaming the uprising on efforts to proselytize (19 July), the paper called the East India Company 'an infernal despotism that has fattened on India during the last century' (6 August). Later (on 29 August), the *Herald* said that the 'poor natives of Hindostan' over whom the Company ruled were treated with 'more cruelty than the slaves of Georgia or Mississippi ever experience'.

But as massacres of English civilians became known, the *Herald* switched its sympathies. By September, the paper thought that the English were fighting for civilization against barbarism, and on 14 November, it urged the British to avenge 'the monstrous cruelties of Nana Sahib and his men'. The next day, the *Herald* claimed that a victorious England would bring about a 'wider diffusion of Christianity' in India. The paper had always feared that if the British were defeated and India lapsed into disorder, America would lose its trade with India and the impact on US prosperity would be 'disastrous' (25 July).

The *New York Times* wrote no fewer than forty editorials in favour of the British in India, called for strong action, and used harsh language against the sepoys.

6 July. The Briton must rule [India] politically and religiously, or he must be overrun by the treacherous and rebellious Indian.

18 September. To the Bengal Sepoy the murder of English women and children is a religious pleasure in which he had never before had an opportunity to indulge.

While also holding (on 12 July) that the Company had 'in so many ways impeded the advance and blighted the fruits of British rule in India', the paper said on 5 September that Americans respected their 'English cousins' who had displayed 'the great virtues of the race'. At stake 'in the East', the *New York Times* wrote on 15 December, were the 'vast interests of civilization, commerce, and Christianity'. Earlier, on 16 September, the paper had offered prayers for 'the heroic defenders of Lucknow'.

Taking a different line, the *New York Daily Tribune*, edited by Horace Greeley, gave space, as we have seen, to pieces sent from England by Marx and Engels. Some of them were however placed unsigned on the edit page. While condemning the rebels (24 August) as 'nothing other than brutal and ferocious savages', the paper argued (1 September) that 'in forcing a critical examination ... of English rule ... [the Sepoys] had certainly rendered a great service at once to India and to England.'

The *Boston Daily Advertiser* presented the rebellion as a logical result of the Company's failure to spread the gospel and rule firmly. It saw pre-British India as 'barbaric' and said (16 September) that India would for long need to remain under the 'strong rule' of 'a civilized' nation like England. In Pennsylvania, Philadelphia's *Public Ledger* thought that India required tougher discipline and that the Revolt was at the heart of a global struggle between civilization and barbarism. In its view (25 August) all in 'the civilized world' were holding 'their breath till they see how this struggle will terminate'. The Revolt had occurred, said the *Ledger* on 3 August, because the Company had 'thwarted the work of the Missionaries'.

There were regional nuances in the American response. In the capital, two prominent newspapers, the *Washington Daily National Intelligencer* and the *Washington Daily Union*, did not show much interest in the news from India, but the *Intelligencer* used the term 'sepoy' pejoratively, referring on 20 November to Mormons who had defied the law in Utah as those 'Utah Sepoys' and to their leader, Brigham Young, as their 'Nena Sahib'. The *Daily Union* worried about shortages of sugar and tea in America if the British were dislodged from India.

Analysing American comments on the Revolt, David Mosler refers to 'the informed opinions of New York editors' and 'the tough Christian tone of Boston and Philadelphia'.[25] In the American South, concern over slavery coloured editorial comments. *The Richmond Whig and Public Advertiser* claimed (on 1 January 1858) that the East India Company, a target of censure in the East Coast press, had 'done much good and suppressed much evil'. Attacking an editor in Lynchburg, Virginia, who had sympathized with the sepoys, the Richmond paper wrote that Nana Sahib 'deserves to be quartered alive', and added on 15 October:

> The British in India are placed in almost the identical position, morally, that we are placed here in Virginia. Physically, the difference is that we are the more numerous class as compared with the inferior race which we govern, while the English in Hindostan are but as one to several thousand of the Hindoos. But in both cases a great, powerful, intellectual race holds in subjection one which is inferior to it in all mental and moral attributes.
>
> The class to which the slave-holder belongs in Virginia is the class to which the Englishman belongs in India. It is strange to us, then, how any Virginian can sympathize with the atrocities of Delhi ...

In South Carolina, the *Charleston Daily Courier* also likened the British in India to the South's slave-holders. To this paper, the Revolt's suppression was a vindication of the southern way of controlling blacks. It asked those British who criticized 'us poor slave-holders' for using allegedly harsh methods to realize that they too finally needed to employ 'vengeance' (1 September). In Alabama, the *Mobile Register* declared (11 October) that 'the records of cannibalism afford no parallel to the hideous barbarities of Cawnpore and Delhi.' Another southern journal, the *New*

Orleans Picayune, thought (1 July) that the 'whole Hindoo race' was 'suspicious, fanatic, and revengeful'.

In what was still considered the country's West rather than the Midwest, the *Chicago Tribune* declared its faith in the quality of the white race. Even though the British in India were hopelessly outnumbered, the paper thought that their 'physical and moral power' would prevail. 'Men of Saxon blood' would control even 'millions of Indians'—a 'Herculean task' not beyond the whites in India.

In San Francisco in the Far West, the *Evening Bulletin* asked (29 September) for 'summary vengeance' on 'the inhuman brutes' who had 'murdered and mutilated innocent children and violated and butchered helpless women'. Earlier (18 September) the *Bulletin* had regretted that American governments dealing with their Indians, the native Americans, had not been as tough as India's Britons, who had brought 'the entire power of the empire' to bear on the task of 'punishing those wretches' in India.

Also bringing up native Americans and their supposed cruelty, the *Sacramento Union* said (24 November), 'For barbarous cruelty and savage brutality, the acts of the revolted Sepoys exceed any of the bloody tragedies recorded of Indians of this continent.'[26] In its very first issue (November 1857), the new *Atlantic Monthly*, destined to acquire much influence, carried an article on 'British India' by Charles Creighton Hazewell, who wrote:

> There is nothing like the rule of the English in India to be found in history ... As against the wrong [of conquest by force] that was perpetrated, and the suffering that was inseparable from wars so numerous and long-continued, are to be set the reign of order and law, under which the mass of the inhabitants have been able to cultivate their fields in quiet, and with the assurance that they should reap where they had sowed, undisturbed by the incursions of robber-bands ...
>
> An indifference to life, and a love of cruelty for cruelty's sake, are common characteristics of most of the Orientals, and are chiefly conspicuous in the ruling classes.[27]

In the following month, the *Atlantic Monthly* carried another article on India by Hazewell. Mentioning the 'general dread of being Christianized' as a factor in the Revolt, Hazewell conceded that 'the tidings of the possession of Delhi by the mutineers' had 'stimulated the daring madness of regiments' in several places in north India. But he spoke once more of 'the malignity of a subtle, acute, semi-civilized race, unrestrained by law or by moral feeling', and pronounced that 'cowardice possessed of strength' had wreaked the 'horrible sufferings upon its [white] victims'. Yet Hazewell ended with a caveat:

> If the close of this revolt be not stained with retaliating cruelties, if English soldiers remember mercy, then the whole history of this time will be a proud addition to the annals of England.[28]

An article, 'The British in India', printed in the *New Englander*, a journal published in New Haven, Connecticut, made no effort to conceal its feelings:

> Throughout a region more extensive than England itself, the English, a few months ago the rulers and masters, are now mangled and dishonored corpses, or hunted fugitives, or fighting for their own and one another's lives. Even this is not the worst . . . the hand of vengeance has not struck only at the instruments of alien dominion; their innocent families have been butchered under circumstances the most horrible; gentle women and tender children have been done to death with a refinement of hideous cruelty of which only North American Indians, or South Sea cannibals, would have been thought capable.
>
> All England is mourning for her dead. All England is roused to take vengeance on the murderers, to vindicate her sullied honor, to re-establish her profaned authority . . .[29]

While sharply split over slavery, American public opinion thus reached a consensus on the Revolt in India. Outraged by the killing of women and children, virtually all white Americans wanted the English to subdue the Indians, and they seemed to agree that the white West as a whole was called upon to extend civilization to the world's coloured, non-Christian peoples.

A play called 'Jessie Brown; or, The Relief of Lucknow' was presented in Washington at the end of 1858, featuring Nana Sahib as the chief villain. For some time, no actor was willing to play the role of the hated Nana Sahib, and at least one terrified woman in the audience, a southerner called Mary Chesnut, feared that American slaves would rebel like the sepoys one day.[30]

An exception to the American consensus was provided by the *Liberator*, the abolitionist weekly appearing from Boston from 1831. Though horrified by the Kanpur brutalities, the weekly's founder editor, William Lloyd Garrison, insisted that it was 'little short of blasphemy' for the British 'to subjugate nations, rob them, apply physical tortures, and goad them to insurrection, and then go over the solemn farce of Fast days and prayers'.[31]

Frederick Douglass, the black abolitionist, offered a somewhat different angle. Speaking in New York on 3 August 1857, well before America understood what was happening in India, Douglass used the news from there to underline racial tensions within the abolitionist movement. He said:

> [I]n some quarters the efforts of colored people meet with very little encouragement. We may fight, but we must fight like the Seapoys of India, under white officers. This class of Abolitionists don't like colored celebrations, they don't like colored conventions, they don't like colored Anti-Slavery fairs . . .[32]

Lincoln and the Revolt. We should note the silence on the Indian Revolt from several influential Americans, including Lincoln and Thoreau. No public or private remark by either Lincoln or Thoreau on India's 1857 events has come to light. It is hard to think that these two were not interested.

Thoreau's warmth for Indian thought and his interest in India have already been marked by us. As for Lincoln, in 1857 and 1858 he was a lawyer-cum-politician living in Springfield, Illinois, but increasingly involved in issues transcending his state. Thus we saw how he reacted to the 1857 Dred Scott judgment with his 'House Divided' speech. The Indian Revolt must have stirred Lincoln's thoughts.

Moreover, two missionaries who returned from India to America, Reverend Dr Joseph Warren and Reverend Mr Hay, gave well-publicized talks on India and its Revolt in Springfield during the winter of 1857–58 on days when (as we know from the Lincoln log) the president-to-be was in his home town. Lincoln *may* have attended one or more of these talks and would certainly have heard of them. We know that at least one of his good friends, Orville Hickman Browning, a lawyer who would serve on the US

Senate from 1861 to 1863, heard several of these Springfield talks given by Warren and Hay.

This evidence, contained in Browning's diaries, reveals that Hay was 'an escaped missionary from Allahabad' while Warren had spent fifteen years in India (it is not clear where). Warren ended up living for short spells in Browning's Springfield home and served from 1858 to 1862 as the pastor of Springfield's Westminster Presbyterian Church. Browning's diary describes one of Warren's lectures ('On the philosophy of Hindooism', 2 March 1858) as 'excellent'. Two days later, Browning writes that he had just heard a 'very interesting lecture from Dr Warren on the Sepoy insurrection'.[33]

The Revolt was thus talked about in the world around Lincoln, even if for some reason he did not himself hear Warren or Hay. However, not given to speaking on a subject until he was sure of what he wanted to say, Lincoln chose to remain silent on the rebellion in India. Something similar probably happened with Thoreau.

RUSSELL

Rejoining the correspondent of The Times, we get something exceptional: a formidable observer's first-hand accounts from the India of 1858–59. His impressions are found in private letters to Delane and his family, in diary jottings, and in reports written for The Times. In 1860, his two-volume Diary in India, drawing on all that he had written during his visit there, was published. Most quotes that follow are from the two-volume Diary, where he says he 'saw India in mourning, lighted up by a blood-red conflagration' (Vol. 1, p. vii).

En route, in Alexandria, Russell heard that Havelock had died five weeks earlier in Lucknow. Like everyone in Britain, Russell had admired the old soldier's push and pluck, and wondered about the honours that Havelock would receive in England. He wrote, 'All our hopes and our anticipations and speculations had been abruptly buried in his grave' (22).

Fellow-passengers did not greatly impress Russell. A major returning to India spoke (on the ship from Suez) of 'rascally'

Muslims and 'slimy, treacherous Hindus', adding, 'Those niggers are such a confounded sensual lazy set—you might as well think to train pigs' (51). Russell noticed women who were going to be married in India allowing liberties to be taken by men who had wives at home; sharp class distinctions among Britons returning to India; contempt for 'the Indian character and way of life'; and missionaries with violent thoughts about Indians and violent reactions towards the ship's servants.

Before reaching India, Russell's reflections had told him that the 'the normal processes of change and decay' were not likely to be 'suspended in the special case of the British empire'.[34] Arriving in Calcutta on 28 January 1858, he was met by a younger brother of his editor, Captain George Delane, a member of the Governor General's bodyguard. George Delane told Russell that he had been made a temporary member of the Bengal Club, where he was given a room.

On that first day itself, Russell noticed that Calcutta's Britons seemed hierarchical, argumentative and quarrelsome, and yet united in their disdain of Indians, including those regarded as high-born or elect. Finding that the Europeans disliked the sight of Indian elites moving about in Calcutta's upscale area, Russell thought of an earlier time when Roman consuls moved haughtily amidst plebeians. He wrote that night in his diary:

28 January 1858. But here on this esplanade, or race-course . . . — whatever it is— . . . there is such insult offered as the arrogance of the most offensive aristocracy—that of complexion—can invent to those who by no means admit themselves to be the plebeians of the race.
    See: there is a feeble young man dressed in white, with a gilded velvet cap in his hand, trying to drive a vehicle which looks like a beehive, [judging] from the cluster of his attendants . . . That is Chuck-el-head Doss, the great little young Bengal merchant, the inheritor of old Head Doss's money, and the acceptor of . . . a Germanic-Hindoo-Christianic philosophy which teaches him that, after all, whatever is is best, and that the use of the senses is the best development of the inner man. Is he a bit nearer to us because he abjures Vishnu, accepts providence, and thinks our avatar very beautiful? Ask 'Who he is.' 'He's one of those nigger merchants— a cheeky set of fellows, and d__d blackguards, all of them' (103–04).

Russell did not quite get Doss's name ('Chakra' something or 'Jag' something?), but evidently the man entertained a mix of Indian and Western beliefs—the Calcutta of the late 1850s contained many of this sort. We should mark too that as a friend of Max Müller, Russell was familiar with some outlines of Hindu thought. His observations continue:

> Then there is a morose old man in a chariot drawn by four horses, with two well-dressed fellows with their backs to the horses, outriders, and runners, and a crowd of servants. He is a handsome, worn-out looking man, with a keen eye, lemon-coloured face and gloves, dressed in rich shawls and curious silks. Who is he? A few Europeans bow to him. 'He is the Raja of Chose—a great rascal' (104).
>
> You show some historic interest when you are shown Tippoo Sultan's son and grandson; but your friend is too busy looking at the pretty fair face of Mrs Jones (104).
>
> Every [British] clerk keeps a buggy, every [British] merchant has a carriage and lives in a style which speaks of enormous profits, or little conscience (106).

The next day, Russell called on the Governor General. To his surprise, all the innumerable servants in the magnificent Government House were Indians, including some carrying swords. Despite the Revolt, 'not a single English domestic was visible' (113). Russell found Canning surrounded by dispatch boxes, files, papers and maps, and assessed him as an analytical and judicial chief, unwilling to believe a report until it was examined to be true.

At this first interview, Canning discredited the stories of rape and mutilations that Russell had brought up, but suggested that Britons recovering in Calcutta's hospitals from the Revolt's incidents might know something about the stories.

On visiting a hospital on Little Russell Street and another in Kidderpore, Russell was struck by the efficiency and cleanliness he saw in both places, a contrast, he thought, from the Crimea. He met patients from Kanpur and Lucknow. 'Not one of them could tell me of a single mutilation of any woman to which they could depose of their personal knowledge' (117). A woman who had been besieged in the Residency in Lucknow spoke instead of class divisions there:

29 January. While some were starving, half fed on unwholesome food, others were living on the good things of the land, and were drinking Champagne and Moselle ... Whilst cannon-shot and shell were rending the walls about their ears ... whilst disease was knocking at the door of every room, artificial rules of life still exercised their force; petty jealousy and 'caste' reigned in the Residency; the 'upper ten' with stoical grandeur would die the 'upper ten', and as they fell composed their robes after the latest fashion (119).

From the city, Russell journeyed to Serampore (he knew of it as a missionary quarter) and to nearby Barrackpore, where Mangal Pandey had fired the Revolt's first shot. In Barrackpore, he saw hundreds of disarmed but uniformed sepoys (most of them from Avadh) standing sullenly at attention. If dismissed, they would have joined the rebels. So they were detained at Barrackpore, with white soldiers standing guard over them.

By now, within three days of landing in India, Russell was missing white faces—none were to be seen on his trip back to Calcutta. Judging from the throngs of Indians he passed, Russell thought that the horrid Hindu customs of which he had heard from Calcutta's Britons could not have been all that destructive, for the race was clearly thriving.

At a dinner in the grand Calcutta home of the advocate-general, Russell noticed pleasant lighting, flags, flowers and fire-arms. 'Dancing vigorous, music good,' he would note, and add:

The supper-rooms gave one an exalted notion of the resources of Calcutta, and one could not help asking himself, 'Has there been a mutiny at all?' (129)

His jottings reveal a scrutinizing eye:

2 February. In India the disturbance caused by the movement of great bodies is widely felt. The Governor General, in moving to Allahabad the other day, absorbed all the bullock-waggons on the road *for five days.* When Lord Dalhousie crossed the Ganges, he had *one hundred elephants* in his train. Sir Colin Campbell's baggage, &c., extended *for eighteen miles,* when he came down from Lucknow (emphasis in the original).

Tonight I hear that the menagerie of the King of Oude, as much his private property as his watch or turban, were sold under discreditable circumstances, and his jewels seized and impounded, though we had no more claim on them than on the Crown diamonds of Russia (130–31).

Aware of the power of *The Times*, Canning and his staff did their best to meet Russell's needs. Colin Campbell, who was in Allahabad to plan another expedition from Kanpur to Lucknow (it was to join him that Canning had commandeered the bullock wagons), was asked to give every assistance to Russell, who intended to cover Campbell's latest venture. Before Russell left Calcutta to join Campbell's army, an Indian servant (a Christian) was found for him: Simon, a 'Madrasi', as he was called.

Russell's westward journey from Calcutta to Kanpur was a four-stage affair—by train to Raniganj (120 miles); a four-day ride in a horse-drawn carriage or *'gharry'*, as Russell called it, to Allahabad (via Benares); again by train half-way to Kanpur; by gharry to Kanpur.

En route to Raniganj, Russell stepped off the train briefly at Burdwan, where he saw an imprisoned Raja. At Raniganj he was told 'by the authorities' that no 'mutilated women' had passed through that station towards Calcutta (135–36). Travelling in a gharry to Allahabad, he found the country bleak, grey-brown, mostly flat and full of mosquitoes. Stopping in traveller's bungalows, he read their registers and found that only whites had stayed there, though, in theory, Indians too were entitled to use them. Russell studied the men, women and children who passed by his gharry.

> *8 February.* In no case is a friendly eye directed to the white man's carriage. Oh, that language of the eye! Who can doubt? who can misinterpret it? It is by it alone that I have learned our race is not even feared at times by many, and that by all it is disliked. Pray God I have read it falsely. These passers-by are wondrously squalid and poorly clad (146).

On the night of 9 February Russell reached Allahabad Fort and marvelled at the fact that Allahabad did not fall to the rebels. He recalled how when the Revolt began, Outram had written a 'most masterly state-paper' on 'the paramount necessity of securing Allahabad'. Yet, Allahabad 'was saved by no act of Government, by no care of man.' Luck, Russell thought, had saved Allahabad for the British (151).

Rail lines were being laid in both directions, west of Allahabad all the way to Kanpur, and east of Allahabad towards Raniganj. Before long, it would be possible to travel the entire distance from Calcutta to Kanpur by train. Looking at the lengthening rail lines and at the Fort that Akbar had built three centuries earlier, Russell was struck by what the British had accomplished.

> *10 February.* Excepting the rise of the United States, I know of nothing so rapid and so wonderful in the history of nations as the growth of our Indian empire (151).

So Russell too came close to thinking of India as another America for the British. In Allahabad, he met Canning again and found him devoted to work, honest, sagacious, and resolved, but also cold and haughty, despising 'the arts of popularization'. Until Campbell regained Lucknow, the Governor General would make Allahabad his headquarters.

Russell took a train going halfway towards Kanpur and saw that it consisted of discarded British second-class carriages. When he alighted in Kharga, he noticed a large retinue of cooks, servants and ayahs looking after 'a luxurious little baby' and 'another little lord of the Indian creation' and 'two little terriers'. 'I was curious to know who this millionaire could be, and was astonished to learn that it was only Captain Smith, of the Mekawattee Irregulars ... The whole of this little camp did not contain more than eight or nine tents; but there were at least 150 domestics and a menagerie of animals' (160).

On an overnight journey by gharry from Kharga to Kanpur, Russell recalled the harsh happenings on that road the previous summer.

> *11 February.* At night the gharrys came round, and we rumbled along in peaceful sleep over the trunk-road by which Neill and Havelock had advanced to attack the Butcher of Cawnpore—a road, by the way, of which many of the trees had been hung with natives' bodies as the columns under Neill and Renaud marched to open the way from Allahabad. I hear many stories, the truth of which I would doubt if I could. Our first spring was terrible; I fear our claws were indiscriminating (162).

Because Sir Colin Campbell was cautious, impatient officers called him Sir Crawling Camel. He was someone Russell had known in the Crimea. Russell was greeted warmly by him on 12 February and given a comfortable tent, a horse, and access to the telegraph.[35]

Visiting the Revolt's sites in Kanpur, Russell was shaken by Bibighar and by the flimsy 'walls' of the entrenchment. At Satichaura, he imagined the sights and screams of that fateful day: 'I turned and left the spot with every vein boiling, and it was long ere I could still the beatings of my heart' (208). Yet, he also remembered earlier massacres of history, including several in Europe, and penned a remarkable analysis of the Revolt.

> *12 February.* In fact, the peculiar aggravation of the Cawnpore massacres was this, that the deed was done by a subject race—by black men who dared to shed the blood of their masters, and that of poor helpless ladies and children. Here we had not only a servile war and a sort of Jacquerie combined, but we had a war of religion, a war of race, and a war of revenge, of hope, of some national promptings to shake off the yoke of a stranger, and to re-establish the full power of native chiefs, and the full sway of native religions (164).

Russell thought that the rebel leaders would have liked to bring about 'the destruction of every white man, woman or child who fell into their hands'. But 'on many remarkable occasions' the 'design' was 'frustrated' either because Indians serving the leaders did not have it in them to carry it out, or because policy goals required a sparing of lives (164).

Studying the inhabitants of Kanpur, Russell noticed 'the scowling, hostile look of the people. The bunniahs bow low with their necks, and salaam with their hands, but not with their eyes' (179). He also felt that racial mingling and mixture had ended. Eurasians, he thought, were going to disappear. At times a few wealthy Indians and 'denationalized' Britons still met socially—Russell had attended a Calcutta dinner where an Indian raja was present—but such occasions were rare.

John Walter Sherer, Kanpur's new magistrate, was installed at Duncan's Hotel. Russell, who liked Sherer, regaled a party at the hotel with songs and Irish stories. Some days later, he dined with British civilians, including one 'fierce-eyed, red-nosed, ferrety, bloodthirsty sort of man' who 'rather boasted of the splendid style in which he hung up niggers'.[36] Russell saw that a Sikh, clearly friendly to the British, who had brought a message to the army camp in Kanpur was treated with suspicion. Yet Russell felt that rethinking was needed at both ends of the divide.

> *14 February*. It may be that the native is more to blame for the gulf between us than we are; for his religion digs it deep. He will walk with us, talk with us; but, like Shylock, he will not eat with us, drink with us, or pray with us (190).

Russell learnt in Kanpur that the stories of words of distress scrawled by white children on the walls of Bibighar—stories that had evoked cries of revenge in Britain and in British bungalows across India—were largely untrue. Yet that detail did not really matter.

> *14 February*. One fact is clearly established; that the writing behind the door, on the walls of the slaughter-house, on which so much stress was laid in Calcutta, did not exist when Havelock entered the place, and therefore was not the work of any of the poor victims . . . God knows the horrors and atrocity of the pitiless slaughter needed no aggravation. Soldiers in the heat of action need little excitement to vengeance (191–92).

March for Lucknow. Nursing a need for action, Russell seemed bored in Kanpur by 'the very hum and no drum sort of life I have been leading' (221), but on 27 February, Campbell finally ordered the march to Lucknow. Repeating an exercise performed by him the previous November and by Havelock several times in September, the General asked his forces—his caravanserai—to proceed on the bridge of boats across the Ganga into Avadh.

As the march commenced, Russell, who had obtained a gharry and a white mare for his own use, recalled Avadh's ex-ruler, now a prisoner in Calcutta, and what he had heard about him—belying his reputation, Wajid Ali Shah had conducted himself with 'dignity and propriety' when he was arrested and his kingdom annexed (226).

British guns blew up temples on the Avadh side of the river lest the rebels used them as shields while attacking Campbell's caravan, which was quite an assemblage of humans, animals and things. Russell referred to its component of Indian helpers:

> *27 February.* Bred in camps, but unwarlike—forever behind guns, and never before them ... Most of these people are Hindoos from Bengal or the north-west provinces. Some are from Central India.

The vast army of servants showed that the British had enlisted the support of sections of the Indian population. Russell identified Afghans, other Muslims, the Sikh protecting 'the precious hairs from the contamination of the dust by tying a handkerchief under his jaws', 'the fat bunneah hurr[ying] on in his bamboo-car to see his store-tent; [and] the wives of the bunneahs who sit straddle-legged on the tiniest of donkeys with their toes almost touching the ground. All these men, women and children, with high delight, were pouring towards Lucknow to aid the Feringhee,' Russell observed (228). In addition, there were 'milch-goats and sheep, a flock of turkeys ... ; this long line of camels present[ing] side-views of many boxes of beer, pickles, potted meats and soda-water', and also pets, monkeys, parrots, dogs, some riding on camels and elephants (229–30).

The caravan had left before dawn. Slowly, the sun lit up the top of the travelling procession; then, just before the sun would become disagreeable, there was a halt—in Avadh territory.

> I alighted at my tent-door, which seemed as if it had never moved from Cawnpore. On entering everything was in its place just as I left it. Our mess-dinner was precisely the same as at Cawnpore; and it was hard to believe we were in an enemy's country (231).

It was an unusual sort of invasion. In the tent mess there were 'tables, snow-white tablecloths, plates, knives and forks, curries smoking' and an array of servants with folded arms waiting for their masters (234). Simon, the Madrasi servant, remained at Russell's side.

Aiming to capture Lucknow and its leaders of rebellion with a minimum of British casualties, Campbell had assembled a large force of about 30,000 men of whom nearly 18,000 were Europeans; the rest were mostly Sikhs and Gurkhas. At least six of his columns were led by generals. Campbell had also gathered heavy guns, a large supply of provisions, sappers to blow up defences, engineers to put up bridges and, since he intended to remain in constant contact with Canning in Allahabad, men who would leave behind telegraph lines as they marched forward.

Campbell planned to move forward in careful stages and cannonade, one by one, Lucknow's palaces (all situated next to one another), where he was sure the rebels would congregate. Once defensive walls crumbled from British shells, his infantry and cavalry would storm across and take over. Avadh's forces, by British estimates, consisted of 30,000 rebelling sepoys and 50,000 volunteers raised by the kingdom's talukdars. These fighters were mingled with approximately 500,000 people of the city, all expected to be sympathetic to the rebels. As his army neared Lucknow, Russell was bowled over by his first sight (from the Dilkusha roof) of the Avadh capital:

> 3 March 1858. A vision of palaces, minars, domes azure and golden, cupolas, colonnade, long facades of fair perspective in pillar and column—all rising up amid a calm still ocean of the brightest verdure . . . The towers of the fairy city gleam in its midst. Spires of gold glitter in the sun . . . There is a city more vast than Paris, as it seems, and more brilliant, lying before us. Is this a city in Oude? Is this the capital of a semi-barbarous race, erected by a corrupt, effete, and degraded dynasty (253–54)?

Russell did not doubt that the British force would succeed, but, as he wrote to *The Times* on 4 March (his reports went by telegram to Calcutta and thence by ship to London), he feared that many 'unfortunate' civilians in Lucknow would be 'handed over to a very excited and irritated soldiery, to the fierce Sikhs and to the wild Ghoorkas of Nepal'. He added, 'The time for indiscriminate blood-shedding must cease, let all that the angry civilians of British India can say be said, with the punishment of the mutinous Sepoys and of those actually taken in arms against us. Justice and even vengeance must after a period rest satisfied.'[37]

The rebels defended with fury, skill and evident preparation. Anticipating Campbell's tactics, they had filled up with stoneworks almost every opening to every palace. They attacked too with their hundred or so guns, and with muskets.

Shortly before Campbell reached the city, Begum Hazrat Mahal, the deposed ruler's wife, rode on an elephant through its streets, trying to maintain morale. Firoz Shah, the surviving Mughal prince, had also played a part, asking (in a proclamation issued on 17 February) all Muslims and Hindus to rally to the standard of Birjis Qadr, Avadh's boy-king, or to join the units nearby that he and Bareilly's Khan Bahadur Khan were leading. Yet, facing the heavy batteries of the British, the rebels of Lucknow could hope only to delay, not prevent, the fall of the city, which was completed by 21 March.

Gurkha assistance caused the British some irritation. On 11 March, having arrived much later than announced at Campbell's camp outside Lucknow, Jung Bahadur, the Nepalese chief, insisted on formal speeches just when, within earshot, a bitter fight was taking place at Begum Kothi. Russell did not like Jung Bahadur's appearance, manner or history:

> [Because of his jewels, Jung Bahadur] blazed like a peacock's tail in the sun. But brighter than any gem the Maharajah wore is his eye, which shines with a cold light, resembling a ball of phosphorus. What a tiger-like, cruel, crafty, subtle eye! ... Sir Colin said, 'Do you wish to be introduced to His Highness?' 'No, your Excellency, I have no wish of the kind,' and so I escaped shaking the hand of a man who has committed cold-blooded murder (310).

On the British side, the killed and wounded in the battle for Lucknow totalled 1,100. The rebels perhaps lost 5,000. Most of them, however, escaped with their arms to Rohilkhand or the Avadh interior. The escapees included the defiance's leading lights: Hazrat Mahal, her son Birjis and a cleric, Maulvi Ahmadullah—a nawab's son who possessed devoted followers, battling skills and a belief in Hindu-Muslim cooperation. Campbell's failure, despite all his planning, to destroy the rebel force took the sheen out of the British triumph.

Plunder, vandalism, and vengeance hurt the triumph even more. At every palace, the victors—Britons, Sikhs and Gurkhas—destroyed its riches (fineries, drapes, chandeliers, paintings) and looted its treasures. Shawls, lace, embroidery, gold, silver, pearls, emeralds, rubies, opals, including some large pieces, worth a million and a quarter sterling in all, were swiftly appropriated. Some in the conquering army took enough, Russell saw, to become independent for life. Under the Empire's rules at the time, the plunder was legitimate.

To his regret, Russell got very little of the loot himself. In Kaisarbagh, a soldier offered him a box of diamonds and pearls for a hundred rupees. Not carrying the money, Russell could not take the box, but he did 'load himself with jade and a diamond drop'.[38]

Moving at times with the troops and at other times staying alongside the chief, Russell portrayed the fighting and the orgies for *The Times*. The destruction was condemned by him, but not the looting. He did record, however, the savagery against the defeated enemy. No prisoners were taken. Sepoys were 'bayoneted on the spot or worse'. One sepoy, Russell learnt, was 'roasted alive by the Sikhs'.[39] And he learnt also of 'equally savage behaviour by some of the British'.[40]

> A Cashmere boy came towards the post leading a blind and ancient man, and throwing himself at the feet of an officer, asked for protection. That officer, as I was informed by his comrades, drew his revolver and snatched it at the wretched supplicant's head. The men cried 'shame' on him. Again he pulled the trigger—again the cap missed; again he pulled and once more the weapon refused its task. The fourth time—thrice had he time to relent—the gallant officer succeeded, and the boy's lifeblood flowed at his feet. [There were cheers from his men.][41]

Earlier, on 9 March, Russell had witnessed 'the amputation of a dooly-bearer's thigh'. This youth, who seemed about twenty to Russell, 'a slight, tall, dark-coloured Hindoo', was carrying a palanquin for the British when a round-shot shattered his thigh.

> He never even moaned when, with rapid sweep of the knife, the principal operator had cut the flesh through to the broken splintered bone . . . In two or three minutes the black leg was lying on the floor of what had once been the Begum's boudoir in the palace of Heart's-ease [the Dilkusha]. In two or three minutes more, the dusky patient, with a slow shiver, passed away quietly to the other world.
>
> Some of my friends in camp would deny he had any soul, or, as one of them put it, 'If niggers have souls, they're not the same as ours' (299–300).

The dead of Lucknow included young William Hodson, a captain by now. Apparently sniffing booty, he had 'dashed into a room [in

Begum Kothi] sabre in hand, and had staggered back, shot through the liver' by a rebel who was inside.[42] A Sikh carried Hodson in his arms to a doctor, but in a few hours the Briton was dead. Referring, in his *Diary*, to a 'really national' loss, Russell would add that he did 'not altogether approve' of Hodson's treatment of the Mughal princes in Delhi (320).

Angered by the support Avadh's landowners had given to the rebels, Canning announced that he would confiscate their lands if they did not surrender at once. But British rule did not extend into their spaces. More work lay ahead for Campbell and his columns, and also, therefore, for Russell, who criticized Canning's measure in *The Times*, adding,

> [N]o foreign power whatever could maintain an army in India without the aid of a considerable portion of the population. We could not march a mile without their assistance ... For the Sepoy let there be justice, and if justice be death, let execution be done, but let us cease to disgrace ourselves by indiscriminate clamouring for 'more heads'.[43]

Congratulating Russell on his dispatches, Delane wrote from London that the fame the correspondent had won in the Crimea had been sustained. The editor added that Russell had helped correct attitudes in Britain:

> The public feeling has righted itself more promptly than was to be expected, and we had before the recess a debate in which the most humane instead of the most bloodthirsty sentiments were expressed. The key to the savage spirit was the 'atrocities', and these seem to have resolved themselves into simple massacre.[44]

Close call. On 13 April 1858, a little over three weeks after the fall of Lucknow, Colin Campbell led a column to subdue the rebels in Rohilkhand. Russell joined the column. Hating the heat and down with dysentery, he had to be carried in a dooly before he tried the back of an elephant, which he did not find comfortable.

On 29 April he was walking towards his horse when a fierce kick from another horse, intended for Russell's animal, landed on our correspondent's thigh. Russell was 'knocked two yards back and over'. Doctors had to bleed him with twenty-five leeches clapped on his calf and thigh, and he was back in his dooly.

The next day, the British column confronted some rebel sowars on the outskirts of Rohilkhand's largest town, Bareilly. Though Russell did not realize it at the time, these sowars were part of a force led by the Mughal prince, Firoz Shah. After a skirmish he observed, Russell, who had removed his trousers because of a sharp pain in his injured leg, was 'just lying down on [his] elbow' in his dooly that had been set on the earth under a tree, conscious of leeches, pain and the heat, when he dozed off. Rebel sowars again approached and Russell's dooly-bearers picked up the dooly, only to drop it in a panic. Woken up by the jolt, Russell heard the cry, 'Sowar! Sowar!' and saw a stampede around him. He also saw, not far from where he lay, 'a billow of sowars, their sabres flashing in the sun'.

Russell began imagining 'an inglorious and miserable death' when his 'faithful syce, with drops of sweat rolling down his black face, ran towards me, dragging my unwilling and plunging horse' towards the dooly. Russell, who was wearing only a shirt and had his head, feet and legs bare, was somehow helped on to his horse by Ramdeen, the syce, and the horse was goaded with 'a long strip of thorn' to run (*Diary*, Vol. II, p. 8).

Within seconds, a sowar with raised sword rode towards Russell. A camel driver who came in between was cut down by the sowar, who again lifted his sword and was bringing it down on Russell's neck when a Highlander's bullet felled the sowar.

> As I rode on (Russell would recall) I felt as if cut down—thought of many fox hounds—recollect a sweet sense of pleasure and gaiety as I tried to keep my seat. A Highlander caught me—'Where are you hit, sir? A doctor, a doctor.' I remember nothing more—awoke on my own dooly, screaming from spasms on the lungs, felt I was going to die (5 May).[45]

The Highlander who had saved Russell was none other than an old Crimean acquaintance of his, Sergeant William Forbes-Mitchell. In a book that Forbes-Mitchell would write, the following account is given:

> I was detached with about a dozen men of No. 7 Company to find the ammunition-guard, and bring our ammunition in rear of the line. Just as I reached the ammunition camels, a large force of the

rebel cavalry, led by Firoz Shah in person, swept the flank and among the baggage, cutting down camels, camel-drivers and camp-followers in all directions ...

We saw Mr. Russell of *The Times*, who was ill and unable to walk from the kick of a horse, trying to escape on horseback. He had got out of his dooly, undressed and bare-headed as he was, and leaped into the saddle as the groom had been leading his horse near him. Several of the enemy's cavalry were dodging through the camels to get at him.

We turned our rifles on them, and I shot down the one nearest to Mr. Russell just as he had cut down an intervening camel-driver and was making for 'Our Special Correspondent'; in fact, his *tulwar* was actually lifted to swoop down on Mr. Russell's bare head when my bullet put a stop to his proceedings.[46]

Unable to write, Russell dictated his reports to willing amanuenses among the soldiers and continued for some days with the attacking column. Bareilly was soon captured by the British, as was its chief, the influential Rohilla, Khan Bahadur Khan. Yet Firoz Shah remained elusive and much of Avadh defiant; and Nana Sahib was still on the loose when the British campaign was halted because of the rising heat and the monsoon that followed in July.

As for Russell, he was ordered to proceed to the hills of Simla to recuperate. This was a long and difficult journey, first—across tracts where rebels roamed—to Delhi in the west, and then north to Ambala, Kalka and Simla. Two other sick officers plus Simon, his servant, and an escort of 100 Sikh soldiers accompanied Russell on his journey to Delhi.[47] En route, in Fatehgarh, Russell heard on 28 May that Kunwar Singh, the old rebel who had harassed the British in what would be today's western Bihar and eastern Uttar Pradesh had died of his wounds. Russell wrote in his diary, 'There was something of the soldier and the general about this old chief, and his men had the honour of inflicting three defeats on British soldiers' (Vol. II, p. 40).

As his gharry entered Delhi and clattered past the walls of the Red Fort, Russell reflected on previous arrivals in Delhi of British and other conquerors.

4 June 1858. We did not come into India, as they did, at the head of great armies, with the avowed intention of subjugating the country. We crept in as humble barterers, whose existence depended on the bounty and favour of the lieutenants of the kings of Delhi (50).

Simon told his master what he had resourcefully discovered—they were going to be accommodated in 'Luddylo Cazzle'. This was Ludlow Castle, one of the buildings north of the Red Fort that Theo Metcalfe's father, Sir Thomas, had built, which now served as the home as well as the office of Delhi's new commissioner, Charles Saunders. Russell, whose ear was as good as his eye, had caught Simon's south Indian pronunciation with precision.

He saw that cannon shots had not spared Ludlow Castle, but found it 'agreeable' to be 'ushered into the presence of a fair Englishwoman, who sat at a well-furnished board, doing the honours of her table to a circle of guests'. Until that moment, from the time of his arrival in Kanpur, he 'had lived in camps and in canvas'. He had come to the house 'dusty—I am afraid dirty— fagged—a hot, unpleasant-looking stranger' and had not 'seen the face of an Englishwoman' since leaving Calcutta (54–55).

Zafar. From Saunders Russell learnt more of what he had no doubt heard of well before arriving in Delhi—the trial of King Zafar that began on 27 January in a court martial in the Red Fort's principal state room, Diwan-i-Khas and the sentence, delivered on 9 March, of exile and lifelong imprisonment.

Zafar was found guilty of playing a prominent role in an international Islamic conspiracy to seize power in Delhi and kill its Christians. The fact that Hindus constituted the bulk of the Bengal army's rebels was excluded from the trial, with the prosecution in fact claiming that 'Hinduism [was] nowhere either reflected or represented' in the Revolt.[48] This line taken by the military prosecutors revealed the keystone of a new, or newly underscored, British policy in India—separate Hindus from Muslims, and never again allow the two to come together.

Looking ill and vacant throughout the trial and supported while walking to it by the shoulders of his favourite son, Jawan Bakht, Zafar offered a brief written defence. He was, he swore in God's name, helpless; he had not ordered the killing of Fraser, the resident, or of anyone else; the sepoys would have killed him if he refused to affix his seal on what they brought to him; he had begged the sepoys to go away when they first came from Meerut; they had been rude to him.

The defence was dismissed and all charges were held proven, but the aged life of the last Mughal was not ordered to be terminated. Hodson's assurance had ruled that out. In the dark of the pre-dawn hours of 7 October, he, Jawan Bakht, Bakht's mother, Zinat Mahal, a few other wives and concubines and some servants—a party of thirty-one in all—were moved out of Delhi by bullock cart. They would end up in Rangoon, where, four years later, Zafar died at the age of eighty-seven.

But on 4 June 1858, when Russell arrived in Delhi, Zafar was alive, incarcerated in the Red Fort. The next morning, Saunders took his guest to the Fort for a view of the royal prisoner.

> 5 June. The moment of our visit was not propitious ... was not calculated to ... throw a halo of romance around the infirm creature who was the symbol of extinguished empire ... In fact the ex-King was sick; with bent body he seemed nearly prostrate over a brass basin, into which he was retching violently ... (58–59)

Russell looked the other way, and saw in 'one corner, stretched on a charpoy, a young man of slight figure, who sat up at the sound of our voices and salaamed respectfully ... He was Jumma Bakht ... that scion of the House of Delhi' (59). The *Diary* continues:

> [Zafar] was still gasping for breath and replied by a wave of the hand and a monosyllable to the Commissioner. That dim-wandering-eyed, dreamy old man with feeble hanging nether lip and toothless gums—was he indeed the one who had ... fomented the most gigantic mutiny in the history of the world?
>
> Recalling youth to that decrepit frame—restoring its freshness to that sunken cheek—one might see the King glowing with all the beauty of the warrior David ... His hands and feet were delicate and fine; his garments, scanty and foul (60–61).[49]
>
> It is certain that for several days he protected the unfortunate (European and Christian) ladies who fled to the palace, and resisted the clamorous demands for their blood which were made by the monsters around him ... but he did not take the step which would have saved their lives. He did not put them into his zenana.
>
> It is said he was afraid of his own begums and the women of the

zenana ... Our countrywomen were murdered in his palace. It may
be that we are to some extent punishing in the father the sins of the
children (66).

One of the begums was talking to Saunders, the commissioner,
and Russell asked for a translation of her remarks. Evidently she
was demanding the right to leave the Fort. 'I am tired of [Zafar],
he is no king now,' she said (67). Returning to Ludlow Castle,
Russell continued with his reflections:

5 June. We denied permission to his royal relatives to enter our
service; we condemned them to a degrading existence, in poverty
and debt, inside the purlieus of their palace, and then we reproached
them with their laziness, meanness and sensuality. We shut the gates
of military preferment upon them—we closed upon them the paths
of every pursuit—we took from them every object of honourable
ambition—and then our papers and our mess-rooms teemed with
invectives against lazy, slothful and sensuous princes of his house.
Better die a hundred deaths than drag on such a contemptible,
degrading existence (51).

His thoughts reminded Russell of something his friend Charles
Dickens had written:

The king was subjected to constant annoyance from his numerous
relatives—the Great Mogul Olivers were always 'asking for more'
... Some of these royal families were in want of their meals (57).

Two days later, Russell went up to the Ridge from where his
compatriots had launched their re-entry into Delhi. There, he was
quite moved.

7 June. I saw it was the pride, self-reliance and greatness of a
conquering race alone which had enabled a handful of men to
sustain and successfully conduct the most hopeless military enterprise
that was ever undertaken ... At every stage the audacity of the siege
grew upon me (71).

But he also thought of the decisive role played (he felt) by the
incompetence of the rebel leaders, and then was reminded too of
British follies, including the brilliant planning that provided Delhi
with defensive bastions and plenty of guns—'and then denuded it
of European troops' (71). The sight of white children playing

about in Delhi stirred him; and he judged the Jama Masjid (the mosque that Palmerston wished to demolish) to be 'one of the grandest temples ever raised by man', noting its 'chaste richness, an elegance of proportion, and grandeur of design' (73). He also made an assessment of a different sort:

> 8 *June*. We do not tread on the feet (of the Hindus) so often and so heavily as on those of the (Muslims). Our antagonism to the followers of Mahomed is far stronger than that between us and the worshippers of Shiva and Vishnu ... The Governor who shall find some healthy use for the energies of Mahomedan nobility and gentry will confer a great benefit on India (74).

The ancient Qutub tower at Mehrauli too impressed Russell. The journey to it (on 9 June) enabled Russell to mark the 'miserable sheds' that lined the path between the city of Delhi and Mehrauli,

> in which the outcast population of the city, forbidden to return to their homes, are now forced to live ... For miles they stretch along the road-side. More squalid and vile nought [nothing] can be, save the wretched creatures who haunt them—once, perhaps, rich bunneahs, merchants, and shopkeepers (77).

Proceeding north towards Simla by gharry and dooly, Russell realized that he was crossing lands the British had recently traversed as they marched south to regain Delhi. In Ambala, a Briton boasted to him that he had 'hanged 54 men in a few hours for plundering a village' (82). From Ambala, no less than 140 men and several animals were involved in carrying Russell and his companion (a Captain Alison) with their servants (one for each) and their belongings to Kalka, which lay at the foot of the Simla hills.

Dogs, jackals, vultures, flies and mosquitoes gave the travellers company, but worst of all for Russell—more challenging even than the reporting, the marches, the rides, the risk, the injury and the trauma he had gone through in India—was *the heat*. Because of it, all travelling took place at night or very early in the morning. From Kalka, teams of coolies carried Russell and Alison up to Simla. The two sahibs were placed in easy chairs to which poles were tied; gripping the poles, the coolies heaved their cargo uphill.

Russell, who noticed varicose veins on the coolies' bare legs, was ecstatic at the sight of the hills:

> *13 June.* How I bow down and worship, and am grateful for the mercy that brought me within sight even of your (the Hill's) grateful shade! Under it give me one moment of time to speak my gratitude, and then, if needs be, let me find my grave. None [but the half-drowned mariner] can imagine what is the pleasure of the master of the poor, shattered, broken bark, tossed in seas of fire, and pierced in every plank by sun and fever's stroke, when at last he sees, after all the dead roll of the plain, the hills—the eternal hills (84–85)!

To taste the pleasure of the hills, wrote Russell the next day in Simla (where he would spend four months), 'we must be sick, wounded, roasted, and worn-out in the dreadful plain of India' (93). He had found in Simla a good host, good food, a library, servants 'and above all—how far above, words cannot say—a cool atmosphere' (94).

For their first few days on the hill, Russell and Alison were the house guests of Lord William Hay, deputy commissioner of the Hill States. At dinner on his second evening in Hay's house, Russell would record, 'a young brute named Mitford ... excited my wrath by declaring he thought it quite right to burn wounded sepoys and declaring he did not want justice but vengeance—that he hated all niggers. I put him down in great style and Hay thanked me for it afterwards.'[50]

On 19 June, Russell and Alison moved to The Priory, a house they rented for 60 pounds for the season. It came with 'some thirty servants for two of us' (101). Incapacitated by his leg, Russell spent long days in the verandah, soon got bored by its view of the Himalayas, but read a lot (including Mrs Gaskell's *Life of Charlotte Bronte*), studied the fauna and flora of the garden, shot crows and kites, and decided, like some aristocrats of his and earlier times, to create a menagerie, for which he ordered cages.

Rani of Jhansi. Some days after moving to The Priory, Russell learnt of a significant setback for the rebels. On 17 June, Lakshmibai, the young Rani of Jhansi and a major British foe in central India, had been defeated and killed in a battle with a force commanded by Major General Sir Hugh Rose. 'This victory will restore our prestige in Central India,' Russell recorded (105).

At death, the Rani was in her middle or late twenties. Widowed in 1853, she had bitterly resented Dalhousie's annexation of Jhansi and the abolition of its throne, to which she felt her adopted son was entitled. However, she kept up cordial relations with British officials, including Major Erskine, commissioner of central India's Saugor division, in which Jhansi had been included. Their goodwill was crucial for her and her son's future.

Built on a plateau in Bundelkhand (a Hindustani-speaking territory south of the Jamuna River), the walled town of Jhansi stood 64 miles due south of the rich city of Gwalior, famous for its rock fort, whose young ruler, twenty-four-year-old Jiyajirao Scindia, had remained loyal to the British. Agra, the British-controlled capital of the North Western Provinces, lay 75 miles to the north of Gwalior. To the north-east of Jhansi, at a distance of 102 miles, was the fort, protected by deep ravines, of Kalpi, on the southern bank of the Jamuna. About 45 miles north-east of the river from Kalpi was Kanpur.

In June of 1857, after Jhansi-based Bengal army sepoys rebelled and killed all sixty or so Britons and Eurasians in the town, including women and children, Lakshmibai sent two secret letters to Erskine, concealed by her agents in walking sticks. In these letters, the Rani expressed regret for the killings (which had been preceded by the victims' pleas to her for succour), explained that she had been helpless, and added that she remained in danger. To this, Erskine's response—similar to British responses in respect of other places they could not secure—was to ask Lakshmibai to govern Jhansi 'on behalf of the British' until the latter's authority was restored.

Was the young Rani, who had trained herself to ride and use a sword, afraid of the rebels? In her letters to Erskine, she had written of their bullying her and extorting money from her. Or, contrary to what she had written, did she in her heart sympathize with their cause? Her father, a Brahmin of the same caste as Bajirao II, had close ties with the Peshwa court before Bajirao was ordered to move to Bithur. Evidently, she herself had spent times with Nana Sahib in Bithur. Like him, she nursed grievances against the British. Did she enjoy being an independent queen and hope that with British defeat her son would eventually succeed her as Jhansi's ruler? Or did she simply want white rule to end?

We can ask such questions, but may never know the answers. In any case, in the opening months of 1858, a large British force led by a fifty-six-year-old general, Sir Hugh Rose, was moving north towards Jhansi. Equipped with heavy guns and assembled in western India, this force had left Bombay the previous autumn. Everyone in Jhansi was aware of its approach.

From what had happened in Kanpur, Delhi and elsewhere in north India, the thousands of rebels entrenched in Jhansi knew that surrender to Rose's army was not an option—the British were taking no prisoners. The rebels would have to fight Rose. Whether or not her heart was wholly with the sepoys, Lakshmibai's fate was inextricably joined to theirs. She could not possibly go against them. Moreover, the British had concluded by now that she was part and parcel of the Revolt. She too would have to fight Rose.

She and the sepoys were not entirely on their own. Ready to bring support was Tatya Tope, then roaming with thousands of rebels in the forests between Kalpi and Jhansi. Tope's chief, Nana Sahib, also accompanied by several thousand fighters, was moving in (or between) the more distant regions of Rohilkhand and Avadh.

Some months earlier, between August and October 1857, two of Nana Sahib's agents, Durgaprasad and Bhagwandas, had gone to Chandernagore, the French territory near Calcutta, where they had pleaded for French 'protection' for Nana Sahib, whose 'ancestors', they claimed, 'were in close ties with France'.[51] If Nana Sahib's goal was to preserve himself, that of the audacious Tatya Tope (to whom Nana Sahib had given his seal) was to prevail over the British.

In March, when Rose brought his heavy guns and large force to the gates of Jhansi and began his siege, Tope also swooped down (from the north) with, it is said, 20,000 men. Though taken by surprise, Rose was able to repulse Tope's army and also, early in April, to storm into Jhansi, but not without noticing that Lakshmibai had personally led the effort to repair Jhansi's cannonaded walls.

British victory was followed by great and ghastly reprisals in Jhansi (within days of the vengeance and vandalism in Lucknow that marked Campbell's victory there). In one incident, a room in Jhansi's fort where forty sowars had sheltered themselves was set on fire; when, with their clothes on fire, the sowars ran out, they were all slaughtered. The European women and children killed in Jhansi ten months earlier had been more than avenged, but Lakshmibai had escaped. In a ride immortalized in the Indian imagination, she galloped all the way from Jhansi to Kalpi, her son strapped to her back. Tatya Tope also got away, as did most of his men.

In May, Rose and his army pursued the rebels to Kalpi and won a hard-fought battle there. Once again, Lakshmibai, Tatya Tope, and most of their soldiers escaped. Even so, on 1 June, Rose felt that he could declare success. His men had marched more than a thousand miles, overcome several towns and forts, and captured numerous guns. They were entitled to praise and a pause.

Yet, on that very day, 1 June 1858, Tatya Tope, Lakshmibai and their force had captured Gwalior, which was more than 120 miles to the west of Kalpi. After a swift and secret march to Gwalior, the rebels won over the bulk of its army and forced young Jiyajirao to flee with his personal bodyguard to Agra. A ceremony proclaimed Gwalior's fealty (as in an earlier time) to the Peshwa—i.e., to Nana Sahib—and Lakshmibai was declared the head of its army. Gwalior's store of treasures was raided for the benefit of the rebel army and Lakshmibai was presented with a pearl necklace of enormous value.

Cancelling the halt he had announced, Rose marched with his army from Kalpi to Gwalior. Though their numbers had been augmented, the rebels defending Gwalior were defeated and Jiyajirao returned as its ruler. Tatya Tope again escaped, but on 17 June, Lakshmibai was killed in battle after being shot in the back and then run through with a sword. When, dressed as a man but wearing the pearl necklace, the Rani received these final strikes, she was riding a horse, holding its reins between her teeth, and waving her sword with both hands.

Describing her end, Canning would record that 'when taken to die under the mango clump' Lakshmibai distributed the necklace among her soldiers. Though her face, Canning would add, showed marks of small-pox, her eyes and figure were beautiful.[52] Most of her British adversaries, including those who thought her pro-rebel from the start—with some even believing that she had connived at

Jhansi's killings of June 1857—acknowledged her valour, which was usually described as manly. Writing in 1858, Thomas Dodd would concede that Lakshmibai possessed 'something like the stamp of heroism' and was capable of 'riding like a man, bearing arms like a man, leading and fighting like a man, and exhorting her troops to contend to the last against the hated Feringhees'.[53]

Accused of aiding the rebels, Lakshmibai's father was hanged, but her son, sheltered by a resourceful maid, would go on to receive a British pension.

Russell in Simla. 'We had a small dinner party this evening,' Russell noted in Simla on 23 June. 'As in the plains, each man brings his bearer . . . nine servants in attendance upon six people at dinner' (105). His *Diary* jottings reveal an interest in the details of birds.

> *24 June.* I shot a very beautiful jay today . . . It is black; head covered with fine black feathers, rising into a high crest and top-knot; bill dark slate colour; underneath the lower mandible some fine white sharp pointed feathers; back of neck and wing-covers grey slate; wing blue with white bars; the extremities black, tipped with white . . . I found in its throat a quantity of wild strawberries (107).

His menagerie was growing. On 25 June he obtained two hill bears and a monkey. One of the bears quickly disappeared and the other became wild from grief. To Russell's wonderment, the monkey tamed the bear.

But the reporter's nose was never off duty, and Russell collected titbits. Thus he learnt on 9 July that an army officer against whom a native servant had complained before a judge remarked in response that he had no intention of 'putting up with such conduct on the part of a dog of a native' (118). A week later, Russell heard an opinion that 'missionary zeal' was impeding other British efforts (125).

In Simla's British community, he found an enthusiasm for argument, scandal and balls. After a dinner for eight or ten that he gave at The Priory, he noted (on 16 July), 'As is usually the case in India, not one man agreed with any other on any one point whatever' (125). Earlier he had observed, 'There are some hundreds of families who for the most part do nothing but talk scandal, promenade for a few hours every evening and wait for ball after ball with eagerness.'[54]

He marked, too, an intense snobbery and the supreme importance given to precedence and protocol. Because he had not first called on them, Simla's Britons refused to call on him at The Priory. It did not seem to matter that he was lame and in no position to call.[55]

Letters from England, especially from his wife Mary gave him some relief. Dickens was among those who had written to him, and also Delane, who said that—as during the Crimean War— Russell's suggestions were being passed on to those in authority in the Cabinet, including Lord Stanley, the colonial secretary. 'It was your first private letter from Cawnpore which led to the order against indiscriminate executions,' Delane claimed.[56]

Interactions with Indians were infrequent, but on 31 July Russell entertained the young adolescent sons of a Hill raja. He found the boys good-looking but spoilt, and 'fat from want of exercise and a diet of vegetables, sweetmeat, and butter'.

> When I advised the eldest to walk a little more, and to begin by walking (from The Priory) to his house, he drew himself up and said, 'It does not become me to walk, Sahib.'

'It is this effeminacy,' Russell concluded, 'which destroys the native aristocracy and causes the women to be the real leaders of the people in any outbreak' (137). In this remark we detect the impact on Russell of the roles played by the Rani of Jhansi and Avadh's Hazrat Mahal.

Visiting an orphanage started by Henry Lawrence in Sonawar near Simla for children (often Eurasian) of dead British soldiers, Russell reflected on the man who after years of work in the Punjab had become a casualty of the Lucknow siege.

> *31 July.* What a grand heroic mould that mind was cast in! What a pure type of the Christian soldier! From what I have heard of his natural infirmities, of his immense efforts to overcome them; of his purity of thought; of his charity, of his love, of the virtues his inner life developed as he increased in years; of his devotion to duty, to friendship, and to Heaven; I am led to think that no such exemplar of a truly good man can be found in the ranks of the servants of any Christian state in the latter ages of this world (138).

The singing of Sonawar's Christian boys and girls produced another thought:

> They were singing, 'All nations who on earth do dwell,' and the chords floating out through the open windows went softly through the pinewoods, falling on the heedless ears of the Hindoo and Mussulman, who regard most of us by our deeds and not by our words (141).

Russell had captured the hopelessly unrealistic, if at times touching, effort of westerners in a country they did not understand, and where large numbers treated the West with suspicion. In early August, he recognized his unease at the rude talk by some of Simla's Britons in the hearing of silent but watchful Indian servants. Britons with whom Russell raised the subject claimed that the Indians just did 'not think or talk about us. Our world does not interest them.'

One day Russell asked an unidentified Indian ('a native gentleman') if he knew what the servants really thought of the British. The Indian replied that he would speak the truth 'if the Sahib will not be displeased at it'. Asked by Russell to say it, the Indian pointed to monkeys playing before them and said that the Indian servants thought that like the monkeys, the British were clever, fierce and unpredictable. It was dangerous to laugh at them (148–49).

Military officers and Company officials also wrote to Russell, so that even while recuperating in Simla, he received interesting information, enabling him to send several 'Letters' on the future of the British in India that *The Times* published. The last, the 'Letter' of 28 August 1858, was entitled 'The Sahib and the Nigger'.[57]

In this Letter, Russell argued that the chief cause of the Revolt and its support by the Indian people was 'our roughness of manner in our intercourse with the natives'. He added, 'It is not a pleasing or popular task to lay bare the defects of one's countrymen but . . . I must say that I have been struck with the arrogant and repellent manner in which we often treat natives of rank, and with the unnecessary harshness of our treatment of inferiors.'

Since Indian victims were afraid to go to the courts for redress, such treatment went unreported. On occasion, however, it caused household servants to turn with the greatest ferocity on white families.

> 'What ungrateful miscreants! They had lived with us for years!' Yes, and each year, ladies and gentlemen, but added to the secret source of bitterness, hatred and malice which your indifference, coldness and harshness were filling up to overflowing ...

The British, Russell added, not only supported the Indian caste system but maintained one of their own which was even more rigid and rooted in colour prejudice:

> But while we assist in maintaining caste and custom, we abhor colour ... There is no association, no intercourse, except of a discreditable kind, between Europeans and natives. Marriages between them now occur only among the lower classes. All society would be frightened from its propriety if at one of its balls there appeared any of those slim, tall, dark-eyed, crepe-haired, and rich-coloured Eurasian ladies who prove that the older generation of British officers did not disdain alliances now regarded with scorn.[58]

But things were getting worse, he warned in the same 'Letter'.

> The habit of speaking of all natives as niggers has recently become quite common ... Every man of the mute, white-turbaned file who with crossed arms, glistening eyes and quick ears stands motionless along the mess-room table, hears it every time a native is named, and knows it to be an expression of contempt.

The British, thought Russell, could be proud of their achievements in India, and a change of heart among the British could yet save everything, but they had to remember that 'Hindoos and Mussalmans are our fellow-creatures'.[59]

Return to the front. In October, his leg having recovered to some extent, Russell, who knew that Campbell would pursue Nana Sahib and Hazrat Mahal as soon as the weather allowed, commenced his journey, along with 'bear, birds, and monkeys', towards the front. On the way, he would take in Patiala, Meerut and Agra.

In Patiala, Russell met its Sikh ruler who had given the British valuable support. Reflecting on remarks by British officials that they could not be sure of the ruler's real feelings, Russell thought that outer support should be deemed sufficient. Inner appreciation of British rule was improbable.

> *9 October.* How can we expect such an abnormal government as that of Great Britain in Hindostan, where our governors are indeed alien in blood, religion and language, to command the absolute love of all classes of natives (253)?

He reached Meerut on 11 October and went directly to the 'very spot itself' where—many Britons felt—Hewett, the old major general in charge of the station, could have forestalled the Revolt by ordering a pursuit of the sowars who had taken off for Delhi. Retrospective indignation filled Russell's mind too:

> I was unable to comprehend how it was that the mutineers were permitted to march off after the commission of murder and arson quietly to Delhi, to inaugurate the reign of terror and bloodshed all over India, whilst a regiment of English dragoons, a famous battalion of British infantry, with an ample support of field artillery, were within a few hundred yards of them.
>
> Everyone talks of the incapacity of the aged veteran, on whom the whole affair produced the effect of a hideous nightmare; but is it not strange that among all the officers there was not a man with courage and coolness enough to have taken on himself the responsibility of action, and to order the pursuit of the mutineers?

And he recalled the shame of 'the miserable demonstration of a march through the bazaar after the rebels had gone off, and the feeble inanity of discharging a few round-shot in the dark night in the direction of voices which were heard among the trees ...' (256–7).

Yet present fury was no remedy for past folly. In his notes, Russell recorded his unease at the 'ferocious howl' of enraged Britons, of those who 'plunge their pens into the seething ink' and shout out, 'Blood! More blood!'

> We cannot punish sympathies; the attempt is sure to quicken animosities and provoke national, deep-rooted antipathy ... Many years will elapse ere the evil passions excited by these disturbances expire (258–59).

On 15 October, he was in Agra and standing before the Taj:

> Write a description of the Taj? As well say, 'Write me a description
> of that lovely dream which flushed the poet's cheek or gently moved
> the painter's hand as he lay trembling in delight . . .' It is wrong to
> call it a dream in marble; it is a thought—an idea—a conception of
> tenderness—a sigh, as it were, of eternal devotion and heroic love,
> caught and imbued with such immortality as the earth can give
> (263–64).

Russell also called the edifice 'an outburst of [Shahjahan's]
magnificent grief and pride' (266) and wrote, 'The eye fills and the
lip quivers, we know not why . . .' (269).

From Agra, Russell went to Kanpur and to Allahabad—by now
the train line between Kanpur and Allahabad was complete. At
Kanpur, he placed his menagerie 'in charge of a trusty coolie', who
agreed 'at an amazingly cheap rate' to carry the animals and birds
to Calcutta, where Russell hoped before long to unite with them
and sail for home (274).

From Allahabad, he would accompany Sir Colin Campbell, who
had recently been made Lord Clyde, in his chase of Nana Sahib
and the Begum of Avadh, but there was a significant event in
Allahabad itself—the reading out of the Queen's Proclamation in
respect of India. The East India Company's rule had ended. In
August 1858, the Queen, through Parliament and her ministers,
had assumed the governance of India. In an address to her, the
East India Company directors wrote:

> Let Her Majesty appreciate the gift—let her take the vast country
> and the teeming millions of India under Her direct control; but let
> her not forget the great corporation from which she has received
> them . . .[60]

Though the teeming millions referred to did not have a say in
being transferred from one set of hands to another, there is no sign
that they resisted the move.

Victoria's Proclamation. Aired in Allahabad on 1 November (six
months after the grisly vengeance in Lucknow and Jhansi), the
Proclamation was addressed to all the chiefs, princes and people of
India. Canning, now described as India's first 'Viceroy and Governor

General', read out the text. Prepared by officials and ministers in Calcutta and London, but also influenced by interventions from Victoria and Albert,[61] it represented a wish to heal wounds and address some of the misgivings that had fed the Revolt.

> We shall respect the rights, dignity and honour of native Princes as our own; and we desire that they, as well as our own subjects, should enjoy the prosperity and that social advancement which can only be secured by internal peace and good government.
>
> Firmly relying ourselves on the truth of Christianity, and acknowledging with gratitude the solace of religion, we disclaim alike the right and desire to impose our convictions on any of our subjects.
>
> We declare it to be our royal will and pleasure that none be in anywise favoured, none molested or disquieted, by reason of their religious faith or observances, but that all alike shall enjoy the equal and impartial protection of the law; and we do strictly charge and enjoin all those who may be in authority under us that they abstain from all interference with the religious belief or worship of any of our subjects on pain of our highest displeasure.
>
> And it is our further will that, so far as may be, our subjects, of whatever race or creed, be freely and impartially admitted to offices in our service, the duties of which they may be qualified, by their education, ability, and integrity, duly to discharge ...
>
> [I]n framing and administering the law, due regard [shall] be paid to the ancient rights, usages, and customs of India.

Addressing the Revolt and its aftermath, the Proclamation said:

> We deeply lament the evils and misery which have been brought upon India by the acts of ambitious men, who have deceived their countrymen by false reports, and led them into open rebellion. Our power has been shown by the suppression of that rebellion in the field; we desire to show our mercy by pardoning the offences of those who have been thus misled, but who desire to return to the path of duty.
>
> Already, in one province, with a view to stop the further effusion of blood, and to hasten the pacification of our Indian dominions, our Viceroy and Governor General has held out the expectation of pardon, on certain terms, to the great majority of those who, in the late unhappy disturbances, have been guilty of offences against our Government ...

We approve and confirm the said act of our Viceroy and Governor General, and do further announce and proclaim as follows: 'Our clemency will be extended to all offenders, save and except those who have been, or shall be, convicted of having directly taken part in the murder of British subjects. With regard to such the demands of justice forbid the exercise of mercy.

'To those who have willingly given asylum to murderers, knowing them to be such, or who may have acted as leaders or instigators in revolt, their lives alone can be guaranteed; but in apportioning the penalty due to such persons, full consideration will be given to the circumstances under which they have been induced to throw off their allegiance; and large indulgence will be shown to those whose crimes may appear to have originated in too credulous acceptance of the false reports circulated by designing men.

'To all others in arms against the Government we hereby promise unconditional pardon, amnesty, and oblivion of all offence against ourselves, our crown and dignity, on their return to their homes and peaceful pursuits.'[62]

That night, Allahabad was treated to a display of fireworks, but Russell noticed that Indians present at the reading of the Proclamation and its 'royal promises of pardon, forgiveness, justice, [and] respect to religious belief' were not very numerous (282). He feared too that for Indians the change would be more verbal than real. London and the Queen were very far; Calcutta and other centres of British power in India were so near. Moreover, even if now acting in the Queen's rather than the Company's name, the same officials would continue to rule (280–81).

Pursuit in Avadh. Russell accompanied the powerful columns, led by Lord Clyde, that left Allahabad on 2 November in pursuit of Avadh's rebel leaders. Clyde wanted either to capture them or to push them into Nepal. Once more, his columns were supported by 'up-towering elephants and camels, made taller than nature by heaps of tents and baggage and furniture' (294). Once more, Simon was at Russell's side. Russell again noticed the laying of the telegraph wire as a column advanced:

2 *November 1858.* A pole of fir is stuck in the ground, and remains there till it is rotted by the white ants, the wire is coiled loosely round the top, and thus the telegraph is carried on[wards] in the rear

of the troops almost as fast as they can march, provided the wire is to be had in sufficient quantities (286).

Clyde's columns also carried the Proclamation—and heavy guns. Surrender could save the lives of Avadh's rebelling talukdars, but these barons were not sure that the Proclamation's promise would be implemented, and some officers in the advancing columns did not want to implement it. In any case, Avadh's rebel leaders did not have the big guns to fight the British cannons, even though they often had thousands of fighters. Their aim was escape or a safe surrender.

Beni Madho Singh successfully eluded three British columns that went after him. His fort in Shankarpur near Rae Bareli was taken on 15 November, but the owner had vanished along with his men, arms and treasure. Earlier, the Raja of Amethi had surrendered and his guns were captured, but most of his soldiers escaped. Russell reflected on sights in the Avadh countryside:

> *19 November.* I always perceive natives stealing through the high corn-fields, and running from our approach in all directions as fast as they can. What a life must be that of the Oude peasant! Whichever side wins, he is sure to lose; and in the operations that determine the conquest, he is harassed and maltreated by both sides (317).

At the end of November, Lord Clyde and his army returned to Lucknow without an impressive collection of rebel talukdars. On 10 December, Commander-in-Chief Clyde set forth again, this time towards Faizabad and Bahraich, hoping to find Nana Sahib, Azimullah, Hazrat Mahal, Avadh's boy-king Birjis, and Beni Madho Singh. There was good evidence of their presence in Bahraich, and reports suggested that they were all moving together, along with thousands of soldiers.

Clyde hoped to get close to their moving camp and then pounce on them. But was it possible for an army with elephants and camels to *sneak into* the edges of a rebel camp? Arriving in Bahraich on 17 December, Clyde found that Nana Sahib—the prize the British most desired—and the others had all moved on. On 23 December, Russell thought that Nana Sahib, must not be startled from his lair—there must be no precipitate hasty move to frighten [him]. He is amid the jungles where his nature must be at home, and his capture will be effected probably by treachery and stratagem rather than by force, if it ever takes place at all (360).

Continuing the chase, Clyde's force moved to villages beyond Bahraich—to Intha and Burjidiah. At Burjidiah, a villager questioned by Russell said:

... he had seen 'the Nana Rao' once, that he was a stout man, with pock-marked face, but that when he went to walk in the garden the villagers were driven away, and that it was very difficult to get a sight of him (374).

The pursuit continued to Banki. Beyond Banki was the Rapti River, and across the river was Nepal. When the British reached Banki, Russell gathered that Nana Sahib had been 'in the wood a couple of miles in the rear' when the sound of British guns was heard. Evidently, Nana Sahib 'at once gave orders for flight, had his eight elephants loaded, and made straight off for the Raptee, which he crossed, no doubt, long before our cavalry reached its banks' (380).

His prey had eluded Clyde. Nana Sahib and Azimullah, Nana Sahib's young wife Kasibai, his sister Saraswatibai, brother Bala Rao and his family, the widows of Bajirao, Hazrat Mahal and her son Birjis, and several rebel leaders of Avadh—all had escaped into Nepal, evidently with quantities of treasure. Though not catching the people he was after, Clyde had regained most of Avadh for the British and cleared the territory of the rebellion's principal leaders. Unsure that Canning would support his moving into Nepal, he declared success and the end of his expedition.

Returning to Calcutta via Lucknow and Kanpur, Russell stayed in the residence of a man he liked, Sir James Outram, the Avadh chief commissioner, who, exhausted from recent labours, was recuperating in the Indian capital. In March 1859, having secured, not without difficulty, a passage for himself and part of his Simla menagerie (including the bear) on a ship of the Peninsular and Oriental Company, and after bidding farewell to Simon, Russell sailed for England. In one of his last 'Letters' to *The Times*, sent from Lucknow, he had tried to invoke the wisdom of history:

Let us not think our empire in India founded on a rock against which the heathen may rage in vain. Compared with the dynasties which have ruled here, our race is but the growth of yesterday. Three years have not elapsed since the kingdom and the city from which I write were the appanage of a dynasty of which no traces now exist except such as may be found in prison or in exile ... Above all, let us beware how we rouse that silent, ever-watchful, slow-working, irresistible power before which no race can maintain its own ... the hate of its subjects.[63]

~

Outperforming all the other rebel leaders in tactics, daring and perseverance, Tatya Tope met his end the way Russell thought Nana Sahib would. After his defeat (and Lakshmibai's death) in Gwalior, Tope and his small but disciplined army had for ten months dodged pursuers across central India. The rebels were helped by excellent horses and by villagers who refused to betray despite promises of large rewards.

In April 1859, however, Tatya Tope was tricked by Man Singh, the chief of Narwar, who was nursing a dispute with the ruler of Gwalior and therefore seemed to be anti-British. Sending Tope a message that he needed advice on whether or not to ally with Firoz Shah, who was now moving about in central India, Man Singh asked for a meeting. Tope agreed. As he 'lay down to sleep after a long talk with Man Singh', the latter's soldiers 'closed in silently and pounced upon [Tope] and his two attendants'.[64]

After Tope was pinned down, Man Singh personally helped to shackle him. Following a quick trial in Shivpuri (about 70 miles south of Gwalior), Major Reade, who had enlisted Man Singh in the stratagem, read out Tope's sentence of death by hanging. In a statement recorded shortly before his death (18 April), Tope exonerated himself and Nana Sahib from the Kanpur massacres of June and July 1857, claiming that the sepoys and sowars had acted on their own.[65] But he took his end with perfect calm. A British eyewitness's account of Tope's hanging has been quoted by Hibbert:

He mounted the rickety ladder with as much firmness as handcuffs would allow him; was then pinioned and his legs tied, he remarking that there was no necessity for these operations; and he then

deliberately put his head into the noose . . . [Later], a great scramble
was made by officers and others to get a lock of [Tope's] hair.[66]

While thought responsible, along with Nana Sahib, for the Kanpur
killings, Tope was nevertheless offered this final accolade by the
British, who could not deny their foe's skill and spirit.

On 23 April, five days after Tope's death, Nana Sahib (who
could not yet have heard of it) sent from his Nepal hideout a
messenger across the Indian border to Major Richardson, a border
military officer. The messenger carried a letter which, though
delivered to Richardson, was addressed, in Nana Sahib's wonted
style, to Queen Victoria, the British Parliament, the directors of
the East India Company (Nana Sahib may not have heard of the
end of Company rule), the Governor General, the governor of the
North Western Provinces, and 'all Civil and Military Officers'.

The first half of the letter declared his innocence and the guilt
of the sepoys and sowars. The second half revealed satisfaction
that by pursuing Nana Sahib the British had given him an
importance they had denied in Bithur: 'If I alone am worthy of
being an enemy to so powerful a nation as the British, it is a great
honour to me, and every wish of my heart is fulfilled.'[67]

Richardson replied that Nana Sahib could take his chances by
returning to India and finding out whether or not the Proclamation's
amnesty applied to him. To this, Nana Sahib's response was that
he would only act if the Queen wrote to him under her seal and
if her letter was brought to him by a French military officer. This
was his last exchange with the British, who refused to send him
another message. If every wish of his heart was indeed fulfilled by
the British treating him as their prime enemy, then it must follow
that ending British rule was not Nana Sahib's prime wish.

Within a year or two, there were reports that Nana Sahib had
died in Nepal, as also Azimullah and Nana Sahib's brother. While
expressing readiness to protect the women who had entered Nepal
with Nana Sahib, Jung Bahadur had indicated that Nana Sahib
himself would have to disappear into the Nepal hinterland,
preferably as a sadhu. He did not wish to incur British hostility by
giving asylum to Nana Sahib or his male colleagues. It seems too
that Jung Bahadur secured for himself most of the treasure that
Nana Sahib had brought with him.[68]

Because there were few reliable eyewitnesses of Nana Sahib's death, stories that he was still alive in Nepal, or had entered India in a sadhu's disguise, would circulate for three decades or more. During this period, three or more 'possible' or 'suspected' Nana Sahibs were detained in different parts of India by the British and inspected by persons who claimed to remember Nana Sahib's appearance, mannerisms and voice. Not matching in these attributes, all the 'suspects' were released. We have to assume that within a few years—or even months—of their arrival in Nepal, he and Azimullah had died in the wilderness.

After an initial period when Jung Bahadur was in two minds, Hazrat Mahal and her son Birjis were given asylum by him. (Earlier, before the Begum and her son were forced out of Avadh, Queen Victoria's Proclamation had been answered by a counter-Proclamation issued in Birjis's name.) The British, who kept a resident in Nepal, asked if Hazrat Mahal and her son were willing to pledge loyalty to the Queen and return to India, in which case, allowances would be provided. Her answer was a firm 'no'.

Hazrat Mahal lived in Nepal until her death in 1874. The son, Birjis Qadr, remained in Nepal for another sixteen years, but returned to Calcutta three or four years after the death there, in 1887, of his deposed father, Wajid Ali Shah. Intending, it seems, to travel to London to press claims for an appropriate pension for himself, he died in or shortly after 1892 in Calcutta, allegedly poisoned by relatives.

Not welcomed by Jung Bahadur, Beni Madho Singh died fighting Gurkhas in Nepal.

We may mark the fate of some other rebel leaders. Captured outside Bareilly in May 1858, the Rohilla chief, Khan Bahadur Khan, a truculent foe of the British, was hanged. Ahmadullah, the fiery Maulvi, retreated from Avadh to Rohilkhand, where for a while he took over the town of Shahjahanpur. Pushed back into Avadh, he was killed there in June 1858 by soldiers of the pro-British Raja of Pawayan, whose fort Ahmadullah had attacked. Taking the Maulvi's head to the British magistrate of Shahjahanpur, the Raja collected the fifty thousand rupees that had been announced for it.

Operating in central India in the autumn of 1857, Firoz Shah moved to Rohilkhand at the start of 1858. Earlier, we saw the May 1858 skirmish near Bareilly between his force and that of the British in which Russell almost lost his life. Forced to leave Rohilkhand, Firoz Shah harassed the British in places near Etawah. In December, there was a dogged fight between his force and a British one, led by none other than Allan Octavian Hume, the magistrate of Etawah. Repulsed by Hume, Firoz Shah was obliged to cross the Jamuna and proceed south to Bundelkhand, where he joined forces with Tatya Tope.

In April, as we saw, Tope was betrayed and killed not far from Gwalior. Seen on 15 April 1859 in Guna, also near Gwalior, Firoz Shah then disappeared, apparently into lands west of India, and is said to have died in Mecca in 1877. This Mughal scion differed from 1857's other rebel leaders in several significant ways. One, as we have just noted, Firoz Shah was never captured. Two, unlike the others, he underlined economic hardships under British rule. Three, he singled out the killing of women and children as a moral wrong and a political folly. Four, he took care to appeal also to the ordinary Indian.

In common with other rebel leaders, Firoz Shah asked Muslims and Hindus to jointly fight the British. Like the others, he too declared that the religions of Islam and Hinduism were at stake. 'Since the real purpose of this war is to save religion,' he said in a proclamation issued on 17 February 1858, 'let every Hindoo and Mussulman render assistance to the utmost.' Like the others, he also highlighted the hardships of landlords. Thus in his August 1857 proclamation, he expressed outrage that 'on the institution of a suit by a common ryot ... a maidservant, or a slave, the respectable zemindars are summoned into court, arrested, put in goal, and disgraced' (*Delhi Gazette*, 29 September 1857). But statements like the following were made only by Firoz Shah:

> It is plain that the infidel and treacherous British government have monopolised the trade of all the fine and valuable merchandise, such as indigo, cloth, and other articles of shipping, leaving only the trade of trifles to the people, and even in this they are not without their share of the profits, which they secure by means of customs and stamp fees, &c., in money suits, so that the people have merely a trade in name ... (August 1857 proclamation)

[A]ll the posts of dignity and emolument in both the departments, are exclusively bestowed upon Englishmen ... (August 1857 proclamation)

[T]he Europeans, by the introduction of English articles into India, have thrown the weavers, the cotton-dressers, the carpenters, the blacksmiths, and the shoemakers, &c., out of employ, and have engrossed their occupations, so that every description of native artisan has been reduced to beggary (August 1857 proclamation).

All who join us should do so solely with a view of promulgating their religion, not with that of worldly avarice ... (February 1858 proclamation)

The delay in defeating the English has been caused by people killing innocent children and women without any permission whatever from the leaders, whose commands were not obeyed. Let us all avoid such practices, and then proclaim a sacred war (February 1858 proclamation).

Lastly, the great and small in this campaign will be equal, for we are waging a religious war. I (the prince) do now proclaim a sacred war, and exhort all, according to the tenets of their religion, to exert themselves. The rest I leave to God (February 1858 proclamation).[69]

Hume and Sayyid Ahmed Khan. In the previous chapter, we left a twenty-eight-year-old Hume secretly communicating from Agra with his Indian contacts in Etawah, then (in July 1857) under rebel control. Though he recovered from a cholera attack in Agra, Hume could not return to his district until January 1858.

Rebels continued to be active there, however. A month after Hume's return, a fierce eight-hour fight took place in Anantram, 21 miles from Etawah town, between about 1,200 rebels on one side and about 300 Britons and Indians on the other. Along with two other Britons, Hume, who rode into Anantram from Etawah, led a rush that precipitated the defeat of the rebels, who lost 121 of their number and many guns.[70]

If Firoz Shah was unique among the rebel leaders, Hume stood out on the British side, thinking that his task was 'to restore peace and order and the Authority of Government with the least possible amount of human suffering'. By the end of 1858, the district seemed wholly pacified. Hume would claim: 'No district in the North Western Provinces has, I believe, been more completely restored to order; none in which so few severe punishments have been inflicted.'[71]

Yet December 1858 saw the attack on Etawah by Firoz Shah's force. In his successful resistance, Hume again showed military ability, yet twenty-one were killed and nineteen wounded on the British side. Firoz Shah lost fifty-eight of his men.[72] Though the rebellion petered out, Hume was criticized in India's British establishment for the schools he had started and especially for taking help for his schools from 'native agencies', i.e., from Indian landlords, who as a class were now suspected of having supported the rebellion.

European critics said that educating the natives was but a way of preparing them to be disobedient, but Hume stood his ground.[73] In 1859, in another unusual step, Hume and one of his Indian contacts, Kunwar Lachman Singh, started *Praja Mitra* or *The People's Friend*, a journal made available at an affordable price in both Hindi and Urdu. The public's voice rather than an official mouthpiece, the journal was read in Gwalior and Bharatpur and other places beyond the NWP, to which Etawah belonged.

We last saw Sayyid Ahmed Khan at the end of September 1857 (when he was forty) as he took his mother from their destroyed Delhi haveli to Meerut, where she died. In the two years that followed, he wrote two short but significant texts, one giving his version of what had happened in Bijnor during the Revolt, and the other (presented to some British officials but not immediately published), containing his explanation for the Revolt.[74]

Sayyid Ahmed told the people of Bijnor that God had 'allowed you to experience again a sample of the Government of former times', to 'recollect how', when Muslim rebels had taken over, 'the Hindus of the District were ruined, murdered, and plundered', and also how, when Hindu landlords had displaced the Muslims, 'you could then taste the government of Hindus, and see what Muslims experienced at Hindu hands: how many houses looted, how many villages razed, and even your own womenfolk ravaged.'

Now that British rule was back, Sayyid Ahmed went on, 'Look how Hindus and Muslims are living with all ease and in peace under English rule. The strong cannot tyrannize the weak now. Each worships God and his Creator according to the requirements of his religion.'[75]

As to why the Revolt broke out, Sayyid Ahmed began by

recognizing (in his as yet private report) that it had evoked wide sympathy—there were 'but few men in truth, even amongst the best of us', who did not 'swerve at heart from respect and loyalty to the Government' or 'withhold from it an active support'. The root cause of the Revolt was the absence of an Indian voice in the government's councils.

> It is from the voice of the people only that Government can learn whether its projects are likely to be well received. The voice of the people can alone check errors in the bud, and warn us of the dangers before they burst upon and destroy us.

Then there was, among Muslims and Hindus alike, the 'firm conviction that the English Government was bent on interfering with their religion and with their old established customs. They believed that Government intended to force the Christian Religion and foreign customs.'

> Many covenanted officers, and many military men, have been in the habit of talking to their subordinates about religion; some of them would bid their servants come to their houses, and listen to the preaching of Missionaries, and thus it happened that in the course of time no man felt sure that his creed would last even his own life time.

The 'great deal of talk . . . about female education' also troubled the public, Sayyid Ahmed wrote. 'Men believed it to be the wish of Government that girls should attend, and be taught at these Schools, and leave off the habit of sitting veiled.' Nothing was 'more obnoxious than this' to the feelings of Muslims. As for the Hindus, they 'were greatly annoyed' by the 1856 Act that permitted widows to remarry.

New land revenue policies were also responsible. 'To resume [revenue collection] on lands [that had been] revenue-free was to set the whole people against us, and to make beggars of the masses.' In Avadh, the decision to 'crush the Talookdars was one of the chief causes of the Rebellion'. 'The Talookdars had long enjoyed the rank of Rajas. They exercised the rights of sovereignty in the villages composing their Talookdaries. From these villages their income was derived. All these rights and all this income alike were suddenly wrested from them.'

The British had failed to learn from Mughal history. Whereas Akbar had established 'a feeling of cordiality' between rulers and the ruled, Aurangzeb's 'rigour and harshness' had ended popular goodwill. 'Now the English Government has been in existence upwards of a century, and up to the present hour has not secured the affections of the people.' Indians 'very generally say that they are treated with contempt'.

Finally, Sayyid Ahmed blamed the Bengal army's policy of recruiting Hindus and Muslims into the same regiment. 'If a portion of the regiment engaged in anything, all the rest joined. If separate regiments of Hindoos and separate regiments of Mahommadans had been raised, this feeling of brotherhood could not have arisen, and, in my opinion, the Mahommadan regiments would not have refused to receive the new cartridges.'[76]

We should mark that at this time Sayyid Ahmed was perhaps the only Indian to offer an explanation of the Revolt. Men like Vidyasagar and Bankim in Calcutta, we saw, chose to remain silent. In Poona, Phule was expressing his unease about the Revolt in conversation, but not yet in writing. For a while, none knew what the outcome was going to be, and in any case the Revolt produced conflicting thoughts in all thinking Indians. As Sayyid Ahmed said, even the 'best' minds, and by 'best' he seems here to mean something like 'most loyal to British rule', had been swayed against that rule. Yet, since neither long-term victory nor order was expected from the Revolt's leaders, Indians could not seriously place their trust in them.

With Sayyid Ahmed as with Hume, with Russell and Phule, and everyone else analysing the Revolt, the explanation revealed something about the analyst as well. Candid as Sayyid Ahmed clearly was, the fact that he had served the Company for many years and was now a servant of the Queen influenced his analysis of Bijnor and of the Revolt as a whole; and we can also sniff, behind his analysis, a Muslim wary of Hindu-Muslim mixing, and perhaps one liable to focus more on the Muslim-British relationship than on the Indian-British one.

Sayyid Ahmed wanted the British to treat all Indians with respect, and landlords and Muslims with sensitivity. Russell, whose reaction to British discourtesy towards Indians was stronger than Sayyid Ahmed's, had reached similar conclusions. Both stressed the need to regain the goodwill of the Indian aristocracy, with Russell stressing also the significance of the Indian domestic.

Frightened—almost terrified—by the possibility of a revival of Brahmin rule, the farmer Phule wanted the British to triumph and to cultivate the peasant's goodwill. Hume seemed to stand between Phule's position and that of Russell and Sayyid Ahmed. While recognizing the influence of landlords and accepting their aid, Hume wanted to take information to a wider public, and education to the children of ordinary Indians. He wished, in short, to trust Indians.

VIEWS IN THE USA

Americans continued with their interest, and sympathies, in the Revolt. After the rebellion's back was broken, Bennett's *New York Herald* wrote (24 May 1858), 'We saw with Saxon pride that England still was true to Saxon pluck, our hearts were with her.' Also praising the British success—Colin Campbell was 'the noblest Roman of them all', and Havelock and Wilson had 'realized the wildest dreams of even Napoleonic ambition' (8 July)—the *New York Times* however claimed that the USA would outperform Britain in the future. 'America . . . will wield over inferior races an influence such as no conquerors of ancient or modern times have ever enjoyed,' it wrote on 12 July 1858, adding that its influence would be based not on force, but on moral greatness.

Not surprisingly, Greeley's *Tribune* cautioned Britons (5 April 1858) that a 'bloodthirsty spirit' when 'adopted by a whole nation becomes horrible indeed'. Yet, even the *Tribune* wanted India to be Christianized to 'shake the confidence of the Hindoos in the dogmas of their priests' and 'to open their eyes to the absurdities and falsehoods' they had come to believe. For this to happen, Europeans should settle in India, the paper proposed (19 May 1858).

In the South, the *New Orleans Picayune* wished (on 21 February 1858) for 'a practical despotism' in India that would prevent a future rebellion. The paper was of the view (10 February 1858) that Indians had to be treated as 'an inferior and dependent race' and taught Christianity.[77]

Consensus in the response to Indian events concealed inner conflicts in many white Americans who harboured unease at the displacement of America's natives, but felt close nonetheless to the British, whom, however, their forefathers had ousted from America. Trying to resolve the conflicts, an article in the *New Englander* of New Haven, said:

> We would by no means maintain the right of national interference; that one people may take upon itself the guardianship of another, however much the latter may mismanage its own affairs; or that a part of the earth's surface of which the resources are neglected or wasted by its present occupants, may be wrested from them by others who feel that they can better administer their inheritance . . .
>
> Were there a whole continent now peopled by savage or half savage tribes, humanity would shudder at the thought of their being deliberately driven out, or swept from existence, to make room for a race of better husbandmen of man's heritage.
>
> Yet the work being once done, as it has been done upon the soil we occupy, on whose conscience presses heavily the burden of the wrongs done to the red man, as we . . . see what a wondrous change civilization has wrought upon his wild and gloomy forests? This is what we are wont to call the hand of Providence in human history, bringing good out of evil . . .
>
> [T]his is certain; no calamity could befall India so great as the withdrawal at present of the British grasp upon her.[78]

A remarkable exception to the American consensus was provided in the April 1858 issue of a literary journal published in Boston, the *North American Review*. The unknown author of this unsigned article entitled 'The Rebellion in India' wrote:

> The breaking out of the present rebellion should not have surprised any one . . . [W]hat great English statesman or general since the time of Warren Hastings's trial, who has paid any attention to the subject, has failed to warn England against the consequences of the East India Company's despotic rule, and its oppressive and cruel exactions?
>
> But no fear of retribution could restrain that rapacious oligarchy, always sustained as they have been by the English nobility, whose junior sons they enabled to accumulate fortunes in a few years, and whose ill-gotten treasure—the money wrung by fraud and torture from rich and poor—has continually been pouring into England . . .

Claiming that blowing men from cannons was not a new practice triggered by the Kanpur killings, the writer said:

> Indeed, it was one of the first inventions of the servants of the East India Company, for the benefit of Hindostan; for we find that so early as 1763 Sir Hector Munro caused twenty-four Sepoys to be blown from the cannon's mouth 'as a caution to others'. It was not pretended that these twenty-four men had murdered either women or children, or that they had murdered any one. All that was alleged against them was that they had 'a mutinous spirit' among them.

Expressing shock at the killing in Delhi of Mughal princes who had surrendered, the article proceeded to discuss the Company's opium monopoly and salt tax.

> Simple as their English masters had hitherto supposed the Hindoos to be, they have long been fully alive to the shameful injustice of the opium monopoly—a monopoly that has not a single redeeming feature. All who cultivate the poppy are obliged, under ruinous penalties, to furnish every particle of the opium which it yields to the government, at its own price. Not only is any reserve seized upon and confiscated, but the party in whose possession it is found is ever after debarred from cultivating the poppy. The drug thus obtained by force is sold at auction at Calcutta by the government, and in recent years has brought a clear annual profit of not less than $25,000,000.
>
> Everyone is aware [of] what has been done to swell up the opium revenue to this amount. Everyone remembers the war waged against China to compel the Chinese government to permit the use of the poisonous drug. For fifty years the importation of opium had been prohibited under severe penalties in China. But the East India Company did not care for this; for it kept a fleet in the Chinese Seas for the express purpose of smuggling the contraband article into all the sea-ports ... [Canton was bombarded] until the Emperor consented to bribe his enemies in order to prevent further loss of life and destruction of property ...
>
> Were we to assume that the government is actuated, as its interested champions pretend, by an honest solicitude for the welfare of the people, in compelling them to surrender their opium crop for about one third of its market value, will the same reasoning apply to the salt monopoly? Is the salt so heavily taxed only for fear the

people might injure themselves by eating it to excess? Is East Indian salt intoxicating or poisonous?

Is it not one of the commonest necessaries of life? Undoubtedly; and this is precisely the reason why it is so heavily taxed. The people are so wretchedly poor, that a tax on mere luxuries would hardly affect them at all, and it would put but little into the coffers of the Company; whereas those who can afford anything will try to procure salt. Hence it is that from this one article the government of India derives, according to its own admission, an annual revenue of over twelve million dollars. It is not too much to say that nine tenths of this sum comes from the miserable, half-naked, half-starved cultivators of the soil.

The article concluded with a reference to demands for executing old Zafar.

Yet it is gravely discussed by the English journals whether the king of Delhi himself—a man upwards of eighty years of age, scarcely able to rise from his couch—ought not also to be executed! It is impossible to believe that any civilized nation—even England, chargeable as she is with many crimes against the weak—would be guilty of so barbarous a deed ...[79]

American attitudes were not influenced by this untypical article. Writing about the Revolt upon visiting its scenes almost four decades later, even Mark Twain focussed almost solely on the fate of the British in Kanpur and their fortitude in Lucknow.[80]

OVERVIEW AGAIN

Hindus and Muslims had allied with one another during the Revolt. Every rebel leader (Nana Sahib, Hazrat Mahal, Tatya Tope, Ahmadullah, Lakshmibai, or whoever) counted on lieutenants and soldiers of both faiths. Large territories in northern and central India rejected British rule. Even so, the Revolt was not a national alternative to that rule. Aimed at destroying British power, it proposed neither an alternative set of rulers for India as a whole nor an alternative way of ruling.

Zafar, in Delhi, conveyed prestige but no authority. Nana Sahib was a king in his own mind, in the minds of a few others in Bithur, and for a few days in Gwalior, but nowhere else. While Hazrat Mahal and her son were acknowledged in Avadh, Khan Bahadur Khan in parts of Rohilkhand, and Lakshmibai in Jhansi, no one led the Revolt as a whole. Tatya Tope was a brilliant leader, but only of his force—the Revolt did not have a unified military command. Most importantly, perhaps, no one seemed to visualize how a liberated 'India' would be ruled or, indeed, how any 'India' would emerge from a sum of several rebellions.

The picture was more complex, of course. Across the land, Indians could not decide what to think, but a national feeling was undoubtedly stirred, as was discovered by a Briton in India at the time, Meredith Townsend, who later edited London's *Spectator*:

> There was not an Indian on the vast continent who did not consider the Sepoys Nationalists, and did not, even if he dreaded their success, feel proud of their victories. An old Hindoo scholar, definitely and openly on the English side, actually cried with rage and pain, in [my] presence, over a report that Delhi was to be razed. He had never seen Delhi, but to him it was '*our* beautiful city, such a possession for *our* country'.[81]

Even so, the lords Canning and Clyde may have had a better conception of 'India' than the Revolt's leaders, and perhaps also of India's path to progress. Restoration of personal ownership was a major impulse for Hazrat Mahal (who had lost Avadh), for Lakshmibai (who had lost Jhansi), for Nana Sahib (who wanted the Peshwa's titles and pension given to him), and for the talukdars of Avadh (who wanted their lands back).

By contrast, Indians as a public stood to benefit from the roads, canals, the telegraph, rail lines and universities launched by the Cannings, Outrams and Lawrences of the time. These Britons were alien rulers, resented for being alien, expensive to keep, often unwise, and unable or unwilling to ensure that their white subordinates treated Indians with dignity. Yet, compared with the Revolt's leaders, they were the party of progress, and also of order.

This verdict of the future was well realized even at the time of the Revolt in cities like Calcutta, Bombay, Madras, Hyderabad, and Poona, which offered no encouragement to the rebels. Even in Delhi and elsewhere in north India, where 'honour' and 'religion' were seen to reside with the rebels, 'order' and 'progress' continued to be associated with the British. Though 'honour' and 'religion' triggered strong emotions and stirred large numbers, the telegraph wire, which quickened communication and reinforcement, and heavy guns, which wrecked rebel defences, ensured British victory.

'War is at an end,' Canning declared in July 1859, and added, 'Rebellion has been put down ... Order is re-established; and peaceful pursuits have everywhere been resumed.' Two years later, he claimed, in respect of Avadh—the Revolt's centrepiece—that the region was 'so thriving and so tranquil that an English child might travel from one end of it to the other in safety'.[82]

Also, the thirst in the British for vengeance subsided. After the Proclamation, surrendering rebels were tried, in some cases executed and in other instances flogged; yet more often than not, they were acquitted or fined or given short terms in prison. As a British writer, John Pemble, would put it:

> The hysterical screams for vengeance had subsided with the fear that had inspired them, and as the British reasserted their strength and repaired their damaged pride their attitude grew more constructive and magnanimous. The old rancour and hatred disappeared.[83]

Russell's writings had played a part in this change. His reports from India had scotched the tales of mutilation and other atrocities and helped change opinion in Britain and, before long, even among India's British. Policy makers were influenced by the logic and passion in his 'Letters'—published in the powerful *Times*—for the right of Indians to be treated as humans. Delane, the editor, said that Russell had given his readers 'a fuller and clearer account of India than they had ever had before; what the country and its peoples looked like; the fascinating variety of cultures; what it felt like to live and march and fight there; the way the British treated the Indians.'[84]

But military policy in India was revised. Henceforth, Britain's Indian armies would have a higher proportion of white soldiers, big guns on India's soil would remain exclusively in British hands, and bonding inside an Indian regiment of different castes and communities would be prevented by instituting exclusive, caste-based regiments. As Charles Wood, Secretary of State for India, said to Canning in April 1861, 'If one regiment mutinies, the next regiment [should be] so alien that it would be ready to fire into it.'[85]

Another lesson was durably engraved on the minds of policy-making Britons—never again allow Hindus and Muslims to revolt together. At a critical moment, Britain had forgotten an unfailing maxim of empires, 'divide and rule', and relied blindly on Hindu-Muslim animosity, not realizing that circumstances could unite Hindus and Muslims as Indians or Asians against foreign, white and Christian rule. The mistake must not be repeated. As early as 9 October 1857, arguing successfully against Palmerston's idea of destroying the Jama Masjid, Governor General Canning had written to London:

> The men who fought against us in Delhi were of both creeds; probably in equal numbers. If we destroy or desecrate Mussulman Mosques or Brahmin Temples, we do exactly what is wanting to band the two antagonist races against ourselves . . . [A]s we must rule 150 million of people by a handful (more or less small) of Englishmen, let us do it in the manner best calculated to leave them divided . . . and to inspire them with the greatest possible awe of our power.[86]

If, after the Revolt had been put down, Hindus wanted to prove that Muslims had initiated it, the British would not object. If Muslims wished to underline the roles of Nana Sahib, Tatya Tope and the Rani of Jhansi, that too would be welcome.

This is just what happened. Highlighting their acts of loyalty during the Revolt, and the 'other' community's disloyalty, Hindus and Muslims separately strove for British favour. They found material for their efforts in conflicting verdicts by British writers on the Revolt, some of whom held that the Muslims had planned it, while others blamed wily Brahmins.

Incorporated in Victoria's Proclamation, the pledge not to impose Christianity became a crucial guideline for India's British rulers. Contrary advice offered in Britain and America was rejected. Their religious belief or beliefs would be left to Indians to decide. Yet, this was more than an acceptance of religious freedom—any impression of a desire to push Christianity would quickly reunite Muslims and Hindus against the British.

Also acknowledged in the Proclamation, and in post-Revolt British policy, was the hold of India's elites, the princes and the landlords. Annexation was forsworn, adoption of heirs was allowed and the idea of levelling Indian society was given up. Landlords, talukdars and zamindars would henceforth be built up as active defenders of the Empire.

These policy changes and the commitment of due regard for 'the ancient rights, usages, and customs of India' reassured influential classes of Indians, but would trouble others in the future, including those working for reform.

'Some say that the Widow Marriage Act was one of the incentive causes of the rebellion.' So wrote S.C. Mitra, Vidyasagar's diligent biographer, in criticism of his subject, within a few years of Vidyasagar's death.[87]

In a summary of the 1857 Revolt composed in the 1930s, Winston Churchill would claim that 'hatred smouldered at the repression of *suttee*'.[88] Reform was thus seen as the harbinger of revolt. In March 1865, the *Friend of India* would write: 'But for the Mutiny the law against polygamy would have been passed.'[89]

Though reform received a setback, the promise in the Proclamation of 'the equal and impartial protection of the law' to all Indians, irrespective of race or creed, would, if implemented, be welcomed by almost everyone.

We will examine in due course how the Revolt and its aftermath impacted Indians in the last four decades of the nineteenth century— how, in particular, the thinking of Sayyid Ahmed Khan, Hume, Vidyasagar, Bankim and Phule evolved.

Before that, however, making a sharp turn in our gaze, we will look at another part of the world—America—and at another series of bitter and bloody clashes. These also involved questions— variously interpreted—of freedom and serfdom, religion and honour, progress versus the status quo, and law versus disorder.

It will not be a leap into the wholly unknown or unfamiliar, for we have looked more than once already at the America of the 1850s. Moreover, ere long in our new journey we will find a familiar companion, William Howard Russell of *The Times*, who would be asked by his paper to cover the American Civil War.

CHAPTER 4

LINCOLN'S RISE TO POWER

AMERICA, 1857–61

Our last image of America's domestic scene, taken from the year 1857, showed opposing reactions to the Supreme Court's Dred Scott verdict from Stephen Douglas and Abraham Lincoln. The Supreme Court had ruled, it will be recalled, that slaves were only property and that barring slavery in new territories was unconstitutional.

Douglas and Lincoln were both lawyers in Springfield, Illinois, and Douglas was a sitting US senator as well. But his term was ending in 1858. Forty-nine at this time, Lincoln seized the chance to run for the seat from Illinois that Douglas, the forty-five-year-old Democrat, expected to retain. His 'house divided' speech of 1857 having made its mark, Lincoln secured the Republican nomination. The relatively unknown challenger asked for a series of debates, the nationally famous incumbent agreed, and between August and October 1858 the two competed before large audiences in each of the seven congressional districts of the state of Illinois.

The performance of Douglas, a likely future President, was a matter of keen interest. Lincoln too had enthusiastic admirers and the issues they debated were a great draw—above all the burning question of extending or containing slavery. 'Bleeding Kansas' was on many lips. The violence in that state, located not very far south-west of Illinois, included the destruction of several anti-slavery settlements and the murder of five pro-slavery settlers.

Ten thousand or more witnessed each verbal contest between Lincoln and Douglas, with many travelling from nearby towns. During the days after a debate, hundreds of thousands followed it in newspapers in Illinois and also across the country. Douglas did not underestimate his opponent. 'I shall have my hands full,' he admitted. Lincoln, he added, 'is as honest as he is shrewd, and if I beat him my victory will be hardly won.'[1]

The two debaters had known each other for long. At one point, they had even shown interest in the same young woman. Raised in an elite family in Kentucky, Mary Todd visited Springfield to be with her sister Elizabeth, who was married to the son of a former Illinois governor. Douglas and Lincoln both saw Mary Todd. In 1842, despite her family's objections concerning the suitor's humbler origins, she married Abraham Lincoln. Though blacks had been owned by her father, Mary Todd shared her husband's aversion of slavery.

On the stage, Douglas and Lincoln provided a dramatic contrast. Though a short five-foot-four, Douglas was stocky and confrontational and the owner of a booming, deep voice. Lincoln's lanky six-foot-four frame was loose rather than firm, and his voice on stage was high-pitched.

Aspiring beyond the Senate to the presidency, Douglas could not afford to displease the South even while seeking support from Illinois voters troubled by the hardening of southern opinion and the Dred Scott verdict. On his part, Lincoln had to win over moderates troubled by extreme abolitionists without disappointing slavery's opponents. As both knew, sentiments in Illinois's all-white electorate varied greatly, with sympathy for abolitionists in the state's northern half contrasting with a feeling in southern Illinois of kinship with the South.

Calling Lincoln an abolitionist-in-disguise and a black Republican, Douglas suggested that his rival was influenced by Frederick Douglass, the African-American author and orator. Douglas also attacked Lincoln's alleged 'warfare' against the Supreme Court over the Dred Scott decision, as well as Lincoln's reluctance, years earlier, to support the war against Mexico.

'Popular sovereignty' in each state was Douglas's solution for the slavery question, with Lincoln countering that America as a whole had to choose between restricting slavery or extending it. In the first debate (in Ottawa in northern Illinois), Douglas criticized Lincoln's use of the 'All men are created equal' sentence in the Declaration of Independence, and added:

> I do not question Mr. Lincoln's conscientious belief that the negro was made his equal, and hence is his brother, but for my own part, I do not regard the negro as my equal, and positively deny that he is my brother or any kin to me whatever.

When Douglas asked if his audience wished to see the prairies of Illinois covered with 'black settlements' or 'to turn this beautiful State into a free negro colony', resounding shouts of 'No!' or 'Never!' were returned. Added Douglas,

> Now, I hold that Illinois had a right to abolish and prohibit slavery as she did, and I hold that Kentucky has the same right to continue and protect slavery ... I hold that New York had as much right to abolish slavery as Virginia has to continue it, and that each and every State of this Union is a sovereign power, with the right to do as it pleases upon this question of slavery, and upon all its domestic institutions.

The incumbent charged that Lincoln's stand that America could not survive as a house divided, half of it permitting slavery and the other half free, was a prescription for civil war, and added that men like Lincoln were

> ... trying to array all the Northern States in one body against the South, to excite a sectional war between the free States and the slave States, in order that the one or the other may be driven to the wall.

In his reply, Lincoln conceded that he did not view African-Americans as the whites' intellectual equals or as being entitled to vote.

> I think I would not hold one in slavery at any rate; yet the point is not clear enough to me to denounce people upon. What next? Free them, and make them politically and socially our equals? My own feelings will not admit of this; and if mine would, we well know that those of the great mass of white people will not ...
>
> We cannot, then, make them equals. It does seem to me that systems of gradual emancipation might be adopted; but for their

tardiness in this, I will not undertake to judge our brethren of the South. When they remind us of their constitutional rights, I acknowledge them, not grudgingly, but fully and fairly . . .

I have no purpose to introduce political and social equality between the white and the black races. There is a physical difference between the two, which, in my judgment, will probably forever forbid their living together upon the footing of perfect equality . . . I, as well as Judge Douglas, am in favor of the race to which I belong having the superior position . . .

[N]otwithstanding all this, there is no reason in the world why the negro is not entitled to all the natural rights enumerated in the Declaration of Independence, the right to life, liberty, and the pursuit of happiness. I hold that he is as much entitled to these as the white man.

I agree with Judge Douglas he is not my equal in many respects— certainly not in color, perhaps not in moral or intellectual endowment. But in the right to eat the bread, without the leave of anybody else, which his own hand earns, he is my equal and the equal of Judge Douglas, and the equal of every living man.

The records tell us that 'great applause' greeted the last sentence, whereas many were appalled by a 'clever' remark by Douglas. 'When the struggle is between the white man and the Negro,' said Douglas, 'I am for the white man; when it is between the Negro and the crocodile, I am for the Negro.'

Lincoln alleged that by forbidding the barring of slavery in the new territory of Nebraska, the Dred Scott judgment had opened the door to a restoration even of the long-banned importation of new slaves. He added that differences between the races furnished

. . . no more excuse for permitting slavery to go into our own free territory, than it would for reviving the African slave-trade by law.

The law which forbids the bringing of slaves *from* Africa, and that which has so long forbid the taking of them to Nebraska, can hardly be distinguished on any moral principle; and the repeal of the former could find quite as plausible excuses as that of the latter.

As for Douglas's notion of 'Popular Sovereignty', its weakness, said Lincoln, was that while it

. . . does allow the people of a Territory to have slavery if they want to, [it] does not allow them *not* to have it if they *do not* want it . . .

[A]s I understand the Dred Scott decision, if any one man wants slaves, all the rest have no way of keeping that one man from holding them.

Douglas replied that recognition of the principle of 'Popular Sovereignty' would lead to 'peace and harmony and fraternal feeling between all the States of this Union'. He added,

[U]ntil you do recognize that doctrine, there will be sectional warfare agitating and distracting the country. What does Mr. Lincoln propose? He says that the Union cannot exist divided into free and slave States. If it cannot endure thus divided, then he must strive to make them all free or all slave, which will inevitably bring about a dissolution of the Union.

Lincoln argued in return that to ask America to choose between extending or containing slavery was a recognition of reality, not a call for a North-South war, whereas Douglas's endorsement of the Dred Scott verdict was a call, even if indirect, for the extension of slavery. In a speech in Springfield before the debate commenced, Lincoln had warned,

[W]e may, ere long, see ... another Supreme Court decision, declaring that the Constitution of the United States does not permit a *State* to exclude slavery from its limits ... We shall lie down pleasantly dreaming that the people of Missouri are on the verge of making their State free, and we shall awake to the reality instead, that the Supreme Court has made Illinois a slave State.

In fact, their minds hardening, some in the South openly sought slavery's extension or 'nationalization', claiming that that system was more humane than the North's system of 'hirelings'. Whereas, their argument went, slaves in the South were given food, clothing, shelter and medical care, and were thus wholly looked after, workers in the North, whether industrial or agricultural, lived 'under a much more stringent and cruel bondage'.

In the cotton-enriched South, slaves did not starve in the streets or sell their bodies or abandon their children, occurrences common, it was alleged, in the North. This attack ignored the fact that a great majority in the North at this time worked for themselves and were not hired hands.[2] It also ignored the views of a southerner like Hilton Helper who wrote in 1857 that slavery and cotton were in the long run ruinous to southern whites. Fearing both a race war and a revolt in the South by non-slave-holding whites, Helper wanted the South to change its culture and economy, and send its slaves back to Africa. In the South, these were seen as a traitor's ideas.[3]

Lincoln claimed he was protecting white self-interest by opposing the extension of slavery into new territories. If African-Americans were taken as slaves into the territories, whites willing to settle there might not find jobs. He would say to white Americans:

> It is due to yourselves as voters, as owners of the new territories, that you shall keep those territories free, in the best condition for all such of your gallant sons as may choose to go there.[4]

Reports of Lincoln's debate with Douglas, including the reporters' parenthetical observations, disclose the style of Lincoln's humour, the temperament of his audience, and Lincoln's willingness to go along with some of his audience's prejudices. In the fourth debate, held in Charleston in central Illinois, he said:

> While I was at the hotel to-day, an elderly gentleman called upon me to know whether I was really in favor of producing a perfect equality between the negroes and white people ... I will say then that I am not, nor ever have been, in favor of bringing about in any way the social and political equality of the white and black races [*applause*], that I am not nor ever have been in favor of making voters or jurors of negroes, nor of qualifying them to hold office, nor to intermarry with white people ...
>
> I say upon this occasion I do not perceive that because the white man is to have the superior position the negro should be denied everything. I do not understand that because I do not want a negro woman for a slave I must necessarily want her for a wife. [*Cheers and laughter.*] My understanding is that I can just let her alone. I am now in my fiftieth year, and I certainly never have had a black woman for either a slave or a wife ...

Another dart was aimed directly at Douglas's bid to re-enter the Senate:

> I have never had the least apprehension that I or my friends would marry negroes if there was no law to keep them from it [*laughter*],

but as Judge Douglas and his friends seem to be in great apprehension that they might, if there were no law to keep them from it [*roars of laughter*], I give him the most solemn pledge that I will to the very last stand by the law of this State, which forbids the marrying of white people with negroes . . . [*Continued laughter and applause.*]

. . . [A]n alteration of the social and political relations of the negro and the white man can be made [only] in the State Legislature—not in the Congress of the United States—and as I do not really apprehend the approach of any such thing myself, and as Judge Douglas seems to be in constant horror that some such danger is rapidly approaching, I propose as the best means to prevent it that the Judge be kept at home and placed in the State Legislature to fight the measure. [*Uproarious laughter and applause.*]

At Jonesboro, the debate's southern-most venue, Lincoln took care to reiterate his acceptance of the rights of southern states:

There is very much in the principles that Judge Douglas has here enunciated that I most cordially approve, and over which I shall have no controversy with him. In so far as he has insisted that all the States have the right to do exactly as they please about all their domestic relations, including that of slavery, I agree entirely with him . . .

But even at Jonesboro Lincoln suggested that the Dred Scott decision was contrary to the spirit of America's founders, who while not banning slavery had sought to limit it, and who expected it eventually to perish.

. . . [A]llow me to repeat one thing that I have stated before. Brooks, the man who assaulted Senator Sumner on the floor of the Senate, and who was complimented with dinners, and silver pitchers, and gold-headed canes, and a good many other things for that feat, in one of his speeches declared that when this Government was originally established, nobody expected that the institution of slavery would last until this day.

That was but the opinion of one man, but it was such an opinion as we can never get from Judge Douglas or anybody in favor of slavery in the North at all. You can sometimes get it from a Southern man. He said at the same time that the framers of our Government did not have the knowledge that experience has taught us—that experience and the invention of the cotton-gin have taught us—that the perpetuation of slavery is a necessity. He insisted, therefore, upon its being changed from the basis upon which the fathers of the Government left it, to the basis of its perpetuation and nationalization.[5]

When elections were held in November, Lincoln, supported by moderates and abolitionists alike, won more *votes* overall for the Republicans than the Democrats received, yet the Senate seat went once again to Douglas, for (thanks to the way electing districts were demarcated) Democrats had won more *seats* in the Illinois legislature, which as a body had to pick the state's senator in Washington. It chose Douglas by a vote of 54 to 46. A deeply disappointed Lincoln wrote on 19 November to an old friend:

> I am glad I made the late race. It gave me a hearing on the great and durable question of the age, which I could have had in no other way; and though I now sink out of view, and shall be forgotten, I believe I have made some marks which will tell for the cause of civil liberty long after I am gone.[6]

Wrong about vanishing from view, and right about the long-term value of his utterances in the debate, Lincoln had also made an immediate impact. Now he was a figure of national stature.

A slave ship. Pro-slavery elements felt blessed by fortune in August 1858 when a ship illegally bringing a few hundred slaves from Africa was impounded by federal officials and taken to South Carolina's principal harbour, Charleston. Its crew were tried for piracy. If the jury acquitted the *Echo*'s sailors, the illegal slave traffic would become legal and the transatlantic slave trade might be revived; if, on the other hand, the sailors were jailed, 'a howl of southern protests would surely shake the Union'.[7]

The court indeed ruled that the sailors were not pirates, but the sight of the naked, sick and terrified slaves the ship had brought underscored—even for slavery advocates—the horror of the transatlantic exercise. The federal marshal responsible for the captive slaves, a man named Daniel Hamilton, called them 'walking skeletons'. He had favoured 'the reopening of the slave-trade', Hamilton would say, 'but a practical, fair evidence of its effects has cured me forever'.[8]

In the end, the *Echo*'s slaves were returned to Africa, minus thirty-five who died in custody and another seventy-one who perished on the voyage back. Henceforth, most slavery advocates would focus on the supposed virtues of slavery in the South—the orderly and prosperous life it was said to make possible—rather than on the benefits of importing fresh batches of slaves, although a few still refused to let go of that dream.

Pull of war. In October 1859 the South howled, and even the North was shaken, when word spread that John Brown and a band of associates, seventeen whites and five African-Americans, all enemies of slavery, had descended with weapons on Harpers Ferry, Virginia, and tried to capture its federal arsenal that stored hundreds of thousands of muskets.

After the Pottawatomie Creek killings of 1856, John Brown had semi-clandestinely moved around New England, where his passion had attracted considerable support from abolitionists. Some provided funds. Brown's plans seemed imprecise, but there was talk of his returning to Kansas to establish a provisional anti-slavery government there.

At some point, the idea of seizing the Harpers Ferry arsenal caught hold of Brown's mind. Evidently he hoped to distribute captured weapons to local non-slave-holding whites, who he believed were ready to rise in rebellion. Expecting slaves also to revolt, Brown had brought to Harpers Ferry a thousand spears for them to use. One of the five blacks in his band wanted to free his wife and child who were enslaved near Harpers Ferry and were expected to be sold; and three of the seventeen whites were Brown's own sons.

On 16 October, Brown's small army surprised defenders, seized the arsenal and took about thirty hostages, who were given food by their captors. A patrol was sent out proclaiming freedom for the slaves, but neither the whites nor the blacks of Harpers Ferry showed any interest in rebelling. In fact, the African-American baggage master at the Harpers Ferry railway station rushed to alert an incoming train that the arsenal had been seized. Brown's band killed the baggage master, but made no attempt to stop the train from proceeding to its destination, Washington.

The next day, federal troops arrived from Washington, led by a fifty-two-year-old colonel called Robert E. Lee, and overcame the guerrilla group that had barricaded itself inside a fire engine house. Ten men from Brown's group were killed, including two of his sons; four residents of Harpers Ferry also perished. But the revolution was over, and its leader, a wounded captive, was quickly charged with murder, attempting a rebellion, and treason against Virginia.

On 2 November, in the Charles Town courthouse of Virginia's Jefferson County, Brown and two accomplices were sentenced to death. On 2 December, he was hanged in public in Charles Town. Many called John Brown mad, but those observing and sentencing him pronounced him sane. Calm throughout his arrest, trial and execution, he had said when first captured, 'You may dispose of me very easily—I am nearly disposed of now. But this question (of slavery) is still to be settled.'[9]

During his trial, Brown said, 'I believe that to have interfered as I have done—and I have always freely admitted I have done—on behalf of His despised poor, was not wrong but right.' He would not mind, he went on, if his blood mingled with 'the blood of millions in this slave country whose rights are disregarded by wicked, cruel, and unjust enactments'. Only blood, he said, indeed 'very much' of it, could purge America's crimes away.[10]

After an initial shock, the South on the whole took heart from the failed raid. Neither slaves nor non-slave-holding whites had supported it, and the federal government had acted swiftly to scotch it. In the North, many sympathized with Brown's goal of ending slavery and were impressed by the demeanour and words with which his life ended; yet, most could not endorse his violent ploy.

Those who had encouraged John Brown, and even the ones who had given him money and weapons, now repudiated or disowned him. Aghast at this disloyalty, Thoreau came out with formidable words. 'Is it not possible,' he asked in Concord, Massachusetts, on 30 October, just days before Brown was sentenced, 'that an individual may be right and a government wrong?' Saying, 'I plead not for his life, but for his character—his immortal life,' and, 'I see now that it was necessary that the bravest and humanest man in all the country should be hung,' Thoreau added, however, that he was not going to weep now. He would control himself until slavery ended; then he would grieve for his friend.[11]

Lincoln refused to defend Brown's action, holding it to be lawless and also futile. While acknowledging Brown's 'great courage, rare unselfishness', he wondered about his sanity.[12] Agreeing that Brown and he were one in judging slavery to be wrong, he thought Brown crossed the boundary by taking the law into his own hands. Motives, Lincoln would say, 'cannot excuse the violence, bloodshed, and treason'.[13]

The discovery of a letter to Brown from Frederick Douglass, the African-American abolitionist, forced Douglass to flee first to Canada and then to England, where he gave lectures. He was not charged, however, when he returned to America in April 1860.

Three months earlier, in a speech in January in Glasgow, Scotland, Douglass had compared John Brown's action with that of India's rebels. Brown's primary aim at Harpers Ferry, said Douglass, was to help slaves to escape, 'not,' he added, 'to shed blood or destroy property, as the insurrectionists in India had done'.[14] Like most Americans, this passionate foe of slavery wished to distance himself from the sepoys.

In the months following his death, Brown's memory stirred an increasing number of slavery-hating northerners. Simultaneously, however, his raid goaded southerners to hit back at 'the meddling North' which, they claimed, Brown typified. The 1856 caning of Senator Sumner by Preston Brooks and the Harpers Ferry raid that came three years later were palpable displays of America's anger.

The possibility of hostility turning to war occurred to many in both halves of America, producing fear, but also a thrill. In engendering the latter emotion, a role had been played by the Revolt in India that Americans had followed for much of 1857 and all of 1858—the period between the caning by Brooks and the raid by Brown.

We have seen that the marches of Havelock and Campbell and the tribulations of Britons trapped in Kanpur and Lucknow stirred their cousins across the Atlantic, who felt that Western or Christian honour was at stake in the distant conflict, but (as Orville Burton suggests) the reports from India featured by 'American newspapers in the late 1850s' also depicted 'something wonderfully exotic and thrilling' about a war for honour. Such a war on American soil was almost something to look forward to.[15]

A new President. It was natural, after the Lincoln–Douglas debate, for Republicans in Illinois to want Lincoln as the party's nominee for President in 1860. Since Douglas was the predictable Democratic nominee, a race between the two Springfield lawyers seemed possible.

Douglas wished to enlist the many Americans, in North and South, who stood in the middle on the slavery question. But his stand that a territory should be allowed to bar slavery, even as it was entitled, in his view, to legalize it, alienated his southern admirers and also the pro-South incumbent President, James Buchanan. Douglas's well-nourished network won him the Democratic nomination nonetheless, but the South's rebelling Democrats decided to run the incumbent Vice-President, John Breckinridge of Kentucky, as a third candidate on a Southern Rights platform.

The Republican establishment on the East Coast assumed that William H. Seward, a long-time foe of slavery who had opposed the Fugitive Slave Law and the Dred Scott decision, would be their party's nominee. A former governor of New York and a two-term US senator, Seward had declared that though slavery was legal under the Constitution, 'a higher law' forbade it. Confident but also complacent, Seward left in 1859 for an eight-month tour of Europe.

Also in the running were Salmon P. Chase, the governor of Ohio, who had taken an even stronger line against slavery; Simon Cameron, senator from Pennsylvania; and Edward Bates of Missouri, who was backed by the *New York Tribune*'s Horace Greeley. Though Lincoln's name was now widely known, and many had read his speeches, people in the East had not seen or heard him. They imagined him as an unlettered frontiersman.

That changed on 27 February 1860 when Lincoln spoke in New York at the Cooper Union. Reports that this tall man from the West was awkward and ungainly were indeed confirmed, and one person in the Cooper Union audience commented that on Lincoln's peculiar frame 'hung clothes that, while new for the trip, were evidently the work of an unskilled tailor'. This observer also thought that Lincoln's feet were extra large, his hands clumsy, and his hair poorly brushed.[16]

But the speech—well-researched, well-argued, sincere and eloquent—was a turning point. Quoting from records of the earliest American debates, Lincoln showed that the founders recognized the federal government's power to control slavery in national territories. Dissociating Republicans from John Brown's raid on Harpers Ferry, he said that the raid was not a slave insurrection, but 'an attempt by white men to get up a revolt among slaves, in which the slaves refused to participate'. It was wrong to try to destroy the government, he said, and equally wrong to fear the slander that opposition to slavery invited. In his concluding sentence he said,

> Let us have faith that right makes might, and in that faith let us, to the end, dare to do our duty as we understand it.

A writer for Greeley's *New York Tribune* felt that he had heard 'the greatest man since St. Paul', and a student from Harvard Law School told his father, 'It was the best speech I ever heard.'[17] Over the next two weeks, Lincoln travelled and spoke widely in New England, including in Cambridge, Massachusetts, where his son Robert was studying at Harvard. In one of these New England speeches, Lincoln employed an analogy to explain why, though a foe of any extension of slavery, he was reluctant to attack it where it existed.

> For instance, out in the street, or in the field, or on the prairie I find a rattlesnake. I take a stake and kill him. Everybody would applaud the act and say I did right. But suppose the snake was in a bed where the children were sleeping. Would I do right to strike him there? I might hurt the children; or I might not kill, but only arouse and exasperate the snake, and he might bite the children. Thus, by meddling with him here, I would do more hurt than good. Slavery is like this. We dare not strike at it where it is.[18]

Lincoln was saying that slaves would be hurt if the South's slave-owners were directly confronted, and that America would be hurt if slavery was left free to crawl into new areas.

Luckily for Lincoln and his supporters, it was in Chicago, from 16 to 18 May, that the Republican convention for choosing a nominee was held. He did not attend—personally soliciting support would seem undignified. Staying at Springfield but eager to know the results, he went first to a newspaper office to find them, and then to the telegraph office.

None among the several candidates in the fray—Seward, Chase, Bates, Lincoln and others—was in a position to win outright. Though Seward led Lincoln comfortably in the first ballot, and very narrowly in the second, the third ballot gave victory to Lincoln, who was the second choice of a majority of delegates.

In the race for the presidency that followed, Douglas, Lincoln and Breckinridge were joined by a fourth contestant, Senator John Bell, also from Kentucky, who called himself a Constitutional Unionist. Though Douglas obtained 29.5 per cent of the popular vote, compared with Lincoln's 39.8 per cent, Missouri (where slavery was lawful) was the only state that Douglas won, apart from New Jersey, where he and Lincoln were joint winners.

The lower South went for Breckinridge, the upper South for Bell. Counting New Jersey, all the free states went for Lincoln, giving him a decisive victory with 180 out of a total of 303 electoral college votes. While in most free states he won more than 60 per cent of the popular vote, Lincoln received hardly any votes in the South.

There, Lincoln's victory, produced by a wave of popular support in the North, was seen as a declaration of hostility. The *Richmond Examiner* warned southerners that 'a party founded on the single sentiment . . . of hatred of African slavery' was 'now the controlling power'.[19]

Assembling in Charleston on 20 December 1860, six weeks after Lincoln's election, the South Carolina legislature unanimously passed an Ordinance of Secession that proclaimed the dissolution of South Carolina's union with all other states, North and South. To its legislators, South Carolina was now a sovereign country. 'This precipitate and mortal act,' Winston Churchill would later write, 'was hailed with delirious enthusiasm. The cannons fired; the bells rang; flags flew on every house. The streets were crowded with cheering multitudes.'[20]

The six other states of the lower South—Mississippi, Alabama, Georgia, Louisiana, Texas and Florida—quickly followed suit. In

February 1861, delegates from these seven 'sovereign' states met in Montgomery, Alabama, and announced the formation of a Confederacy—with the Mississippi senator (and former military officer), Jefferson Davis, as its President; Montgomery as its capital; a new flag (stars and bars instead of stars and stripes); and a new Constitution. While mostly a reproduction of the Union Constitution, this document departed from it by explicitly protecting slavery. Interestingly, however, the ban on international slave trading was retained.

These brave new constructs in the South rested on three shaky assumptions. One was that the North would not coerce the South over the Union. Another was that the Yankees were no match for southern arms. The third was that if the North, with its undoubted advantage in merchant ships and warships, imposed a blockade to prevent cotton from leaving southern ports and arms from arriving there, Europe would intervene for the South. The Confederates 'cherished the notion that "King Cotton" was so vital to Britain and France that neither country could peaceably allow its supplies to be cut off.'[21]

Southern activists took over federal ports and garrison posts in the South. Buchanan, who continued as President until Lincoln's inauguration in March, rejected the secession and deplored the takeover of federal property. But he felt he could only watch and wait, which is what he did as numerous pro-Confederacy officials left Washington to join its new set-up, and large quantities of muskets were moved from Washington to the South.

Also waiting, and wondering whether they should support the seceding units or the Union, were the four states of the upper South—Virginia (the birthplace of George Washington and the fount of American tradition), North Carolina, Tennessee and Arkansas—and the four border states: Kentucky, Missouri, Maryland and Delaware.

Meanwhile, in Springfield, Illinois, the fifty-one-year-old President-elect addressed practical tasks. He had to prepare and outfit his family for life in the White House, wind up his legal practice in the Illinois capital, and appoint Cabinet colleagues and personal aides. He also faced what no predecessor President of America had encountered—the reality of secession and the possibility of civil war. Could judicious concessions undo one and avert the other? Or was war the only way of undoing the secession?

Lincoln was about to exchange a place where he had found warmth, encouragement and, above all, assurance, for another where he would face dilemmas and loneliness.

On the morning of 11 February 1861, as he took a train to Indianapolis for the first leg of a twelve-day journey to Washington, he spoke, in response to requests, to about a thousand people who had assembled at Springfield station. 'My friends,' Lincoln said, 'no one not in my situation can appreciate my feeling of sadness at this parting. To this place, and the kindness of these people, I owe everything. Here I have lived a quarter of a century, and have passed from a young to an old man. Here my children have been born, and one is buried.'[22]

He added that he was leaving 'with a task before me greater than that which rested upon Washington'. But, he concluded, he was 'trusting in Him who can go with me and remain with you'.[23]

Before proceeding towards Washington, Lincoln had travelled (by himself) to east central Illinois to visit his father's grave and also to see his stepmother, Sarah Bush Johnston Lincoln, who had raised Lincoln after the death, when he was nine, of his mother Nancy. At the end of an emotional meeting not far from Charleston, the stepmother, who like many Americans had felt the brush of ominous winds, cried in fear for his future, wishing (but not telling him) that he hadn't been elected President.[24]

During a twelve-day train journey (with numerous stops) to Washington, Lincoln heard (on 18 February) that Jefferson Davis had been inaugurated as the Confederate President and that in Texas a general had surrendered all the federal military outposts to secessionists. In seemingly impromptu talks along the way, Lincoln said that he would do his best to remove grievances that southerners might point out, but would not—as President-elect, he could not—accept secession or the takeover of federal forts.

In Lincoln's understanding, the Union, born with the Declaration of Independence, was older than the Constitution and also paramount, which meant that no state could leave the Union without the consent of the other states. When his train stopped briefly at Dunkirk in the state of New York, he reached out to take hold of an American flag and asked those hearing him 'to stand by me as long as I stand by it', and in New York city he said that nothing could 'ever willingly bring me to consent to the destruction of the Union'.[25]

Lincoln's *emotional* conviction that the American Union had a role in the story of humanity, and his *legal* conviction that a state could not unilaterally exit the Union, were joined by a compelling *political* conviction. Opposition to the extension of slavery was the only question on which all Republicans agreed. It was the central plank of the party's platform in 1860 and voters in free states had overwhelmingly endorsed it. Going back on that platform would destroy the party. Moreover, having given his pledge, his honour was at stake. On 22 February he said (in Philadelphia) that he was ready to be assassinated for his stand.[26]

Unwilling, however, to offer himself to assassins, Lincoln adopted a ruse on the last stage of his long journey to Washington. Following a report of a possible attempt to kill the President, Lincoln was slipped out of his hotel in Harrisburg, Pennsylvania, and put on a special train to Philadelphia, where, in disguise, he boarded the sleeping car of a train to Baltimore. Transferring to another train at Camden station, he reached Washington during the early morning quiet of 23 February.

Word of the dodge got out, and there was much amusement about a President-elect—a six-foot-four man who usually wore a stovepipe hat and had recently started to sport a beard—being obliged to change his appearance. Cartoonists had a great time, especially in the South, but rage was never far from a laugh in the America of February 1861.

Lincoln was lodged, until his inauguration, at Willard's Hotel, where Mary and the boys joined him on the afternoon of 23 February. Over the next few days, job seekers besieged him, and politicians and diplomats tried to size him up. While Lord Lyons, the British minister, formed a favourable impression, the ambassador from Holland noted that the President-elect laughed 'uproariously' at his own jokes, which seemed to dominate his conversation.[27] The Dutchman would later learn that Lincoln used jokes to avoid direct answers or to signal that an interview should end.

Old Winfield Scott, general-in-chief of the US Army—a war

hero who had served in the 1812 war against Britain and the Mexican war in the 1840s, and run for President as a Whig in 1852—called on Lincoln. So did Stephen Douglas, who asked Lincoln to do his best to conciliate the South. On his part, Douglas promised he would not seek political advantage for the Democrats from the country's crisis. 'Our Union,' he solemnly added, 'must be preserved.' A touched Lincoln told another visitor that his old rival was 'a noble man'.[28]

Having surprised many by defeating Seward, Chase and Bates for the Republican nomination, Lincoln now surprised them again by enlisting these competitors into his Cabinet. Prickly with one another, all three were older than the President. Seward became Secretary of State, Chase Treasury Secretary, and Bates Attorney General. Lincoln's Vice-President, elected with him on the same ticket and of the same age as Lincoln, was Hannibal Hamlin from Maine, who had previously served as governor and senator.

On 4 March, the outgoing and incoming Presidents drove down Pennsylvania Avenue to the Capitol. To prevent any bid on Lincoln's life, General Scott had placed sharpshooters on rooftops.

The speech that Lincoln gave—his first inaugural—had profited from ideas and cuts suggested by Cabinet members and others to whom Lincoln had shown a draft. His goal with the speech—an impossible one—was simultaneously to assuage southerners who felt cornered into secession and Unionists who felt overthrown by the South.

He accepted advice to delete a precise pledge that federal forts taken over in the South would be repossessed—such an announcement, he was told, would be interpreted as a call to war and prompt Virginia also to secede. Yet, he felt he had to say, in general terms at least, that his administration would 'hold, occupy, and possess the property and places belonging to the government'.

He would avoid bloodshed, he added, 'unless it be forced upon the national authority'. The idea for the last paragraph, a fervent appeal for ending discord, was suggested by Seward, but the final phrasing was Lincoln's own.

I have no purpose, directly or indirectly to interfere with the institution of slavery in the States where it exists. I believe I have no lawful right to do so, and I have no inclination to do so . . .

217

If the United States be not a government proper, but an association of States in the nature of contract merely, can it, as a contract, be peaceably unmade by less than all the parties who made it? One party to a contract may violate it—break it, so to speak—but does it not require all to lawfully rescind it?

The Union is much older than the Constitution. It was formed, in fact, by the Articles of Association in 1774. It was matured and continued by the Declaration of Independence in 1776. It was further matured, and the faith of all the then thirteen States expressly plighted and engaged that it should be perpetual, by the Articles of Confederation in 1778. And finally, in 1787, one of the declared objects for ordaining and establishing the Constitution was 'to form a more perfect Union'.

One section of our country believes slavery is right and ought to be extended, while the other believes it is wrong and ought not to be extended. This is the only substantial dispute.

Directly addressing anti-Union southerners, he said:

In your hands, my dissatisfied fellow-countrymen, and not in mine, is the momentous issue of civil war. The Government will not assail you. You can have no conflict without being yourselves the aggressors. You have no oath registered in heaven to destroy the Government, while I shall have the most solemn one to 'preserve, protect, and defend' it.

I am loath to close. We are not enemies, but friends. We must not be enemies. Though passion may have strained it must not break our bonds of affection. The mystic chords of memory, stretching from every battlefield and patriot grave to every living heart and hearthstone all over this broad land, will yet swell the chorus of the Union, when again touched, as surely they will be, by the better angels of our nature.

The concluding lines did not placate the South. In South Carolina, a correspondent of the *Charleston Mercury* wrote that Lincoln, described contemptuously as 'the Ourang-Outang of the White House', had sounded 'the tocsin of battle'. In crucial Virginia, the *Richmond Dispatch* charged that the speech 'inaugurates civil war'. In the North, newspapers called the inaugural 'firm' yet also 'conciliatory', though one paper, the *Providence Daily Post*, felt that 'some plain talk' had been followed by 'obscurely stated qualifications'.[29]

To avert (if he could) what now seemed inevitable, Lincoln was willing to reiterate his view that the Fugitive Slave Law of 1850 was constitutional and should be enforced. He would accept, he told Seward, steps towards conciliation that were 'not altogether outrageous', and might even let New Mexico, a territory in the south-west, be admitted without prohibition of slavery, if further extension was abjured.[30] To the South's secessionists, these offers did not merit a second's look.

Russell again. After returning to England from India, William Howard Russell had assumed, in addition to his work for *The Times*, the editorship of a new journal, the *Army and Navy Gazette*, started by the proprietors of *Punch*. When it seemed that a civil war was approaching in America, *The Times* sounded Russell out about going there.

Though a New York lawyer, J.C. Bancroft Davis, was sending weekly reports from America to *The Times*, he was a loyal pro-North Republican whose views did not sit well with the bulk of the paper's British readers, who, while disapproving of slavery, were unwilling, as far as America was concerned, to side with the North against the South.

America's earlier quarrels with the British were not wholly forgotten in the old country where many, 'particularly among the ruling classes ... wanted America's democratic experiment to fail'.[31] Although the Prince of Wales had made a successful visit to America in 1860, not many Britons prayed, as 1861 began, for the Union's survival, while others remembered that two-thirds of the cotton for Lancashire's mills came from the American South.

Some feared that if the Union won and grew strong, it could eventually push Britain to second place in the world and also strengthen egalitarian forces inside England. Elements in the British establishment therefore 'took some pleasure and much comfort in the prospect of the destruction of a Union that was rapidly developing into a powerful state'.[32]

Within *The Times* there were differences of opinion. '*Why* should we be so very anxious to see the Union preserved?' John Walter, the proprietor who involved himself in the paper's policy, wanted to know. 'What has it done to command our sympathy?'[33] That Lincoln was not openly attacking slavery as such gave

Britons an excuse for not supporting the North. Moreover, the suppression of the Revolt in India had greatly strengthened beliefs in Britain in the superiority of whites and the inferiority of non-whites.

The general manager of *The Times*, Mowbray Morris, who had been raised in the West Indies, 'actively approved of the slave system and made no secret of his feelings'. 'The Northern government and its policy are an abomination to me,' he said, 'and I greatly enjoy to hear them abused.'[34] While more open to the North, editor Delane felt that the paper should reflect the opinions of the upper middle class that read *The Times* and ruled Britain. This class was ambivalent in its attitude to the American conflict, but thought of southerners as underdogs who possessed 'the Cavalier qualities, brave and dashing and aristocratic, based on a landed and hierarchical society'—attributes for which the British upper class felt an instinctive attraction.[35]

Russell, who had not crossed the Atlantic thus far, was more than willing to provide a first-hand assessment. The Irishman in him was revolted by the idea of slavery, his instincts were pro-Union, and, as we have seen, colour prejudice repelled him. Yet, Russell, proud of the old history of Britain, found it hard to imagine a country surviving for long without a monarch. Also, as we have found, he enjoyed hierarchical and aristocratic set-ups. Sensing conflicting reactions within himself, he claimed all the same that he had 'no theories to uphold, no prejudices to subserve, [and] no interests to advance' in respect of what was happening in America.[36]

During an 1859 trip to Switzerland, Russell had made friends with John Bigelow, a New York lawyer who owned a share in an evening paper in his city; and in the summer of 1860, he formed a friendship with another American visiting Europe, also from New York, forty-six-year-old Samuel Ward. After making and losing more than one fortune and then making another in South America, Ward had settled in Washington as a 'one-man pressure group', the prototype of the future lobbyist. Bigelow and Ward were enthusiastic about Russell covering events in a country where 'his graphic descriptions of the Crimea and the Indian revolt' in *The Times* were well-known to many.[37]

Thackeray raised a farewell toast in his honour, and on 2 March (two days before Lincoln's inauguration), Russell set off on the *Arabia* for America. Even as he had done three years earlier on his voyage to India, he studied fellow passengers. The 'bellicose determination of the southerners' on the ship impressed him, and he was surprised at the disrespect many northerners showed for the recently elected President.[38]

On 14 March, Bigelow and Sam Ward met Russell off the boat in New York and introduced him to his fellow *Times* correspondent, Bancroft Davis. New York was much smaller than London, and *The Times* of the latter city was the biggest newspaper in the world. A writer in the city where he had landed called Russell 'the most famous newspaper correspondent the world has ever seen'.[39]

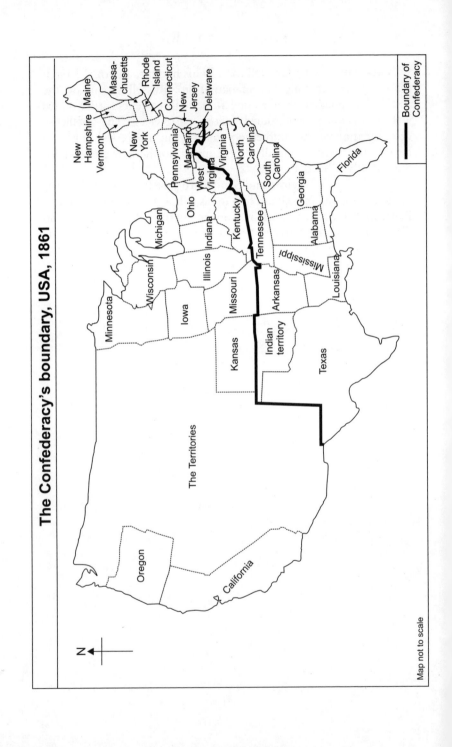

The Confederacy's boundary, USA, 1861

New Hampshire
Vermont
Maine
Massachusetts
Rhode Island
Connecticut
New Jersey
Delaware
New York
Pennsylvania
Maryland
West Virginia
Virginia
North Carolina
South Carolina
Georgia
Florida
Ohio
Michigan
Kentucky
Tennessee
Alabama
Mississippi
Wisconsin
Illinois
Indiana
Missouri
Arkansas
Louisiana
Minnesota
Iowa
Kansas
Indian territory
Texas
The Territories
Oregon
California

N

Boundary of Confederacy

Map not to scale

CHAPTER 5

AMERICA SHEDS ITS BLOOD
THE CIVIL WAR, 1861–65

Russell landed in New York on St Patrick's Day. At a celebratory dinner in the evening, there was a good deal of eating, drinking, singing and speech-making, with Russell entering into all the activities. Later, he could not remember what he had said—newspapers the next day would give different versions—but it seems clear that the visitor 'delivered himself of the fervent hope that the Union would survive intact'.

What delighted northern eyes the next morning produced penitence in Russell, who had wished to be seen as an impartial recorder of events, while at *The Times* in London there was shock and anger. Mowbray Morris wrote to Russell: '*I am very sorry you attended that SP dinner and made that speech.*'

Descriptions in New York's newspapers help us picture the newly arrived forty-one-year-old correspondent. One reporter said that Russell had

> short iron locks parted down the middle, a grayish moustache and a strong tendency to double-chin, a very broad and very full but not lofty forehead, eyes of a clear, keen blue, sharply observant in their expression, rather prominently set and indicating abundant language.

Another wrote:

> This substantial and slightly protuberant figure may stand about five feet seven inches in his boots ... As a speaker he is rather nervous

and hesitating ... he is given to humming and hawing before the commencement of each sentence ... but in the *matter* of his speech we have seldom heard any orator more lucid, compact and self-balanced than Mr. Russell.[1]

No matter what London thought, Russell's 'fervent hope' had won the North's goodwill. Arriving in Washington on 26 March, he booked himself at Willard's Hotel and in the evening met Secretary of State, William Seward. The next day, Seward took Russell to the White House to meet Lincoln. In his diary Russell would write:

Soon afterwards there entered, with a shambling, loose, irregular, almost unsteady gait, a tall, lank, lean man, considerably over six feet on height, with stooping shoulders, long pendulous arms, terminating in hands of extraordinary dimensions, which however, were far exceeded in proportion by his feet. He was dressed in an ill-fitting wrinkled suit of black ...

The impression produced by the size of his extremities, and by his flapping and wide projecting ears, may be removed by the appearance of kindliness, sagacity and the awkward bonhomie of his face; the mouth is absolutely prodigious; the lips, straggling and extending almost from one line of black beard to the other, are only kept in order by two deep furrows from the nostril to the chin; the nose itself—a prominent organ—stands out from the face, with an anxious, inquiring air, as though it were sniffing for some good things in the wind; the eyes, dark, full and deeply set, are penetrating, but full of an expression which almost amounts to tenderness.[2]

When Seward introduced Russell to him, Lincoln shrewdly but also correctly remarked that *The Times* was 'one of the greatest powers in the world', perhaps next only, he added, to the Mississippi; Russell, continued the President, was 'a minister' of that power. In the ensuing conversation, Lincoln offered 'two or three peculiar little sallies'. Russell would record (with a hint of surprise) that he was 'agreeably impressed' with Lincoln's 'shrewdness, humour, and natural sagacity'.[3]

Wooed by the Union, Russell was invited to dine with the Seward family and, on 28 March, to attend Lincoln's first official dinner, where Cabinet members, General Winfield Scott, the head of the Union army, and Russell were the only guests. Within days,

Russell had talked with all the leading men in the government, and with Scott and Lord Lyons, the British minister.

However, his first Letter published in *The Times* referred not to any of these meetings, but to the ambience of Washington and of Willard's Hotel, with people of all types, accents and clothes—'long-limbed, nervous, eager-looking men ... in vast conceptions in hatting and booting' trying to grab 'some pet appointment under Government'.[4] He detected no unity among the northerners, who seemed to range, he observed, from abolitionists to moderate Lincolnians to those wanting peace above all and thus ready to let the 'errant sisters' of the South go; also much drunkenness and amateurish military preparations.

In Washington, Russell also met the commissioners sent by Jefferson Davis to negotiate terms of secession. He found these southerners (whom Lincoln would not meet) to be determined and united, undeterred by the prospect of war, disdainful of northerners who they thought had been corrupted by trade and industry—and fervent about slavery. In his Diary, though not yet in his dispatches, he would write about these southern leaders:

> [S]lavery is their *summum bonum* of morality, physical excellence, and social purity, I was inclined to question the correctness of [their] standard, and to inquire whether the virtue which needed this murderous use of the pistol and the dagger to defend it, was not open to some doubt; but I found there was very little sympathy with my views among the company.

Meeting these commissioners convinced Russell of the inevitability of war. He wrote to Bigelow in New York of the 'immortal smash' about to occur, and also offered to his friend a prediction about Republicanism—influenced no doubt by his own monarchical bias—that would not hold up:

> The world will only see in it all the failure of republican institutions in time of pressure as demonstrated by all history—that history which America vainly thought she was going to set right and re-establish on new grounds and principles. I fail to discover among the men I have come in contact with any 'veneration' for anything—it's a useful bump—good government grows under it.[5]

When Russell was introduced to him, and for several days before and after, Lincoln was getting to know the Presidency from the inside—he was discovering the possibilities and limits of his new office. He was also debating what he should do about Fort Sumter, a federal post on an island off the South Carolina coast.

On 5 March, the day after his inauguration, he learnt that the officer in charge at the fort, Major Robert Anderson of Kentucky, had sent word that provisions for his garrison would only last for six weeks. If not resupplied, he would be forced to surrender to the secessionists. However, Anderson added, a force of 20,000 well-disciplined men could secure the fort for the Union.

Knowing that even a force sent solely to resupply Fort Sumter would provoke war, Lincoln took time to obtain counsel. Withdrawing the Fort Sumter garrison was one option. Attempting to provision it clandestinely was another. Sending a force to secure the fort, and thereby starting war, was a third. Many advised Lincoln to take the first option. Douglas said in the Senate that South Carolina was entitled to Fort Sumter. Greeley's *New York Tribune* wrote that the southern states should be allowed to go in peace. Others strongly urged the opposite, telling him that failure to reinforce Fort Sumter would be disastrous for the North and for the Republican Party.

Lincoln wanted to probe the intentions of Virginia, which was yet to declare its stand. Would it abjure secession if the Union withdrew from Fort Sumter? General Scott, a Virginian, offered his assessment that to satisfy Virginia, the Union would also need to give up Fort Pickens in the Gulf of Mexico, off Florida, which was firmly in Union hands and easy to reinforce.

There was no complete assurance, however, that the handover of Forts Sumter and Pickens would persuade Virginia to stay with the Union. Moreover, withdrawal from Fort Sumter would not only violate Lincoln's pledge regarding federal property, thereby demoralizing the North; it would also raise the Confederacy's prestige, which could help it gain recognition from European powers.[6]

Another consideration was perhaps even more important. If, as was likely, South Carolina attacked a Fort to which food was being sent, 'the government will stand justified before the entire

Bahadur Shah Zafar

Nana Sahib

Rani of Jhansi

Sayyid Ahmed Khan

Allan Octavian Hume

Vidyasagar

Bankimchandra Chatterjee

Jotiba Phule

Lord Dalhousie

General Henry Havelock

Lord Canning

Colonel James Neill

Lord Clyde (Colin Campbell)

Abraham Lincoln

Frederick Douglass

George McClellan

Robert E. Lee

Ulysses S. Grant

Queen Victoria

William Howard Russell

Leo Tolstoy

Karl Marx

country in repelling that aggression and retaking the forts'.[7] These are not Lincoln's words. They were written to him, before his inauguration, by an old if critical friend from Illinois, Orville Hickman Browning (the one, we may recall, who closely followed the Indian Revolt). But they seem to represent Lincoln's reasoning. He was anxious that the first shots of an apparently inescapable war should come from the other side.

Aware that his decision was likely to—was in some ways expected to—provoke war, Lincoln lived under an almost unbearable strain. On the night of 28 March (following the official dinner to which Russell had been invited), he 'slept not at all'. In the morning, he felt he was 'in the dumps',[8] but he had reached a decision—a bid would be made to supply Fort Sumter with provisions. His Cabinet agreed with him, some (including Seward) less wholeheartedly than others.

On 6 April, Lincoln sent a clerk in the State Department called Robert Chew to Charleston with instructions to inform Governor Francis Pickens of South Carolina that an attempt would be made to supply Fort Sumter. If the attempt was not resisted, so went Lincoln's carefully worded message, the Union government would make 'no effort to throw in men, arms or ammunition . . . without further notice'. The same day, a fleet capable of provisioning Fort Sumter sailed from New York. On 12 April, South Carolina answered the message brought by Chew by firing at Fort Sumter. The Civil War had begun, and Anderson and his garrison were forced to surrender within thirty-six hours.

The North was united in outrage. Douglas 'hastened to the White House to grasp Lincoln's hand'.[9] Ex-President Buchanan vowed to back Lincoln, and Lincoln himself issued a proclamation calling for a militia of 75,000 to suppress 'combinations' in seven states—he was not going to recognize the Confederacy or legitimize its name.

But the proclamation set off the secession of the Upper South. Claiming that every state enjoyed sovereign rights, North Carolina, Virginia, Tennessee and Arkansas left the Union and offered their military forces to the Confederacy. The secession of his state, Virginia, settled the mind of Robert E. Lee. During the hectic days of March, when plans to expand armies were set in motion in both

North and South, General Scott had offered Lee the chief command of the Union army. In April, the offer was repeated, and Lee was informed that Lincoln had authorized it.

But Lee declined the offer. And when Virginia seceded, Lee resigned his commission in the Union army, left his home in Arlington, and took the train for Richmond. Eighteen months earlier, when he had arrived in Virginia to subdue John Brown, he represented the Union. Now he was ready, if need be, to fight the Union on behalf of Virginia.

~

Russell visited Fort Sumter soon after it had surrendered. His friend Sam Ward was already in the South on an 'unofficial one-man peace mission'.[10] Russell joined him. Like their counterparts in the North, southerners, including generals, colonels and their families, courted Russell, and 'one man studied up his Thackeray to converse with him on equal terms'.[11] But Russell was more interested in how the war would proceed, and in studying southern attitudes.

He thought southerners to be united in their beliefs that they would 'lick the cowardly Yankees' and that need for cotton would bring England to the South's side.[12] Indeed, England had by this time declared neutrality, which to the North seemed to imply recognition of secession. It was natural for Lord Palmerston, seventy-seven but still the British Prime Minister, to picture America through Seward, who had visited England, rather than through Lincoln, who had never left America and was yet to be adequately known. Judging Seward to be 'rabidly anti-British', Palmerston also suspected that the Secretary of State had been 'contemplating a war against Britain as a diversion from the impending Civil War'.[13] Seward seems indeed to have suggested something approaching that to Lincoln, but there is no record of Lincoln considering it seriously.[14]

According to Pemberton, Palmerston's biographer, 'It seemed to Palmerston (and the majority of enlightened Englishmen) that if five and a half million people wished to manage their own affairs and pursue their own manner of life they should be allowed to do so.'[15] A member of Palmerston's Cabinet saw 'the determination of the North to prevent secession' as 'the most singular action for the restitution of conjugal rights that the world has ever heard of'.[16]

As for Russell, despite his instinctive sympathy for the North and hatred of slavery, he wrote in his diary:

> I am more satisfied than ever that the Union can never be restored as it was, and that it has gone to pieces, never to be put together again, in the old shape at all events, by any power on earth.[17]

An unnamed person in South Carolina told Russell that all that the South needed was for 'one of the Royal race of England to rule over us'. We do not know whether this was a genuine sentiment or a card to draw British support. In any case, Russell, who referred also to the South's 'grace' and 'charm', duly reported the remark. However, southerners dissociated themselves from it when it was published.[18]

When war was officially declared on 7 May, Russell was in Montgomery, Alabama, where he met the Confederate President, Jefferson Davis, 'a very calm, resolute man', as Russell described him. Said Davis to him:

> We do not seek the sympathy of England by unworthy means, for we respect ourselves, and we are glad to invite the scrutiny of men into our acts; as for our motives, we meet the eye of heaven.[19]

After witnessing in Montgomery the auction of 'a stout young negro, badly dressed and ill-shod', Russell wrote in *The Times*:

> I am neither sentimentalist nor Black Republican nor negro worshipper but I confess the sight caused a strange thrill through my heart . . . There was no sophistry which could persuade me the man was not a man—he was, indeed, by no means my brother, but assuredly he was a fellow-creature.

Later in the day, Russell saw a black girl put up for sale, but nobody offered the reserve price, which was $610. 'Niggers is cheap,' people said.[20]

There being no war yet to report, Russell took the chance to see as much as he could of the South. Travelling with Sam Ward, he journeyed from Montgomery to the Gulf Coast, where he saw Fort Pickens (the federal post), Alabama's coastal town Mobile, and the

South's largest city, also on the Gulf Coast, New Orleans. From New Orleans, the two travellers went up the Mississippi River to Baton Rouge (also in the state of Louisiana), Vicksburg (in Mississippi), and Memphis (Tennessee).

Southerners were told by Russell that Lincoln was a man with 'will and intelligence'. Observing slaves during the long journey, Russell thought that they often seemed well cared for. But he could not accept justifications of slavery and had repeated disputes with his hosts. Letters that Ward sent to friends in the North, signing himself 'Carlos Lopez', stated that through his forensic skill, Russell was 'fighting secession sword in hand'. In 'controversy', Ward wrote, Russell was 'the ablest general logician I ever heard converse'.

Russell's reports from the South took weeks to reach London and sometimes got lost on the way. Their central political theme was that the South would fight and fight hard. Readers of *The Times* were told that 'there is no people in the world so crazy with military madness' as the southerners. Coming from the only non-southern journalist in the South, the assessment was of interest to England and of value in Washington and New York. 'I don't believe you ever wrote better,' said Delane in a letter to Russell.[21]

By the end of June, Russell and Ward were back in the North, where Russell noticed a somewhat more resolute spirit than before, but he saw too that new immigrants, the Irish and the Germans, were enlisting more than Yankees in the militia. Russell had reached some conclusions by this time. Slavery was bad. America should remain united. Because of its numbers, industry and navy, the North was likely to win eventually. The fight would be long, hard and bitter; and in the end, the victorious Union would not be secure or contented.[22]

Fighting had not commenced, but there had been major political developments. Lincoln and his allies had managed to retain in the Union the crucial 'border' states of Kentucky, Missouri, Maryland and Delaware. In addition, Virginia's western counties had left Virginia to form a new state, West Virginia, which chose to remain in the Union.

Linked by birth to Kentucky (like Jefferson Davis), Lincoln was supposed to have said, 'I should like to have God on my side, but

I must have Kentucky.'[23] Although Kentucky and the other 'border' states permitted slavery and contained influential pro-Confederacy elements, the balance was tilted in the Union's favour by geography, military pressure and Lincoln's political astuteness.

And Lincoln had held on to the view, which he wanted Europe to accept, that America was facing an illegal rebellion. An illegal rebellion is also what India's British governors thought they had faced in 1857, even though for a while King Zafar claimed that the British were the rebels and he the rightful ruler. Insisting that he remained President of all of the USA and that the unfolding war was not one between two lawful entities, Lincoln argued that while elements in the South had indeed seceded, the states themselves remained in the Union.

India's rebellion was recalled to buttress the Union's case and, in particular, to caution England against treating North and South as equally lawful belligerents. A Democrat who was also a strong Unionist, Joel Parker of New Jersey wrote:

> There were millions of people in India engaged in a war against the government of Great Britain ... and they were all, kings, princes, and sepoys, held alike as rebels against the paramount government ... Now suppose that at about the time when Havelock began to move effectively for the suppression of the rebellion ... the United States had concluded to recognize the king of India and his adherents as belligerents. The English government would undoubtedly have regarded this as an evidence of hostility ...[24]

Keeping European powers in mind, Lincoln ordered a blockade rather than a closure of the South's seaports. As President of all the states he was entitled to order the ports closed, yet foreign vessels were likely to test such an order, and the testing could provoke naval conflict between America and a European country.

Mounting a blockade was a safer policy, but capable foreign vessels could skirt a blockade. In the event, blockade-running in the South's interests developed 'upon a large scale', both 'in cotton outwards and arms inwards'. Yet 'not a single European Government received the envoys of the Confederate states'.[25]

The pragmatic Lincoln was again seen when, despite his view that secession was illegal, he chose to treat captured soldiers or sailors as prisoners of war, not criminals or pirates. He knew that the South could retaliate in kind.

And though refusing to admit a legal war, Lincoln claimed a war-time right to curb personal freedoms. When Maryland was making up its mind and some in that state seemed about to join the southern revolt, Lincoln was ready not only to have them arrested, but also to deny them release under a writ of habeas corpus. He said he did not want to show 'such extreme tenderness' towards 'the citizen's liberty' as might let 'the government itself go to pieces'.[26]

Convinced that the South still contained many who cherished a united American nation and numerous yeomen who opposed slavery, and conscious of the North's clear superiority in wealth and strength, Lincoln expected an early defeat of the rebels. One or two great battles and the thing would be over.

~

In tiny rooms he had rented on Washington's Pennsylvania Avenue (the street on which the White House stood), Russell waited for the fighting to begin. Though both sides had spoken of war, neither had prepared for it. 'The American people had enjoyed a long peace, and their warfare had been to reclaim the wilderness and draw wealth from the soil.'[27] Men had been mobilized but not trained (recruits on both sides included some Britons who had fought India's sepoys), and while many officers (on both sides) had taken part in the Mexican war, their expertise had rusted. Moreover, weapons and munitions were not in large supply.

The North's advantages were in numbers (a population of 23 million against 9 million in the South, of whom 4 million were slaves), on the sea (the South had almost no navy), in infrastructure (the North's roads, canals and rail lines were better and longer), and in manufacturing, including of what a war required (clothes, footwear, firearms). On the other hand, the Confederate states felt that they 'were defending hearth and home against invasion and overlordship'.[28] Loss in a battle, or even in a series of battles, would not spell their end. The North would have to conquer all of the South, bit by bit. It would be a clash of will, stamina and patience, not just of numbers or resources. And the smaller side had often won in history, including in the Revolutionary War against England.

The southern states imagined too that they were stronger in martial spirit, military tradition and, importantly, in leadership. Davis, the Confederate President, had not only served in the Mexican war but had also been Secretary of War from 1853 to 1857. As a result, he was aware of the qualities and weaknesses of senior officers he would deploy. In contrast, Lincoln had acquired no knowledge, during his career in law and politics, of war or of military officers.

Then there was cotton, grown only in the South. Deprived of it, would not workers in the North and in Europe revolt, demanding an end to war? However, in 1861, Europe not only had ample cotton reserves, it expected additional supplies from India, Egypt and Australia. Moreover, cotton cloth was no longer Britain's main export to Asia, where (in 1861) markets contained a surplus of cotton goods. It was India-grown opium that now constituted Britain's chief export to China.

~

In April 1861, after Virginia declared secession, the Confederate capital was shifted from Montgomery to Richmond. Only a hundred miles south-west of Washington, Richmond was an inviting target, even though a series of rivers and defence lines blocked the path to it. Northern public opinion clamoured for action and Lincoln himself felt that the soldiers he had summoned in April for ninety days of duty should be used in an assault before they returned home. Though Winfield Scott advised waiting, Lincoln and the Cabinet demanded a move in the direction of Richmond.

Brigadier General Irvin McDowell was asked to lead an advance that finally took place on 21 July. His army of 35,000 moved towards a town and rail junction, about 30 miles west of Washington, called Manassas, which stood beside a stream called Bull Run or Bull's Run. Hoping to enjoy a triumphal outing, many civilians from Washington, including some members of Congress and their families, joined the westward advance, which, however, they impeded by crowding the road.

Russell too rode forth from Washington—now he would report an actual war. But he ran into heavy traffic—McDowell's supplies moving forward, Congressmen and families wanting to see the fun, other picnicking families, and some Union soldiers returning because their tour of duty was over. At noon, he passed Centreville, about 9 miles short of Manassas. In the afternoon, he was surprised to see some Union wagons moving against the traffic and coming towards him.

Two opposing streams of traffic met on a bridge, causing a jam, and Russell heard from some soldiers returning to Centreville (on their way back to Washington) that they had been 'whipped'. 'The teamsters of the advancing waggons now took up the cry ... "Turn back—turn your horses," was the shout up the whole line.'[29] Russell pushed himself forward, but again encountered 'waves of soldiers' passing him 'who had abandoned their guns and equipment in the rush to get away'. They seemed convinced that the enemy cavalry was at their heels. Russell also then rode back to Centreville and on to Washington to write his report for *The Times*.

What had happened? To begin with, in fact, McDowell's advance had surprised the Confederates, but a brigade led by a thirty-seven-year-old Confederate officer called Thomas Jackson and based on Henry House Hill, about 4 miles west of Centreville, stopped McDowell's force. Then, reinforced by new arrivals by rail, Jackson's brigade repulsed the Unionists. But Confederate forces did not pursue the retreating Unionists.

The Confederate army 'was more disorganized by victory than the Federals by defeat'. The truth for both sides was that 'the day was hot, the troops raw, [and] the staffs inexperienced'.[30] About 500 Unionists and 400 Confederates were killed that day in what the North would call (after the stream) the First Battle of Bull Run, while the South called it the Battle of Manassas (after the town). It was also the battle that would earn Jackson, a man with Ulster origins, who was both a practitioner and a scholar of war, the nickname 'Stonewall'.

When, after midnight, Russell returned to his rented rooms on Pennsylvania Avenue, he did not have all this information. But he had picked up a lot of stuff. A long Letter written in his small room and completed at three on the morning of 23 July was delivered to a mail steamer in Boston just before it sailed for England. It was published in *The Times* on 6 August.

Filling nine columns, Russell's report spoke of 'both a defeat and a disgrace'. The confusion and panic in Unionist ranks was mentioned, with Russell referring to 'the runaways of an utterly demoralized army'. But the Letter said that Bull Run was not the end of the war and added:

> The North must put its best men into the battle, or she will inevitably fall before the energy, the personal hatred, and the superior fighting powers of her antagonist ... But though the North may reel under the shock, I cannot think it will make her desist from the struggle, unless it be speedily followed by blows more deadly than the repulse from Manassas.

Delane wrote to Russell of the 'delight' with which everyone in England read 'the vivid report' of the 'debacle' and wondered whether Americans would be able 'to bear the truth so plainly told'. Even more delighted, Mowbray Morris feared that Russell would be lynched by angry Unionists.

As Churchill the historian would later observe, 'Europe was astonished; the South was overjoyed; and a wave of fury swept the Union.'[31] Lord Palmerston felt that his preference for the South had been vindicated. 'If the Northerners had been inspired by noble ideals,' he argued, 'they would never have fled in disorder from the field.'[32]

Four weeks after he had written it, copies of *The Times* carrying Russell's account reached America. By this time, the North had recovered its confidence and was trying to forget Bull Run. But there was great curiosity about what Russell had reported. In fact, the *New York Times* had written, 'We scarcely exaggerate the fact when we say, the first and foremost thought on the minds of a very large portion of our people after the repulse of Bull Run was, what will Russell say.'

After Russell's account was seen in America, many strongly attacked him. The *Chicago Tribune* claimed that Russell had made up the story without going to Bull Run. Bennett's *New York Herald* wrote, 'As for running away, Mr Russell himself set the example, and, riding a foaming steed, was foremost in the line of retreat.' But the *New York Times* defended Russell unreservedly, saying, 'He gives a clear, fair, and perfectly just and accurate, as it is spirited and graphic, account.'[33]

~

A long lull followed, during which Russell faced vilification and received several threatening letters. He was lampooned in the North as 'Bull Run Russell'. Yet southerners were not pleased either. One of them, Mary Boykin Chesnut (the woman who had been terrified by the play about Nana Sahib), wrote in her diary:

> Russell, I think in his capacity of Englishman, despises both sides. He derides us equally. He prefers to attribute Bull's Run to Yankee cowardice rather than to Southern courage. He gives no credit to either side. After all, we are mere Americans![34]

What most displeased Russell was that after Bull Run Union generals were unwilling to facilitate his reporting—he had become persona non grata. Not that there were major new battles to cover. Russell utilized his time to socialize and also to read books, including a new novel called *Great Expectations* by a friend in London called Charles Dickens.

Bull Run destroyed the myth of a dramatic short war. Though thousands had been killed, neither side had gained an inch. Following the fiasco, a sobered Lincoln replaced McDowell with thirty-four-year-old George B. McClellan. A dashing veteran of the Mexican War (where, as a twenty-year-old, he had served in a company of engineers) and a Democrat in politics, McClellan pondered over a grand plan of old Winfield Scott that envisaged the Union navy paralysing all the South's seaports from Richmond to New Orleans, and a large new army moving from the coast to the interior to crush the rebellion.

In October, when Winfield Scott retired, McClellan succeeded as general-in-chief of all the Union armies and 'bent himself with zeal and capacity' to organize brigades, divisions and army corps, along with artillery, engineers and supply trains.[35] But McClellan was taking his own time. Eager for the general to come up with a plan of attack, Lincoln, and northerners as a whole, were getting impatient. After great early popularity, which had been aided by the sight of the general in full uniform riding a magnificent horse, McClellan was seen as dragging his feet.

Treating him nonetheless with extraordinary courtesy, Lincoln called a few times at McClellan's house to discuss options until one famous night (13 November 1861) when the general, on reaching his home and learning that Lincoln, accompanied by Seward and John Hay (the President's secretary), was there, waiting for him, sent word to the visitors that he was going to bed. While declining to express 'points of etiquette and personal dignity', Lincoln lost respect for McClellan.[36]

Yet, as months passed without visible action, many were also losing their confidence in Lincoln. Alleging incompetence, some linked it to Lincoln's plain origins, with Benjamin Wade, an abolitionist senator from Ohio, recalling that after all, Lincoln had been born 'of "poor white trash" and educated in a slave state'.[37]

Also controversial was Lincoln's response to developments in the key 'border' state of Missouri, where slavery was permitted. Commanding the army in 'the western region' that included Missouri, John Charles Fremont not only ousted the state's governor for being feeble in his support for the Union, he declared in August 1861 that Missouri was under martial law and that its slaves were free. These dramatic decrees by Fremont (who had earned fame earlier as an explorer and military officer and in 1856 as the unsuccessful Republican nominee for the presidency) were welcomed by many in the North and especially by the Republican Party's radicals. However, not only did Lincoln object to a military commander dictating policy, he was certain that Fremont's orders would push opinion in Missouri and Kentucky against the Union. Revoking the orders, Lincoln also relieved Fremont of his military command. This displeased many Republicans who backed a policy of emancipating slaves, which they believed would induce blacks in the North and the 'border' states to join the Union's armies, and help trigger rebellion inside the South.

Lincoln suffered too from the impact of his wife's zeal for improving the White House's decor. There could only be praise when Mary Todd Lincoln 'personally oversaw the scrubbing, painting, and plastering' of a house that was in sorry shape when the Lincolns arrived and now, for 'the first time in years', looked 'sparklingly clean'.[38] But the husband was furious when large bills came in for carpets, china and other items that Mary had ordered without his knowledge. He wanted to pay out of his own pocket, but finally agreed, not without embarrassment, to Congress authorizing the money needed.

War with England? In November 1861, Russell had a real story to cover. James Mason and John Slidell, two Confederate emissaries proceeding to Europe to explain the South's cause and highlight the cotton angle, evaded the Union blockade and reached Havana where they boarded a British mail packet, the *Trent*. However, after it left Havana, the *Trent* was stopped by a Union gunboat, and Mason and Slidell, plus two assistants, were removed as Union prisoners. Northerners regarded the arrests off the *Trent* as a bold coup, but the British saw it as an affront, if not a direct attack.

Palmerston's 'immediate reaction', beyond demanding the return of Mason and Slidell, was 'to move battleships and troops'. England thought it 'possessed immeasurably the greatest fighting fleet in the world'. This fleet 'received instant orders to hold itself in readiness, and within a week the first reinforcements were on their way to Canada', which was viewed as the 'immediate American objective' if war between England and America occurred.[39] 'If the Federal Government refuse compliance,' the Prime Minister privately remarked, 'Great Britain is in a better state to inflict a severe blow and to read a lesson to the United States which will not soon be forgotten.'[40]

Yet the government of neither country was eager for war. Veiled threats had indeed been issued, and international maritime law invoked in opposing ways, but, thanks to an intervention by Prince Albert, London agreed to use politer language to seek the release of the Confederate emissaries. On his part, Lincoln required some persuading to release Mason and Slidell. In the end, however, after sagely remarking, 'One war at a time,' he ordered their release.

But it had been close. In a letter to Russell written before the crisis had passed, Delane described public feeling in Britain: 'It is a real, downright, honest desire to avenge old scores ... [T]he whole Army, Navy and Volunteers are of one mind, and all mad for service in America.'[41] Palmerston and some others in England thought that without the reinforcements he had sent, the 'tactfully worded dispatch' would not have worked, and hostilities might have commenced. Palmerston's biographer, however, offers another explanation for the absence of war:

> Yet, viewing the crisis in its proper perspective, it is difficult to escape the impression that what really preserved peace was the absence of telegraphic communications (across the ocean). Had the news of the American response and British military measures reached London and Washington simultaneously at the peak of national excitement . . . [nothing] could have prevented a war.[42]

Though continuing to be slandered in some northern newspapers for his Bull Run account, and shunned even more because *The Times* was taking a pro-South line, Russell was upset by the possibility that the South might win with British support. He wrote to Delane, 'I am much exercised about the Southern people becoming independent and a slave power—and we the authors of it! That touches me nearly.'[43]

Keeping daily contact with Lord Lyons and others at the British embassy, Russell learnt on 27 December of the Union's decision to release the four captives. He rushed to Boston hoping to interview Mason and Slidell before their transfer to a British ship, but was not in time.

While relieved that the crisis was over, Russell was disappointed that he would not cover an Anglo-American war from the battlefront. Now his ability to write was back in the hands of Union officers who disliked the line *The Times* took and were unwilling to give him a reporter's pass. Annoyed at his situation, Russell went to Canada, where he spent a few happy weeks before returning to the USA.

A peculiar sequence of events terminated Russell's American stay. Immediately on learning of the resolution of the *Trent* crisis, he had sent off a telegram to his friend in New York, Sam Ward, who was distraught at the possibility of an Anglo-American war. Russell's telegram read, 'Act as if you heard some very good news for yourself. Dine as soon as you get this.'

Russell's consistent adversary, the *New York Herald*, somehow got hold of the telegram and charged in a story published in March that Russell was in fact advising Ward, described by the

Herald as a well-known speculator, to buy stocks just before they soared in value. Russell's biographer, Alan Hankinson, is convinced that the charge was 'entirely groundless'. The news that war clouds had disappeared, he argues, was no longer confidential by the time Russell sent the telegram. Moreover, Ward was no longer an active speculator, and in any case the imagined 'tip' reached him too late in the day to be of use. In Hankinson's view, through the telegram Russell was only trying to reassure a troubled friend.

Whatever the truth, the *Herald* story, which was repeated in other American newspapers, damaged Russell's standing in America. Even Lord Lyons was now unwilling to meet him. Russell rebuked himself and wrote in his diary, 'Oh, William Russell, where was your sense? Why did not your pride kill you?' In a letter to Russell, Delane too regretted the correspondent's 'indiscretion' and added, 'how keenly we felt the tarnish it cast on a reputation in which we take so warm and affectionate an interest'. 'Remember,' Delane said, 'that of all the weaknesses poor mankind is cursed with, good nature is the most dangerous.'[44]

Coming on top of the North's unfriendliness to *The Times* and its correspondent, this personal slur drove Russell back to Britain. Delane and Mowbray Morris urged him to remain in America, but Russell had had enough. On 9 April 1862, he sailed for home, thereby denying himself the possibility of offsetting, as a reporter from the scene of action, *The Times*'s anti-Union bent.

Lincoln. Militarily, Lincoln needed a Union commander who brought victories on the ground. On the diplomatic front, he had to ensure that England and France did not intervene in support of the South. Politically, he had to satisfy the North's anti-slavery wing as well as the largely pro-slavery border states, and, in addition, preserve a modicum of unity among the ambitious politicians in his Cabinet and the Congress.

Then there was his family. Early in February 1862, less than a year after they had moved into the White House, Willie, his lively eleven-year-old son, fell seriously ill, most probably from the mansion's unclean water. On 5 February, when the President and his wife received hundreds of visitors at a grand party that had been planned weeks earlier ('the most superb affair of its kind ever seen here', the *Washington Star* would write[45]), the parents slipped away several times to be with Willie. Fifteen days later, Willie died, the second of the Lincoln boys to go very young.

For weeks the devastated mother was unable to leave her bed. The father is reported to have remarked, 'My poor boy. He was too good for this earth ... I know that he is much better off in heaven, but then we loved him so.' To cry, Lincoln would on occasion shut himself in a room. For solace he was obliged to turn more than before to God and to the task of caring for Tad, who was not yet nine. The oldest of the boys, eighteen-year-old Robert, was still at Harvard.

Also wrenching Lincoln's soul was the slavery question, which lay at the heart of the Civil War and yet was intentionally absent from its rhetoric. Hating slavery, but uncertain whether American whites were ready to accept free blacks, Lincoln alternated between waiting for a solution and questing for it. Though he looked for an opportunity to liberate at least some slaves, he was afraid that hostility would surround them when they were freed.

The War. Broadly speaking, the Union's forces had three possible paths into the South. One was by ships along the Atlantic and Gulf coasts, to be followed by forays from the shore into the South's hinterland. Another was overland, from Washington and its neighbourhood, towards Richmond. Further to the west lay a third route, down the Ohio and Mississippi Rivers.

The South responded to the blockade of its ports by building small fast ships that could go around the Union's larger vessels. Yet it could not prevent Union warships from capturing several vital positions. By the end of 1861, all the sea islands of South Carolina were under Union control. Fort Pulaski, off the port city of Savannah in Georgia, was battered into submission in April 1862. While Savannah remained in Confederate hands, it could no longer be used for the South's international commerce.

Also in April 1862, Admiral David Farragut—'southern born and reared'[46]—easily captured the Gulf Coast city of New Orleans, which contained more people than any other southern city. In May, Farragut went up the Mississippi River all the way to the fort city of Vicksburg. Though the admiral was forced to return to New Orleans, the Confederates realized that they could be hit from the South as well.

Ways to enter the South

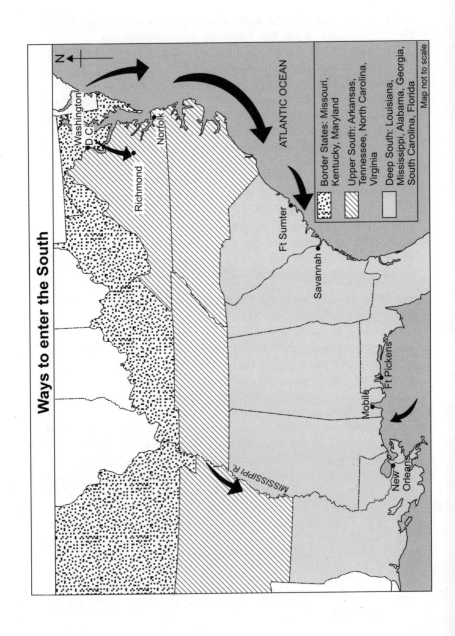

Washington D.C.

Richmond

Norfolk

ATLANTIC OCEAN

Ft Sumter

Savannah

Mobile

Ft Pickens

New Orleans

MISSISSIPPI R.

N

Border States: Missouri, Kentucky, Maryland

Upper South: Arkansas, Tennessee, North Carolina, Virginia

Deep South: Louisiana, Mississippi, Alabama, Georgia, South Carolina, Florida

Map not to scale

They had missed a chance to strike at Washington in the fall of 1861. Believing that foreign intervention in their favour was near at hand, Davis and his colleagues also assumed that if the North moved towards Richmond, the South would be able to repeat the Bull Run repulse. So instead of attacking they waited.

In the western theatre, where General Henry Halleck was in command of the Union's forces, their blue-clad soldiers and steel-clad boats began to show up near the South's river-front defences. In February 1862, Brigadier General Ulysses S. Grant of Illinois won significant victories in this theatre. First he seized Fort Henry in northern Tennessee, down the Tennessee River, which flowed southward off the Mississippi and the Ohio. Only 10 miles east, defended by 17,000 Confederates, lay a crucial southern stronghold, Fort Donelson, on the river Cumberland, which flowed off the Ohio. After four days of fighting, Fort Donelson surrendered, with the Union taking 14,000 prisoners and 60 guns, and Grant becoming famous.

In April, in an encounter at Shiloh in south-western Tennessee, Confederate forces seemed at first to have surprised Grant, but were forced in the end to yield another 7,000 prisoners in what proved to be the Civil War's bloodiest battle thus far. Most of the 3,500 or so killed were teenagers. Still, by the summer of 1862, Union forces in the western theatre had moved about 200 miles southwards across a 300-mile front.

Occurring far away from Washington, and taking a heavy toll, these successes did not satisfy Lincoln, who desired early blows in the direction of Richmond. Already, he had made major changes in military command. Edwin Stanton of Ohio had become Secretary of War, replacing Cameron, who was seen as being corrupt. Radical Republicans demanded a new general-in-chief as well and wanted John Fremont, Missouri's anti-slavery general, to replace General McClellan, a Democrat who was known to be opposed to a growing demand for a proclamation emancipating all slaves.

Judging McClellan to be too slow and cautious, yet not careful enough about protecting Washington, Lincoln removed him in March as general-in-chief while retaining him as the head of the forces in and around Washington—the so-called Army of the Potomac. Halleck was named the head of the Army of the West, and Fremont was made the head of a new 'Mountain' army. The civilian Secretary of War, Stanton, was expected to guide the trio of generals.

Preferring to attack the Confederate capital from the east—from the Atlantic coast of south Virginia—McClellan finally, at the end of March, landed with a large force in Fortress Monroe, between the mouths of the rivers York and James. But he claimed he could not advance towards Richmond without reinforcements from the Washington area that Lincoln was reluctant to spare.

By the middle of May, however, McClellan had reached within 25 miles from Richmond. Earlier, on 3 May, to demonstrate to the general his sense of urgency, Lincoln had himself sailed to Fortress Monroe on a new Treasury cutter, the *Miami*. Treasury Secretary Chase and War Secretary Stanton had gone with the President. At night, Lincoln insisted on 'climbing out on what Virginians called their "sacred soil"'. To Lincoln, it was Union soil as well. He walked up and down on the beach under a bright moon.[47]

McClellan was about to receive reinforcements for a final push when, unexpectedly, Washington was confronted by a threat. In the Shenandoah Valley nearby, 'Stonewall' Jackson had mounted a sudden Confederate attack. Jackson's aim was to relieve the pressure on Richmond, and in this he was wholly successful. The idea of reinforcing McClellan was quickly given up.

At the end of May, following serious injuries to their commander, Joseph E. Johnston, the Confederate 'Army of Northern Virginia', as it came to be called, found a new commander, Robert E. Lee. On 26 June, Lee launched the first of a week-long series of attacks on McClellan's forces, which were forced to retreat, step by step, all the way back to the coast. Both sides suffered heavy casualties in these battles—Lee's army of about 90,000 lost nearly 3,500, with 16,000 wounded, and McClellan's 105,000-strong army counted nearly 2,000 dead and 8,000 wounded.

On 11 July, in another rebuff to McClellan, Lincoln, who by now had discarded the idea of a civilian directing the Union's armies, elevated Halleck as the new general-in-chief. A third blow to McClellan was the appointment at the end of June of John Pope of Illinois as the head of a new Unionist Army of Virginia. At the end of August, however, Pope lost what would become known as the Second Battle of Bull Run. Looking for one or two major victories—no matter what their cost—that could draw England or France onto the southern side, Lee mauled Pope's bigger forces. Bitter recrimination broke out between Pope and McClellan, with the former alleging that McClellan had withheld aid.

Lincoln fully shared the politicians' mistrust of McClellan, yet the general from Pennsylvania was greatly liked by the soldiers, who were convinced of his interest in their lives and morale, and also of his abilities as a leader. Though he was McClellan's superior in rank, Halleck too was inclined to defer to him. When, therefore, it became clear as the summer ended that Lee was about to take the offensive and attack Maryland, McClellan was the only officer that Lincoln could turn to.

On 17 September, the bloodiest day of the Civil War, McClellan's Army of the Potomac fought Lee's Army of Northern Virginia in the Battle of Antietam near Sharpsburg, Maryland. Over 3,600 soldiers were killed and more than 17,000 were wounded on a single day, with the Union army's casualties exceeding those of the Confederates; but since Lee was obliged to return to Virginia, Antietam was seen as a Union victory achieved by McClellan, even though Lee had managed to take the bulk of his forces back with him. And though the North claimed a triumph, there was acknowledgment of Lee's generalship and of the spirit, over a series of battles, of the outnumbered soldiers of the Army of Virginia, which was usually short of weapons, food, clothes and boots.

Indians in the Civil War. Recent research at military archives in America (done by Terry Fenander of Australia, Francis C. Assisi of Kerala and others) suggests that scores of Indians born in places like Calcutta, Bombay, Madras, Burhampur, Pondicherry and Bangalore, but brought by their British masters to America, may have enlisted in the Civil War. In the war's record books, these men from India are described as having 'mulatto, creole, negro, swarthy, bronze or dark' complexions. They all bore Western names, came from 'a variety of backgrounds: sailors, mariners, machinists, farmers, cooks, laborers, as well as the occasional student', and enlisted in the navy, the cavalry, artillery and infantry, serving as sergeant, seaman, fireman, steward or cook.

One of them, Charles Simons, would earn a medal of honour from President Lincoln in 1864; he had attained the rank of a sergeant in Company A of the 9th New Hampshire Infantry. The muster rolls of the USS *Minnesota* show a 'John Burns of Madras, India' as having served in that ship. Then there was a Conjee Rustumjee Cohoujee Bey, apparently a Parsi claiming 'Punjabi royalty as part of his Indian heritage' who landed in New York (via London) in 1848, got converted, acquired the name of Gomez, enlisted in 1862 as a steward in the USS *North Carolina*, and settled after the war in San Francisco, where he died.[48]

Black soldiers and slavery. Despite a 1792 law barring them from bearing arms for US forces, blacks had fought in the 1812 war against England. Yet when, after the Civil War began, many blacks wanted to volunteer, they were prevented or discouraged: it was thought that the sight of armed blacks would alienate northern and border-state whites.

We saw earlier that Fremont's 1861 bid in Missouri to invite slaves to rebel and join the Union army was scotched by Lincoln, who feared secession by the border states. In April and May 1862, Lincoln showed a similar reaction when General David Hunter, commanding Union soldiers in footholds gained on the Atlantic coasts of Georgia and South Carolina, began enlisting blacks in the area.

Hunter was ordered to disband a black unit he had assembled. The general was also ordered to retract a proclamation he had issued that declared slaves in Georgia, South Carolina and Florida to be free. Such declarations were in the President's province and not to be made by a general, and certainly not without consulting Lincoln.

By mid-1862, however, a new policy seemed necessary. An increase in the number of former slaves in areas won by Union forces had combined with a decline in white volunteers, and soldiers were urgently needed. Pressure for taking steps to emancipate slaves had also grown, with influential northerners insisting that white recruitment too would go up if a fight against slavery was joined to the fight against secession.

Moreover, federal commanders were demanding clarity over their obligations to former slaves in newly acquired areas. While some commanders freed the slaves, others sent them back to their masters, either because slaves were seen as their masters' property or because commanders lacked the means to care for them. But was it defensible not to free all slaves in liberated areas? Indeed, was it justifiable for a Union engaged in a war that everyone knew was linked to slavery to accept slavery in the border states?

Acknowledging that the Fugitive Slave Law could not apply to the slaves of rebels, Lincoln had at first canvassed for support for a solution of emancipation-cum-migration. This envisaged the freeing of slaves in the border states plus their voluntary migration to a country in Central America or the Caribbean willing to take them. Such a scheme, thought Lincoln, would solve the question of what should happen with freed blacks and would be welcomed in the border states.

Working patiently during the 1861–62 winter, he won support in his Cabinet and in the Senate for what with some ingenuity he called 'a plan of gradual abolishment of slavery'—'abolition' was still a controversial term. The plan gave each border state the option of emancipating its slaves and, with their consent, deporting them to a place willing to accept them, provided the state found the money for the exercise. But nothing came of it. Though Congress endorsed the scheme, no border state opted for it. Blacks too disliked the scheme, and white radicals attacked it. Some said that any separate space for freed blacks should be created within the USA, not in another country.

In the summer of 1862, as sentiment for a direct challenge to slavery grew, Congress passed the Second Confiscation Act, which laid down that Confederates who did not surrender within sixty days of the Act's passage would be punished by the confiscation of their property and the freeing of their slaves. A slave's foray off the coast of Charleston, South Carolina, had helped create the new mood. On 13 May 1862, after persuading the captain of a transport steamer, the *Planter*, to take him as a deckhand, Robert Smalls stole the boat, which his family and some other blacks had quietly boarded, sailed it past Confederate vessels and lookouts without drawing suspicion, and surrendered it, along with cannon, guns and maps, to a federal fleet.

By now, Lincoln had advanced his own position. After having

been convinced for years that the Constitution entitled a state to permit slavery, he now satisfied himself that 'as commander-in-chief of the army and navy in time of war' he had the 'right to take any measure which may best subdue the enemy'[49]—including a measure declaring that slaves in a seceding or enemy state were free.

On many days in June and July, while waiting in the telegraph office of the War Department for news from the fronts, he quietly worked on a proclamation of emancipation. If slaves anywhere were to be freed, the President should give the order, not a general, not even the legislature. He showed his draft to the Cabinet on 22 July, consulted a few other close friends, and received the sound advice that the proposed proclamation—radical in principle even if limited in application—would go down better if it followed a major military victory. The 17 September battle of Antietam opened his way and Lincoln issued the proclamation by executive order on 22 September.

It declared the freedom of all slaves in any seceding state that did not rejoin the Union by 1 January 1863. A subsequent executive order issued on 1 January declared that the slaves of all eleven seceding states were free. Addressed to areas over which the Union had no control, the proclamation did not free border-state slaves or even slaves in places that Union forces had captured in seceding states. All it amounted to, it seemed, was a threat that secessionists would be punished by emancipation, joined to a promise that re-entering the Union by 1 January would protect slavery.

Yet it wasn't all bark and no bite. For the South's blacks, the proclamation transformed the Union's forces into a liberating army whose arrival they could pray for and assist. In fact, they could do more. By escaping to Union lines, they could join the liberating army.

The proclamation had other effects. Terminating a long and uneasy national silence, it committed the Union to ending slavery. It also had an international impact. Once slavery was declared to be the issue in America, governments in England and France lost the option of helping the South. They could not afford to be seen by their peoples as supporting the cause of slavery.

Horace Greeley, the *New York Tribune* editor, was among those who had been disappointed by Lincoln's caution over slavery. Though thinking for a brief period that seceding states should be allowed to go their way, Greeley was a consistent foe of slavery. On 19 August, in a piece entitled 'The Prayer of Twenty Millions', he had criticized Lincoln for not making slavery the war's dominant issue and had argued that freeing the slaves was the best way of weakening the Confederacy.

The carefully honed answer that Lincoln sent to Greeley gave no hint of the proclamation, ready for release at a moment's notice, that had lain for over a month at his side. Aware that his reply would be seen by everyone, not just the *Tribune*'s readers, Lincoln said on 22 August:

> My paramount object in this struggle *is* to save the Union, and is *not* either to save or to destroy slavery. If I could save the Union without freeing *any* slave I would do it, and if I could save it by freeing *all* the slaves I would do it; and if I could save it by freeing some and leaving others alone I would also do that. What I do about slavery, and the colored race, I do because I believe it helps to save the Union; and what I forbear, I forbear because I do *not* believe it would help to save the Union.
>
> I have here stated my purpose according to my view of *official* duty; and I intend no modification of my oft-expressed *personal* wish that all men everywhere could be free.

In conveying that the Union mattered more to him than slavery, Lincoln was astutely preparing white America for his still secret proclamation. When it came upon them, they should remember its author's commitment to the Union. An attentive reader of the reply to Greeley might have also marked that Lincoln—a careful chooser of words—had said 'paramount', not 'sole', thereby leaving room for an additional purpose for the struggle.[50] And even casual readers would have noticed Lincoln's insertion of his personal dislike of slavery.

In August 1862, this was hardly a rare expression in the American North—radicals were using much stronger language. Yet, other northern whites were having second thoughts. A policy of not talking about slavery had been followed by firm declarations against its extension, including by Lincoln; still, the declarations had led to secession, war, dislocation and shortages.

Democrats were beginning to argue that there were better responses. In retrospect, the Stephen Douglas platform of 1860 appeared to many to be wiser than it had seemed when Lincoln crushed him in the North. Though Douglas had unexpectedly died in June 1861, several were willing to fill his place at the head of the Democratic Party. General McClellan was thought to be one of them. Learning of the proclamation before it was issued, he strongly urged Lincoln to withhold it.[51]

Despite second thoughts in the North over confronting slavery, Lincoln moved in measured yet clear steps towards making slavery more rather than less of an issue. The reply to Greeley was one step. Coming a month later, the emancipation proclamation was the next.

'Indian' revolt. As we know, Lincoln saw the South's secession as rebellion, even as India's British rulers had seen the 1857 events. However, it was a revolt by the Sioux or Dakota 'Indians' of Minnesota in August 1862 that seemed to provide the closest parallel to the India story.

Very much a frontier territory in 1862, far in the north-west for most Americans, Minnesota had annexed lands belonging to the Sioux and other indigenous communities. Delays in the payment of annuities promised when the Sioux yielded their lands led to hunger and anger, and in August, a group of young Sioux men raided a farm, took away eggs and killed five settlers.

The violence quickly spread. Skilfully led by a man called Little Crow, who felt that his standing among his people had been damaged by white men, the Sioux conducted raids and fought battles that took several hundred white lives in August and September. It was the largest massacre of whites by natives in American history. Mail carriers, stage drivers, and women and children were among the whites killed, as also many armed men. Pressed for aid, Lincoln sent General John Pope with a force to Minnesota in September. By early October, the rebellion was put down, and a hundred or so of the Sioux had been killed, but Little Crow managed to slip away to Canada. When he returned with his son the following year, he was shot dead by a settler.

Pope employed pitiless force against the Sioux. 'It is my purpose utterly to exterminate the Sioux if I have the power to do so,' he declared. 'They are to be treated as maniacs or wild beasts.'[52] Little Crow's defiance entered native history, but the Minnesota authorities had found an opportunity for revenge and also for obtaining more land. Minnesota's Republican governor, Alexander Ramsey, called the Sioux 'assassins' and worse, and declared that the community would not be allowed to live in the area. It was expelled to Nebraska and South Dakota.

A military commission tried more than 1,500 captured Sioux, including women and children. Lincoln's instruction was that no one was to be executed without his sanction. On 8 November, he was given a list of 303 Sioux condemned to die. Asking Pope for details, Lincoln also wanted an identification of the guiltier and more influential ones on the list. Pope replied that if the whole lot were not executed, the white population would launch 'an indiscriminate massacre of all the Indians' including 'old men, women, and children'. Agreeing with Pope, Morton Wilkinson, senator from Minnesota, said, 'Either the Indians must be punished according to law, or they will be murdered without law.'

Going through the record of each convicted man, and giving weight to the murder of innocent farmers and to rape, Lincoln selected thirty-nine Sioux to be executed. Writing out each name in his own hand, he 'warned the telegraph operator to be particularly careful, since even a slight error might send the wrong man to his death'.[53] One was pardoned at the last minute, but on 26 December, there occurred the largest public execution in American history, ending the lives of thirty-eight men. Yet Lincoln was told that by not authorizing more executions he had lost popularity and hurt all Republicans in Minnesota.

McClellan removed. In fact, the Republican Party had lost ground all across the country. Lee's attacks in Virginia and Maryland had led to doubts about any early Union victory and it was not possible to hide the lack of trust between the President and McClellan, who had reverted to passivity after the costly Antietam success.

The general's objections to Lincoln's policies went beyond the emancipation proclamation, which others in the Union army also ridiculed. McClellan was critical, at least in private, of the suspension of habeas corpus, which Lincoln felt was justified in theatres of war. McClellan would have spoken publicly of the danger of 'our free institutions' turning into 'a despotism' had he not been counselled that he was under oath to obey his commander-in-chief.[54]

But was the general disloyal as well? There were moments when Lincoln seemed to think so. On 1 October, he made a sudden visit to McClellan's Army of the Potomac in the vicinity of Antietam and spent three nights close to the general and his soldiers. At dawn on 2 October, he took O.M. Hatch, an old friend from Springfield who was accompanying the presidential party, on a walk up a hill from where the two could see the entire camp.

Asked what he saw, Hatch replied, 'The Army of the Potomac.' 'No, Hatch, no,' said Lincoln, 'this is General McClellan's bodyguard.'[55]

Though he never found evidence that McClellan was disloyal, Lincoln doubted his commitment to crushing the Confederacy.[56] More importantly, the soldiers' warm reception to Lincoln in Antietam satisfied him that removing McClellan would not cause a mutiny. On 5 November, Halleck was asked to relieve McClellan and General Ambrose Burnside was given the command of the Army of the Potomac.

Unpopularity. Elections held in October and November 1862 brought large gains to the Democratic Party in the states of New York, Pennsylvania, Ohio, and Lincoln's own Illinois. New York and New Jersey chose Democrats as governors. The *New York Times* called the result a 'vote of want of confidence' in Lincoln.[57]

Lincoln was thankful, however, that Europe had not intervened in the South's favour. England's neutrality did not impress many in the North, where there was sarcasm about the 'neutral English gentleman' who 'deals in Christianity—Episcopalian brand', 'sends his missionaries to bully heathen-land', declares slavery to be 'horrid and scandalous' but is ready to 'fight for the cotton raised by slaves'—and 'forgets how he blew the Sepoys from the guns'.[58]

Still, recognition of the South or even any active mediation by England or France would have been a serious blow to the Union. Neither seemed ruled out. By now, Lancashire was 'feeling the cotton famine',[59] and 'Lord Palmerston in England had decided that summer (1862) on mediation.' Gladstone, Chancellor of the Exchequer in Palmerston's government, had said more:

> We may have our own opinions about slavery, we may be for or against the South, but there is no doubt that Jefferson Davis and other leaders of the South have made an army; they are making, it appears, a Navy; and they have made what is more than either; they have made a Nation.[60]

The North was outraged. But the result of the battle of Antietam helped change minds across the Atlantic, averting 'the danger to the North that the Confederacy would be recognized by the Powers of Europe'.[61] Lincoln's proclamation expelled that danger into the remote distance. Though aristocrats across Europe harboured sympathy for supposed southern gallantry, 'even despotic Russians were opposed to slavery'.[62]

A ploy. Before the proclamation's implementation on 1 January, Lincoln gave the South and the border states another chance, and also showed that he was a man of the centre. The proclamation and the removal of McClellan had offended moderates without pleasing Republican radicals. To remain effective, Lincoln needed to regain America's middle ground.

In a State of the Union address that he sent to Congress on 1 December, he asked for three constitutional amendments. The first would allow any state that abolished slavery by 1900 (in thirty-seven years, that is) to receive US bonds. The second would guarantee the freedom of all slaves who now 'enjoyed actual freedom by the chances of the war' but authorize compensation to masters loyal to the Union. The third would allow Congress to appropriate expenses for any voluntary resettlement of free blacks outside the United States. Aiming to win Americans in the political centre, Lincoln was conveying his keenness on restoring the Union. Once the Union was restored, he believed, slavery would inevitably, if also gradually, disappear.

There was another consideration. If victory came before long, Lincoln's wartime powers would end. During peacetime, the emancipation proclamation, which drew on the legal doctrine of military necessity, would probably be overturned by the courts.

His amendments, on the other hand, would end slavery permanently. Lincoln hoped, too, that portions of the South would secede from the Confederacy and freely rejoin the Union. By now, Union forces had taken parts of Tennessee, Arkansas and Louisiana, and the Norfolk region of Virginia. Would not the whites of these areas vote for the Union, thereby also earning the right to continue with slavery until it died a natural death?

Yet it seemed hardly possible, in the climate of war, to hold calm elections for allowing parts of the South to secede from the South. And, in fact, there was no chance for Lincoln's proposed amendments to get a two-thirds vote in Congress or to pass in two-thirds of the states. Still, Lincoln had underlined his goal of ending slavery and his preference for ending it gradually, with the support of as many Americans as possible.

Though his State of the Union message had an immediate political purpose, in its conclusion, Lincoln inserted words declaring that America's struggle mattered to all of humanity:

> In giving freedom to the slave, we assure freedom to the free—honorable alike in what we give, and what we preserve ... We shall nobly save, or meanly lose, the last best hope of earth.

Setback. The whiskers of McClellan's reluctant replacement, General Burnside, gave birth to the term 'sideburns'. But the general let Lincoln down badly. On 13 December, against the President's advice, he hurled the Army of the Potomac across the Rappahannock River into Fredericksburg in Virginia (halfway to Richmond) and ordered his soldiers to advance up a hill to Marye's Heights, where the Confederates were waiting for them.

Their defeat was total. While a tenth of Burnside's army were left dead, wounded or missing, the Confederates emerged with far fewer losses. The northern public erupted in anger, though not at Burnside or Lincoln. Jokes were still being made about the President's awkward appearance and manner, and a few attacked his competence, with Wilkinson, the Minnesota senator, who hated Lincoln's refusal to send more Sioux Indians to death, even saying that only 'the death of the President and a new administration' could bring about change.[63] But Wilkinson's fuming was an exception and Lincoln's prestige remained fairly high.

His Cabinet was another story. With despondency and hardship increasing—'failure of the army, weight of taxes, depreciation of money, want of cotton ... the continued closure of the Mississippi [River]' and more[64]—a target for wrath was needed, and the Cabinet seemed to provide it. The Cabinet did not function as a team, it was charged, and Seward, the Secretary of State, was accused of undermining Union policies. Smarting at attacks that spared the President, Chase, who was Seward's and indeed Lincoln's rival, told a caucus of Republican senators that on major decisions Lincoln was consulting only Seward, not the Cabinet.

Seward resigned, precipitating a crisis at a difficult moment, but Lincoln resolved it with a brazen move. In the presence of other Cabinet members and a group of senators, Lincoln pointedly asked Chase to say 'whether there had been any want of unity or of sufficient consultation' in the Cabinet. Not really, said Chase. Thus having lost face with the senators, Chase had no option but to resign. After securing two resignations, Lincoln refused to accept either, and the storm passed.[65] If he had let Seward alone or Seward and Chase both go, Lincoln himself would have been the next target of attack.

He learnt some lessons from this episode. Thus far, his Cabinet meetings had been quite informal, with Lincoln at times putting his feet up on a table while other members rested their legs on nearby chairs. After the Chase–Seward episode, the meetings became more regular and more formal. And that direct challenge to Chase notwithstanding, Lincoln became a little more correct and respectful towards his colleagues, who after first swallowing the tale of a lanky rustic somehow stumbling into high office had discovered, to their humiliation, that the casual President was in fact conscious of his intellectual superiority. Following the incident, Lincoln was willing to be more courteous.

Nonetheless, as 1862 ended and the memory of Fredericksburg continued to hurt, Lincoln could at least remind himself that his skills were intact.

~

Ice and snow interrupted the war, but left scope for thought. While Lincoln concluded from the Fredericksburg defeat that he needed a more capable general, Lee inferred that another defiant or daring victory would rekindle the possibility of European intervention.

In January, Lincoln gave command of the Army of the Potomac to General Joseph Hooker, despite reports that Hooker had hindered Burnside's effort at Fredericksburg and had, in fact, spoken out in favour of a dictatorship. In a letter to Hooker, Lincoln recalled the reports, said that the question of a dictatorship would be taken care of after victory, and ended with advice and a call: 'Beware of rashness, but with energy and sleepless vigilance go forward and give us victories.'[66]

At the end of April, Hooker led forces totalling more than 130,000 across the Rappahannock River in the direction of Richmond. The Confederates facing the attack numbered 61,000 in all, but in what admirers would call Lee's 'perfect battle'—he split his limited forces and jumped on an unprotected Union flank—the Army of the Potomac was pushed right back.

'My God! It is horrible—horrible; and to think of it, 130,000 magnificent soldiers cut to pieces by less than 60,000 half-starved ragamuffins,' wrote Greeley in the *New York Tribune*. 'My God! My God!' Lincoln groaned. 'What will the country say?'

By 6 May, when this Battle of Chancellorsville (8 miles to the west of Fredericksburg) ended, each side had seen more than 1,600 killed and more than 9,000 wounded, with more than 8,000 missing in all. Striking though Lee's triumph was, he lost his most valuable colleague, 'Stonewall' Jackson, in this battle. Even more importantly for the Union, the bulk of the Army of the Potomac was left intact, while Lee's much smaller forces had been badly depleted.

Having resisted the Union's attack dramatically, Lee now chose to attack daringly. If he defeated Union forces in the North—if a victory there could crown the Fredericksburg and Chancellorsville results—Europe might indeed still intervene, the Emancipation Proclamation notwithstanding. And northerners might tire of war. Already, as Lee knew, northern newspapers like the *New York World* and the *Chicago Times* were asking for an end to the war.

What followed was the Battle of Gettysburg in Pennsylvania's Adams county, fought from 1 to 3 July between Lee's forces and

The Western Theatre

Eastern cities and battle sites

the Army of the Potomac led by General George Meade (Hooker was removed by Lincoln at the last minute). Marked by swings of fortune, great slaughter, and blunders and bravery on both sides, the battle ended in Unionist victory.

Evidently aiming at Harrisburg, the Pennsylvania capital, which was more than 160 miles north from Fredericksburg (where the bulk of his soldiers were camped), Lee was forced to clash with Meade's army at Gettysburg, 36 miles south of Harrisburg. Like Lee, Meade too had marched north, but along a more eastward line. In this Gettysburg battle, a fifth of the Unionist army of nearly 94,000 were killed, wounded or missing, while the Confederates lost a full third of their 71,000 men, if losses during Lee's retreat are also counted.

In one critical engagement of this epic battle, a Minnesota regiment, outnumbered five-to-one by Confederates, lost 215 of its 262 men. Yet, the North destroyed Lee's hopes of conquering adversity by audacity, and the Civil War's turning point had been reached. However, Meade's failure after victory to pursue Lee's retreating army would for long be cited as a reason for the war's continuance for another two years.

Here we may remember that complaints of the defeated enemy being allowed to get away also featured in the Revolt in India, along with the stories of the many killed and maimed.

At the same time that the Gettysburg battle was being waged, an equally crucial fight took place in the western theatre. Commanding the Union's 'Army of the Tennessee', Major General Ulysses Grant had taken his forces across the Mississippi River and compelled Confederate forces to retreat to the fort city of Vicksburg in the state of Mississippi. A two-month siege that Grant enforced deprived Vicksburg's civilians—women and children included—of goods and supplies, enraging the South.

After 4 July 1863, when Vicksburg surrendered to Grant, the entire length of the great Mississippi River, which started in a lake in the USA's extreme north and entered the sea in New Orleans in the far south, became available to the Union—New Orleans had been in Unionist hands since April 1862. Union ships could now sail freely down the Mississippi from Minnesota all the way to the Gulf.

The Mississippi River formed a natural boundary for several states including Lincoln's Illinois and was central to their economies. Earlier, we noticed Lincoln's warmth for the river when, on meeting Russell for the first time, he remarked that the power of *The Times* was exceeded only by that of the Mississippi. Now he could declare: 'The Father of waters again runs unvexed to the sea.'[67] Control over the Mississippi was as crucial to this war as control over the Ganga had been in India in 1857–59.

Also in July 1863, scores of African-Americans forming the 54th Massachusetts Regiment earned glory though not victory when, commanded by Robert Gould Shaw, son of white abolitionist parents, they stormed Fort Wagner on Morris Island off the South Carolina coast. Though outnumbered and in the end killed or repulsed by Confederate defenders, they had managed to hoist the regiment's colours on a parapet of the fort. Nine days earlier (on 9 July), another lot of black soldiers had gone into combat at Port Hudson in Louisiana.

The South took combat by blacks as a great offence—a black man taking up arms against the Confederates was a capital crime—and southern sentiment 'stiffened'.[68] Yet the North had seen what African-Americans could do in the war, and the events aided their increased mobilization. Despite urgings to Lincoln by Frederick Douglass, the black abolitionist, African-American recruitment had, in fact, received little encouragement until abolitionists in Massachusetts, including Ralph Waldo Emerson, started to assemble the 54th Regiment. Frederick Douglass had been actively involved in this effort, and two of his sons joined the 54th. Both survived. One of them, Lewis Douglass, would later write a first-hand account of the Fort Wagner assault, describing the brave death of Shaw and the courage of black soldiers.

But blacks were not popular with all northern whites. In New York city, where 'Peace Now' was a strong sentiment—especially among the Irish and other immigrants, many of whom had no jobs—African-Americans were seen as having caused the war. Riots over a draft announced in the wake of the Gettysburg battle took a number of black lives in the city.

In August, calling on Lincoln at the White House, Frederick Douglass complained that the President was vacillating about the value of black troops. Lincoln replied, 'I think it cannot be shown that once when I have taken a position I have ever retreated from it.'[69] By the end of the year, more than 100,000 blacks were serving in the Union armies.

Atrocities. 'Conduct warfare on the most chivalrous principles,' Russell would write, 'there must be a touch of murder about it, and the assassin will lurk under fine phrases. The most civilized troops will commit excesses and cruelties, which must go unpunished . . .'[70]

The atrocities committed by both sides in the Indian Revolt were not absent in the American Civil War. Fury at the involvement of black soldiers increased the willingness to perpetrate them. The North was viewed as having made up its mind to destroy southern civilization itself—Grant's siege of Vicksburg was cited as proof.

The adversary's civilian sympathizers were not always safe. August 1863 saw a massacre in the anti-slavery town of Lawrence, Kansas; it had been ordered by a Confederate guerrilla, William Quantrill, in revenge for the deaths in prison (from a floor collapse) of four women related to Quantrill's men. Although Lawrence's women and children were spared, no fewer than 150 men were killed on a single day.

Black prisoners of war were killed in Ocala, Florida, and surrendering black and white soldiers at Fort Pillow in Tennessee were shown no mercy. 'Human blood stood about in pools,' a Confederate soldier would record.'[71] Later, in revenge, a dozen bayonets and a dozen bullets silenced a captured southern soldier begging for his life.[72]

Gettysburg Address. Gettysburg had made a critical difference and relieved Lincoln, but for some time he found it hard to forgive Meade for not chasing the retreating Lee. He had even written out a letter blaming the general: '[Lee] was within your grasp, and to have closed upon him would . . . have ended the war. As it is the war will be prolonged indefinitely.'

Recognizing, however, that he did not know all the circumstances, Lincoln did not sign or post the letter. The truth was that having lost innumerable soldiers and some of his ablest generals, and having had 'on many nights not a wink of sleep' or any time during the day to wash his hands or face, Meade was in no position to attack Lee's forces on the run.[73] With an eventual Unionist victory no more in doubt, popular longing in the North was simple: 'Let the war end and the Union be restored.' To most, including a majority of politicians, the terms of peace did not greatly matter. All they desired was an early return to what existed before the costly war.

Also wanting the war to end and the Union restored, Lincoln wanted something more: a fresh commitment to equality. White Americans needed to recognize the truth of their forefathers' word, so often denied in practice, that all humans were created equal. Without such a realization, the costly war would turn out to be a war in vain. He hinted at this need in a few 'public' letters to politicians in different parts of America, but spotted an ideal platform for articulating it when he was invited to the dedication of a new cemetery in Gettysburg where thousands of 'imperfectly identified and hastily buried' bodies of American soldiers were going to be reinterred.[74]

Set for 19 November 1863 on the grounds adjoining one of Gettysburg's battlefields, the ceremony was bound to be both solemn and stirring. A famous orator, someone with few equals in the knowledge of history or in eloquence, had been selected for the occasion—Edward Everett, former president of Harvard College, former Secretary of State, and former senator. As the nation's President, Lincoln was invited to offer a few remarks dedicating the grounds to their sacred use.

Lincoln agreed. What he wanted to say could be clothed in 'a few remarks'. We are told that 'he took the assignment very seriously'.[75] To learn the detailed topography of the site, he summoned to the White House the landscape architect designing the new cemetery, and he started jotting down his ideas several days before the event.

His son Tad fell ill the day Lincoln was to leave for Gettysburg. Remembering the deaths of two of her boys, Mary Todd Lincoln demanded that her husband cancel his journey, but Lincoln ignored her pleas and on the afternoon of 18 November, took the special four-coach train in which some members of his Cabinet and of the diplomatic corps, the President's secretaries, Nicolay and Hay, and his black manservant, William Johnson, also travelled.

A telegram stating that Tad was doing better relieved Lincoln shortly after he reached Gettysburg at night, and he wrote out a final version of his speech. In the morning, he put on a new black suit, white gloves, and his trademark stovepipe hat that had a black band showing that the father was still mourning for Willie. Then Lincoln mounted a horse that seemed too small for him, waited for others to assemble, and rode slowly with them to the burial ground, which was less than a mile away.

The living and the dead merge at a cemetery, and the merger can hit very hard when those to be buried are counted in the thousands. The countryside cemetery of Gettysburg with its far horizons and fresh history would have produced the profoundest emotions in Lincoln, who was always stirred even by a plain rural scene. As a young man, he had written a poem on seeing a stretch of land that had nurtured him in childhood:

> The very spot where grew the bread
> That formed my bones, I see.
> How strange, old field, on thee to tread
> And feel I'm part of thee.[76]

Since humans tread also on fellow humans, wars result, and grain fields are turned into burial grounds. The American who best knew the history of battles, battlefields and burials, and who knew also how to tell that history, was Edward Everett. So dedicated was Everett to oratory that it was said that he 'ran for and held office in order to attract an audience for his speeches'.[77] To do justice to the battle and the dead of Gettysburg at what would be his crowning oratorical offering, Everett had talked at length with General Meade.

'Standing beneath this serene sky,' his oration began, 'overlooking these broad fields now reposing from the labors of the waning year, the mighty Alleghenies dimly towering before us, the graves of our brethren beneath our feet, it is with hesitation that I raise my poor voice to break the eloquent silence of God and Nature.'

The two-hour oration contained a description of burials of heroes in ancient Greece, an analysis of why the Civil War had occurred, a day-by-day story of the battle of Gettysburg, and reflections on how America was likely to be reunited. Everett did not read from his notes, which lay next to him; he had committed everything to memory. In conclusion, he said:

> [W]herever throughout the civilized world the accounts of this great warfare are read, and down to the latest period of recorded time, in the glorious annals of our common country, there will be no brighter page than that which relates The Battles of Gettysburg.[78]

Though towards the end of Everett's performance there was some mild movement in the audience, which was of thousands, his words had been gripping. Some in the audience were at times in tears. According to Nicolay and Hay, Lincoln's young secretaries, '[F]or the space of two hours [Everett] held his listeners spellbound by the rare power of his art.'[79] When the oration ended, Lincoln pressed Everett's hand with great fervour.

Lincoln's own speech, delivered in 'his high, penetrating voice' with, it seems, a Kentucky accent,[80] lasted less than three minutes. Witnesses later recalled that Lincoln held the text in his hands, but disagreed on whether he looked at it while speaking.

> Fourscore and seven years ago our fathers brought forth on this continent a new nation, conceived in liberty and dedicated to the proposition that all men are created equal. Now we are engaged in a great civil war, testing whether that nation or any nation so conceived and so dedicated can long endure. We are met on a great battlefield of that war. We have come to dedicate a portion of that field as a final resting-place for those who here gave their lives that that nation might live.
>
> It is altogether fitting and proper that we should do this. But in a larger sense, we cannot dedicate, we cannot consecrate, we cannot hallow this ground. The brave men, living and dead who struggled here have consecrated it far above our poor power to add or detract. The world will little note nor long remember what we say here, but it can never forget what they did here.
>
> It is for us the living rather to be dedicated here to the unfinished work which they who fought here have thus far so nobly advanced. It is rather for us to be here dedicated to the great task remaining before us—that from these honored dead we take increased devotion to that cause for which they gave the last full measure of devotion— that we here highly resolve that these dead shall not have died in vain, that this nation under God shall have a new birth of freedom,

and that government of the people, by the people, for the people shall not perish from the earth.

Why, proving Lincoln wrong, his 270 or so words of 19 November 1863 are remembered more than the deeds that called for them is the theme of several books, including Garry Wills' brilliant *Lincoln at Gettysburg*, and need not detain us. Yet we may note that the name 'Gettysburg' does not feature in Lincoln's short speech, nor does slavery, or the Union, or the South, or even the USA.

Unlike Everett, Lincoln was more than a scholar—he was an artist. At Gettysburg, despite learning what he could about its topography, despite a searing awareness of the sacrifice at Gettysburg, despite the significance of its outcome in the North's favour, Lincoln addressed not so much the particular as the general, not so much an immediate question as an ever-present one, not so much a national mood as a universal wish. And he compressed his ideas into bare bones, retaining only the essential, and restraining his passion in order to deepen its effect.

This very human, apparently laid-back and yet oft-impatient President had arrived at Gettysburg with clear ideas that he wanted engraved on minds. Looking for a meaning for America's cumulative killings—for a purpose for the war and also for America as a nation and a Union—he had rediscovered that meaning in the Declaration's proposition, 'All Men Are Created Equal.'

They may not have all realized it, but the soldiers dying for the Union and the citizens working and paying taxes for it were, to Lincoln, engaged in proclaiming that belief. And all hearing or reading the speech realized that 'the people' mentioned thrice in its final phrase included persons of every race.

On receiving the invitation to Gettysburg, Lincoln had known *instinctively* that there he would connect at once to the soldier and his family, but he also saw *prophetically* that from there he might connect to all of America and perhaps to people everywhere. Where Everett magnificently told the story of *a* battle in *a* place at *a* time, Lincoln spelled out an idea for all places and all times. The setting of a great battle and a great cemetery *was* needed to give power to his words. Yet the words transcended their setting, so that today they, the words, provide the setting for the event and the place.

Not everyone present on 19 November grasped the power of the address, but quite a few did, as did others who read it, and as did much of the press. 'The dedicatory remarks by President Lincoln will live among the annals of men,' said the *Chicago Tribune*. A paper in Springfield, Massachusetts, the *Republican*, wrote that Lincoln's 'little speech' was 'deep in feeling, compact in thought and expression, and tasteful and elegant in every word and comma'. And Ralph Waldo Emerson thought, in an appraisal echoed in later decades, that the 'brief speech at Gettysburg will not easily be surpassed by words on any recorded occasion.'[81]

Fully understanding Lincoln's meaning and goal, critics like the *New York World* and the *Chicago Times* challenged his reading of history, with the former claiming that '*This* United States' was the product *not* of the Declaration of Independence but 'of a compact known as the Constitution'. Attacking the speech as a 'perversion of history', the *Chicago Times* insisted that the officers and soldiers who died at Gettysburg were upholding the Constitution and the Union, not 'the proposition that all men are created equal'.[82]

Next President. At least in a couple of respects, the America we are looking at was the same as present-day America—an ongoing war did not dampen curiosity about the next presidential election, which was due at the end of 1864, and electoral prospects seemed tied to the war's results.

Lincoln was eager to be re-elected. But he did not say this freely even to himself, and certainly not to others. That sort of honesty was contrary to American conventions in the 1860s. Searching his heart, he would truthfully admit some 'personal vanity or ambition'. Re-election would mean endorsement of his performance and he had 'the common pride of humanity' to desire that endorsement.[83]

But it was more than vanity: Lincoln felt he could 'better serve the nation in its need and peril than any new man'.[84] The presidency of nearly three years had been a difficult burden. But Mary Todd was keen to continue in the White House, and apart from personal desires Lincoln thought that as one who had been 'severely schooled' he might 'better finish a difficult task'.[85] We have to infer, in addition, that he thought himself more fitted than the others to reunite a bitterly divided people.

When, therefore, in Fall 1863 a friend wanted to know, on behalf also of other friends, what his private thinking was, Lincoln replied that a second term would be both 'a great honor' and 'a great labor' but, if offered, he 'perhaps ... would not decline'.[86]

But was he going to be offered it? Would the Republicans renominate, and American voters re-elect, him? In large part that depended on the war's results—on the time, lives, and money needed to overpower a South that was defeated but defiant. McClellan, the general dismissed by Lincoln, had emerged as the leading Democratic contender. However, Democrats were divided between supporters of the war and others who wanted immediate peace by settling with the South.

For ten difficult months after the Gettysburg Address, prospects for Lincoln's re-election or an early conclusion of the war did not look bright. He was observed in moods of dejection, pessimism, or, at times, of something close to fatalism. These moods reflected the depth of his longings and did not affect his political instincts, which remained sharp.

In December 1863, Lincoln addressed the tough question of how Southern states might return to the Union. In the North, opinions ranged from (at one extreme) unconditionally welcoming back every southern state willing to rejoin to (at the other end) treating the whole of the South as a conquered province.

In a politically adroit proclamation of amnesty, Lincoln announced that, barring senior Confederate officers, every rebel swearing allegiance to the Union and acceptance of Union laws regarding slavery would be pardoned. The proclamation added that a government established in a southern state by voters taking the pledge would be recognized by the Union, provided such voters comprised at least one-tenth of the state's 1860 voting list.

During the 1863–64 winter, the Lincolns took care to entertain a number of the influential at the White House. Thinking about another term helped Mary in her battles with grief and with a discontent that did not seem to leave her. She also drew some consolation from comparing her state with that of her youngest half sister, Emilie Todd Helm, who passed through the White

House in the fall of 1863, after her husband, a Confederate general, had been killed in combat. Emilie's week-long stay in the White House, en route to her home in Kentucky, was not however appreciated by battle-scarred Unionists who heard that she spoke freely in the White House of her loyalty to the South.

Though nurturing his prospects, Lincoln was far from sure that he would be asked to run again. The war's length and cost had created a desire for change among Republicans. Salmon Chase, the Treasury Secretary, thought that the White House needed a clear mind and firm hands—like his own, for example. General Fremont, the radical Republican who had unsuccessfully sought the presidency in 1856, thought he could bring the war to a speedy conclusion.

Less likely than Lincoln to attract the national electorate, Chase and Fremont were however capable of obstructing Lincoln's nomination, and of seeking advantage from an old American sentiment, which had nothing to do with Lincoln's performance, in favour of rotation.

In general, dissatisfied Republicans were divided between those who thought that Lincoln was too conservative and others who thought him too radical. Radical Republicans blamed Lincoln for, among other things, not involving the blacks enough. Conservative Republicans criticized Lincoln for failing to offer an olive branch to a South that knew it could not win and was ready, they believed, to end the war if assured of generous terms, including over slavery. This was also the Democrats' charge against Lincoln.

Within the Republican Party, the radicals were more influential than the Conservatives, but American voters overall were more cautious. Recognizing that Lincoln's desire to steer a middle course, joined now to a clear commitment to end slavery, was probably wise, many Americans were nonetheless disappointed by the war's slow progress. Only a few, however, held the President personally responsible. For most Americans, the war was the generals' business.

In November 1863, Generals Ulysses Grant, William Sherman and George Thomas had indeed given the Unionists a notable victory, clearing most of Tennessee of Confederates and opening the path for a march into Georgia, the South's heartland. Two months before that, yielding to diplomatic pressure from Lincoln and Seward, British authorities had seized two ironclad warships, fitted with lethal underwater rams and capable of disabling the Union's blockading vessels, that were being built for the Confederates in an English shipyard.

But for many months after November, Unionist forces failed to advance. Looking for a new army leader, Lincoln thought of Grant. But the general had been spoken of as a possible President, including by the *New York Herald*. Would political ambition affect the general's judgement on military strategy? Even if it did not, should Lincoln be gifting a springboard to a possible rival? He sent an intermediary to probe Grant's intentions.

Once he was shown a letter from Grant pledging that nothing would persuade him to be a candidate for President, Lincoln summoned the general from the western front, appointed him as general-in-chief *and* the head of the Army of the Potomac, and backed his promotion as the country's first lieutenant general since George Washington.

Grant, who like Lincoln hailed from Illinois, had fought in the Mexican War of the 1840s, but had not liked its goal. He was convinced that that war had been waged 'to acquire territory out of which [additional] slave states might be formed'.[87] As we had seen much earlier, this was also Lincoln's view of the Mexican War. In March 1864, Grant became the general-in-chief of a war waged at first to end secession, but now aimed also at ending slavery. However, military gains did not follow Grant's elevation.

In April, a daring Unionist raid on Richmond (approved by Lincoln) ended in complete failure and in embarrassing allegations that the raiders had intended to abduct Jefferson Davis, the Confederate President. Then, in May, in another fierce battle fought in Virginia, Robert E. Lee's smaller forces again triumphed over the Unionist side, this time led by Grant. Not only that, over a two-week period, the Army of the Potomac lost, through death and injury, nearly 32,000 men.

Lincoln tried to make sense of these jolting reverses and asked himself whether 'this terrible, bloody war' could have been avoided. An observer found the President 'pacing back and forth a narrow passage leading to one of the windows, his hands behind him, great black rings under his eyes, his head bent forward upon his breast . . . a picture of . . . sorrow, care, and anxiety'.[88]

Much of America was now 'wild for peace'[89] and Republican prospects seemed bleak. Though they did not add up to much, some of Lincoln's radical critics met in Cleveland, Ohio, at the end of May, nominated Fremont for President, and demanded a constitutional amendment to ban slavery. A few days later, however, many more Republicans and also several pro-war Democrats assembled at a convention in Baltimore, Maryland, and chose Lincoln as the nominee of a new 'National Union' party that incorporated the old Republican Party. Interestingly, participants at this convention included a few southern delegates from Louisiana, Tennessee and Arkansas who had emerged out of Lincoln's 'ten per cent' scheme for southern representation.

At the suggestion of Lincoln (who did not attend), the convention stole the Cleveland gathering's chief agenda and asked for a constitutional amendment against slavery. Also, the convention voted for Andrew Johnson, a southern pro-war Democrat, as its vice-presidential nominee. A Tennessee senator who remained loyal to the Union, Johnson had been named military governor of Tennessee by Lincoln after portions of that state were captured by the North in 1862.

Though some Republicans disputed the legitimacy of the Baltimore convention and its nomination of Lincoln, they could not put forward an alternative name. The Republican keenest to replace Lincoln, Treasury Secretary Salmon Chase, lacked the courage to declare his candidacy, but he could not resist undermining Lincoln in conversations with fellow Republicans.

Chase's innuendos did not remain a secret. Mary Lincoln said he should not be invited to White House occasions and the President himself felt he had had enough of the Secretary. After being renominated at Baltimore, Lincoln moved against Chase by rejecting the latter's candidate for a vacant post in Chase's own Treasury Department. When Chase sent in his resignation, it was, to his surprise, accepted.

Yet, Grant's defeat in Virginia in May and subsequent inability to push Lee into retreat had disappointed Lincoln. The general from Illinois did have a strategy—attrition. He would squeeze Lee's forces in Virginia through unceasing pressure applied by the Union's larger numbers. But attrition was not going to yield quick results. In July, Grant again seemed to let Lincoln down. With the general-in-chief engaged deep inside Virginia, Confederate bands freely raided Washington's outskirts. Despite Lincoln's urgent messages, Grant seemed slow in sending reinforcements to the capital.

That Republicans seemed unenthusiastic about his re-election didn't help Lincoln's low spirits, and dejection may have contributed to the ruthlessness and short temper seen in him at this time. Some of the harshness was unavoidable. With death and desertions depleting the Union's seemingly motionless army, Lincoln was forced to order a draft of 500,000 men in February 1864, and of another 200,000 in March.

It was widely understood that conscription was needed to coerce a defiant South, but when the draft faced hurdles from judges willing to employ the writ of habeas corpus, and Lincoln sounded ready to jail or exile the judges, quite a few felt that he was going too far. Chase (before his resignation) and other Cabinet members succeeded in persuading Lincoln against the idea of punishing judges, yet habeas corpus was suspended throughout the country.

When the South threatened to shoot captured black soldiers, Lincoln issued an order for retaliation, declaring that for every captured Union soldier killed, a rebel soldier would be executed, and that for every soldier enslaved by the South, a rebel would face hard labour. Later, recognizing that 'blood cannot restore blood', he would regret this order, which was never carried out.[90]

In May, he ordered stern action against two newspapers in New York, the *World* and the *Journal of Commerce*, for publishing a bogus presidential 'proclamation' for a draft of another 400,000 men. Authored by two reporters who had imitated Lincoln's style, the 'proclamation' was designed to generate a fortune in the gold market. As anticipated, the price of gold rose sharply. An enraged Lincoln, supported by Stanton, the War Secretary, directed the army to seize 'by military force' the premises of the two papers and ordered the arrest of their editors and owners. They were set free as soon as the reporters' responsibility was discovered, and the papers quickly resumed publication, but the reporters were sent to a military prison. Lincoln had displayed his tough and perhaps also authoritarian side.[91]

Often, however, he was thwarted. Despite Lincoln's strong urging and the call from the Baltimore convention, a sufficient majority could not be found in Congress to adopt the Thirteenth Amendment abolishing slavery.

In July, Horace Greeley of the *Tribune*, now writing increasingly critically of the cost of the war, asked Lincoln to respond positively to what Greeley claimed was a peace feeler from the Confederates. Three Confederate emissaries, Greeley reported, were on the Canadian side of the Niagara Falls with full authority to negotiate peace. The editor advised that Lincoln should offer them generous conditions for ending the war. It would prove his keenness for peace and improve prospects for his re-election.

Lincoln suspected (rightly, it would later be found) that the real aim of the Confederate emissaries was to influence the presidential election, not to probe peace. Yet Greeley had put him on the spot. If he did not respond as advised, Greeley and the *Tribune* would allege before all of America that Lincoln was not interested in peace.

The President's solution was to send Greeley a note addressed 'To Whom It May Concern' which said that his government would consider 'any proposition' from the South 'which embraces the restoration of peace, the integrity of the whole Union, and the abandonment of slavery'.[92] As expected by Lincoln, the Confederates not only dismissed, but also published his note. Lincoln was 'exposed' as one linking peace to the ending of slavery.

In the summer of 1864, Lincoln did not wholly mind such an image, but the 'To Whom It May Concern' note killed his alliance with the pro-war Democrats, who objected to making the abandonment of slavery a precondition for talks with the South. The *New York Herald* declared that the note had 'sealed Lincoln's fate in the coming Presidential campaign'.[93]

For a while Lincoln thought he might rephrase his note to mollify the pro-war Democrats, but when he tried out a new wording on Frederick Douglass, the African-American spokesman replied, his eyes flashing with anger, that it would 'be taken as a complete surrender of your anti-slavery policy'.[94]

At this, and remembering also that by this time about 200,000 blacks were fighting for the Union, Lincoln abandoned the idea of amending his note. As a result, he lost the support not only of the pro-war Democrats, but also of many conservative or moderate Republicans. Yet, prompted by Douglass, he had lived up to his Gettysburg Address. Moreover, and this was of practical relevance, it was now harder for Chase or someone like him to snatch the mantle of slavery abolition from Lincoln.

Another political storm was created when, also in July, Lincoln chose not to sign the Wade–Davis Bill, a congressional measure named after the Republican chairmen of the House and Senate committees that sponsored it. The bill sought to replace Lincoln's requirements for a southern state to return to the Union with far more stringent criteria. Lincoln followed up with a proclamation defending his refusal to sign. Unabashedly seeing himself as a person America needed at this time, Lincoln was not going to allow his standing to be damaged, or his careful work spoilt, by politicians to whom headlines seemed to matter more than results.

Many Republican leaders were outraged, however. And Lincoln's prospects were not improved when, at the end of July, a large number of new casualties were reported from Virginia, where Grant had been trying for weeks to take the strategically located town of Petersburg, about 30 miles south of Richmond. The casualties were the consequence of a desperate effort to shatter Petersburg's defences. A huge mine was exploded under the Confederate line, and about 15,000 Union soldiers were led into the crater created by the explosion; but within hours about 4,000 of them were killed or wounded, and the rest were obliged to withdraw.

As if this was not bad enough, Wade and Davis came out on 5 August with a 'manifesto' fiercely criticizing Lincoln's treatment of their bill, whereupon the *Herald* wrote of Lincoln as 'an egregious failure' who should 'retire from the position to which, in an evil hour, he was exalted'.[95]

Weighed down during this dreadful summer by the casualties for which, as President, he felt ultimate responsibility, and also by the mounting criticism directed at him—and at times also at his wife for her apparent extravagance—Lincoln became 'more and more gaunt and the furrows on his cheek and brow bit deep'. [96] His ready humour and ever-present sense of irony helping, but not sufficing, Lincoln again, it seems, sought succour from a power higher than human.

Lincoln needed an assurance, or an explanation, beyond what his reasoning provided. Why so many lives had been lost, how many more would go, how long the war would go on, why good and able people were unhappy with him—questions like these did not have clear replies. Even a much simpler question, why he, Lincoln, departing from the inaugural pledge not to interfere with slavery, had called for emancipation and abolition, did not have an obvious answer. A Kentucky editor had asked that question. Lincoln answered, 'I claim not to have controlled events, but confess plainly that events have controlled me.'[97] A higher, if at times baffling, purpose, he thought, was at work, in his mind and in America's life.

Yet by August, Lincoln was quite pessimistic. Stories surfaced that Grant (who remained popular despite the May defeat and the July deaths) would again be tapped, this time by a new Republican convention. On 18 August, about twenty-five leading radicals and Lincoln-foes met in New York in the home of the city's mayor to devise a plan to replace Lincoln. They included Wade, Davis, Massachusetts Governor John Andrew, editor Greeley, and a few others. Though Chase and Sumner, the Massachusetts senator, did not join, their support was assumed, and the conclave decided to organize another Republican convention at the end of September.

Learning of what was being planned, Lincoln once more asked a close friend of Grant to sound out the general. To Lincoln's huge relief, Grant's unqualified response was that Lincoln's re-election was as important as the army's victory.[98]

But even if there would not be a serious Republican challenger, would Lincoln defeat the Democratic candidate, who was to be named at the end of August? On 22 August, Lincoln was warned by Raymond, the head of the executive committee of his party, that the tide was running 'strongly against us'. They were likely to lose New York, Illinois, Indiana, and Pennsylvania to the Democrats, Lincoln was informed. His own assessment was even more adverse. Lincoln thought that without some great change, he would be 'badly beaten'.[99] On 23 August, he actually drafted and signed a memorandum that said that his defeat was 'exceedingly probable' and assured his cooperation to the winner for saving the Union.

Lincoln was certain that the likely Democratic nominee—and likely victor—General George McClellan, would be pressed by his party to seek an armistice and, if need be, concede Confederate independence. Believing that McClellan would not want to go that far, Lincoln committed himself to supporting him during the critical days between election and inauguration.

The tide turned in Lincoln's favour at the Democratic National Convention, held in Chicago at the end of August. McClellan, the pro-war Democrat, was indeed nominated, but anti-war Democrats dictated a suicidal platform that demanded 'a cessation of hostilities' because, it was claimed, the four-year effort 'to restore the Union by the experiment of war' had failed.[100] Not willing to tell the men he had led into battle that their effort had failed or that their fellows had died in vain, McClellan tried to reject his party's platform, but the damage had been done.

Within days, on 4 September, came a message from General Sherman in Georgia: 'Atlanta is ours.' Partially besieged by Sherman's troops, a great southern city had evacuated and the Unionists had moved in. Almost immediately thereafter, word came that Mobile, Alabama, the last important Gulf port that the Confederates controlled, had been taken by Rear Admiral David Farragut.

Lincoln announced a day of thanksgiving for 'the signal success that Divine Providence' had made possible, and almost everyone realized that his prospects had suddenly become much brighter.

For a few days Lincoln's Republican foes tried to continue in opposition or suggested that he should 'kindly and patriotically withdraw'.[101] But the plan for a new convention and candidate fizzled out, and before long, all the rivals and critics—including Chase, Sumner, Wade, Davis and Greeley—one by one voiced their support for Lincoln, some more feebly than others and some without taking his name.

If Providence had intervened in Lincoln's favour, it also forced his hand. Several anti-Lincoln men obtained a price for their switch—an appointment here of a favourite, a removal there of a foe, or whatever. Salmon Chase, for one, became Chief Justice of

America, replacing Taney (linked forever to the Dred Scott judgment), who died in October. The radicals obtained the ouster of Montgomery Blair, postmaster general in the Lincoln Cabinet, who had criticized abolitionists. To placate influential holdouts, the collector of customs in New York city had to be replaced. Fremont, who sought no price, also withdrew from the race, saying that though Lincoln had been a failure, McClellan would restore the Union with slavery intact.

On election day in November, Lincoln won every state except New Jersey, Delaware, and Kentucky. Despite the handicap of his platform, McClellan won 45 per cent of the vote, an index of the dislike of the war's cost. Yet Lincoln's victory was clear. In the electoral college, it was overwhelming—212 against 21.

Inside the South. From the summer of 1863—after Lee's failure to win at Gettysburg in the east and the fall of Vicksburg in the west—the South had known clearly and well that its subjugation could be delayed, but not prevented. Yet it chose to fight on. Let there be more destruction and new devastation, said the spirit ruling its heart, but let not history record that the South had yielded.

For another year, the South defied and delayed the North, but morale fell and anger rose at Lincoln's re-election, which was interpreted as evidence that northerners were 'insatiable for our blood'.[102] Earlier, Confederate agents had used money to influence Chicago's Democratic convention and later, on election day, to incite violence in Chicago and New York. With Unionist forces closing in, some minds in the South turned to the idea of assassinating or kidnapping Lincoln.

But faith in the virtues of slavery had ebbed. In fact, the South needed slaves as soldiers. Blacks were drafted into Confederate units, and at the end of December, Jefferson Davis, the Confederate President, sent Duncan Kenner, a rich Louisiana planter, to Europe with an offer to emancipate all slaves if England and France would recognize the Confederacy. The offer was at least two years too late.

Though he typified the South's unyielding mood, Mississippi's Davis had not given Virginia's Lee the authority or support deserved by the brilliant general. Having served as an officer in the war with Mexico in the 1840s and as Secretary of War in the mid-1850s, President Davis thought himself qualified, not merely entitled, to take military decisions. It was not until 31 January 1865 that he made Lee general-in-chief in the Confederacy.

In December 1864, Grant was applying ever greater pressure on Lee's forces and on Richmond, while Sherman in Georgia and Thomas in Tennessee continued to penetrate deeper inside southern territory. On 15 November, Sherman had begun his 300-mile march with more than 60,000 soldiers from Atlanta to Georgia's Atlantic coast.

The Union army set Atlanta ablaze as the march to the southeast commenced. Instructed to prevent the state from sending any assistance whatsoever to Lee in Richmond, the army confiscated food, burnt farms, and destroyed Georgia's bridges and rail lines along the way. Thousands of slaves left their plantations and joined Sherman's advancing columns (some of these deserting slaves would die in the countryside during the march), but the whites of Georgia would not forget the destruction wrought by the marching columns.

The 13,000 or so Confederate soldiers who remained in the area to fight Sherman's army could do nothing as rail lines were broken up, heated over fires, and twisted around tree trunks. These would be remembered as Sherman's neckties. 'He left behind him a blackened trail, and hatreds which pursue his memory to this day,' Churchill would write almost a century later.[103]

On 10 December, Sherman's army reached the outskirts of Savannah, Georgia's biggest port city. About 10,000 Confederates were entrenched inside, but Sherman's notice that he would not hesitate to cannonade and starve the city produced its surrender in eleven days. In a message to Lincoln, Sherman spoke of Savannah as a Christmas present for the Union.

A Confederate general called John Bell 'Sam' Hood, a Kentucky-born Texan and one of the South's fiercest fighters, had eased Sherman's passage across Georgia by removing his troops from Atlanta before Sherman took that city. Hood thought he would use his troops, numbering about 22,000, in attack, not in defence. He would blast the Unionists out of Tennessee.

It was a reckless idea. On 30 November in Franklin, Tennessee, and two weeks later in Nashville, Tennessee, Hood's forces were slaughtered by the 55,000 or so Unionists led by a Virginian, George Thomas. Not the Unionists, but the Confederates had been eliminated from Tennessee, while in Georgia, Sherman had been freed from any serious resistance.

The governors of Georgia and North Carolina said they would make peace with the Unionists on their own if Davis did not, and individual members in the Confederate House of Representatives asked for a cessation of hostilities. At the end of the year, Lincoln encouraged such voices by declaring that southern soldiers could 'at any moment have peace simply by laying down their arms and submitting to the national authority'.[104]

Refusing to surrender, Jefferson Davis was nonetheless willing to send negotiators. On 3 February 1865, for the first time after the start of the war, Lincoln met three Confederate leaders, including Alexander Stephens, their Vice-President. Held just outside Washington on the *River Queen*, the Presidential boat, the talks failed, largely over the question of slavery. Reminding the delegation that the South had in effect given up slavery, Lincoln also indicated that money might be advanced for emancipation, but a formal rejection of slavery was too much for the delegation to swallow.

For the Union, the rejection was about to be enshrined in the Constitution as the Thirteenth Amendment, which Congress passed on 1 February. Lincoln had worked hard to obtain the necessary two-thirds majority which, as we saw, Congress had denied him nine months earlier. Using all his authority and charm, he persuaded several doubting Democratic and border-state congressmen to now support the amendment.

Later, it would be alleged, we do not know how factually, that Lincoln used something more—that he obtained the withdrawal of a bill for regulating a railroad company in order to win a few congressional votes for the amendment—and it would be said, on the basis of the allegation, that 'the greatest measure of the 19th century was passed by corruption, aided and abetted by the purest man in America'.[105]

The Richmond to which the Confederate emissaries returned in February 1865 was solemn but doomed. The news from Petersburg, a vital gate for Richmond's supplies, was that it would not hold out for much longer against the squeeze that Grant had been applying for nine continuous months. Once Petersburg went, Richmond would go too.

South Carolina, the first state to secede, lay just to the north of Savannah. To Sherman it merited all the wrath his army could summon, and his marching columns razed the state in January and February. On 17 February, the city of Columbia surrendered. Much of it was burnt down, with some fires evidently started by Confederates to deny supplies to the army of one they saw as the devil. Two weeks later, Charleston, a pride of the South and the port from where Confederates had fired the Civil War's first shots, fell without a fight.

Urge to heal. Like Jefferson Davis, Lincoln could have done better at handling his generals. Yet his clarity and firmness had saved the Union. Despite a predisposition against war, he had led the Union 'with steel and flame'.[106] Now, thanks to a combination of his armies' timely victories, his standing as a person and his astuteness, he would begin another four years as President.

Upon re-election, his thoughts turned at once to healing America's deep wounds. Overcoming an innate tendency to pessimism, he had performed superbly as a politician, reading people clearly, knowing when to be silent, when to relate a joke, when to yield, and when to say 'no'. Yet he had an even greater gift for insights for the long run.

Lincoln the thinker was greater than Lincoln the tactician; the questing Lincoln—the one asking why so many lives had been lost, how many more would go, and how long the war would last—was even more interesting than the Lincoln guiding the war.

We have to admire his ability to switch as required between these roles. Even while his instincts served him by the hour, he was thinking of the years that lay ahead, and of the America of the future. For this Unionist was also, or even more, an American, never forgetting his southern roots and able, thanks to these roots and his wife's live connections, to identify with the South even while ordering its conquest.

Reflections that accompanied his war role reinforced Lincoln's belief that slavery was not only a great iniquity; at its depth it was an American rather than a southern iniquity, in fact, a human offence that people anywhere were capable of committing.

This was not a new thought. A series of Fast Day and Thanksgiving Day proclamations issued by Lincoln throughout the war called the people as a whole to repent of the sins that led to bloodshed. Previous governments in America and elsewhere had also at times asked for penitent prayers from the populace. We saw how, shaken by the Revolt in India, Victoria and numerous British preachers asked the British in 1857 to fast and pray for a day.

In March 1863, four months before the Gettysburg battle, Senator James Harlan of Iowa (whose daughter Mary would five years later marry Robert Lincoln) had introduced a resolution asking President Lincoln to proclaim a national day of prayer and fasting. Adopted by the Senate on 3 March and signed by Lincoln on 30 March, the resolution said:

> [M]ay we not justly fear that the awful calamity of civil war, which now desolates the land, may be but a punishment, inflicted upon us, for our presumptuous sins, to the needful end of our national reformation as a whole People?

Whether or not these were Lincoln's own words, they indicate his thinking. Two years later, in March 1865, when Lincoln had to provide an address to inaugurate his second term, he was ready to translate his wartime reflections into precise words and to name the presumptuous sin.

The Second Inaugural. On the morning of 4 March, 'cheer upon cheer' greeted Lincoln's towering figure as it emerged on the platform on the eastern side of the Capitol in Washington. As Lincoln stepped forward, a half-sheet of paper in his hand, the sun pierced the clouds, bathing the arena with light, and he spoke:

> [F]our years ago all thoughts were anxiously directed to an impending civil war. All dreaded it, all sought to avert it ... One-eighth of the whole population were colored slaves, not distributed generally over the Union, but localized in the southern part of it. These slaves constituted a peculiar and powerful interest. All knew that this interest was somehow the cause of the war ...

Neither party expected for the war the magnitude or the duration which it has already attained. Neither anticipated that the cause of the conflict might cease with or even before the conflict itself should cease.

Each looked for an easier triumph, and a result less fundamental and astounding. Both read the same Bible and pray to the same God, and each invokes His aid against the other.

It may seem strange that any men should dare to ask a just God's assistance in wringing their bread from the sweat of other men's faces, but let us judge not, that we be not judged. The prayers of both could not be answered. That of neither has been answered fully.

The Almighty has His own purposes. 'Woe unto the world because of offenses; for it must needs be that offenses come, but woe to that man by whom the offense cometh.' If we shall suppose that American slavery is one of those offenses which, in the providence of God, must needs come, but which, having continued through His appointed time, He now wills to remove, and that He gives to both North and South this terrible war as the woe due to those by whom the offense came, shall we discern therein any departure from those divine attributes which the believers in a living God always ascribe to Him?

Fondly do we hope, fervently do we pray, that this mighty scourge of war may speedily pass away. Yet, if God wills that it continue until all the wealth piled by the bondsman's two hundred and fifty years of unrequited toil shall be sunk, and until every drop of blood drawn with the lash shall be paid by another drawn with the sword, as was said three thousand years ago, so still it must be said, 'The judgments of the Lord are true and righteous altogether.'

With malice toward none, with charity for all, with firmness in the right as God gives us to see the right, let us strive on to finish the work we are in, to bind up the nation's wounds, to care for him who shall have borne the battle and for his widow and his orphan, to do all which may achieve and cherish a just and lasting peace among ourselves and with all nations.

Immense applause followed, and then Lincoln took the oath of office, administered by none other than Salmon Chase, the new Chief Justice. Unable to summon Lincoln's inclusiveness, many American newspapers seemed puzzled by the address, although most commented respectfully on it. The *Chicago Times*, however, called the address 'slipshod' and 'puerile', adding, 'by the side of it, mediocrity is superb'.[107]

British newspapers, by contrast, were quite stirred. Despite a four-year record of pro-Confederate bias, *The Times* reported the speech favourably, while the *Spectator* said, in a comment written after Lincoln's death in April:

> We cannot read it without a renewed conviction that it is the noblest political document known to history, and should have for the nation and the statesmen he left behind him something of a sacred and almost prophetic character ... [No other document] written in a period of passionate conflict ever so completely excluded the partiality of victorious faction, and breathed so pure a strain of mingled justice and mercy.[108]

This is also how many others in subsequent decades have responded to an address so remarkably free of 'triumphalism, righteousness, or vilification of the foe'.[109] Its anguished yet stern conclusion that the war's destruction was a price for the sin of slavery does not spare the North, for that sin was 'American' rather than southern slavery. And when for a brief moment Lincoln specifies those who dared to pray for 'God's assistance in wringing their bread from the sweat of other men's faces', he quickly adds—even before concluding the sentence—'but let us judge not, that we be not judged'.

Standing in the throng at a White House reception after the inauguration was Frederick Douglass. Hailed by Lincoln, Douglass told him that the address was 'a sacred effort'.[110]

Lee surrenders. Petersburg fell on 2 April. The next day, Davis and his Cabinet escaped to Danville, Virginia. On the run and hunted, Davis moved between pockets still under Confederate control in Virginia, the Carolinas and Georgia.

On 3 April, Lee abandoned Richmond and moved westward. The next day, taking the coastal route from Washington, Lincoln journeyed into what had been the Confederate capital. There, a black man bowed to the President, and Lincoln bowed back, until then an impossible occurrence in Richmond and an improbable one even in Washington. Another black man knelt down before

Lincoln, by now Father Abraham to many African-Americans. 'Don't kneel to me,' Lincoln said, 'you must kneel to God only.'[111]

In Richmond, Lincoln visited what had been the Confederate White House, where Davis had lived before escaping. Before leaving for Washington by the *River Queen*, Lincoln asked the band that had accompanied the President's party to play what in effect had become the South's anthem, 'Dixie'. It was his way of saying that the South's whites would not lose their dignity though its blacks could now expect to be respected. A few days earlier, at a conference on 28 March aboard the *River Queen*, Lincoln had told Generals Grant and Sherman that he wanted the Confederates' submission, but no more bloodshed.

The surrender of the fatigued but still proud balance of Lee's Army of Northern Virginia took place on 9 April in the courthouse of Appomattox, about 75 miles west of Richmond. Lee told his men that any further sacrifice in fighting 'overwhelming numbers and resources' would be 'useless'.[112] Grant took Lee's surrender. His terms required Lee's soldiers to give up their arms and go home on parole. Officers could keep their swords. Union wagons would provide food. History remembers what Grant added:

> Your men must keep their horses and mules. They will need them for the spring ploughing.[113]

Lee, on his part, voiced acceptance of the abolition of slavery. On or around 12 April, a letter from Lee announcing the surrender reached Jefferson Davis in his hideout.

John Wilkes Booth. A handsome twenty-six-year-old actor who had enjoyed fair popularity in Richmond, John Wilkes Booth was the son of an eminent Shakespearean actor, Junius Brutus Booth. The father had left England and his first wife in 1821 and settled in Maryland. Southerners seemed to love the wholeheartedness of the son's acting as well as his ability to leap and fence on stage. They gave John Wilkes Booth the importance he craved for.

Imagining himself a member of the South's ruling class, John Wilkes Booth thought slavery to be a great blessing for slave-owners and also for slaves, and he viewed Lincoln with contempt. To him, Lincoln's 'appearance, his pedigree, his coarse low jokes and anecdotes' were as repulsive as his efforts 'to crush out slavery'.[114]

When, five years earlier, he heard, while acting in a Richmond theatre, that John Brown was to be executed elsewhere in Virginia, John Wilkes Booth left promptly to witness the execution. During the Civil War, he smuggled medicines to Confederate soldiers while acting in New York and Washington. No questions were aroused, for Booth had been born in Maryland. In November 1863, President Lincoln saw Booth on stage in *The Marble Heart* in Washington's Ford's Theatre; from the stage, the actor saw Lincoln in the President's box.

On Lincoln's re-election, Booth decided that the President had to be kidnapped as a hostage for the release of thousands of Confederates held in the North, and enlisted several co-conspirators for the project. Twice the idea came close to being attempted but had to be abandoned because, on both occasions, Lincoln's plans changed at the last minute.

On 3 March, Booth went to Lincoln's inauguration at the Capitol, stood quite close to the President, and thought that assassination might be a better idea than abduction.

~

After the inauguration, Lincoln felt exhausted and ill, and Mary thought he would not survive another four years in Washington. He relaxed, however, during visits to the theatre (with a party that usually included his wife and son Tad, who was now twelve) or at afternoon carriage rides with Mary.

Sometimes, the couple talked of the future. Lincoln had saved and invested most of his salary drawn over the previous four years (Congress paid for almost all the White House expenses); and for real estate he had the house in Springfield plus 200 acres in Iowa. Not aware that Mary had piled up a large debt, Lincoln felt that the family was comfortably off. He spoke to Mary of visits they would make, once the second term ended, to California and, across the Atlantic, to Europe.

Husband and wife had differed over the plans of Robert, their older son, who had graduated from Harvard in 1864 and was keen to enlist as a soldier. Afraid that she would lose a third son,

Mary opposed the idea, but Lincoln could not afford talk of a twenty-one-year-old son of a President kept back from the war. In January 1865, he wrote to Grant 'as though I was not President, but only a friend' and asked whether Robert could join the general's 'military family'. Giving Robert a captain's rank, Grant made sure that he was not exposed to danger.[115]

On 8 April, returning to Washington from his visit to Richmond, Lincoln read out passages from Shakespeare to companions on the *River Queen*. From *Macbeth*, one of Lincoln's favourites, he read the lines where, after murdering Duncan, Macbeth contrasts Duncan's undisturbed sleep with the torture in his own mind. After commenting admiringly on the lines, Lincoln read them aloud again.

Two days later, Washington celebrated Lee's surrender with volleys of cannon fire, and the next day, 11 April, thousands, including numerous freed blacks, streamed into the White House grounds and demanded a speech from Lincoln. Appearing at a second-floor window, Lincoln offered his thanks to Providence and praised Grant and his brave men. Then he proceeded to describe his plans for reconstruction, and added his hope that 'the very intelligent' among the blacks as well as blacks 'who serve our cause as soldiers' would obtain the right to vote.

In the crowd was John Wilkes Booth. When he heard the remark about some blacks voting, Booth muttered, 'That means nigger citizenship,' adding, '. . . that is the last speech he will ever make.'[116]

~

On 14 April, which happened to be Good Friday, Lincoln was in unusually good spirits. Robert, just returned from Grant's army, gave details of Lee's surrender at Appomattox. In the afternoon, Lincoln took a ride with Mary in an open carriage. When she asked if he wanted others to join, he said he preferred 'to ride by ourselves today'. Almost 'startled' by his mood, Mary asked him why he seemed happy. The war had ended, Lincoln replied. 'We must both,' he added, 'be more cheerful in the future. Between the war and the loss of our darling Willie, we have both been very miserable.'

Returning from the ride, he did what he always enjoyed doing, which was to read aloud, in company, literary passages that he liked. On this day, visitors from Illinois were the favoured listeners. Dinner was had early, for he and Mary were going to Ford's Theatre to see a comedy, *Our American Cousin*.

He had asked the Grants to go with them but having made other plans they declined. Stanton, the War Secretary, and his wife, when they were invited, also expressed regrets. Lincoln next asked Major Thomas Eckert, chief of the War Department's telegraph bureau, to join. The President had become familiar with Eckert after numerous visits to the telegraph bureau for the latest war news. Besides, Eckert was exceptionally strong and would be useful in the event of an attack in the theatre, which, Lincoln had been warned, was always possible.

But Stanton had given Eckert work and he too declined. The Lincolns then turned, successfully, to a couple they liked—Clara Harris, daughter of a senator from New York, and her fiancée, Major Henry Rathbone, who too could guard the President.

In the afternoon, John Wilkes Booth learnt that Lincoln would be seeing the play at night. Quickly summoning three close associates, George Atzerodt, David Herold and Lewis Paine (also known as Lewis Powell), Booth instructed them. That night, Atzerodt was to kill Vice-President Andrew Johnson in his residence, Paine was to murder Seward in his home, and he, Booth, assisted by Herold, would kill Lincoln in the theatre.

With the announcement that the President, the Vice-President and the Secretary of State (who was responsible for new elections) were all dead, the Union (Booth thought) would descend into chaos, and the still-at-large Jefferson Davis, supported by Joseph Johnston, the general in the Carolinas who had not yet surrendered to Sherman, would reignite Confederate defiance.

The Lincolns were wildly cheered inside Ford's Theatre as they climbed the steps to the dress circle and walked to their box, but it was noticed that the President looked tired and thin. His liking for it known, a rocking chair had been placed in the box for the President. As the comedy got going on the stage, which was nearly 12 feet below their box, Mary frequently applauded, while her husband laughed heartily.

Known well to the theatre's hands, John Wilkes Booth had no difficulty sidling up to the dress circle ninety minutes or so after the play had started and walking right to the entrance of the presidential box, where a White House footman stood. Booth showed the footman his calling card and was let inside.

He crept noiselessly to a position two or three feet behind the rocking chair. At about 10:13 p.m., when Lincoln was leaning forward, his chin cupped by his right hand and his arm on the velvet-covered banister at the edge of the box, Booth aimed a Derringer at the President's head and pulled the trigger.

When Rathbone tried to catch hold of him, Booth slashed the major with a dagger. Then, dagger in hand, he jumped down from the banister to the stage below, shouted to the audience 'Sic semper tyrannis' ('Thus always to tyrants'—Virginia's motto), exited by the stage door, mounted a waiting horse and rode away.

By now, smoke was rising out of the presidential box and Mary was shouting, 'They have shot the President! They have shot the President!' even as she tried to prop him up in the rocking chair. An army doctor who was in the audience ran up to the box and saw that Lincoln was still alive. Carried to a house across the street and placed diagonally on a bed that was too short for him, Lincoln survived for nine hours until 7:22 in the morning of 15 April.

Moved by train through scores of American cities and towns before burial in Springfield, Illinois, Lincoln's coffin was saluted by millions of stunned, mourning and revering Americans.

~

Atzerodt had made no attempt to kill Andrew Johnson, who succeeded as President, but Paine attacked Seward in his home and left him bleeding, though fated to recover. Paine and Atzerodt were quickly arrested, but Booth and Herold (who had gone with Booth to the theatre) remained on the run until 26 April, when they were cornered in a farm in northern Virginia. While Herold gave himself up, Booth refused to surrender and was shot dead. Herold, Paine, Atzerodt and a fourth person charged in the conspiracy, Mary Surratt, were tried and executed in July.

In the days before his end, Booth expressed surprise that the

South did not hail his deed or follow it up with an uprising. He was not the first (or last) assassin to encounter reactions he had not anticipated. If the South was reluctant to celebrate, and the rest of America erupted in grief at Lincoln's killing (politicians were astonished at the love and respect he evoked), anger too was roused. The single bullet fired by Booth had done the work of a whole Union army, destroying the slenderest hope of Confederate recovery and advancing the recognition of black rights.

On 5 May, somewhere in Georgia, Jefferson Davis met for the last time with his Confederate Cabinet. The Confederacy was formally dissolved. Five days later, Davis was captured in Irwin County, Georgia. Let out after a two-year imprisonment, Davis lived until 1889, spending time travelling (including to Europe), writing (about the Confederate years), and promoting trade with South America.

Joseph Johnston also belied Booth's hopes. Before April ended, he surrendered all Confederates under his command to Sherman. Johnston lived on until 1891, long enough to attend Sherman's funeral.

In October 1865, Robert E. Lee signed and sent to Seward an allegiance pledge that was expected to earn him amnesty. Not receiving a reply, he thought he remained subject to prosecution. However, from October 1865 until his death five years later, Lee served as president of Washington College (now Washington and Lee College) in Lexington, Virginia.

In 1868, two years before his death, Lee endorsed a Democrat running for President against Ulysses Grant, but the latter won. Four years later, Grant was re-elected President, this time running against Horace Greeley, who represented a breakaway Liberal Republican Party. Grant's presidency invited charges of corruption, but it also saw firm action against the Ku Klux Klan, a secret terrorist organization started in 1865 to revive white supremacy. Grant lived until 1885.

A strong supporter of Grant's actions against the Ku Klux Klan, Frederick Douglass lived until 1895. In 1884, two years after the death of his wife Anna, Douglass married Helen Pitts, a white feminist twenty years younger than he. Before his death in 1895, Douglass served as minister to Haiti.

Six years after her husband's death, Mary Lincoln lost eighteen-year-old Tad, the third of her sons to die early. Assailed by acute depression, she died in 1882 in Springfield, Illinois. Robert Lincoln, who rose to be Secretary of War and minister to England, would live on until 1926.

In 1868, the Fourteenth Amendment gave national citizenship rights to former slaves. The Fifteenth Amendment of 1870 gave black men the right to vote. Freed blacks were soon voting and taking office, and many southern states were governed by Republican blacks and whites.

But a counter-campaign was rapidly organized, poor governance did not help and intimidating paramilitary groups in the South succeeded in barring most blacks from voting. By 1877, to the bitter disappointment of Frederick Douglass and numerous others, the South was once more ruled by conservative white Democrats.

Racial segregation would mark the South for decades thereafter, all the way into the 1960s. But the mark would be recognized as ugly, a blot on America's face that had to go one day. If Americans saw this—if they saw that honour lay not in racial purity but in ending an injustice that was also a national shame—it was in fair part because of Abraham Lincoln.

Starting himself with prejudice and ignorance about African-Americans, Lincoln had put his country on a path to equality by the time he died. In the decades that followed, race-based supremacy, hierarchy and discrimination would continue to be defended, but mostly in subtle or roundabout fashion. America had become committed to the goal of equal rights for all.

CHAPTER 6

CONNECTIONS

THE TWO REVOLTS;
AND INDIA, 1860 TO 1900

In this concluding chapter, we will first compare and connect the India of the Revolt with the America of the Civil War. Then, in a longer section, we will examine links between the period of our study and the India of our times.

In our day, Indians familiar with the American Civil War easily outnumber Americans aware of India's 1857 Revolt. The opposite was the case in the 1850s and 1860s. During that period, American interest in the Indian Revolt was not quite matched by Indian interest in the American Civil War. However, many Indians followed the course of that war. Not just Calcutta's British-owned press, but also the Indian weekly, the *Hindoo Patriot*, carried stories about the American conflict, often on the front page.

Thus *Hindoo Patriot* readers were informed in July 1861 that 'large bodies of Slaves have joined the Camp of the Federal Army in America.' Reproducing an uncorroborated report in the *Englishman* that 'a steamer of war carrying the Confederate flag' and ready to attack any merchant vessels under the federal flag was cruising in the Bay of Bengal, the *Hindoo Patriot* wondered whether America's 'fratricidal war' would 'extend its gory limits even over the waters of British dominions'. On 15 September 1862, the paper wrote:

> The cause of emancipation of the slaves is still trembling in the balance. The Confederates are daily gaining ground, and the pluck and energy of their Generals are adding fresh wreaths to their laurels . . . . We need not however despond. We cannot believe that the countrymen of Lincoln and Seward will die tame game to the slave-holding Confederates . . . Let it be remembered that on the side of the Federals are truth, justice, and humanity.

Although clearly sympathizing with the Unionists, and quite angry at an 'extra-official' remark by Lord Russell, the British foreign secretary, that 'the Southern states are in arms for independence, the Northern for domination' (17 November 1862), the *Hindoo Patriot* remained uncertain for quite some time as to the war's final result.

The British-owned *Bengal Hurkaru* was less willing to cheer the American North. On 4 April 1862, it wrote, '[I]t is now tolerably evident to the most heated partisans of the North that the war cannot be carried on much longer, and that the necessity of letting the South go free, in order to avert worse consequences, is absolutely irresistible.'

Many Indians were aware of the link between the American war and India's cotton exports, and the *Hindoo Patriot* noted (8 September 1862) that after having for long 'encouraged a trade in slave-grown produce', Manchester was finally impressed 'with the necessity of having a second string to the bow', that is, of importing cotton from India. While conceding the relative inferiority of Indian cotton, the paper recalled a past when India exported cloth, not raw cotton: 'The productions of the Indian loom went at one time almost to clothe the world.'

Interestingly, in comments on widely reported barbarities in America's 'fratricidal war' (an expression frequently used by the paper), the *Hindoo Patriot* recalled that the British press in India had 'declared that the "Cawnpore Massacre" was unparalleled in the history of military atrocities'. Now whites of European origin had provided a parallel (10 November 1862). Frequently expressing hopes for a truce in America, but seeing little signs of it, and clear-sightedly concluding that England and France were unlikely to intervene, the *Hindoo Patriot* spoke (10 November 1862) of 'a terrible evil spirit' that had 'possessed' the 'American body politic', producing from both sides the cry of 'war to the death'. Though troubled by Lincoln's suspension of habeas corpus, the *Hindoo Patriot* gave space in its columns to his 'noble words', as it described them (26 January 1863), and could not conceal its admiration for the man.

Elsewhere in India, British-owned newspapers and the few Indian journals that existed carried news of the Civil War. India-based Americans—merchants, consuls and missionaries, not however adding up to a large number—offered their own accounts to Indians with whom they interacted. One remarkable result was that a few unnamed 'Parsees and Hindoos' of Bombay contributed money for a Union field hospital.[1]

Yet in the early 1860s, the number of Indians touched either by the press or by the Americans living in India was small. For the bulk of Indians, the village or *mohalla* was their world. The burdens of daily life were too pressing, and their education too poor, for them to harbour curiosity about events in America. Knowledgeable and thinking Indians, however, saluted Lincoln from afar, like the editors of the *Hindoo Patriot*. Aware that 'niggers' was a common expression for Indians when India-based Britons talked among themselves, informed Indians desired a slave-liberating Unionist victory in America.

~

An independent USA was very different from an India ruled by aliens. Yet there were similarities between the Revolt and the Civil War. For a start, the outcomes were similar. As Susan Bean, a scholar of the India–America relationship in 'the Age of Sail' (before steamships became the norm), says, 'Both the American Civil War and the Rebellion of 1857 ... ended with affirmations of existing power relations, of the industrial North over the agricultural South in the United States, and of the government of British India over rebellious native rulers and soldiers.'[2]

Immense bloodshed marked both clashes. In India, most rebels but also many British privates perished without any record of their death. America lost more lives in the Civil War than it would in World Wars I and II combined. In both conflicts, tradition was often deemed more important than life, with Hindu and Muslim sepoys in India and white southerners in the US preferring death to the destruction of a way of life. Less significantly, perhaps, victors in both conflicts grumbled about the many on the opposite side who got away.

Both countries saw contests between freedom and oppression, equality and indignity, authority and rebellion, and order and anarchy. Blowing across both ends of the earth, the same time spirit seemed to stir up confrontations that were fundamental and also emotional. America's slaves wanted freedom, and many American whites supported their demand. 'Freedom' or, to be accurate, 'independence' was a cry in India too, but we saw that it was not yet a united or a national cry; and we also saw that with many leaders of the Indian rebellion, restoration of lost personal privileges seemed a stronger urge than independence.

We have marked that many Americans followed the Indian rebellion closely. Though at that time not many educated Indians travelled or migrated to the United States, the Indian 'rebellion was engrained in American minds'.[3] Intellectually there was a bridge between India and America in the 1850s and 1860s. This did not have much to do with trade between India and America, which though declining was still significant. Americans had sensed that the future of India, and of British rule there, would somehow touch their world, and they were riveted by the clash between Indian sepoys and British masters.

Also, as we noted, stories in the American press of British valour in the Indian Revolt produced in many Americans a thrill about a war for honour. That thrill may have made the thought of a civil war less horrifying to them.

Pro-slavery voices in the US equated slaves with India's sepoys and presented sepoy violence as an argument against freeing slaves. On the other hand, opponents of slavery likened the American South to India's rebels and saw both as violent foes of established authority. Thus, abolitionists and Confederates alike saw the sepoys as the villains in the Indian drama. Though some Americans saw serfdom in Britain's hold over India, and viewed the Indian rebellion as its natural consequence, the sepoys evoked no sympathy in America, whether among northerners or southerners.

Once the Civil War commenced, Unionists reminded the British of popular American sympathy for their position in India when rebels had challenged it in 1857, and asked, as we saw, for a similar understanding from the British in their effort to subdue the Confederacy.

American emotions were stirred by the sepoys' British victims or opponents, not by the sepoys' bid for independence, which did not register in America as a progressive step. By contrast, the Union's fight against slavery was seen by Indian intellectuals as an advance for the world as a whole. Although records of Indian comment on the Civil War are not easy to locate, there was, as we have noted, disapproval of American slavery and approval of Abraham Lincoln.

Willing to confront the moral question behind slavery and yet anxious to conciliate southerners, Lincoln was able to initiate a healing process in the United States. He also helped Americans to reflect—through his Second Inaugural and in other ways—on why the Civil War had cost so much in life, limb and treasure.

The India of his time, or the British Empire of his time, had no Lincoln equivalent, no one in authority who reached out to all sides or looked for the clash's deeper meanings. Remote from the scene in any case, Prime Minister Palmerston did not even bother to do so—his mind refused to acknowledge an Indian side. Once or twice, as we saw, Canning made the attempt from Calcutta, and so did Victoria from afar through her proclamation.

However, such attempts were drowned in the British clamour for security, for which total domination was seen as the only way. It is not surprising, then, that no British figure, whether Canning or Victoria or any other, was able to articulate a profounder meaning for the totality of the 1857–59 deaths, or to identify, in line with what Lincoln had done for America, the chief 'sin' in the Indian situation.

In some ways, the American situation was 'easier'. Despite the bitter North-South divide, there was a common religion to appeal to, as Lincoln well understood. Finding common ground for rulers of an alien race and subjects different from them in colour, faith, and customs was an almost impossible task, tougher even than speaking to an America divided over slavery.

Certainly it seemed out of the question for a principal player on the rebel side to think of reaching out to the British. Tragically, however, even winning the confidence of the Indian mainstream was not on the rebel agenda. No doubt Indians across the land felt a tingle of pride when Zafar was installed as an autonomous king, yet anxiety followed quickly and troubled most Indian minds. Except for the people of Avadh, Indians in general seemed to fear the tyranny of anarchy under rebel 'rule' more than they disliked the oppression of British control.

We saw that Calcutta's elite and non-elite Indians did not trust the rebels. In Delhi and Bijnor, Sayyid Ahmed Khan claimed that dominant Indian groups, whether Muslim or Hindu, were more oppressive than the British whom they had temporarily displaced. And in Poona, Joti Phule was relieved that Nana Sahib had failed to re-establish Brahmin rule and that British control would continue.

Oppression was an issue in India, but for all the dislike of alien rule, Indians could not agree on the identity of the immediate oppressor. Was a British sahib always worse than a local bully from a dominant caste? Although there was as yet no organized movement of 'low' castes or 'untouchables' against the 'high' castes, it seems likely that even in north India many from the 'lower' castes shared the relief felt by Phule in western India at the rebellion's failure.

A British author quoted by Phule, Henry Mead, asserted in 1857, 'It might be hard for us (the British) to make out a claim to be considered the friends of the Indian peasant, but the Sepoy is his hereditary enemy.'[4] Mead's picture of a non-Brahmin peasant standing up against a Brahmin sepoy was greatly over-simplified— we know that many sepoys were not Brahmins. Nevertheless, there is no evidence that the peasantry of India as a whole backed the rebels.

As for urban centres, a historian of Calcutta's popular culture would find that the streets of Calcutta displayed 'waggish glee at the expense of the leaders of the 1857 Sepoy rebellion' in the 1880s.[5]

Comparison enables us to recognize that unlike the American Civil War, where slavery quickly emerged as *the* central issue, the Indian Revolt revealed, as it progressed after its initial eruption, *two* central wrongs. One was the British sense of racial superiority;

the other was the rebels' sense of caste and class superiority. The Indian people found both hurtful.

Firoz Shah and some other rebel leaders criticized the British for not admitting Indians into higher-grade jobs and for hurting Indian artisans and traders, but the equality that most rebel leaders sought was between elite Indians and the British, not between ordinary Indians and the British, or even between ordinary and elite Indians. That men from the 'lower' classes were entering privileged areas of Indian life was, in fact, one of their complaints against the British.

Though more progressive than any other rebel leader, even Firoz Shah was outraged, we saw, that under British rule 'respectable zamindars' could be challenged in a court of law by a common peasant, maidservant or slave. We noticed too the vast gulf between top salaries and bottom wages in the 'budget' that a temporarily crowned Nana Sahib had drawn up.

The effort for Hindu-Muslim unity was undoubtedly an impressive feature of the Indian rebellion. Almost all the leaders, including Zafar, the Rani of Jhansi, Hazrat Mahal and Tatya Tope, called for unity—a plea that may sound similar to Lincoln's call for Union in America. India's Christians, a tiny minority, were however excluded and often killed by the rebels. If, therefore, the unity sought by the rebel leaders was restricted, it also seemed to require the glue of rage, and it lacked the promise of permanence. Appeals for it were generally tactical exercises, stressing joint action against the white or Christian enemy rather than long-term cooperation between Muslims and Hindus.

Religion was a major factor in both revolts, but its impact was not simple. In America, the South cited the Bible in defence of slavery, but many northerners saw abolition as a Christian duty. A feeling that Hinduism and Islam were in danger fostered the Revolt in India, and the use of force against Christians and the British was presented as a religious obligation, but in the end, most Hindus and Muslims did not feel that their religion was compromised by British rule.

The impression that the British intended to turn all Indians into Christians enjoyed only a short life. Clear pronouncements by Canning and the proclamation by Victoria played a part in dispelling it; also, when passions died down, many Indians saw for themselves that the average British civilian or officer posted in India, no matter his other faults, was not looking for converts.

Once the rebellion was suppressed, the British were quick to deepen and enlarge India's divides. Indians, on their part, became eager to demonstrate to the British that *they*, Indians of their particular stripe, were loyal and reliable, unlike Indians of 'that other' stripe. Security and strength for *their* group—achievable, they thought, through British blessing—soon elbowed out unity as the Indian urge, while divide-and-rule was enshrined as a central British tenet. A weapon employed against the British during the Revolt, religion would now be used by the British to split Indians.

The question of order or anarchy was resolved in most Indian minds in favour of the alien ruler and against the indigenous rebel. We saw in America that southern whites persisted for some time with the claim that theirs was a well-ordered, in fact divinely ordained, society, but in the end America's Union government emerged as the source of order. In India, the rebels, while emphasizing tradition and custom, were never in a position to speak in the name of order or stability. That platform belonged squarely to India's British rulers.

And if the American contest was, among other things, one between the old and the new, between (as some saw it) a decaying if stubborn feudalism and a blooming if also oft-callous capitalism, with the South representing the former and the North the latter, in India the British, despite the bitter story of their uninvited conquest of the land, signified the new order, and the rebels the old. In both conflicts, feudal ways and rebel leaders seemed to be on one side, and change and opportunity on the opposite flank. If a new order meant the demise of the East India Company, the British were prepared to pay that price. And if a new order meant postponing ideas of confronting British rule, by 1859 most people in India seemed willing to meet that condition.

From a Marxian point of view, both revolts were reactions to the advance in technology. At both ends of the earth, feudal forces made a last stand against a burgeoning bourgeoisie profiting from steam engines and the railway. Equally, a scholar of millenarian movements might say that both India and America witnessed a failed bid to build a nobler future on the foundation of an imagined past.

~

We have noted that in the 1850s and 1860s, the time spirit favoured capitalism. Another idea fuelled worldwide in that age was nationalism. These two 'isms' profited from a third god of the time, science. The 1860s and 1870s would see, in Europe, the rise of Germany and Italy as nation states, and in Asia the emergence of modern Japan. While these 'new' nations competed with Britain, France and America, the combination of capitalism and nationalism produced a fresh thrust of European imperialism, this time into Africa. It also intensified jealousies within Europe, which resulted periodically in war, fought with more scientific weapons.

Numerous gifted minds saluted the new trinity of capitalism, nationalism and science—often reduced to a single word, progress— but there were two notable exceptions, Karl Marx and Leo Tolstoy, both encountered previously in our survey. Here, in this final chapter, we will quickly look at the rest of the lives of Marx and Tolstoy, if only because of their subsequent influence on the thinking of Indians. We will glance also at the remainder of the lives of five others we met during our survey of India, individuals who were relatively young when we last lingered with them.

Though Marx and Tolstoy and these five others all died around the end of the nineteenth century—around a hundred years ago, that is—their varied and at times conflicting ideas affected Indian thinking in the twentieth century. *They connect the period we have looked at to the period in which we live.*

MARX

Our last encounter with Marx was through his comments on the Indian Revolt sent from London and published in the *Tribune* of New York. Marx's Manchester-based friend Engels continued to support him in London. But with a wife and six children to look after, Marx also needed the payments fetched by his *Tribune* pieces. During the American Civil War, these pieces, and articles he also wrote for *Die Presse* of Vienna, revealed a Marx who pored over maps, battles and strategies and made predictions. This, we may remember, is what he had also done with the Indian Revolt.

During the Civil War he rooted unabashedly for the Union, declared that the Confederates, not Lincoln, had started the conflict, pronounced, over the *Trent* crisis, that Britain had no legal right to intervene, and predicted correctly that it would not be able to intervene. Later on in the war, he suggested that McClellan, the Union general, was not a sincere foe of slavery. Though Marx himself was not wholly free from his time's notions of civilized and uncivilized races, he pushed in his Civil War articles for a Union edict freeing the slaves of rebels, and expressed impatience with Lincoln's restrictions on abolitionist generals like Fremont.

The sympathy shown to the South by much of the British press and by Prime Minister Palmerston infuriated Marx. In February 1862, he expressed relief (*Tribune*, 1 February) that 'the true character of the civil war has been brought home to the (British) working classes, and . . . the dangerous period when Palmerston rules single-headed without being checked by Parliament is rapidly drawing to an end.'

But Marx was more than a forceful and engaged journalist. He was also a philosopher who wished to unlock the secrets of history, economics and politics. There was, moreover, a third Marx—the one who encouraged revolutionary groups in Europe and took part in the founding (in 1864) of the International Workingmen's Association, or the First International, an alliance of socialists and leftists of many persuasions.

Not nationalism but working-class solidarity across national borders was Marx's icon. He wrote of the class enemy's oppressive nature and called for action against it everywhere. Many were stirred. In 1871, seven years after the First International was launched, a group in Calcutta contacted Marx to ask how they could start a branch. Although no branch emerged, this may be seen as Marx's first Indian connection.[6]

Most American readers of his *Tribune* articles were unaware of Marx's revolutionary side. Though first published in 1848 (in German), his *Communist Manifesto*, with 'Workers of the World,

Unite!' as its last line, was little known in the America of the 1860s. Books and pamphlets that he wrote in the 1840s and 1850s were followed in 1862 by *Theories of Surplus Value*, where Marx argued that employers or capitalists appropriated the value that labour bestowed on things.

Published in 1867, the first volume of Marx's *Das Capital* elaborated the argument. Thanks to Engels, two more volumes of *Das Kapital* would be brought out after Marx's death. That capitalism was going to kill itself was part of the law of history identified by Marx, who expected a revolution to occur first in one of Europe's leading industrial powers, either France, Germany or England. Marx claimed, too, that compared with idealists advocating a brotherly or religious socialism, his approach to socialism was more scientific.

After a Franco-Prussian war in 1870–71 ended in a German victory, Marx wrote *The Civil War in France*, a discussion of the workers' Commune that bravely ran the city of Paris for two months, defying the Prussian victors and also the rest of France, which had accepted defeat. Marx, who had championed Paris's militant workers, had to explain why their revolution ended so quickly. Following this writing, Marx was more closely watched by the British police, and illnesses also dogged him.

He died in London in March 1883, two years after the death of his wife Jenny. Speaking at his burial, Engels called Marx 'the greatest thinker' of his time. His passion had indeed convinced many everywhere that history was on the side of the downtrodden and that struggle would be rewarded.

In the century to follow, Marxism would be proclaimed as the dominant ideology of several countries, including the world's largest, Russia, and the world's most populous, China, though not in any of the lands he thought were riper for a communist revolution—England, Germany and France. Twentieth-century India too would contain numerous and influential adherents of Marxism as well as non-Marxists who liked his denunciation of imperialism.

Others, however, would question Marx's theories of class enmity and the dictatorship of the proletariat. Marxism would experience more schisms, and more bitter ones, than any church; in its name, the world would witness numerous cruelties. Russia and other lands that turned Marxist would eventually renounce Marx's theories, and China, too, would abandon Marxism in practice, if not in name.

TOLSTOY

Though his words have been quoted since, we had left the young count in the mid-1850s during the Crimean War, where he saw that vanity and fear rather than nobility marked the soldiers. Before that war, Tolstoy had served as an officer in the Caucasus, where the Russian army was trying to suppress Chechen rebels, who were Muslim by religion. During that operation, Tolstoy soaked up an incident that invites a comparison with India 1857.

After a fight with Shamil, who was his chief, a Chechen rebel called Hadji Murad had crossed over to the Russian side, which however decided to use him as a bait to lure Shamil. Though he managed to escape from them, Murad was captured by his Russian 'protectors' and decapitated. This was in 1852. Seven years later (in April 1859), the British in India would, as we saw, successfully use Man Singh, supposedly a rebel, to entice and execute the deadliest rebel, Tatya Tope.

Unexcited by a god of nation or race, a twenty-four-year-old Tolstoy had fastened on to a powerful human story where the central character was a non-white non-Russian. He saved the Murad story in his mind for half a century until it became the basis for his last novel, *Hadji Murad*, which was completed six years before his death but only published posthumously.

Even in his late twenties, Tolstoy with his bony head and lined cheeks conveyed a 'hard ascetic air' and people apparently felt uncomfortable under his 'extraordinarily piercing gaze'.[7] By this time he had mastered French and English and, interestingly, also made a study of eastern languages and religions.

Travelling provided other lessons. During an excursion in 1857 to France, Switzerland and Germany, he went to a public execution in Paris and saw 'the head parting from the body and fall into the basket'. The sight convinced the twenty-nine-year-old count of 'the emptiness of the superstition of progress'.[8]

Three months later, in July 1857 (when, far away in India, Delhi was in rebel hands and Kanpur witnessed brutalities, while passions over slavery were on the boil in America), Tolstoy was again shocked when he saw wealthy English visitors in Lucerne in Switzerland 'refusing alms to a little perambulating singer'. Satisfied with their correct beliefs ('civilization is good, barbarism is bad; liberty is good, slavery is bad'), such 'Liberals', as Tolstoy called them, did not seem interested in the actual humans they encountered.[9]

The young count started schools near his estate for the children of peasants, wrote stories for them, and decided to be a public champion of the peasants, who remained at the mercy of landowners and the state despite an 1861 decree in Russia abolishing serfdom. But Tolstoy desired pleasure too ('women, money, fame') and enjoyed it.[10]

He wanted to defend the idea of art for art's sake, an art freed from any moral intention, and in one debate, strongly did so, but his conscience refuted him, and the death in 1860 of a loved brother shook his faith in beauty or art. 'Art is a lie, and I can no longer love a beautiful lie,' he declared.[11]

But he also fell in love, and in 1862, when he was thirty-four and the object of his love, Sophie Behrs, was twenty-one, they married. Not only did Sophie too love literature, she provided a combination of assistance, companionship, peace and security that enabled Tolstoy to produce, during the next seventeen years, two of the masterpieces of nineteenth-century fiction—*War and Peace* (which Sophie copied seven times until it was 'final') and *Anna Karenina*. These classics were written in Yasnaya Polyana, the estate that Tolstoy had inherited, about 120 miles south of Moscow.

War and Peace, its Russian text sprinkled with French sentences, recreates the historical period around Napoleon's invasion of Russia (1812). In this vast epic, Tolstoy's mind reigns over an ocean—now stormy, now calm—of human passions. The tempest rises or abates as the author's mind dictates. Dissolving into his characters, the novelist 'falls in love together with them, suffers with them, dies with them'.[12]

But the novelist is also a historian, and the lives of the five aristocratic families of Russia that he closely follows intersect with history's events. The individual destinies of scores of distinct characters are woven together with the destinies of armies and peoples; the Russian psyche in peace and war is revealed; and war itself emerges as alternately soul-stirring and soul-destroying.

Napoleon and the tsar are not the heroes of *War and Peace*, which shows history being made not by a few individuals or events but by bigger (and often unexplainable) currents. Searching (in 1910) for a comparison for the conflicts of *War and Peace*, where 'a hidden destiny hurls the blind nations together', the French thinker Romain Rolland felt he had to go past the *Iliad* to the Mahabharata.[13]

Completed in 1879, eight years after *War and Peace* had been brought to an end, *Anna Karenina* traces two parallel and yet connected lives, one of which, though given another name, is largely Tolstoy's own. The other life is that of a beautiful but tragic woman 'consumed by love and crushed by the law of God' even though she is conscious of 'an almost holy moral strength' inside of her (Tolstoy's words in the novel). Her end saddens the reader, as it seemed to sadden the writer.

While again providing the spectacle of life in all its shades, speeds and sorrows, in *Anna Karenina* Tolstoy presents (more so than in *War and Peace*) his own moral evolution and his personal views. A key moment in *Anna Karenina* occurs when, during a conversation with a group of people, Levin (the character based on Tolstoy) hears a peasant speak naturally of those 'who live not for self, but for God'. The sentence gives Levin confidence and peace.

Before finishing *Anna Karenina*, Tolstoy experienced, at the age of fifty or fifty-one, a personal crisis. He felt suicidal and had to hide a cord lest he hanged himself with it, and avoided picking up 'a gun for a little shooting'—hunting was a passion with him—lest he used it on himself.[14] Neither family nor art could solace him, but eventually—as would happen to Levin in *Anna Karenina*—the peasants restored his faith in life and in God. (The hidden cord and the unused gun figure in the novel also.)

After regaining confidence, Tolstoy tried for three years to become a conventional Russian Christian. The attempt was a complete failure. Dogmas alienated him; despite a deep love for Christ, he had been unwilling from his youth to accept that Jesus was God. He was offended, too, by hates within Christianity, and by the church's blessing of war and capital punishment.

But he was moved by the Sermon of the Mount's rejection of lust, hate and revenge, and by its elevation of 'Love God, and thy neighbour as thyself,' as the highest commandments. To Tolstoy, moreover, the Asiatic or the African was a neighbour too. In fact none could be happy unless all were.[15]

Sophie, whose feelings were much wounded when, on the eve of their marriage, he showed her a journal that recorded occasions when he had yielded to lust, found the new Tolstoy even harder to accept. Yet the creator of *War and Peace* and *Anna Karenina* had accepted a new calling. It was expressed in 1882 in *A Confession*, which recounted the moral and spiritual struggles that preceded Tolstoy's recapture of confidence.

To his annoyance, disciples and followers emerged. But the church attacked and finally excommunicated Tolstoy. In his reply to the church, Tolstoy expressed his belief that Christ—better than anyone else—had helped human beings to do the will of God, but he was a man still. Questioning the church, Tolstoy questioned the state too, and its armies.

Even as tension between Tolstoy and his family grew, Russia's writers begged him to return to literature. Tolstoy did not feel he had abandoned it. *The Death of Ivan Ilyich* was published in 1886, *The Kreutzer Sonata* in 1889, and *Resurrection* in 1899. However, he would not confine himself to novels. *The Kingdom of God is Within You* appeared in 1894 (in Germany to begin with, because the Russian church was against its publication), and *Readings for Every Day of the Year*, an anthology of wisdom from West and East, in 1904–05. He also wrote philosophical essays such as *What is Art?*—which came out in 1897—and short stories like *What Men Live By* and *Where Love is, God is*, both published in 1885.

Though focusing on the needy and elevating the poor peasant, Tolstoy refused to accept the socialism to which the inequalities of industrialized Europe had driven Marx and some other nineteenth-century thinkers. He accused socialists of valorizing hate and rejecting the individual conscience, and said they did not allow any doubt to enter their beliefs. Constitutionalists and liberals fared little better at his hands. Tolstoy judged 'parliamentary slavery', as he called it, to be worse than the serfdom of Russians under a tsar, for it was legitimized slavery, flaunting the stamp of approval given by a restricted and usually self-centred electorate.[16]

It is unlikely that Tolstoy was thrilled by Russia's expansion, between the 1860s and the 1880s, into Central Asia, when places like Tashkent, Samarkand, Bukhara and Ashkabad were annexed. Later, during Russia's 1904–05 war with Japan, which was an offshoot of the Russian desire for a year-round port in East Asia, Tolstoy's views on nationalism and war were powerfully expressed.

Tolstoy indeed wept when Port Arthur in Manchuria fell to the Japanese,[17] for Russian honour still stirred the seventy-six-year-old who was about to write *Hadji Murad* and who cherished memories from the 1850s of battle fronts in the Caucasus and the Crimea. But he could not defend the waste of life. In a 1904 tract entitled *Bethink Yourselves!* he wrote:

> Again war. Again sufferings, necessary to nobody, utterly uncalled for; again fraud; again the universal stupefaction and brutalization of men.
>
> Men who are separated from each other by thousands of miles, hundreds of thousands of such men (on the one hand Buddhists, whose law forbids the killing, not only of men, but of animals; on the other hand Christians, professing the law of brotherhood and love) like wild beasts on land and on sea are seeking out each other, in order to kill, torture, and mutilate each other in the most cruel way. What can this be? Is it a dream or a reality? Something is taking place which should not, cannot be; one longs to believe that it is a dream and to awake from it. But no, it is not a dream, it is a dreadful reality! . . .
>
> Scientists, historians, and philosophers, on their side, comparing the present with the past, deduce from these comparisons profound conclusions, and argue interminably about the laws of the movement of nations, about the relation between the yellow and white races, or about Buddhism and Christianity, and on the basis of these deductions and arguments justify the slaughter of those belonging to the yellow race by Christians; while in the same way the Japanese scientists and philosophers justify the slaughter of those of the white race.

Making 'that simple appeal to the consciousness of each separate man which, nineteen hundred years ago, was proposed by Jesus', that he 'bethink himself, and ask himself, who is he, why he lives, and what he should and should not do', Tolstoy concluded by quoting a letter he had received from 'a simple seaman':

'You should have seen what took place yesterday at the station,' he said; 'it was dreadful. Wives, children, more than a thousand of them, weeping. They surrounded the train, but were allowed no further. Strangers wept, looking on. One woman from Toula gasped and fell down dead. [She had] five children. They have since been placed in various institutions; but the father was driven away all the same.'[18]

What Tolstoy had thought of the loss of life in the American Civil War is apparently not recorded, but there is evidence of his admiration for Lincoln. In an interview in 1908 to the *New York World*, he seems to have spoken of a visit 'to a wild and remote area of the North Caucasus' where local tribesmen evidently asked Tolstoy to speak about Lincoln. Surprised that they had heard of Lincoln, Tolstoy told them everything he knew about Lincoln's difficult upbringing, his politics, and the Emancipation Proclamation, and saw that they were greatly impressed.

After recalling this encounter in the Caucasus, Tolstoy seems to have told his interviewer from the *New York World* that Lincoln 'overshadow[ed] all other national heroes' because of 'his peculiar moral power'. While George Washington was 'a typical American' and Napoleon 'a typical Frenchman', Lincoln was 'a humanitarian as broad as the world. He was bigger than his country.'[19]

As to what Tolstoy may have felt about the 1857 Revolt, his 'Letter to a Hindu', written in 1908, gives a clue. Arguing that Indian participation in British rule was perpetuating that rule, Tolstoy asked Indians to reject violent rebellion and adopt instead a strategy of nonviolent non-cooperation in their struggle for independence. He wrote:

A commercial company enslaved a nation comprising two hundred millions . . . . What does it mean that thirty thousand men, not athletes but rather weak and ordinary people, have subdued two hundred million vigorous, clever, capable, and freedom-loving people? Do not the figures make it clear that it is not the English who have enslaved the Indians, but the Indians who have enslaved themselves? . . .

305

As soon as men live entirely in accord with the law of love natural to their hearts and now revealed to them, which excludes all resistance by violence, and therefore hold aloof from all participation in violence—as soon as this happens, not only will hundreds be unable to enslave millions, but not even millions will be able to enslave a single individual. Do not resist the evil-doer and take no part . . . in the violent deeds of the administration, in the law courts, the collection of taxes, or above all in soldiering, and no one in the world will be able to enslave you.[20]

Tolstoy had written this 'Letter' in response to a request from a twenty-four-year-old Bengali living in North America, Taraknath Das, who was bringing out an insurrectionary journal from Canada called *Free Hindustan*. Asked to explain his belief in nonviolence, which Das disliked, Tolstoy put a lot of thought into the article and revised it several times.

It is not clear if Tolstoy's piece was printed in *Free Hindustan*, but in 1909, a typed copy reached Mohandas Karamchand Gandhi in England, where he was trying to create awareness of the nonviolent struggle he had initiated in South Africa. Gandhi was interested in Tolstoy, having read him from the time of his arrival in South Africa in 1893, when he was twenty-four.

The Kingdom of God is Within You, in particular, had influenced Gandhi in his journey towards nonviolence, and though he had not communicated with Tolstoy, his views seemed to correspond with the Russian's. On Lincoln and America's anti-slavery struggle, for example, Gandhi had written in 1905 (in *Indian Opinion*, his journal in South Africa), 'It is believed that the greatest and the noblest man of the last century was Abraham Lincoln.'[21]

Greatly taken with the 'Letter to a Hindu', Gandhi, now forty, wrote to Tolstoy asking for confirmation that the text was his and also for permission to publish it. On receiving the Russian's consent, Gandhi issued it in South Africa in December 1909.

Ever since 1880, Tolstoy's wife and all except one of his many children had continued to oppose him. In November 1910, after three decades of strained relations, he felt he had to part from them. Accompanied by daughter Alexandra, he left his ancestral home and estate, Yasnaya Polyana, aiming, it seems, to reach a convent where the superior was a sister of his. Falling ill on the journey, the old count was obliged to get off at a small station called Astapovo. There, in the stationmaster's home, Tolstoy died on 20 November 1910. He was eighty-two.

His last long letter, written in September 1910, was to Gandhi, who gave the name 'Tolstoy Farm' to a new 1,000-acre centre outside Johannesburg, created by the generosity of a friend, Hermann Kallenbach, a German Jew and architect who recognized himself (so Gandhi had informed Tolstoy) in *A Confession*.

BANKIM

Seven years younger than Tolstoy, and in fact the youngest of our links to the two revolts, Bankimchandra Chatterji was twenty-one when, in 1859, the Indian rebellion ended, and twenty-seven when the American Civil War was over. By this time, he had already published his first novel. Much later, when 'as a mere boy', Rabindranath Tagore, the future Nobel laureate, first saw him, the lad noticed in Bankim 'a keen and fierce brilliance, like that of a scimitar raised to strike'.[22]

Bankim, we may remember, was a judicial officer in Bengal. As he moved from place to place in the presidency's districts and wrote his novels (portraying adventure, chivalry, romance and deceit in the India of earlier centuries or in Europe-ruled India), his British superiors assessed him, in confidential notings, as efficient, clever, talented, prompt and brilliant in his work.[23] Having obtained a law degree in 1869 with flying colours, in 1874 he won a case against a Colonel Duffin who had insulted him.

He was not interested, however, in defying British rule. Belonging to 'the highest caste of Hindu orthodoxy, a powerful civilian in the British administrative machinery, a famed novelist and an erudite scholar', he was 'a respectable citizen' and 'reserved taciturn person' who had to protect his status.[24]

Earlier, we observed that Bankim had remained totally silent on the Revolt. Though greatly impressed by the Rani of Jhansi and wanting to write about her, he gave up that risky idea. So were 'independence and dependence' the same to him? To this question, which was put to him, Bankim's answer was, 'We are a dependent nation and shall remain in a state of dependence for a long time yet. It is not for us to debate such issues.'[25]

We have already noted that this opinion was widely shared. A comment in March 1870 in the new Bengali journal, *Amrita Bazar Patrika*, to the effect that the 1857 uprising was 'not merely a revolt of the sepoys but a war of independence'[26] was an exception to the rule of prudent silence that Bankim and almost everyone else observed on such questions. As Bhabatosh Chatterjee, literature professor, Bankim scholar and editor of a major volume honouring Bankim, puts it, 'It is beyond contention that the dead weight of tradition, the social climate and the hazards of a writer who was also a government official in a country under tyrannical foreign domination set limits to his utterances.'[27]

Within those limits, Bankim wrote with vigour. He would be called 'beyond question the greatest novelist of India during the 19th century'[28] and 'the acknowledged Master who ... brought Bengali into the arena of world literature'.[29] His romances 'ease[d] off the tedium of the dreary evenings in the houses of the big landlords in the districts of British Bengal'.[30] Yet Bankim was also a thinker whose essays have been regarded by some as more important than his novels, and a writing maestro whose literary journal, *Bangadarsan*, is said to have 'set a standard that has not been surpassed'.[31]

His essays, sociological and philosophical, were products of an independent yet questing mind, a mind rationalist but also nationalist, that paid attention to Western thinkers such as Jean Jacques Rousseau, John Stuart Mill, Auguste Comte and Herbert Spencer, and also to early Indian texts. However, because his essays seemed to say different and opposing things, Bankim's philosophy cannot be spelt out with any precision. According to Bhabatosh Chatterjee, 'his philosophy [has] no well-knit content'.[32]

One of Bankim's oft-quoted short texts is on the condition of the Bengali peasant. Written in 1872, the year when *Bangadarsan* was launched, and after three of Bankim's novels had been published, the lines are a comment on the prosperity that British rule had evidently brought to a section of Indians.

> Whose is this prosperity? Hasim Sheikh and Rama Kaivarta, with their blunt-edged ploughs and two skin-and-bone oxen, plough knee-deep in mud, bare-footed and bare-headed in midday sun— have they prospered? ... I see your prosperity and mine, but are you and I the country?[33]

Adds Bankim:

> The animal's enemy is animal; man's enemy is man; the Bengali landlords are the enemies of the Bengali peasants ... A big man called a landlord devours a small man called a peasant.[34]

In 1879, when he was forty-one, Bankim published a booklet on equality, *Samya*, where he declared that the root of human misery lay in inequality 'between man and man, between the rich and the poor, the ruler and the ruled, the high-born and the low-born, the oppressor and the oppressed, and the male and the female'. Three figures in history, Bankim added, had effectively challenged inequality—Buddha, Jesus and Rousseau. According to Bhabatosh Chatterjee, this 'tract on equality shines like an unsheathed sword' and 'holds a unique position in sociological literature in 19th-century India'.[35]

But Bankim soon disavowed *Samya* and excluded most of it from his collected works published in his lifetime.

We must mark, too, that *Samya* is silent not only about the 1857 Revolt but also about the American Civil War. On the other hand, six years before *Samya* was published, Jotiba Phule in Poona had come out with his book *Gulamgiri* ('Slavery'), dedicating it to Americans who had fought slavery and writing admiringly in it of Lincoln and his associates.

The absence in Bankim's writings (not just in *Samya*) of any reference to the plight of America's slaves or the struggle in America against slavery suggests that many of India's finest thinkers of the time lived in a Eurocentric world. England and France had conquered far continents, and Germany and Italy were moving towards unification. These nations of Europe merited study. America was an aberration, and probably unstable.

This, as we know, was the British view, and elite Indians in the nineteenth century—and later—were inclined to look at the world with British eyes. But another factor was also at work. By the 1870s, Indian elites had accepted the theory (pressed by our friend Russell's friend Max Müller) that north Indian Aryans were connected to the 'White' races of Central Asia and Europe. Blacks, in contrast, were complete strangers, and perhaps inferior as well. Indians prized a light or 'fair' skin, which proved the Aryan connection. When British officers or soldiers called the Indian sepoy a 'nigger'—we noted several examples of this—both abuser and abused assumed that being black was a misfortune.

But it is not as if the American Civil War was played out without Calcutta or Bankim knowing about it. On the economic front, India's cotton exports had boomed as a direct result of that war. On the cultural-literary front, *Uncle Tom's Cabin* was known to prominent Indians, who knew also that slavery had strong opponents in Europe and America.

In 1843, a decade before that novel was published, Dwarkanath Tagore, Rabindranath's grandfather, just returned from a visit to England, presented to audiences in Calcutta a British opponent of slavery, George Thompson, who had accompanied Tagore to India and who wanted trade between India and Britain to grow. Earlier, when Thompson had lectured in America, a slavery supporter there called him 'an infamous foreign scoundrel'.[36]

At least some in India saw similarities between cotton plantations in the American South and eastern India's indigo plantations. Addressing a gathering in Calcutta's Town Hall early in 1857, just before the Revolt broke out, Rajendralal Mitter likened 'the Anglo-Saxon planters' of indigo in Bengal, who he said were ruining 'inoffensive and helpless peasants', to 'the slave owners of Virginia'.[37] Two years earlier, concluding that 'the behavior of the planters had retarded the spread of Christianity', European missionaries in Calcutta had asked for a description of planter intimidation that would equal in impact the scenes painted in *Uncle Tom's Cabin*.[38]

As a judicial officer posted at times in indigo country, Bankim was well aware of planter violence, and he would have closely followed a series of indigo disturbances that occurred in Bengal between 1859 and 1862. The American Civil War had begun by the time these disturbances ended, and newspapers in India, including the *Hindoo Patriot* and *Somprakas*, perhaps the leading Bengali paper of the time, were commenting on it.[39] Also, similarities between the American South's cotton plantations and British-run indigo plantations in India were being pointed out. Even so Bankim was not induced to reflect, publicly at any rate, on slavery in America.

On women, Bankim's position was both impressive and ambivalent. After initially championing equality for women in *Samya*, he felt he had gone too far and withdrew his text. Women are central and even dominant in his novels, and he portrays a remarkable range of female characters, including 'cooks, servant women, children and girls with tinkling ankle bells [who] vie with each other to keep the decibel level permanently high'.[40]

Bankim's women can be powerful as well, 'torn between love and conscience . . . bruised by betrayal; stoical but passionate; racked with desire; wounded but forgiving; courageous and adventurous'.[41] However, sinners receive stern punishment in his novels, and the liveliest woman is in the end returned to her interior place within closed walls.

An irremovable traditionalism in Bankim's formidable and in many ways modern mind prevented him from endorsing widow remarriage, a cause taken up, as we know, by Vidyasagar, who was older than Bankim by eighteen years. In June 1880, Bankim used harsh language in *Bangadarsan* while objecting to the reform:

> We do not think that the hardships of the widows are intolerable. Supposing they are really intolerable, but at the same time highly beneficial to society, what necessity is there for removing them? . . . If it is cruelty not to relieve the miseries of a handful of widows, then it must be a barbarous inhumanity to cause mischief to thousands of individuals . . . by inaugurating widow remarriage.[42]

Observing that Bankim's accent 'changes all the time', Bhabatosh Chatterjee wants us to understand the 'alternation of trenchant upbraiding and propitiation, of defiance and adjustment, of challenge and conventionality, of advance and retreat' in his subject-hero.[43]

Still, these arguments and explanations may not be all that important. Bankim's fame rests in the end not on his novels or essays, but on a single poem, *Vande* (or *Bande*) *Mataram*. He wrote its first two stanzas in 1874 or thereabouts and used the text to fill an empty space in *Bangadarsan*. It is said that his daughter and the compositor at the press told him that they were not particularly impressed with the lines. Apparently Bankim replied that they would grasp the meaning one day.[44]

Written spontaneously in an unprecedented blend of Sanskrit and Bangla, the lines were addressed to a Mother who could be seen as the Mother either of Bengal or of India as a whole. Aurobindo Ghose's literal prose translation is as follows:

I bow to thee, Mother,
richly-watered, richly-fruited,
cool with the winds of the South,
dark with the crops of the harvests,
the Mother!

Her nights rejoicing in the glory of the moonlight,
her lands clothed beautifully with her trees in flowering bloom,
sweet of laughter, sweet of speech,
the Mother, giver of boons, giver of bliss!

Terrible with the clamorous shouts of seventy million throats,
And the sharpness of swords raised in twice seventy million hands,
Who sayeth to thee, Mother, that thou art weak?
Holder of multitudinous strength,
I bow to her who saves,
To her who drives from her the armies of her foemen,
The Mother!

When the song was written, seventy million was the population of Bengal Presidency, which included today's Bangladesh and the Indian states of West Bengal, Assam, Bihar and Orissa. Later, Bankim produced more words for the poem, and the full song entered his novel *Anandamath*, published in 1882.

But problems arose. With the additional lines, Mother India became Mother Goddess as well, a Goddess Durga who held ten weapons of war in her hands. Moreover, the novel made it clear that the Mother Goddess would enable Hindus to defeat Muslims.

Set in the Bengal of the 1770s, which saw a rebellion of ascetics against the newly established British rule, *Anandamath* features Hindu men and women—'Santans', as they are called, or 'Offspring', the Mother's children—who take vows of severe austerity but who also rob, plunder and kill, for their aim is to oust British and Muslim influence in Bengal and set up a Hindu kingdom. The following excerpts from the novel are from the translation by the brothers Aurobindo Ghose and Barindra Kumar Ghose.

Bhavananda (a leader of the ascetic band, speaking to Mohendra): In every country the relation with the ruler is that of protector and protected, but what protection do the Mussalman rulers give us? Our religion is destroyed, our caste defiled, our honour polluted, our family honour shamed; and now our very lives are going the same way. Unless we drive out these vice-besodden long-beards, the Hinduism of the Hindu is doomed.

Mohendra: How will you drive them out?

Bhavananda: By blows.

Mohendra: You will drive them out single-handed? With one slap, I suppose (34).

To this, the response of Bhavananda, also described as 'the robber', is to sing the second stanza of *Vande Mataram*: 'Who hath said thou art weak in thy land/ When the swords flash out in seventy million hands/ And seventy million voices roar/ Thy dreadful name from shore to shore?' (Aurobindo Ghose's verse translation, p. 34) Later on in the novel, Satyananda, who is Bhavananda's leader, says:

We do not want kingly power. Only because the Mussalmans are the enemies of God we want to destroy them totally (97–98).

Elsewhere in the novel, Muslim heads are cut off by Santans who also set fire to Muslim villages and burn them to ashes (114). 'At that time,' the novel adds, 'the Santans did not realize that the British had come for the salvation of India. How could they understand this? . . . This thought was only in the mind of God' (117). However, another character in the novel, the fearless woman Santi or Shanti (perhaps partly modelled, as we have previously speculated, on Lakshmibai of Jhansi) speaks of Englishmen as monkeys (119).[45]

Anandamath ends with the defeat of the Muslims. 'The Mussalmans are defeated, the country again belongs to the Hindus' (161). While many of the Muslims were killed, others 'smeared themselves with Ganges clay and began singing, "Hari, Hari," and claimed they were Hindus'. The sage or teacher who had mysteriously guided the rebellion asks Satyananda and the others to go home.

The Sage: 'Your work is accomplished. The Mussalman kingdom is destroyed. You have no other work now.'

Satyananda: 'The Mussalman domination is done away with but no Hindu kingdom has yet been established. The English are strong in Calcutta now.'

The Sage: 'The Hindu kingdom is not destined yet to be established ... The English will rule India now .... The Santan rebellion has come only to put the British on the throne ... The British are our ally and friendly power. Besides, none has the requisite power to be victorious in the long run in a war against the British' (191–93).

~

No translation in prose or verse, even one by Aurobindo Ghose (Sri Aurobindo), can reproduce the force of the *Vande Mataram* song, where sound (in two languages, Sanskrit and Bangla), rhythm, and melody all become one, and singer and listener are both stirred.

Then there is the historical fact that in 1905–06 (about twelve years after Bankim's death), large numbers of Bengali Hindus spontaneously cried 'Vande Mataram!' as they demonstrated against the British decision to partition Bengal (in 1911 the decision was reversed); and the further historical fact that in subsequent decades, right up to independence in 1947, the cry was, for a great many Hindus across India, the most popular patriotic call, with several repeating Bankim's utterance even as they embraced the gallows.

Yet Muslim unease with the song and the novel that featured it is also a historical and understandable fact. Apart from the anti-Muslim context in which the song enters the novel, the idea of worshipping the image of a goddess seems directly opposed to Islamic doctrine.

Arguing that a novel should be seen as only a novel, and that a novel's version of history should not be taken as the writer's personal or lasting view, a few Muslims have defended Bankim and recalled his sympathy for Muslim peasants such as Hasim Sheikh.[46] Other scholars have asked for a different reading of *Anandamath*, pointing out that the tension in the novel between erotic and ascetic impulses may be more significant than its portrayal of Hindu-Muslim conflict. Muslims generally have however not been convinced.

Modern India's 'solution' has been to dismiss the *Anandamath* context and focus exclusively on the song's first two stanzas, if not on the first alone. The solution has worked up to a point, yet *Vande Mataram* remains a perfect example of the nearness between patriotic passion and religious tension. In any case, what is relevant for our study is the speed with which the joint Hindu-Muslim Revolt of 1857 morphed into 'the Hindu-Muslim question', and the passion with which a brilliant Indian mind entered into that discussion.

Most scholars agree that with the years Bankim became more of a staunch Hindu. Never losing his intellectual sharpness or gift for satire, he poked fun at the Bengali babu eager for Western approval and claimed that 'much that was truly worthy in modern Western ideas was already anticipated in traditional Hindu thought.'[47] Dissecting Hindu texts and mythic literature, he asserted that Krishna was a historical person, a human worthy of deification, and added:

> There does not exist in the history or poetry of any country an ideal character as all-qualified, as sinless as Krishna . . . No religious text of any country has such dharma-nourishing ideals as the sastras of the Hindus.[48]

He also said, 'It is the duty of all Hindus to act unitedly, with one counsel and one view—awareness of this is the first half of founding a nation.'[49] Referring to four of Bankim's novels, Bhabatosh Chatterjee says, 'In *Mrinalini*, *Anandamath* and *Devi Chaudhurani*, the idea of a theocratic state lies just below the surface . . . and the idea comes in the foreground in certain passages and dialogues. In *Sitaram*, it is the leading theme and is given the fullest expression.'[50] Published in 1887, *Sitaram* was the last of Bankim's novels.

India's Hindus should concern themselves with building a Hindu nation rather than an India for all its inhabitants. For building it, their texts offer a foundation and British rule provides a strong scaffolding. And yes, Hindus should master science and learn, if need be from the West, how to acquire power and use force. This seemed to be his message. Bankim's rationalism may have shaped his human yet godlike Krishna, a picture quite different from the traditional Hindu view of God incarnating himself as Krishna; but Hindu nationalism rather than a new Hindu theology appears to be his legacy—Hindu rather than Indian nationalism.

Before judging Bankim for his views, we should recall his times. In Bankim's 1860–90 Bengal, an intellectual and judicial officer like him would spend little time with Muslim counterparts, who were very few in any case. Though Muslims were a majority in much of Bengal, poverty, resentment and suspicion had kept them from educating their children in British-run schools. As a consequence, most Indians in Bengal's administrative machinery were Hindus.

Earlier, while British rule in Bengal was still being consolidated, the Brahmin thinker Rammohan Roy (who died five years before Bankim's birth) had associated with Muslim scholars. Once the British were firmly in charge, Hindu intellectuals saw no need to work with Muslims. Socially, in any case, there was little Hindu-Muslim mingling. This was especially true among elites. Muslim men were warned to stay away from occasions where unveiled Hindu women might be present, and high-caste Hindus were taught that contact with Muslims was polluting.

Bankim's normal day would thus not have included interactions with Muslims. He must have seen Muslims brought to his court, and they feature in his novels, but there is no indication that he had Muslim friends. The Revolt and its Hindu-Muslim alliance notwithstanding, it was not natural for Bankim to imagine a composite Indian nationalism.

Thanks in fair part to the labours of Allan Octavian Hume, the Indian National Congress (INC) emerged in 1885, a story we will soon get to. We do not seem to have a record of what Bankim thought of the INC's plea for an Indian role in India's governance, but he seems to have avoided associating himself with such pleas. It would have been risky for a functionary like him.

Bankim died in 1894 at the age of fifty-six, some months after receiving the British title, Companion in the Order of the Indian

Empire. Victoria, the Queen who approved the award, was still living and was in fact, since 1877, the Empress of India rather than a mere queen. Born nineteen years before Bankim, Victoria owed *her* elevated title to a Prime Minister she liked, Benjamin Disraeli. A Prime Minister she did not much care for, Palmerston, had died in October 1865, some months after Lincoln's assassination.

SAYYID AHMED

Two years older than Victoria, Sayyid Ahmed Khan watched her open a viaduct during a seventeen-month-long visit he made to Britain in 1869–70. We last saw Sayyid Ahmed in 1859, when he provided his noteworthy explanation of the Revolt. Though he had correctly foreseen its outcome, shame at the extinction of the Mughal throne made him think of migrating to a Muslim-run country (he considered Egypt), but he resisted the urge. India's Muslims seemed to need help, and he would live amidst them to provide it.

He also turned down a large estate the British had offered in appreciation of his role during the Revolt, and remained a judicial officer. This added to the respect he had earned among India's Britons. In 1860 he wrote *The Loyal Mahomedans of India*, which informed the Raj that not all Muslims had backed the Revolt, and in 1863 he asked a Muslim audience in Calcutta to look above all for the facts.

> The student will discover that truth is many-sided and that the world is a good deal wider than his own sect, or society or class . . . If the natives of India had known anything of the mighty power which England possesses . . . the unhappy events of 1857 would never have occurred.[51]

In 1861 (in line with a policy change that Sayyid Ahmed had advocated in his assessment of the Revolt), three Indians were named to the viceroy's legislative council. Two were princes, the third, Sir Dinkar Rao, was the diwan of Gwalior who had remained loyal to the British when Gwalior's army revolted, and all three were Hindus, but Sayyid Ahmed was able to 'rejoice' and give 'thanks to the Almighty' for their work in the council.[52]

As a judicial officer, Sayyid Ahmed was moved from district to district in what is today's Uttar Pradesh the way Bankim had been transferred within Bengal. In Moradabad and Ghazipur, Sayyid Ahmed started schools, as Vidyasagar and Phule had done. Financed by Hindu and Muslim friends of his, Sayyid Ahmed's schools were open to all communities. Like Bankim he wrote, without however attempting novels or poetry, and like Vidyasagar and Bankim he acquired a printing press (in Ghazipur). An Urdu commentary by him on the Bible pointed out similarities in Islam and Christianity to his Muslim readers.

A translation society he started in 1864, soon to be called the Scientific Society, would translate, for readers of Urdu, forty Western books on subjects such as agriculture, meteorology and electricity. Posted to Aligarh (about 80 miles south-east of Delhi), Sayyid Ahmed found a valuable Hindu backer there, Raja Jaikishen Das. Sayyid Ahmed's Scientific Society was moved to Aligarh, where he also started (in 1866) a British India Association (we earlier saw that in 1851 a group of zamindars had created a British India Association in Calcutta), saying that the platform would enable both Hindus and Muslims to 'honestly, openly and respectfully speak out their grievances' to their British rulers. Referring to 'the great God above', Sayyid Ahmed added that this God was 'equally the God of the Jew, the Hindu, the Christian and the Mohammedan'.[53]

Unwilling (again like Bankim) to be insulted, in 1867 he led, though still a functionary in the Empire, a walk-out at a function in Agra because Indian guests had been given inferior places. Both Hindus and Muslims left with him. Soon thereafter, however, following a new posting in Benares, he appeared to be focussed on 'the welfare of Muslims alone'.

This was the impression created on his old friend from Bijnor, Shakespeare, also now posted in Benares. 'Before this,' the Briton evidently said to Sayyid Ahmed, 'you were always keen about the welfare of your countrymen in general.' Shakespeare wished to know why the change had occurred. A campaign by Hindus in Benares to replace Urdu with Hindi in the courts brought it about, replied Sayyid Ahmed. To him, Urdu was not only a 'memento of Muslim rule', it was a product of Hindu-Muslim interaction down the centuries.[54]

Not that Urdu and Hindi were very different from each other. Both used the same words, though some Hindus peppered their speech with Sanskrit terms while some Muslims introduced fancy Arabic and Persian sounds into their language. It was perfectly possible, at this stage, for a single language in two scripts to develop in northern and central India. It was equally possible for Hindi and Urdu to be driven along separate channels.

On both sides, separateness was preferred to a common language. The Hindu-Muslim partnership of the Revolt ten years earlier had vanished. India's Muslims, rather than India's inhabitants, would become the community or *qaum* that Sayyid Ahmed would primarily work for. On the Hindu side, the Benares-born poet, Bharatendu Harishchandra (1850–82)—often referred to as the father of modern Hindi literature—and other writers in Bharatendu's circle preferred a Sanskritized Hindi. Also, rather like Bankim and others in Bengal (and like Sayyid Ahmed), these Hindu writers either remained silent about 1857 or praised the British victory. Bharatendu's sole direct reference to 1857 occurs in a cryptic stanza: 'The fires of the sepoy revolt were put down brutally. For terror, Indians dare not move their heads.'[55]

Badri Narain Upadhyaya (1855–1921), Bharatendu's close associate, thought that the rebellion had been a folly. He wrote, 'Those who thought that religion and caste were in danger . . . took with them a few foolish soldiers and some evil men and caused a great havoc.' While another close associate, Pratap Narain Mishra (1859–1923), '. . . reacted sharply to official suspicions of the loyalty of Indians to British rule' and 'compared [viceroy] Lord Ripon not only to Akbar but also to Ram', Radha Charan Goswami (1859–1923), who came from a family of priests in Brindavan and was 'highly inspired' by Bharatendu, wrote a fantasy in 1880 in which he said that Yama, Hinduism's god of death, had created 'a special hell for those who had fought against the British in 1857'.[56]

When, in 1881, the Sikh entrepreneur, Dyal Singh Majithia, started the *Tribune* as a public trust in Lahore, the English-language paper declared in its opening editorial: 'Towards the rulers of our country our conduct will be marked by staunch and unswerving loyalty.'[57] Thus, separately, did Muslim, Hindu and Sikh intellectuals woo India's British rulers.

~

Sayyid Ahmed's journey to England (1869) was sparked off by the award of a scholarship for Cambridge to his son Mahmud, a student at Calcutta University, who was one of nine Indians, and the first from the North Western Provinces, to get such an opportunity. George Graham, a police officer who had been friends with Sayyid Ahmed, suggested that the father too should travel to England. Agreeing, the father obtained furlough, mortgaged the ancestral home in Delhi, borrowed money, and travelled with Mahmud, another son, Hamed, a friend, Khudadad Beg, and a servant called Chajju.

By now, Sayyid Ahmed was fifty-two and his beard had turned white. Graham, who also took leave and joined his friend in England, speaks of Sayyid Ahmed's 'massive build', 'medium height', 'leonine face' and 'hearty laugh'. Later, Graham would write his friend's biography—perhaps the first 'by a Victorian gentleman in praise of a "native"'.[58] We can picture Sayyid Ahmed's expensive journey to England and his time there thanks to Graham's book and thanks to letters that Sayyid Ahmed wrote (to Raja Jaikishen Das among others), which were published in the *Aligarh Institute Gazette*, the journal of the Scientific Society.

The party took three days to get to Nagpur from Benares, proceeding by train to Jabalpur and by bullock cart thereafter. From Nagpur, they took a train that went through numerous tunnels (which awed Sayyid Ahmed) to Bombay. Taking the *Baroda* to Suez, a train to Alexandria, another ship, the *Poona*, to Marseilles, and another train to Paris, where they took time to see the Palace of Versailles, they finally arrived, by a new train, in Calais, where they crossed the English Channel. On the *Baroda*, Sayyid Ahmed was impressed by a Sunday service on the deck.

All the English seated themselves on chairs and the clergyman read prayers . . . I stood silently and respectfully near them, walking every now and then. I saw the way God was prayed to, and admired His catholicity. Some men bow down to idols; others address him seated in chairs, with head uncovered; some address Him with head covered and beads on, with hands clasped in profound respect; many abuse Him but He cares not . . .[59]

The sight of the Arab coast affected Sayyid Ahmed—'I thought of God having caused our blessed Prophet to be born in it.' And Europe bowled him over. He wrote of 'the beauty of the buildings, the brilliancy of the lamps, and the number of well-dressed good-looking men and women', and said that he had been 'struck dumb with amazement' by 'the life-like fidelity' of the paintings in the Versailles Palace. Comparing the canals of this palace with 'the famous canal in the Delhi Fort in whose waters I used in former days to play', he thought that the one in Delhi 'was undoubtedly far inferior'.[60]

Graham took his friend to the Derby. Now retired in England, John Lawrence from the Punjab (Henry Lawrence's brother) called on the Indian visitor. Unlike Bankim or Vidyasagar, Sayyid Ahmed never mastered English, but he attended the last reading given by Charles Dickens (who would die in June 1870), and met Thomas Carlyle (1795–1881), who had written of the Prophet of Islam as a hero. Also, as we have already noted, Sayyid Ahmed was present when Queen Victoria opened a viaduct.

Regrettably, we do not have an account by Russell of Sayyid Ahmed's visit to England, where he spent many pounds hiring carriages for calls on the high and important. In fact, it is unlikely that Russell met him—he was away from England for much of this time, reporting first-hand on the new Suez Canal and accompanying Albert Edward, the Prince of Wales, to Egypt and the Middle East.

While in England Sayyid Ahmed was decorated with the Star of India—clearly the British were keen to woo him. On his part, he was impressed by much in England, including the curiosity and education of the maids in the house where he had rented rooms.

The first, Anne Smith, is very clever, reads the papers and does her work like a watch or machine . . . She calls us all 'sir'. Khudadad Beg she calls Mr Beg, and on hearing that that was not his full name, said, 'Sir, please pardon me, but your full name is very difficult.' There was great fun over this, and we have all taken to calling Khudadad Beg 'Mr Beg' . . . The other, Elizabeth Matthews, very young and modest, maid-of-all-work, in spite of her poverty invariably buys a half-penny paper called the 'Echo'.[61]

Education was the English secret, he concluded, a conviction reinforced on visits to Cambridge, where Mahmud was dropped off, Oxford, and several schools including Harrow and Eton. He would start a modern college for India's Muslims. And through a new journal he would reform his qaum's manners, even as, he was told, Addison and Steele had done in England through the *Tatler* and the *Spectator*.

On 24 December 1870, within three months of his return to Benares, the first issue of *Tahdhib-al-Akhlaq* or *Mohammedan Social Reformer* appeared. The journal kicked up a storm, for among other things, Sayyid Ahmed said in it that the slavery Muslims had practised in the past was forbidden by the Qur'an. Six years after the end of the American Civil War, Sayyid Ahmed, for one, had written about slavery.

He wrote too that polygamy was permissible only if the husband was sure he could be equally just towards each wife. It was not irreligious for Muslims, he further argued, to dress like non-Muslims, and he added that contemporary Muslims were entitled to exercise independent judgement, *ijtihad*, on modern questions not covered by the Qur'an or some authentic pronouncement.

The orthodox were up in arms. Sayyid Ahmed was called an infidel, an atheist and a Christian, but attacks on him subsided once it became clear that he was serious about a Muslim college, and that the British were helping him.

The governor of the NWP, Sir William Muir, released 75 acres of land. Lord Northbrook, the viceroy, gave Rs 10,000 from personal funds. Indian princes contributed, including the Muslim ruler of Rampur, the Sikh ruler of Patiala, and the Hindu ruler of Vizianagaram. Raja Jaikishen Das helped, too, and Sayyid Ahmed Khan went door to door with a bag round his neck to collect donations.

In June 1875, the Mohammedan Anglo Oriental College (MAO) of Aligarh held its first classes. The following year Sayyid Ahmed retired from service to give all his time to MAO, and in January 1877, Northbrook's successor as viceroy, Lord Lytton, visited the college.

This was shortly after a great durbar in Delhi, held on 1 January 1877, when princes from different parts of the land gathered to acknowledge the assumption by Queen Victoria of the title of Empress of India, or Kaiser-i-Hind. Already the Revolt seemed an old story.

That the princes assembled not in Calcutta, the traditional seat of British power, but in Delhi, the Mughal capital, was an expression of British confidence. Yet chiefs from across the land gathering under a Delhi umbrella was also a suggestion, rare in Indian history but not unknown, of national unity. Interestingly enough, 'the Indian press compared the durbar to the *rajsuya yagna* of Yudhishthira (portrayed in the Mahabharata) and to the assemblage of nobles from all parts of India at the Mughal court'.[62]

～

In practice, MAO did not prove as reformist as some hoped and others feared. Only males could enter it. Their religious education was handled not by Sayyid Ahmed but by a committee of orthodox Muslims. However, the teaching of arts, science and law courses was in English; both Shia and Sunni were welcomed and treated alike (Sayyid Ahmed was a Sunni); Hindus were included in the student body, the faculty and the managing committee; to gain Hindu confidence, the slaughter of cows on the campus was forbidden.

Despite the impact made on him by England's newspaper-reading maidservants, Sayyid Ahmed was educating Muslims from India's higher classes, not persons like Chajju, the servant who had accompanied him to England. And despite the concessions that Sayyid Ahmed had made to orthodoxy, a modern Muslim college outraged some people.

Anonymous letters reached him that spoke of oaths on the Qur'an to kill him. But the qaum as a whole welcomed a college that would enable young Muslims to find jobs, and liked the man who had become a bridge between India's Muslims and their clearly irremovable British rulers. In 1920, MAO would become the Aligarh Muslim University. In time, some of its graduates would become Prime Ministers or Presidents in independent India and Pakistan. Exponents of both Muslim nationalism and Indian nationalism would cite their Aligarh connection. Yet one of its products, the scholar Mohammed Mujeeb, would criticize Sayyid Ahmed for putting his college ahead of religious and social reform.

> It appeared as if he had made a bargain, and asked his community to accept his college, where the 'new' education was offered on condition that new ideas on Islam were not offered as a part of this education ... The higher value was discarded for the lower, a few hundred acres of dusty lands and buildings without character were exchanged for the infinite spaces of religious and moral speculation; the reconstruction of the social and economic life of a whole community was sacrificed to secure recruitment in the lower grades of government service for the sons of a few hundred Muslim families.[63]

With the opening of MAO, Sayyid Ahmed was seen as a leader of the country's Muslims and named to the Imperial Legislative Council, where he initiated a bill for compulsory vaccination against smallpox and spoke out against racial discrimination in Indian courts.

When Allan Octavian Hume (a part, like Sayyid Ahmed and Bankim, of the machinery of British rule) proposed a native volunteer corps, Sayyid Ahmed backed the idea even though his friend George Graham was against it. Indians had to be trusted if they were to trust the British, he told Graham.

But later, when Hume succeeded, after being thrown out of government, in encouraging his numerous Indians friends, including many in Calcutta, to launch the Indian National Congress, Sayyid Ahmed spent much energy opposing the new body. He seemed shocked by the Congress's demands for a place for elected members on local and provincial councils, and for greater opportunities for Indians to enter the civil service.

Expressed at public meetings, Sayyid Ahmed's opposition sprang from fear. Men from the lower ranks would win in elections. Bengali Hindus, better educated than other communities, would monopolize the civil service. An India run by Indians would be dominated by Hindus, who were far more numerous than Muslims. It was much better that Britons continued to govern far into the future, and Muslims at any rate should stay clear of the Congress.

Lucknow, 18 December 1887. Would our aristocracy like that a man of low caste or insignificant origin, though he be a B.A. or M.A., and have the requisite ability, should be in a position of authority above them and have power in making laws that affect their lives and property? Never! Nobody would like it. (*Cheers.*) A seat in the Council of the Viceroy is a position of great honour and prestige. None but a man of good breeding can the Viceroy take as his colleague, treat as his brother, and invite to entertainments at which he may have to dine with Dukes and Earls.

Now, I ask you, have Mahomedans attained to such a position as regards higher English education, which is necessary for higher appointments, as to put them on a level with Hindus or not? Most certainly not. Now I take Mahomedans and the Hindus of our Province together, and ask whether they are able to compete with the Bengalis or not? Most certainly not. When this is the case, how can competitive examination be introduced into our country? (*Cheers.*)

Now, we will suppose [an] election . . . [T]here will be one number for us to every four for the Hindus . . . . Then they will have four votes and we shall have one.

For Sayyid Ahmed, the continuance of British rule was essential for preventing strife.

Now, suppose that all English, and the whole English army, were to leave India, taking with them all their cannon and their splendid weapons and everything, then who would be rulers of India? Is it possible that under these circumstances two *qaums*—the Mahomedans and the Hindus—could sit on the same throne and remain equal in power? Most certainly not. It is necessary that one of them should conquer the other and thrust it down.[64]

If Hindus were coming together in the Congress, crossing provincial divides, Muslims would need not only to unite among themselves, but also to get closer to the British, who were Christians, no matter what had happened during the Revolt.

Meerut, 14 March 1888. Our Hindu brothers of these provinces are leaving us and are joining the Bengalis. Then we ought to unite with that *qaum* with whom we can unite. No Mahomedan can say that the English are not 'People of the Book'. No Mahomedan can deny this: that God has said that no people of other religions can be friends of Mahomedans except the Christians.[65]

Sayyid Ahmed's remarks notwithstanding, the Congress was not primarily a Hindu body. 'The eradication of all possible racial, religious or provincial prejudices' was in fact one of its aims, and a Muslim barrister from Bombay, Badruddin Tyabji, presided at its third session in Madras in 1887. In a letter to Sayyid Ahmed, Tyabji said:

> If any proposal is made which would subject the Mussalmans to the Hindus or would vest the exclusive power in Hindus to the detriment of the Mussalmans, I would oppose it with all my strength, but the Congress proposes to do no such thing. Its aims are and must be for the benefit of all communities equally.[66]

But Sayyid Ahmed's attacks contributed to Muslim wariness towards the Congress. In 1888, a year when he was knighted, Sayyid Ahmed helped create the United Indian Patriotic Association (UIPA) for prominent and mostly rich Muslims and Hindus who too were troubled by the formation of the Congress. Rather like Sayyid Ahmed, the Hindu Maharaja of Benares said that 'representative institutions was an occidental idea'.[67] Within a month, fifty local groups joined the apex body of the UIPA.

Within a few years, however, the UIPA gave way to the Mohammedan Defence Association, with Theodore Beck, a Briton from Cambridge who was the MAO principal, as its secretary. Without Beck, in fact, the new body would not have got going. The Briton seemed even less convinced than Sayyid Ahmed of the likelihood of Hindu-Muslim cooperation. 'Anglo-Mohammedan friendship was possible,' Beck seems to have said, 'but friendship between Muslims and the followers of Hindu and Sikh religions was impossible.'[68]

Even as Hindus like Bankim saw British rule as an opportunity to build Hindu strength vis-à-vis Muslims, Sayyid Ahmed, scion of Mughal nobility, sought a Muslim-British alliance to keep both Hindu rule, and rule by uncultured voters, at bay. He would do nothing to upset the qaum-Empire relationship for which he had patiently and successfully toiled.

~

In 1883, Graham enjoyed 'a right pleasant sight' of the viceroy, Lord Ripon, seated on Sayyid Ahmed's right at an Aligarh function, and Sayyid Mahmud (who became a judge), sitting on the viceroy's right. The scene symbolized a change. The qaum had recovered influence, thanks in part to Sayyid Ahmed.

'I am an utter nothing,' he said in 1884, 'yet I am a descendant of the Messenger who is the mercy of the two worlds. I shall walk on the path of my ancestor.' But it was not only a matter of descent. 'Considerable reflection and thought with an open mind' had led him, he claimed, to 'full certainty' about his faith.[69]

Between 1880 and 1888, he wrote four volumes on the Qur'an, offering a commentary that strove to emphasize the scripture's conformity with nature and with reason. Mujeeb, who thought that Sayyid Ahmed's was a non-religious mind that 'sought to achieve essentially secular values', felt nonetheless that the commentary identified important issues.[70] Another Sayyid Ahmed scholar, Christian Troll, thinks that the ethics advocated in the commentary gives 'due importance to the intentions of the heart' and goes beyond 'mere formalism and legalism'.[71]

Because Sayyid Ahmed was such a major figure, and his views were known, the commentary invited less hostility than his *Reformer* had done. Still, Maulana Rashid Ahmed, head of the influential Deoband seminary, said in 1889 that between the Congress, which seemed to be led by Hindus, and Sayyid Ahmed's MDA, the former was preferable. 'Sayyid Ahmed administers sweet poison,' he added.[72] The Maulana's comment reflected a continuing resentment of British rule in important sections of the qaum. Living to the age of eighty-one, Sayyid Ahmed died in Aligarh in March 1898.

HUME

We had left young Hume in Etawah in 1859, when, to the dismay of his British peers, he and an Indian landlord started *The People's Friend*, a journal in Hindi and Urdu that was read in places far away from Etawah. But in 1860, when Hume was thirty-one, the government recognized his bravery in the Revolt with a 'Commander of the Bath' decoration.

His spirit remaining independent, Hume criticized the Raj's practice of giving judicial powers to police officers, and he also objected to torturous methods of investigation, but ill health forced him to repair to England, where he stayed on leave for two years.

Returning to Etawah in 1863, Hume devoted much energy to an old interest—the study of birds. His personal collection of bird skins and eggs had been destroyed during the Revolt. Now he embarked on a larger project—a survey and documentation, with the help of interested friends, of the birds of the Indian subcontinent. The project received a boost in 1867, when Hume was made commissioner of Inland Customs for upper India, and again in 1870, when he rose to become the Government of India's Agriculture and Commerce Secretary, positions that put him in contact with officers, fieldworkers and potential birdwatchers across the land, Indians as well as Britons.

His new responsibilities took Hume and his wife to Simla, where they bought Rothney Castle on Jakko Hill. This mansion became a museum for a rapidly growing number of bird skins and eggs. Many were sent by a network of ornithologists enlisted by Hume. He also collected numerous specimens himself as he travelled widely for work and sometimes solely for ornithology, including to the banks of the Indus in the north-west, the Khasi Hills and Manipur in the north-east, the Andaman and Nicobar Islands in the Bay of Bengal and what were called the Laccadive Islands (now Lakshadweep) in the Arabian Sea.

Hume's natural history collection in Simla's Rothney Castle in the 1870s may remind us of Russell's menagerie in a smaller house in Simla in the summer of 1858, and of Russell's fascination with the birds he shot while living there.

To return to Hume, in 1869 he published *Rough Notes on Indian Ornithology*. Three years later, he started a quarterly journal for the study of birds, *Stray Feathers*. The early 1880s saw Hume's *Game Birds of India, Burmah and Ceylon* (co-authored by C.H.T. Marshall) and *Nests and Eggs of Indian Birds*. Hume was preparing another volume containing the life histories of 700 birds—he hoped it might prove to be the greatest work on ornithology[73]—but in 1884, a servant stole the manuscript and apparently sold it as waste paper.

A crushed Hume said nothing but abandoned the book. Birds

were no longer allowed to tease his mind, and he decided to donate his entire collection to the British Museum of Natural History.

Acting on Hume's request, R. Bowdler Sharpe, head of the Museum's ornithological department, journeyed in 1885 from London to Simla, took over the gift of 82,000 birds and eggs, and brought the precious cargo safely to London. 'All students of Indian ornithology bless the name of Hume when they go to work in the Museum,'[74] and quite a few are surprised to learn that he also helped found the Indian National Congress.

Charismatic, assertive (arrogant and cantankerous to his critics) and ever curious, Hume would say of himself (when fifty-seven), 'I still remain a boy at heart.'[75] We have seen that unlike most British officers, Hume had Indian friends, and also that a readiness to trust Indians was part of his make-up. This did not always please his superiors, even though his abilities were recognized.

The years as Agriculture Secretary, requiring journeys to different parts of the land, enhanced Hume's knowledge of the needs of the Indian peasant and produced ideas for agricultural reform. They also kept him abreast of the thinking of a new middle class of educated Indians emerging from the universities of Calcutta, Bombay and Madras. He noticed, too, the appearance of new Indian journals. The days when zamindars and princes were the only influential Indians were ending.

Occurring in February 1872 in the Andaman Islands, the assassination by a Muslim extremist of Lord Mayo, the viceroy, was a reminder that not all Indians had given up violence. Hume, on his part, never needed a reminder. The possibility of 'another bloody revolt' remained an 'obsession' with one who could never forget 1857.[76] He had concluded that maintaining relationships with Indians and involving them in their country's governance were the ways to avert a recurrence.

Hume frankly told Mayo's successor as viceroy, Lord Northbrook, that 'anarchy and devastation' were on the cards if taxes on the peasantry were not reduced and if 'a substantial Indian element' was not brought into the government.[77] Famines that occurred later in the 1870s in eastern, western and southern India only confirmed Hume's views.

Like many in his time, Hume nursed an admiration for the 'Aryan' virtues, which, it was believed, had descended alike to classes of Europeans and Indians. Hume's future biographer, William Wedderburn, a civilian in western India, thought that Hume himself, 'fair and blue-eyed, stalwart and active, a dauntless lover of freedom', displayed 'the true Aryan breed'. Adding that Hume was 'in full brotherly accord with the Aryan of the East, the meditative and saintly type', Wedderburn felt that 'it pained [Hume]'s very soul that West should deny to East the joys of freedom, which should be the common heritage of both.'[78]

Hume was struck also by the peaceful Meiji revolution that occurred in Japan in the 1860s, converting a military despotism into a constitutional government. He wondered why India's alien bureaucracy should not also yield place, gradually and peacefully, to a national government, which could become 'a tower of strength to the Empire'.[79] Britons governing India and Indian elites agreed about the Aryan race and the usefulness of the British Empire, but, unusually for a Briton, Hume also wanted a role for Indians in India's governance.

Despite his views, Hume was offered, it appears, the governorship of the Punjab by Lord Lytton, Northbrook's successor as viceroy. Replying that the large entertaining expected from a governor would not suit him or his wife, Hume said he would rather be home member, an idea that Lytton seemed open to. But Lord Salisbury, Secretary of State for India and a future Prime Minister, turned it down on the ground that Hume had opposed a reduction of Indian duties on British textiles.[80]

His sympathy for Indians and unconcealed dissatisfaction with British policies having won Hume the dislike of several colleagues, a bid to 'suppress Mr Hume' was launched.[81] Finally, in June 1879, Lytton demoted Hume, sending him to Allahabad as a member of the NWP's Revenue Board. When Hume asked for the reason, Lytton replied through his private secretary that the step 'was in the public interest'.[82] Nothing else was said, and no dereliction of duty or incapacity was suggested.

The *Statesman* commented that Hume had been treated 'shamefully and cruelly', and the *Englishman* reasoned that Hume's offence was that he 'expressed his views with great freedom, without regard to what might be the wishes or intentions of his superiors'. The *Englishman* added that Hume was thought of as 'insubordinate' merely because he refused to suppress 'even in most confidential notes' his dissent from official steps.[83]

He was unwilling to serve in Allahabad for any length of time. Taking furlough, he returned to Simla and his Rothney Castle, but not before forming relationships with westerners and Indians prominent in the Theosophical movement, including the Russia-born Helena Blavatsky and the American, Henry Olcott.

Impressed by these personalities and by the Theosophical movement's declared openness to truth from all sides and its belief in universal brotherhood, Hume was also willing to believe some dire but dubious pronouncements shown to him by persons in the movement. Made by supposed but unnamed (and evidently fake) gurus, these statements claimed that another violent rising, similar to that of 1857–59, was being planned.[84]

An actual attempt to ignite a violent rebellion in the Marathi country had failed in the summer of 1879, and the bid's captured leader, Vasudev Balwant Phadke (1845–83), died in detention; but in 1879 and 1880 it was possible for a man like Hume to believe, at least for a while, the scary stories he was hearing. Though Hume's connections with the Theosophical movement would end by 1884, his keenness on a partnership with Indians to remove the ground for a fresh rebellion would only grow.

Edward Robert Lytton, the viceroy who demoted Hume, had organized (with the blessings of Prime Minister Disraeli) the imperial durbar in Delhi in 1877. In 1878, Lytton raised a storm with his Vernacular Press Act that authorized a magistrate who felt that an Indian-language newspaper was preaching disaffection to fine its press and confiscate its machinery.

Opposition to the measure was organized by the newly formed Indian Association, where the England-educated Surendranath Banerjea (1848–1925), editor of a new weekly, the *Bengalee*, was a prominent leader. Unlike the zamindar-dominated British Indian Association, the new body represented sections of Calcutta's educated middle class.

The passage of the Vernacular Press Act energized Indian intellectuals. In an ingenious response, the *Amrita Bazar Patrika* converted itself into an English-language journal. In Madras, the *Hindu* was started in 1878, also in English. The *Tribune*, another Indian-owned English-language journal, would start in Lahore in 1881. Significantly, the new journals carried reports of events occurring even in distant provinces.

Following appeals by the Indian Association and others to Gladstone, the Liberal Party in Britain decided to oppose the Act, and many Indians imagined a bright future for India if only the Liberals obtained control in England. Their wish was granted in April 1880, when Gladstone led the Liberals to a large victory over Disraeli's Conservatives. One consequence of Disraeli's defeat was Lytton's resignation as viceroy.

He was succeeded by fifty-three-year-old Lord Ripon, a staunch liberal-radical who had earlier served in the India Office in London. A grandfather of his had been a governor of Madras. A recent convert to Catholicism, Ripon divided his term in India between Calcutta and Simla. The new viceroy found a good deal of sense in the opinions of a Simla resident he met, the bird-keeper of Rothney Castle. 'Extremely friendly relations' grew between Ripon and Hume.[85]

In January 1882, the viceroy repealed the hated Press Act, and in May of that year he committed himself to local self-government through municipal and rural boards where at least two-thirds would be non-officials, chosen if possible by election. Excitement over Ripon's local self-government initiative of May 1882 drowned out a suggestion that Surendranath Banerjea had made in his paper, the *Bengalee*. Noting that ties among educated Indians of different provinces had strengthened, he wrote (on 27 May) that something else was needed.

> The time indeed has truly come when a great national congress, meeting once every year, may cement still further the bonds of unity among the Indian races, and prepare the way for concerted action in reference to political matters . . .[86]

That Ripon was aiming at something larger than local self-government was spelt out in a private letter he wrote to his close friend (and author of *Tom Brown's Schooldays*), Thomas Hughes, the Christian Socialist.

I am laying the foundation upon which may hereafter be built a more complete system of self-government for India which may convert what is now a successful administration by foreigners into a real government of the country by itself.[87]

Whether Hume too was made aware of this bold but undisclosed thought is not known. What is clear is that Hume's involvement in Indian politics began with Ripon's scheme for local self-government, which Hume saw as just the sort of initiative needed for removing the reason for another revolt.

Predictably, however, the India Office in London and the British establishment in India tried to impede the reform. Ripon asked for Hume's help to mobilize Indian support, and the result was an extraordinary letter by Hume in the *Pioneer*, British-owned but read widely in northern India by Indians and whites. The letter called upon educated Indians to embrace the opportunity to govern their localities and to realize that Ripon was facing strong critics in England and in India. It concluded with these words:

My friends, the game is in our own hands; the ball is at your feet, and the question is, '*What will you do with it?*'[88]

Indian newspapers publicized the letter throughout the land, and Hume (who now formally resigned from the civil service) emerged as a Briton who thought of Indians as *his* people ('the game is in *our* hands') and wanted them to begin to run their country—and who, moreover, seemed to be the viceroy's ally.

Another Ripon ally was the law member in his executive, C.P. Ilbert. In December 1882, Ilbert told the Imperial Legislative Council that he welcomed the Indian press as 'the best source of information' on what was happening, and in February 1883 he introduced a bill that Indians, especially in Bengal, had long asked for. It sought to empower an Indian district magistrate or sessions judge in the mofussil (hinterland) to try Europeans accused of a criminal offence.

The few Indian district magistrates or sessions judges that existed had been granted such a power in a city like Calcutta, but the idea of giving them authority over whites in the countryside triggered a 'white mutiny'. Disturbed already by Ripon's initiatives, most of India's Britons saw in the Ilbert Bill a mentality that would destroy the hierarchy that had enabled a white minority to dominate a large population. They revolted.

At meeting after meeting in different parts of India, Ripon as well as the land's natives were roundly abused. After the first of these meetings, held in Calcutta on 29 February 1883, the correspondent of *The Times* reported that 'no such excitement has been witnessed among the Europeans since the time of the Mutiny.'[89]

But a Parsi visitor to Calcutta who had gone to the meeting just 'to see the fun' left, as he would write in a Bombay newspaper, 'as soon as I heard the Bengalis abused'. He added, 'There is no difference between Bengalis and Parsis. All are Indians.'[90] The racism in the anti-Ilbert rhetoric of India's Britons, widely reproduced in the Indian press, was producing a new sense of Indianness.

Observing the 'white mutiny' from Simla was an Indian-in-spirit. On 1 March, Hume penned a hard-hitting letter to 'Graduates of the Calcutta University'.

> [I]t is to you, her most cultured and enlightened minds, her most favoured sons, that your country must look for the initiative. In vain may aliens like myself love India and her children as well as the most loving of these; in vain may they, for her and their good, give time and trouble, money and thought; in vain may they struggle and sacrifice . . . they may place their experience, abilities and knowledge at the disposal of the workers, but they lack the essential of nationality, and the real work must be done by the people of the country themselves.

Since individuals could not do what an organization could, Hume proposed, for a start, an association with say fifty 'founders'.

> You are the salt of the land. And if amongst even you, the elite, fifty men cannot be found with sufficient power of self-sacrifice, sufficient love for and pride in their country . . . to take the initiative and if needs be devote the rest of their lives to the Cause, then there is no hope for India. Her sons must and will remain humble and helpless instruments in the hands of foreign rulers, for 'they [who] would be free, *themselves* must strike the blow'.
>
> And if even the leaders of thought are all either such poor creatures, or so selfishly wedded to personal concerns, that they dare not or will not strike a blow for their country's sake, then justly and

rightly are they kept down and trampled on ... ; then we your friends are wrong, and our adversaries right ... If this be so, let us hear no more fractious, peevish complaints that you are kept in leading strings, and treated like children, for you will have proved yourselves such. *Men* know how to act.[91]

This letter was not published but sent privately to a circle of trusted friends. About three months later, an almost identical idea was expressed in a letter sent from England to Ripon by Arthur Hobhouse, who had served as law member in Lytton's executive. Concerned that India's small but growing community of Britons would 'get the ear of their countrymen to the exclusion of the enormous mass of the real owners of the country', Hobhouse hoped that 'the educated Natives may form a sufficiently compact and intelligent body to exercise political pressure' on London.[92]

Hume's letter probably influenced two subsequent events. On 8 March, six of Calcutta's Indian bodies, hitherto at odds with one another, sent a joint memorial to Lord Ripon thanking him for the Ilbert Bill. And in April, one of Hume's closest friends, Womesh Chandra Bonnerjee (1844–1906), a barrister from London's Middle Temple, quietly put together a 'United Indian Committee' to campaign in favour of the Ilbert Bill.[93]

Meetings welcoming the Bill were held in Bombay and elsewhere, but stories of white unrest dominated the media. The press in Britain offered strong backing to the Bill's foes. The *Daily Telegraph* wrote, 'On the day when we surrender the rights and privileges of superior strength and ethnical rank in India we invite our own expulsion.' *The Times* said, 'India can be governed by Englishmen only as a conquered country ... [T]he privileges of the English who are resident there ... are not anomalies at all ...'[94]

Ripon's Liberal Party friends in Britain capitulated before a fierce opposition mounted by the Conservatives, which was matched in India by white solidarity against the Ilbert Bill. In 1884, Ripon was forced to accept a compromise that retained little of what he and Ilbert had put into the bill. Ripon felt he had detected in fellow Britons in India 'the true ring of the old feeling of American slave-holders'.[95]

In September 1884, Ripon announced that he was ending his viceroyalty early: he wanted Gladstone to appoint a Liberal successor before new British elections brought the Conservatives back in power.

His departure was a triumphal march, with large crowds bidding him farewell as he travelled from Simla to Calcutta and Calcutta to Bombay, the Indian press praising him, a meeting in Serampore resolving to call him a mahatma, and temple priests performing ceremonies for his well-being. Some Indians were in tears, and in Bombay no fewer than 154 addresses were presented to him.

But more than a send-off had occurred. Thanks to Ripon, the Ilbert Bill, and the agitation for and against that bill, 'the first beginning of national life' had been glimpsed in India. This was the comment of the *Hindu* of Madras. The paper added that 'a powerful native opinion' conscious of 'its importance and strength' now existed. '[H]ow to secure this ground' was the question.[96]

~

That, of course, was the question that Hume had raised in his letter to the graduates of Calcutta University. He was among those who saw Ripon off in Bombay in December 1884, but he stayed on in that city for three months, for he had sensed that Bombay and Poona would have to play a major role in organizing what he was now aiming for—a meeting where India's best would get to know one another, form an Indian National Union, and agree on necessary political steps.

Was this entirely Hume's idea? Or had Ripon inspired it, in line with Hobhouse's letter to him? We may never know for certain. The thought was on more than one mind. We have seen that in May 1882 Surendranath Banerjea had publicly asked for 'a great national congress'. Others were expressing a similar wish. In December 1884, when Hume and many leading Indians were present in Bombay for Ripon's send-off, Dadabhai Naoroji (1825–1917), the Parsi who would become the first Indian to enter the British Parliament, seems to have broached the idea of an annual all-India gathering.[97]

Whether or not his original idea, Hume pursued it with energy, to which the loss that year of his manuscript of 'The Birds of India' may have contributed. He also pursued the plan with secrecy until it was safe to announce it. Remarkably, caution was also observed by the many with whom he discussed the plan, or who discussed it with one another in Hume's absence.

During several months before his journey to Bombay, Hume was evidently writing to Indians in Calcutta, Poona, Bombay, Madras and elsewhere in order to link them with one another. One of the letters we know of was written on 16 November 1884 to Chiplonkar, the secretary of the Poona Sarvajanik Sabha. In this letter, Hume stated that in order to advance 'the National Cause' and the 'linking-in' idea, as he called it, he intended to travel to 'Bombay, Poona, Madras, Calcutta, Patna (perhaps Dacca), Benares, Allahabad, Agra, Delhi, Amritsar and Lahore' and possibly some other places.[98]

In Poona, the Sarvajanik Sabha (Public Association), which was principally led by Mahadev Govind Ranade (1840–1901), a Brahmin judge and social reformer, 'was conducted with great energy and ability'.[99] Though Jotiba Phule was critical of Brahmin dominance in the body, the Sabha's influence was large.

In Bombay, three barristers, Pherozeshah Mehta (a Parsi), K.T. Telang (a Hindu), and Badruddin Tyabji (a Muslim)—spoken of as the three brothers in law—were providing impressive leadership. Moreover, Bombay seemed 'less bedevilled by factionalism' than Calcutta, and its Britons appeared less hostile to natives than those in the capital city.[100]

On 31 January 1885, during Hume's visit, a new political body was formed in Bombay, the Presidency Association. Soon afterwards, the men of Poona agreed to host the all-India meeting at the end of 1885. Early in March, Hume arrived in Madras, where he found a number of prominent men already prepared to take part in an all-India get-together.

A steamer of the Peninsular and Oriental Company took Hume from Madras to Calcutta. Largely because of personal rivalries, Bengal, the country's largest, richest and most populous province, was no longer the undisputed leader of political India. Yet, an all-India meeting without Bengal's representatives was unthinkable. W.C. Bonnerjee and some others agreed to go to Poona, but it seems that Hume did not meet Surendranath Banerjea in Calcutta.

On his way back to Simla, Hume talked with leading Indians in several places in north India, prompting the *Pioneer* to speculate, in June, on what he was up to. Reporting a rumour that Hume would be going to England to try to enter Parliament and form an 'Indian' party, the *Pioneer* added that such a goal might explain Hume's 'mysterious movements' of the preceding months.

Hume's answer, published in the *Pioneer*, did not reveal the whole truth. Confirming that he was going to visit England, but denying any interest in the House of Commons, he protested at mystery being attached to the movements of 'a quiet old retired officer like myself'. Claiming that 'my home is in India', Hume explained what he had recently done:

> I merely went from place to place to renew, or, in some cases, to make, the *personal* acquaintance of native gentlemen with whom, directly or indirectly, I had long been in communication.[101]

In fact, however, Hume had already sent a confidential note to what he called 'the inner circle' of 'the National Party' or 'the Indian National Union', announcing a conference in Poona in the last week of December, expressing the hope that it would 'form the germ of a Native Parliament' and adding that in addition to attendees from Poona, twenty from Bengal, twenty from Bombay Presidency, twenty from the Madras Presidency, and ten from north India would take part.[102]

He had also taken care to inform the new viceroy, Lord Dufferin, a Liberal like Ripon, of what was being organized. Hume's talk with Dufferin resulted in the abandonment of a plan to ask the governor of Bombay, Lord Reay, to preside at the conference—the viceroy and Hume agreed that a high functionary of the Empire could not preside over a conference likely to criticize its functioning.

In July, Hume sailed for England, where his aims were (1) to inform Liberal leaders of the Indian National Union project, (2) to organize an 'Indian party' in Britain to act as a pressure group, and (3) to persuade editors of leading newspapers to give space to Indian points of view, not just the opinions of India's Britons. Among the scores of people he met in Britain were Ripon, John Bright and Florence Nightingale.

Without naming him, Bright would say publicly of Hume (in Birmingham in November), 'I have never met with [another] man—and I have met with scores—who appeared to know so much about all parts of India.' After listening to Hume on his project, Florence Nightingale wrote to William Wedderburn in Bombay, 'We are watching the birth of a new nationality in the oldest civilization in the world. How critical will be its first meeting at Poona.'[103]

However, hurdles arose. In November, Surendranath Banerjea, still unaware of the Poona plan, announced that his Indian Association would hold a National Conference in Calcutta on 25, 26 and 27 December. After consulting Hume, who returned to Bombay on 2 December, the Poona hosts agreed to postpone the start of *their* meeting to 28 December, and to call it a *Congress* rather than a Conference, which is what Calcutta was holding.

On 5 December, the *Hindu* of Madras gave the first public notice of the Poona gathering, but a cholera outbreak in Poona in the third week of December forced a change of venue. Fortunately, Bombay was ready, and the Gokuldas Tejpal Sanskrit College Trust offered its buildings above Gowalia Tank in central Bombay for the first session of the Indian National Congress.

Of the 'very close on one hundred gentlemen' who gathered, thirty-eight came from six centres in the western presidency, twenty-one from thirteen different places in the southern presidency, three from Calcutta, three from different towns in the Punjab, and seven from four principal towns in the NWP and Avadh. The rest, close to thirty, were (Indian) officials, again from different parts of the country. Their role was to listen and if need be to advise, not to speak on record.

Hume's proposal that Womesh Chandra Bonnerjee should preside was unanimously accepted. Bonnerjee said that misfortunes and illnesses had prevented Bengal from sending a larger delegation— he was no doubt alluding, among other things, to a failure of teamwork with Banerjea.

Proceedings were conducted in camera in the hall of the Sanskrit College and only summaries were provided to the press, yet some contemporary accounts bring to us the flavour of the event. Writing in the *Bombay Gazette*, a European onlooker referred to 'the men from Madras, the blackness of whose complexion seemed to be made blacker by spotless white turbans', 'bearded, bulky, and large-limbed men' from the NWP, 'Marathas in their cart-wheel turbans', 'stalwart Sindhis from Kurrachee' and Parsis in a headdress 'which they themselves have likened to a slanting roof'. A delegate from Bengal would write:

> It was as if every member had inwardly resolved upon having less of words and more of work, every one of them inspired with an inward feeling that it was real work for his country which had called them to that hall ... There was an attempt in almost every speech to be brief, concise and to the point ... and a ring of true patriotic earnestness which thrilled through the sympathetic chords of all listeners ...[104]

In his remarks, Bonnerjee was quick to refute the charge that the Congress was 'a nest of conspirators and disloyalists'. To wish to be governed according to principles prevalent in Europe was 'in no way incompatible with thorough loyalty to the British Government', he declared. Dadabhai Naoroji said that the Congress was asking for 'the rights of British subjects, as British subjects'.[105] Resolutions were passed, including one asking for the inclusion of elected members in provincial councils and another asking for a cut in the military budget, which Indian revenues were financing.

At the end, three cheers were raised for Hume, the lone European in the assembly. (Another Briton who helped in Bombay, the judge William Wedderburn, was obliged to remain in the background.) The Bengal delegate quoted above wrote of Hume that his face beamed 'with intelligence and frankness', that 'sympathy' came across 'from his lustrous eyes', and that Hume was 'the first to cheer and first to appreciate a joke or a sentiment'.[106]

Eight years earlier, another Briton, Viceroy Lytton, the man who demoted Hume, had organized in Delhi an imperial durbar that was grander by far, and where maharajas and nawabs displayed their splendour. Yet it was this much humbler event in Bombay that the *Hindustani* of Lucknow picked out as crucial. In an article in January 1886, the paper said:

> When the historian of the future sets himself to write ... he will not fail to mention prominently the 28th, 29th, and 30th December 1885, when the various forces of the country were brought together. We

have very often used the word 'nation' . . . and we know also that there are many Anglo-Indians who will not believe that there is anything like a nation in India. But if any of these gentlemen had been present at the National Congress [in Bombay], he would have been convinced of the existence of something like a nation in India. The assembling of Sindhis, Punjabis, Bengalis, Madrasis, Guzeratis, Mahrattas, Parsis, Marwaris, Hindus and Mahomedans under the same roof, and for a common object, is by no means a trifling thing.[107]

~

His association merging ere long with the INC, Surendranath Banerjea presided twice at its sessions, in 1895 and 1902. Wedderburn also presided twice, in 1889 and 1910. Hume never became president but served as general secretary from 1885 until 1909.

Relations between the INC and the Raj fluctuated between uneasy cordiality and coldness. Only in the next century would the Congress defy the Raj. At the second Congress, held in Calcutta in December 1886, with Dadabhai Naoroji presiding, the delegates were invited to a garden party by Viceroy Dufferin. Badruddin Tyabji, the Muslim barrister, chaired the third Congress, which was held in December 1887 in Madras, where the governor, Lord Connemara, again entertained the delegates.

When an outreach programme adopted in Madras was criticized by the Raj, Hume replied that the Congress provided an alternative to 'illegal or anarchical proceedings' and would seek to ensure that the 'surging tide' that Western education and ideas of liberty had let loose would 'flow not to ravage and destroy but to fertilize and regenerate'.[108]

Cautioning Hume against the 'bold and drastic policy of appealing to the masses', Auckland Colvin, a Liberal who was the governor of the NWP and a supporter of the INC until its Madras session, also pointed to the opposition shown to the Congress in his province by Sayyid Ahmed (which we saw), and suggested that the Congress was alienating Muslims.

In his reply, Hume claimed that Muslim opposition would die down with time, and he charged that the 'hostile stimulus (to Muslims) came from the outside, from a few ill-advised (British)

officials who clung to the pestilent doctrine of Divide et impera.'
Since there were not many Muslims among English-speaking
Indians, the class to which the INC was appealing, it was natural,
Hume conceded, for Muslims to think of the INC as pro-Hindu.
Once, however, the Muslims gave up their suspicion of Western
education, they would hold their own against the Hindus. To
Hume, who always recalled that Muslims had protected him in
1857, the argument of Muslim inferiority was 'wretched',
'monstrous' and 'a shameful libel'.[109]

Wedderburn, whose older brother John was killed in the 1857
Revolt, would argue that while men like Colvin looked at India
from the viewpoint of the ruler, Hume did so from the angle of the
ruled. Surrounded by yes-men, the official could never find out
what the people really went through or felt. Hume, on the other
hand, sought out independent and critical Indian minds aware of
the misery of the masses.[110] Wedderburn would speak too, without
naming anyone, of 'excitable and high-handed functionaries, who
put their trust in espionage' or 'stimulated among Mahomedans a
class hostility to the movement' or 'who recommended that Mr
Hume should be deported'.[111]

In the end, it was of his own will that Hume left India. His INC
colleagues did not insist on his staying on. They felt the need to
stand on their own feet, and he realized the need to let go. His
helpful and untiring hand had also been a controlling one.
Moreover, suggestions by him that 'well-to-do Congressmen would
be among the first victims of hunger-induced anarchy' and his
'reminders that nationalists were not making sufficient sacrifices'
had needled many of his colleagues.[112]

There were differences too. The 1857 trauma never left Hume's
psyche and he again spoke in 1891–92 of the likelihood of a large-
scale rebellion. The assessment was repudiated, in a letter to *The
Times*, by Dadabhai Naoroji, who by now was in London, where
he had taken charge of the British Committee of the INC.[113]

Hume's psyche had been affected, too, by a personal void. 'I
never had a son,' he wrote to Dufferin in 1886. '[T]his, though I
have carefully hid it for my dear wife's sake, has been a great grief
to me, and has altered the whole course of my life . . .'[114]

Returning to England in 1892, Hume helped with *India*, a

journal presenting the realities of his other country, and continued, formally at least, to serve as an INC general secretary. Scores of heads and horns he had collected in India were given to the British Museum and he also started a botanic institute in south London. The Indian National Congress's 'father', as all Congressmen continued to call him, died in July 1912 at the age of eighty-three.

PHULE

A political platform for the educated elite of more than a score of India's far-flung cities was a notable advance from provincial associations of landlords, but the peasants, untouchables and tribals constituting the country's overwhelming majority had no way of mounting the new platform or speaking from it, and most of them remained unaware of its existence.

One man, however, was continually beating the drum for peasants and untouchables, and for the widow—Poona's Jotiba Phule, who was thirty-three in 1860. We saw him last in the late 1850s as the Indian Revolt petered out, an outcome he welcomed. He had dreaded the possibility of Brahmin rule returning to his Marathi country.

Phule saw British supremacy as a providential opportunity for India's peasant castes (the so-called Shudras) and untouchables (the so-called Ati-Shudras) to shake off high-caste domination, but he grumbled that the British had absorbed the high castes into their ruling machinery and were collecting taxes from the peasantry to pay the salaries of high-caste clerks, accountants and teachers.

During the Revolt, British officers previously friendly to Phule had cut him dead, not realizing that he wanted their side to win. After the Revolt, they had continued to work through Brahmin teachers and accountants.

Always ugly to him, India's caste equations seemed more offensive to Phule's mind once the American Civil War began. He felt there was no difference between the enslavement of blacks in America and the oppression of Shudras and Ati-Shudras in India. Just as the slaves and the Union had joined hands to end slavery in America, he wanted India's peasant and untouchable castes and the British government to unite and overthrow Brahmin domination.

343

In contrast with the other Indians we have focussed on, who seemed to remain wholly silent about the American Civil War, Phule followed that war with his heart and soul. He tried to imagine the 'divine satisfaction' of a Negro mother reunited with her sons and daughters, and a black husband with his wife. When the slaves were freed, Phule (his biographer Dhananjay Keer informs us) sang of Lincoln and 'the glory of the American heroes and statesmen who nobly and untiringly fought for the liberation of the Negroes'.[115]

Published in June 1873, his book *Gulamgiri* (Slavery), with the subtitle '*Slavery within the Indian Empire, under the cloak of Brahminism*', was dedicated

> To the good people of the United States as a token of admiration for their sublime, disinterested and self-sacrificing devotion in the cause of Negro Slavery; and with an earnest desire that my countrymen may take their noble example as their guide in the emancipation of these Shudra brethren from the trammels of Brahmin thraldom.[116]

About the ending of slavery, he wrote:

> The down-trodden people of India feel specially happy at this auspicious development because they alone or the slaves in America have experienced the inhuman hardships and tortures . . .[117]

Pointing out that 'half the . . . people of America had to wage a bloody war against their own compatriots for three years to emancipate the Negro slaves from their thraldom', he charged that Brahmins were 'torturing the Shudras and Ati-Shudras in India more cruelly than the treatment meted out by the American slave-owners to their Negro slaves'.[118] If the story of what Shudras and Ati-Shudras had gone through were told, 'streams of tears will burst forth from within the black hard rock which will inundate the whole earth.'[119]

Phule's openness to Western voices in India, whether missionary or secular, also set him apart. He did not feel he was disrespecting his Indian ancestors when he read Western works on the 1857 Revolt or on Indian religions and society. Accepting (along with almost all the intellectuals of his time, Western or Indian) the theory of Aryan migration into India, he again stood out by rejecting the alleged superiority of the Aryans over the natives they had subjugated, a superiority that Western scholars too had assumed.

Viewing several of the supposedly Aryan heroes and gods of Hindu legends as unworthy, Phule in particular attacked Parasurama, the god of the axe. Listed in the texts as an incarnation of Vishnu, Parasurama (assumed to be an Aryan Brahmin) had filled five large ponds with the blood of Kshatriyas to avenge his father's killing. Claiming the Kshatriyas as sons of the soil and as his ancestors, and the ancestors also of all of India's peasants and untouchables, Phule charged that by decimating the Kshatriyas, Aryan Brahmins had made India easy prey for Central Asia's Muslim invaders.

The attack on Parasurama was part of a forty-five-page ballad that Phule wrote in 1869 in honour of Shivaji, the seventeenth-century hero of the Marathi country who rose from a peasant caste to defy the Mughal empire. The ballad was composed following Phule's visit to Raigad, Shivaji's old capital, where he found the Shivaji sites in a state of complete neglect.

Brahmin writers had portrayed Shivaji as a chieftain blessed with a brilliant Brahmin guide, Ramdas, and with the good sense to carry out the guide's directions. Phule's ballad, which would be recited across the Marathi country, presented Shivaji as a Kshatriya hero who cared for the peasants, neglected no one, and made soldiering open to all. Also, Phule's Shivaji was a commander who in battle was cautious or daring as needed, and took no liberties with captive females.

Phule, the grower-cum-vendor of flowers who educated the daughters and the sons of the humble, went on to become a contractor and also a member of the Poona Municipal Committee. But his passion was spent on the peasant. Liberating the peasant from the moneylender's debt and the Brahmin's ideology became the theme of Phule's writing—in Marathi verse and prose—and of his activities.

He wrote *Priestcraft Exposed* in 1869, which was also the year when he wrote the Shivaji ballad. Four years later came *Gulamgiri*, offering Phule's view of Indian history and society. Describing Brahmins as Aryan invaders who had cleverly divided native non-Brahmins in order to rule them, the book questioned the truthfulness and morality of Hindu texts. The 1857 Revolt was not in the people's interest, he observed, but the British advent was.

However, he wrote that it was wrong of the British to fill government departments with Brahmins. If skilled non-Brahmins were not available for essential jobs, let more Britons be imported, Phule wrote, especially those with the character and spirit of service shown by his missionary friends. That the British had not spent more money and effort on schooling the children of the Shudras and the Ati-Shudras was a major complaint of the wide-ranging *Gulamgiri*, which espoused a morality of assisting the needy.

Attacks on *Gulamgiri* combined sarcasm with a charge that Phule was an agent of Christians. A Brahmin critic wrote in November 1873 of Phule's 'colossally incomparable knowledge of language, religion, history and logic' and added that the book had probably emerged from 'the brains of a jealous, disappointed, dwarfish Christian, newly converted but frustrated, and Phule must be a mere tool in his hand.'[120] The suggestion was that an intellectual critique, whether or not sound, could originate only from one with a high-caste origin, not from a Mali like Phule.

To rescue Shudras and Ati-Shudras from false doctrine, as Phule saw it, and from rituals requiring Brahmin priests, he and his friends started the Satya Shodhak Samaj (SSS) or the 'Truth Seeking Society', which would teach the fatherhood of God and the brotherhood of man, attack the caste system and idol worship, advocate temperance, and raise non-Brahmin priests who would wear a peasant's dhoti and turban. Open to all (Shudras, Mahars, Mangs, Brahmins, Jews, Muslims, and others), the SSS held its first meeting in Poona in September 1873, the year when *Gulamgiri* came out. Sixty people met and elected Phule, by then forty-five, as their president.

In another significant 1873 event, Jotiba and his wife Savitribai adopted a boy, Yashwant, to whom Kashibai, a Brahmin widow, had given birth in their home. The story was this: before Phule's father died, he had asked Jotiba to take a second wife for obtaining a son. Replying that childlessness may originate with the husband rather than the wife, he had refused to remarry. Soon thereafter, spurred by what Vidyasagar had done for widows in

Calcutta, the Phules had reached out to Poona's widows. Handbills informed widows forced into pregnancy that the Phule home was there to aid them:

O you widows! Come and deliver here safely and secretly. Take your child or leave it here at your sweet will.[121]

Not surprisingly, the orthodox in Poona 'went wild',[122] but, without naming the Phules, a Poona journal, *Dnyanaprakash*, wrote in 1871 of 'a benevolent gentleman' who had opened a house for sheltering orphans and pregnant widows.[123] Kashibai was one of the widows who went there for help, and her baby was adopted by the Phules.

At least some Brahmin voices were now willing to acknowledge that a Shudra and his wife were helping Brahmin widows in need, and willing also to support widow remarriage. They were bitterly opposed by a young man in his early twenties, Vishnushastri Chiplunkar (b. 1850), who defended the rule of the Peshwas, attacked Phule not only for his views but also for his language and grammar, and mocked him as 'a Shudra founder of a new religion' and 'a world teacher'.[124] Some critics called Phule's candid writings coarse as well, but earthiness in style was part of his message.

In any case, he and the SSS went ahead with their agenda. Marriages without Brahmin priests were performed by the SSS in December 1873 and May 1874. Talented non-Brahmins emerging from new universities were drawn to the SSS, including Dr Vishram Ramji Gholay, a surgeon. In 1875, on Phule's proposal, Gholay became the SSS president. The body now had 232 members.

This was the year when William Russsell Howard and Phule were geographically in the same place, for Russell had accompanied the Prince of Wales on a tour of India that included a day in Poona. We know that members of Phule's SSS sang songs in Poona in praise of the prince,[125] but there is no confirmation that Phule met either the prince or Russell.

Occurring in the late 1870s, the abortive revolt led by Vasudev Phadke created quite a stir in Poona and the neighbouring countryside. Though Phadke's bands included several Shudras and Ati-Shudras, Phule refused to cheer or condone Phadke. Soon Phule would stir up the countryside himself with the message of the SSS, urging peasants not to hire Brahmin priests and encouraging barbers to refuse to shave the heads of Brahmin widows. His calls were not instantly hailed, and Phule found that 'like the American slave' the Indian Shudra was apt at times to resist 'any attempt that may be made for his deliverance and fight even against his benefactor'.[126]

In another tract, *The Cultivator's Whipcord* (1883), Phule described Brahmin oppression, but also wrote on farming methods and rural sanitation, and said that if enough educated Shudras were not available, Britons, Muslims and other non-Brahmin Hindus should fill government positions in the countryside.[127]

In this book and in a later 1885 booklet, *Satsar* (Essence of Truth), Phule expressed 'joy at the defeat and discomfiture of Hindu reformers who could not retain Pandita Ramabai in Arya Dharma'.[128] He was referring to Ramabai, gifted daughter of a well-known Poona Brahmin, who had won attention first for her learning and eloquence and then, in 1883, for her conversion to Christianity. Those who had earlier praised Ramabai's gifts now attacked her as a feeble woman. Phule defended Ramabai's right to decide for herself but did not advocate conversion or embrace Christianity himself. Faith in God and human brotherhood seemed to be his religious belief and sensitivity towards poor children, untouchables and beggars, his religious practice.

Continuing to compose poems (*akhandas* as he called them), Phule sang the glory of Muhammad in one of them and said that Muhammad fought single-handedly for truth, bestowed equality on his followers, and rejected the notion of high and low.[129] Other poems included Marathi verses that a bridal pair could together recite at marriage ceremonies in lieu of Sanskrit verses pronounced by a priest but understood by no one.

The launch of the Indian National Congress did not excite Phule. The chief Poona constituent of the INC was the Sarvajanik Sabha, where Brahmins dominated. The story was not very different elsewhere. In September 1885, three months before the first session of the Congress, Ranade, the Sabha's leading light, and Phule had clashed over the caste system and the state of the peasantry. After the INC's opening session, Phule said that the Congress could become national only if it addressed the hardships of the peasants and the Dalits, and if it was 'formed of men of all religions'.[130]

Always looking for Mahar and Mang talent that he could encourage, Phule tried to combine Shudra and Ati-Shudra energies for a united non-Brahmin front. This impulse for non-Brahmin unity, and an allied resentment of Brahmin influence, come across from the will that Phule drew up in 1887, when he turned sixty. The will gave the fruits of Phule's estate to thirteen-year-old Yashwant, the adopted son. But if he became irresponsible, Savitri was to find a worthy Shudra boy who would then inherit the fruits of the estate, and who would be required to look after Mahars and Mangs. No Brahmin was to be allowed to touch Phule's dead body.[131]

This exclusionary will should be balanced by our knowledge of Phule's continuing friendship with individual Brahmins and their backing of his work. Through the will, he wished to demonstrate that key rites did not require a Brahmin presence.

Phule also travelled often to Bombay, where men from rural Maharashtra were finding work in mills. There, Phule joined in the exertions of a close friend and SSS colleague, Narayan Meghaji Lokhande, for a better deal for the millhands. Lokhande would later be called a pioneer of India's working-class movement, and it would be said that 'the Indian labour movement in its early stages was a branch or an offshoot of the Satya Shodhak Samaj.'[132]

Despite obstacles, including a legal challenge, marriages performed by the SSS were taking place in the countryside around Poona. In June 1887, Phule went to Talegaon village to perform a barber's wedding, which the area's priests tried to prevent. Angry at the priests' unsuccessful attempt, barbers in the area said they would not shave Brahmins anymore. Claiming that *they* had boycotted the barbers, the Brahmins barbered themselves for a while before pleading (successfully) for a return to earlier arrangements.

In the summer of 1888, leaders of Bombay's non-Brahmin communities discussed how to recognize Phule's sustained work for the lowly and decided that he should be formally called a Mahatma, or great soul. Four years earlier, we saw, people in Serampore (near Calcutta) had resolved to call Lord Ripon a

Mahatma. Now, in a ceremony in Bombay in May 1888, the son of a flower-grower was given that title. Two months later, Phule had a stroke. But he recovered sufficiently to write a final book, the *Satya-Dharma Pustaka* (Book of the Truth-Religion), which spoke of a God who is one, unknowable, unreachable, kind and just, of the human goals of gender equality and caste abolition, and of truth being a seeker's watchword.

During Jotiba's illness, Savitri managed his affairs. This was in accordance with his wish but in opposition to prevalent custom, which allowed a male relative but not the wife to take charge.

In February 1889, Yashwant, seventeen, was married in his father's presence to the twelve-year-old daughter of a non-Brahmin colleague. In January 1890, Sir Charles Sargent, Chief Justice of Bombay, ruled that marriages conducted by the SSS were valid. And in the summer that followed, the barbers of Bombay agreed not to shave the heads of widows.

On 28 November 1890, not long after tasting satisfaction and vindication, Jotiba Phule died. At the last rites, the pyre was lit by his adopted son Yashwant, who by birth was at least half a Brahmin.

VIDYASAGAR

In August 1858, when he was only thirty-eight (and the Revolt not yet fully suppressed), Vidyasagar quit his government jobs as the Sanskrit College principal and an inspector of Bengal's schools. The resignation was accepted, but Vidyasagar was asked to translate Victoria's Proclamation of November 1858, a service he was willing to render.

By this time, he had set up model public schools and a chain of girls' schools across Bengal. His resignation had nothing to do with the Revolt. He simply felt he was not receiving the respect or salary he deserved. 'My heart is not in my work,' he told his superior, W. Gordon Young, the director of public instruction.[133]

Part of Vidyasagar's heart was in his village, Birsingha, where he had established 'a free English school, a night school, a girls' school and a charitable dispensary'. Another part stayed close to Bengal's widows. Within a year of retirement, bearing all the expenses himself, he had arranged the marriages of fifteen widows.[134]

Occurring at about the same time, the death of his father's mother, who had taken care of him in childhood without ever upbraiding him, deeply shook this man. Friends admiring Vidyasagar's manliness seemed surprised.

The theatre had never attracted him, but Vidyasagar went again and again to see a play he had inspired, where a young widow confined to a tiny room forms an attachment for a young neighbour, becomes pregnant, confesses the fact, and commits suicide. Evidently, the vigorous man was in floods of tears each time he saw the drama.

When Harish Chunder Mukherjee died, Vidyasagar found a new editor and owner for the *Hindoo Patriot*. He also helped other Bengali and English journals and had a role in launching *Somprakas*, which 'attained the foremost place among the Bengali newspapers' of the time.[135] But the active man needed a full-time job. He asked the governor of Bengal for a professorship at Presidency College on the salary a European professor would draw, but was turned down.

In a future appraisal, Tagore would say that Vidyasagar's 'chief glory was neither compassion nor learning but his invincible manliness and his indelible humanity'.[136] Many had felt sorry for the Hindu widow but only Vidyasagar was forceful enough to fight for her. Identifying with humanity rather than only with Indians, not observing Hinduism's rites and forms and 'never seen to tell mantras or to worship a Hindu god or goddess', he yet refused to accept a second-class status for Indians. He freed his mind but held his head high.

Referring also to Vidyasagar's 'robust physique' and 'bold heart', the scholar Santosh Kumar Adhikari echoes Tagore's verdict by underlining the 'stubborn manliness' which enabled Vidyasagar 'to break the age-old walls of orthodox ritualism'.[137]

In both Vidyasagar and Phule, we have noticed self-respect, sympathy for the widow, openness to wisdom from non-Indian sources, and a critical assessment of Indian society. Both were sharply attacked. In a generally positive biography written a decade after Vidyasagar's death, Subal Chandra Mitra would nevertheless say that Vidyasagar had 'materially injured [and] disorganized Hindu society and Hindu religion' and claim that 'the whole Hindu community was disappointed in him'.[138]

Unlike Phule, who was seven years younger, Vidyasagar did not form an organization for changing Hindu society. He was content with wielding an individual's influence. Again unlike Phule, who seemed to believe in a merciful God, Vidyasagar often revealed an agnosticism which was sharply expressed in 1867, when the rains failed and many innocents in Bengal died of famine. Like Phule, however, Vidyasagar too was attacked for using 'indecent language'. Criticizing one of Vidyasagar's tracts against polygamy, Bankim wrote in his journal, *Bangadarshan*, 'We are crusading to purge Bengali literature of its obscene tendencies and hence have dared to condemn Vidyasagar. The language used . . . is unemployable in any discussions conducted by a society of *bhadralok* [gentlemen].'[139]

Yet the two, Vidyasagar and Phule, one in eastern India and the other in the west, had given Hindu society a long-missing ideal of social service. As was the case with Phule, stories of Vidyasagar's warmth for the needy of any background had spread far and wide, and he began to be called Dayasagar (ocean of mercy) as well.

In some important encounters, however, as with the governor over his wish to be a professor, rejection was Vidyasagar's fate, which the widely loved yet lonely man took with dignity and at times with caustic humour. 'Why should that man abuse me?' he asked once, adding, 'I have never done him a good turn.'[140] Less easy for him was the refusal of family members to accept his views. 'Incessant inhaling and exhaling of tobacco smoke' was apparently one way in which Vidyasagar expressed displeasure.[141] He was however (like Phule) a teetotaller and temperance advocate.

In 1864, during the period of the Civil War, Vidyasagar had cordial meetings in Calcutta with a Unitarian missionary from Boston, Charles Dall. We must assume that Lincoln and slavery came up—most American Unitarians were abolitionists—but we have no record of the conversations. Two years later, Mary Carpenter, whose father had hosted Rammohan Roy in Bristol, arrived in Calcutta and not only met Vidyasagar, but also nursed him after he was thrown off a buggy.

Vidyasagar's 'heart was always drawn', said K.C. Sen—the man who had helped produce that play about the widow, and who often visited Vidyasagar's home—to any 'spirited, amiable, kind, truthful and honest' person, be that person 'a Hindu, Brahmo, Christian or Mussalman', a 'native of his fatherland or of a foreign country'.[142]

Earnings from Vidyasagar's press and bookshop more than covered his and his family's needs, but appeals to his charity rarely failed, and he also paid several individuals he had personally hired to teach in girls' schools in different parts of Bengal. (These teachers were all men; training women to teach was an innovation for which even Vidyasagar was not ready.) The result was a debt that grew to Rs 50,000 until he cleared it, not long before his death.

One recipient of Vidyasagar's generosity was the brilliant poet and dramatist, Michael Madhusudan Dutt (1824–73), who had run short of money while in Paris in 1864. In a letter to Vidyasagar asking for help, Dutt wrote, 'The man to whom I have appealed has the genius and wisdom of an ancient sage, the energy of an Englishman, and the heart of a Bengali mother.'[143]

That heart quickly melted, but Dutt's poetry too had captured Vidyasagar, who sent Rs 6,000 to Dutt in Europe. Becoming a barrister in London two years later, Dutt wrote to his benefactor, 'You have saved me.' Dutt returned to Calcutta. Unable, however, to organize his life, he died a pauper in a charitable hospital in 1873. 'I can't help any more,' Vidyasagar had written to him a year earlier.[144]

Out of the Sanskrit College and barred from the Presidency College faculty, Vidyasagar was free to put his energy, in the 1860s and 1870s, into starting a new school—the Metropolitan Institution (MI), where pupils were taught in English. It grew quickly into India's first non-governmental college and won affiliation to Calcutta University. Between 1881 and 1892, the MI, for which Vidyasagar put up an impressive building with money he raised, produced 492 graduates and thirty-three postgraduates.

In 1869, two years after getting his daughter married, Vidyasagar left Birsingha, his village, for good. Flouting his word, its residents had gone ahead with a widow's marriage that he had initially blessed and then for some reason disapproved. He showed his displeasure by walking out of Birsingha. The following year saw a bitter family dispute over the marriage of his twenty-one-year-old son, Narayanchandra, with Bhavasundari, a sixteen-year-old Brahmin widow, who had been chosen by the son. What Vidyasagar's parents thought of this marriage is not known, but it is likely that they opposed it. We know for certain that his wife, Dinomayee, was against it, as also his brother, Sambhuchandra. The wife and the brother absented themselves from the event, which took place in Vidyasagar's Calcutta home. His parents probably kept themselves in Benares. Unfazed by the rejection, Vidyasagar wrote to his brother:

> I consider the inauguration of widow marriage into Hindu society the most virtuous deed of my life.[145]

~

In an earlier comment on the Indian National Congress, we noted its distance from India's peasant castes, Dalits and tribals, as well as Phule's argument that the INC would become 'national' only if it addressed their needs. Even as Phule tried to do his bit for the peasant and untouchable castes, Vidyasagar embraced the tribals.

He had befriended Santhals in Karmatar, a tribal town 80 or so miles to Calcutta's north-west, where, for a change from family tensions, he had bought a home in the 1870s. 'He fled to Santhal Parganas for peace. The simple cares and joys of the Santhals were balm to a world-weary soul. They had the free run of his house at Karmatar. He bought for them little presents and organized for them little feasts.'[146] Inevitably, the Karmatar home became also a school for Santhal youngsters. 'But the idyll did not last long. He ceased to visit Karmatar in the last years of his life.'[147]

In 1880, fourteen years before Bankim was similarly honoured, Vidyasagar was made a Companion in the Order of the Indian Empire. He was sixty at the time and 'the greatest Indian then living', in the assessment of Romesh Chunder Dutt, the author and historian who would preside over the INC in 1899.[148] Almost a century later, Bhabatosh Chatterjee, devoted compiler of a valuable Bankim volume, would similarly call Vidyasagar 'the greatest man of nineteenth-century Bengal'.[149]

He was, too, as we saw earlier, the author of the Bengali primer 'on which four generations and more have been brought up', a writer who 'drew his material from the Ramayana and the Mahabharata, from the works of Kalidasa as well as from Aesop's fables and from Shakespeare'.[150]

His mother died in 1871, his father in 1876, both finding their end, in fulfilment of an old Brahmin longing, in the holy city of Benares. Dinomayee, Vidyasagar's wife, died in 1888. By now, moreover, his son Narayanchandra, whose marriage to a widow had meant everything to the father, had managed to offend Vidyasagar sufficiently enough to be disinherited. However, in his last lonely days the father was loyally nursed by Narayanchandra, who after his father's death won a suit for Vidyasagar's assets. Occurring in 1891, Vidyasagar's death at the age of seventy-one seemed to sadden all in Calcutta, whether they were poor or rich, Hindu or non-Hindu, Indian or non-Indian.

PENULTIMATE THOUGHTS

The Vidyasagar Bridge across the Hooghly is today one of Calcutta's finest sights and blessings, Bankim's *Vande Mataram* is sung across India, Hume's Congress has endured, as has Sayyid Ahmed's university, and Phule remains an icon of political and social movements. These five are not, of course, our only links to the period when the Indian Revolt and the American Civil War occurred. Nor are they the only figures from their times to have influenced the India of our day.

If we have focussed more on them than on others—at the expense, regrettably, not only of remarkable individuals but also of a few crucial parts of India, like the South—that is largely because a book's size and a writer's range both have limits. Within those limits, however, it is hoped that these pages may have offered a flavour of an important part of India's story, and also America's, and of some connections between the two.

At the start of this chapter, it was suggested that India, or India and Britain taken together, had missed in the 1850s and 1860s a Lincoln-like figure reaching out to all sides and exploring, with some promise, a deeper meaning for the pain of 1857. None of our five may have been a Lincoln, yet each tried to discover a path forward for *his* people in an India stratified by caste, divided by religion, and ruled by aliens. The five did not quite agree, or remain consistent themselves, on who their people were. At one stage or another, even if not throughout their lives, all five seemed interested in Indians as a whole, with a few of them harbouring this interest throughout their lives.

In a 1927 piece entitled 'Lincoln in India', the American poet Vachel Lindsay would envision Abraham Lincoln on the banks of the Ganga in Benares, surrounded by a multitude of Brahmins, Kshatriyas, Vaishyas and Shudras, all gathered to anoint Lincoln as 'a great priest or chieftain of India'. 'He is a Brahmin,' the Brahmins assert. Each of three other castes also claims Lincoln as its own. Then the scavengers appear, 'the outcasts, the men from the dust of the dust, the servants of the lowest'. They are shouted at by the others, and dust is thrown on their heads.

Peace is restored when an old woman, 'worn and bowed', arrives. All make way for her, and the lanky Lincoln takes off his familiar hat and bows his head. Pointing to Lincoln, the old woman says to everyone, 'I am his mother. I was born in the dust ... He was born, with tears, in the dust.' At this, in a twinkling of an eye, the circles change, and the hierarchies disappear.[151]

By the time (September 1927) when Vachel Lindsay's piece was published in America, many thought that a Lincolnesque figure had in fact surfaced in India, someone confronting alien rule but also Indian flaws, someone eager to identify with all sides and especially with the lowest—and someone, moreover, who, referring in 1916 to untouchability, had said, in the spirit of the Second Inaugural:

Every affliction that we labour under in this sacred land is a fit and proper punishment for this great and indelible crime that we are committing.[152]

But Gandhi's story does not belong here. What belongs is the story of the Irishman with whom we began and with whom we will end.

RUSSELL

We may recall William Howard Russell leaving America in unpleasant mood in April 1962, three years before the end of the Civil War. Anti-Union editorials in *The Times* had provoked an intensification of attacks in the American press on Russell, who personally was pro-Union, as we know. No longer able to take the attacks, he sailed for home, even though editor Delane wanted him to stay on in America.

Back in London, he resumed editing the *Army and Navy Gazette*, before long also becoming the journal's owner, and clubbing with men like Thackeray, Dickens and Trollope. Russell's 'quick mind and ready tongue' made him a prized companion, with Thackeray saying that it was worth a guinea a day to have Russell dining at his table, and Trollope writing in his autobiography that among people he knew only one man, also an Irishman, who equalled Russell 'in the quickness and continuance of witty speech'.[153]

Overlooking his disobedience in America, *The Times* asked Russell to review special books or cover grand events and even arranged a pension for him. Shortly before the March 1863 wedding of Albert, the Prince of Wales, Delane sent a note to him: 'But you—you who wrote the Coronation at Moscow as never man wrote—don't you feel it is a duty to scribble the marriage of the Prince of Wales . . .?' The morning after the royal wedding thus found *The Times* carrying an eleven-column description by Russell of the Windsor Castle event.[154]

One of the scores of scenes from the event that Russell captured in his massive handwritten account was of old Palmerston, the Prime Minister, 'as he stepped up lightly into his seat, and looked round him with a brisk joviality, as if about to quell a troublesome member, or evade by a most voluminous reply an awkward question'.[155]

In two years, Palmerston and the man governing the large nation across the Atlantic would both die. In March 1863, the Gettysburg battle was about four months into the future. It is unlikely that either Palmerston or Russell guessed how history would compare the Empire's Prime Minister with his American contemporary. We can, however, recall Russell's graphic word portrait of Lincoln, done in 1861.

In August 1863, Russell covered the funeral of the general whose Indian campaign he had reported—Lord Clyde, formerly Sir Colin Campbell. And in 1865, after the Lincoln assassination, he again journeyed across the Atlantic. Although it lay as yet in the future, some by now could glimpse America's displacement of England and Europe at the top of the world.

Russell's purpose on this voyage, made on the *Great Eastern*, the world's biggest ship, was to describe for readers of *The Times* a bid from that ship to lay a cable across the ocean. Though that attempt failed, Russell's account, soon published also as a book called *The Atlantic Telegraph*, was a triumph; in a fresh bid made in the following year, the *Great Eastern* managed to lay the ocean cable.

It was on the *Great Eastern*, at the launch of the 1865 bid, that Russell first met Prince Albert, whose wedding he had documented two years earlier. The conversation led to a friendship that would last long, without always proving easy.

In 1866, Russell covered another war, this time on the European continent, where Prussia defeated Austria. His reporting stood out once more, but that was not the case a few years later during the Franco-Prussian War of 1870–71. Now fifty-one, Russell was no longer as energetic as before; other correspondents were better at using the cable; and readers preferred a new, more concise, style.

When Prince Albert went to India in 1875–76, Russell accompanied him as private secretary as well as a correspondent for *The Times*. Formal occasions, banquets and, above all, hunting filled the tour. Russell was required to take notes of every speech by the Prince. 'Not a natural courtier', Russell found it a strain to have to defer always to the Prince, who was apt to blame Russell for the tiniest misprint in *The Times*' accounts of the royal tour.[156]

Though even in 1875 it was 'a small world', India was large. We lack solid evidence of Russell running into any of our 'five'— Sayyid Ahmed, Vidyasagar, Hume, Phule, or Bankim—but we recognized, while viewing Phule's life, that he and Russell may at least have seen each other during the prince's Poona visit.

Russell's doubts about 'empiring', as he would call it, and about the British attitude to the world, had persisted. Thus he had noted in an 1868 diary entry that Delane, while a 'capital' human being, was 'a typical' man of the English middle class and 'very ferocious and foolish and narrow in his views' about Ireland.[157] On his 1875 visit to India, Russell found that British attitudes had 'changed little in the eighteen years since the Mutiny'. Towards the end of the tour, he wrote in his diary about the dignitary he was accompanying, 'It is much to be regretted that the Prince has never had a talk with a peasant. What a flood of light the ryot could have let in! He has never even spoken to a Baboo!'[158]

In 1879, after hearing that the British resident in Kabul had been killed by the Afghans, Russell would write:

> If we go on empiring it all over the world we must expect such startling news and deeds. And we are talking of a Burmese War and a Maori War! Queen Victoria's reign has been an incessant record of bloodshed.[159]

Mixing with the great and famous did not give Russell unalloyed or lasting satisfaction, but he enjoyed it. When Thackeray, who was a good friend, died in December 1863, it was a big blow. Even after the passage of two months, Russell would write, 'Never more will the world be to me as once it was. No, not with all the happiness of wife and children—or even if fame and fortune came instead of this dull drab inglorious struggle with the present which leaves no hope for the future.'[160]

Four years later, in 1867, Mary Russell, his wife, too died. Another friend, Charles Dickens, passed away in 1870, and Delane, perhaps Russell's greatest friend, died in 1880, three years after retiring from *The Times*. Russell was in South Africa at the time, reporting on the 1879–80 Zulu War, though he arrived after the main battle was over.

This was the last war that Russell, now sixty, would cover. Once more, his sympathies seemed to lie with the underdog. He had positive words for Cetewayo, the Zulu leader who dared to defy the British, and admiring words for Bishop John William Colenso, the white pastor advocating the Zulu cause.

When he was sixty-three, Russell married Countess Antoinette Malvezzi, a thirty-six-year-old Italian Catholic, in three ceremonies,

Catholic, Protestant and civil. Eleven years later, in 1895, Russell was knighted. By this time, young Mohandas Gandhi had completed a three-year course of law in London and was in South Africa. In 1900, Russell's German friend, Max Müller, died. Another German who entered our story, Karl Marx, had died much earlier, in 1883.

When the British fought the Dutch Boers in South Africa in 1900–01, Sir William Russell, now eighty and following the war from London, stayed true to his Irish bent and sympathized with the Boers. In 1901, Queen Victoria died and Russell's friend Albert became King Edward VII. Despite a surfeit of travelling, injuries, drinking and eating, Russell lived on, Antoinette looking after him, as also some of Russell's grandchildren, 'with practical devotion'.[161]

Having survived Phule, Vidyasagar, Bankim and Sayyid Ahmed, and also Lincoln, Marx and Victoria—but not Hume or Tolstoy—William Howard Russell, our guide to much of the nineteenth century, died in London in his Cromwell Road home on 10 February 1907, shortly before his eighty-seventh birthday.

NOTES

CHAPTER 1: BRITANNIA RULES THE WAVES

1. W. Baring Pemberton, *Lord Palmerston* (London: The Batchworth Press, 1954), p. 181.
2. HANSARD CXII [3d Ser.], pp. 380–444.
3. Pemberton also notes that British hearts were stirred 'wherever the British flag flew or a British merchantman sailed or British subjects foregathered in a foreign land'. See Pemberton, *Palmerston*, pp. 179–80.
4. Ibid., p. 167.
5. Ibid., p. x.
6. Ibid., p. 349.
7. Ibid., pp. 169–70.
8. Ibid., p. ix.
9. Alan Hankinson, *Man of Wars: William Howard Russell of* The Times (London: Heinemann, 1982), p. 21.
10. Ibid., pp. 1–2.
11. Karl Marx and Friedrich Engels, *Collected Works*, Volume 1, pp. 3–9. Accessed at http://www.marxists.org/archive/marx/works/cw/index.htm
12. Karl Marx, *Critique of Hegel's Philosophy of Right*, 1843.
13. Brian A. Hatcher, *Idioms of Improvement: Vidyasagar and Cultural Encounter in Bengal* (New Delhi: Oxford University Press, 1996), pp. 28–29.
14. Santosh Kumar Adhikari, *Vidyasagar and the Regeneration of Bengal* (Calcutta: Subarnarekha, 1980), p. 5.
15. Akshaykumar Maitreya in *Sirajuddowla* (Calcutta: 1898), quoted in Ranajit Guha, *An Indian Historiography* (Calcutta: K.P. Bagchi & Company, 1988), p. 54.
16. Hatcher, *Vidyasagar*, p. 48.
17. Ibid., p. 50.
18. Edward Said, *Orientalism* (New York: Vintage Books, 1979), pp. 123 ff., quoted in Hatcher, *Vidyasagar*, p. 50.

19. Hatcher, *Vidyasagar*, p. 193.
20. Ibid., pp. 178–79.
21. Foreword by Sibnarayan Ray in Subal Chandra Mitra, *Isvar Chandra Vidyasagar: The Story of his Life and Work*, reprint (Kolkata: Parul Prakashani, 2008; first ed., 1902).
22. See Penderel Moon, *The British Conquest and Dominion of India* (London: Duckworth, 1989), pp. 609–10.
23. See Elizabeth Kelly Gray, '"Whisper to him the word 'India'"': Trans-Atlantic Critics and American Slavery, 1830–1860', *Journal of the Early Republic* (Fall 2008), Philadelphia, pp. 384–88.
24. Quoted in Hatcher, *Vidyasagar*, p. 28.
25. Ibid., p. 42.
26. See article 'Ishwarchandra Vidyasagar' by M.K. Gandhi in *Collected Works of Mahatma Gandhi*, Vol. 4 (New Delhi: Publications Division, n.d.) pp. 411–14. The article was first published in *Indian Opinion* (Durban, South Africa) on 16 September 1905.
27. Adhikari, *Vidyasagar*, p. 77.
28. Hatcher, *Vidyasagar*, p. 95.
29. Ibid., pp. 104–05.
30. Ibid., p. 97.
31. Ibid., pp. 6, 168–70.
32. See article by William Radice in Manik Mukhopadhyay (ed.), *The Golden Book of Vidyasagar* (Calcutta: All Bengal Vidyasagar Death Centenary Committee, 1993), p. 194.
33. Mukhopadhyay (ed.), *The Golden Book of Vidyasagar*, p. 201.
34. Hatcher, *Vidyasagar*, p. 101.
35. Ibid., pp. 268–74.
36. Vidyasagar made this comment in 1859. Quoted in Ibid., p. 112.
37. William Howard Russell, *My Diary in India, in the year 1858–9*, Vol. 2 (London: Routledge, Warne, and Routledge, 1860), p. 49.
38. http://www.cyberamu.com/ulc/sirsyed.php
39. William Wedderburn, *Allan Octavian Hume: Father of the Indian National Congress, 1829–1912* (London: T. Fisher Unwin, 1913), p. 5.
40. Maratha: (1) Someone from Maharashtra; (2) belonging to a Marathi-speaking peasant caste.
41. Dhananjay Keer, *Mahatma Jotirao Phooley: Father of Our Social Revolution* (Bombay: Popular Prakashan, 1964), pp. 4–7.
42. Rajmohan Gandhi, *Revenge & Reconciliation: Understanding South Asian History* (New Delhi: Penguin, 1999), p. 125.
43. Pratul Chandra Gupta, *Nana Sahib and the Rising at Cawnpore* (Oxford: Clarendon Press, 1963), p. 2.

44. Keer, *Phooley*, p. 13.
45. Ibid., pp. 13–14.
46. Ibid., pp. 15, 17.
47. Jotirao Phule, *Slavery*, translated by P.G. Patil, included in *Collected Works of Mahatma Jotirao Phule*, Vol. 1 (Bombay: Department of Education, Government of Maharashtra, 1991), pp. 57–9.
48. Phule, *Slavery*, p.58.
49. Keer, *Phooley*, p. 23.
50. Ibid., p. 23.
51. The *Bombay Guardian*, 16 December 1853, quoted in Keer, *Phooley*, p. 27.
52. Keer, *Phooley*, p. 26.
53. Ibid., p. 35.
54. Garry Wills, *Lincoln at Gettysburg: The Words that Remade America* (New York: Touchstone, 1992), pp. 177–78.
55. Henry David Thoreau, *Journal*, Vol. 2, General editor, John Broderick (Princeton: Princeton University Press, 1981), p. 371.
56. Quoted in the lead editorial, *New York Times*, 7 December 2007, p. A30.
57. Thoreau, *Journal*, Vol. 2, p. 371.
58. Winston S. Churchill, *A History of the English-Speaking Peoples*, Vol. 4: *The Great Democracies* (New York: Dodd, Mead and Company, 1954), p. 150.
59. Ibid., p. 151.
60. Ibid., p. 150.
61. Ibid., p. 152.
62. Ibid., pp. 150–51.
63. In the 1850s in the American South, 'Yankee', originally a term for a resident of New England, usually meant anyone from the North.
64. Churchill, *A History*, p. 155.
65. Wills, *Gettysburg*, p. 132.
66. Ibid., p. 123.
67. Ibid., p. 179.
68. Churchill, *A History*, p. 155.
69. See article by Francis C. Assisi in *Span* (New Delhi), May–June 2007, pp. 6–7.
70. From a report citing the *Asiatic Journal* in the *Mechanics' Magazine: Museum, Register, Journal, and Gazette* (UK), No. 661, 9 April 1836.
71. Susan Bean, *Yankee India: American Commercial and Cultural Encounters with India in the Age of Sail, 1784–1860* (Salem, MA: Peabody Essex Museum, and Ahmedabad: Mapin, 2001), p. 11.

72. Charles Dickens, *American Notes*, Ch. 6.
73. Gray, 'Whisper to him the word "India"', p. 389.
74. Ibid., p. 391.
75. Hankinson, *Russell*, p. 42.
76. Ibid., pp. 42–43.
77. Ibid., p. 44.
78. Ibid., p. 46.
79. Ibid., pp. 71–72.
80. Ibid., p. 83.
81. Ibid., p. 84.
82. Ibid., p. 84.
83. Ibid., p. 104.
84. Ibid., p. 54.
85. Ibid., p. 99.
86. Ibid., pp. 100–01.
87. Romain Rolland, *Tolstoy*, translated by Bernard Miall (New York: E.P. Dutton, 1910), pp. 59–60.
88. Ibid., pp. 60–62.
89. Ibid., p. 63.
90. Hankinson, *Russell*, pp. 110–11.
91. Ibid., p. 110.
92. Ibid., p. 109.
93. Quoted in Bean, *Yankee India*, p. 255.
94. Christopher Hibbert, *The Great Mutiny: India 1857* (London: Penguin, 1980), p. 378.
95. Gupta, *Nana Sahib*, p. 25.
96. William Howard Russell, *My Diary in India, in the year 1858–9*, Vol. 1 (London: Routledge, Warne, and Routledge, 1860), pp. 165–67.
97. Russell, *Diary in India*, Vol. 1, pp. 167–68.
98. Hibbert, *Mutiny*, p. 218.
99. Ibid., p. 49.
100. See Churchill, *A History*, Vol. 4, p. 83.
101. Ibid., p. 81.
102. Hibbert, *Mutiny*, p. 24.
103. Russell, *Diary in India*, Vol. 1, p. 130.
104. Gautam Chattopadhyay in Mukhopadhyay (ed.), *The Golden Book of Vidyasagar*, pp. 229–30.
105. Benoy Ghose in *Studies in the Bengal Renaissance* (Kolkata: National Council of Education), p. 46.
106. S.R. Mehrotra, *The Emergence of the Indian National Congress* (New Delhi: Vikas, 1971), p. 89.

107. Benoy Ghose, *Bengal Renaissance*, p. 42.
108. Rajmohan Gandhi, *Understanding the Muslim Mind* (New Delhi: Penguin, 1987), p. 22.
109. See William Dalrymple, *The Last Mughal: The Fall of a Dynasty, Delhi, 1857* (New Delhi: Penguin, 2007), pp. 129–30. Dalrymple cites Hali's story as from Ralph Russell and Khurshidul Islam (eds and trans), *Ghalib: Life and Letters* (London: George Allen and Unwin, 1969), p. 63.
110. Dalrymple, *Last Mughal*, p. 61.
111. Ibid., p. 75.
112. Ibid.
113. Wedderburn, *Hume*, p. 16.
114. Ibid., pp. 16–17.
115. Phule, *Slavery*, pp. 66–67.
116. Keer, *Phooley*, pp. 74–75.
117. Ibid., p. 41.
118. Howard Zinn, *A People's History of the United States: 1492– Present* (New York: Harper, 1995), p. 171.
119. Orville Vernon Burton, *The Age of Lincoln* (New York: Hill and Wang, 2007), p. 70.
120. David Herbert Donald, *Lincoln* (London: Jonathan Cape, 1995), pp. 176–7.
121. Donald, *Lincoln*, p. 166.
122. Ibid.
123. Burton, *Age of Lincoln*, p. 65.
124. Ibid., p. 96.
125. Wills, *Gettysburg*, p. 114.
126. Burton, *Age of Lincoln*, p. 70.
127. Zinn, *History*, p. 179.
128. Quoted in Gray, 'Whisper to him the word "India"', p. 393.
129. Ibid., p. 392.
130. Pemberton, *Palmerston*, p. 247.
131. Ibid., p. 248.
132. Ibid., p. 249.
133. Ibid.

CHAPTER 2: GALLOPING FURY

1. Leo Tolstoy, *War and Peace*, translated by Aylmer Maude (New York: W.W. Norton, 1996), pp. 1371–72.
2. Thomas Frost, 'Complete Narrative of the Mutiny in India,' *Quarterly Review*, 102 (October 1857), Art. VIII, pp. 534–70; http://www.victorianweb.org/history/empire/1857/qr1.html

3. Governor General Canning is quoted stating that the fears regarding the grease 'were well founded' in Rudrangshu Mukherjee, *Mangal Pandey: Brave Martyr or Accidental Hero?* (New Delhi: Penguin, 2005), p. 35. Also cited by William Dalrymple, *Last Mughal*, p. 134.

4. Frost, 'Complete Narrative', pp. 534–70.

5. Ibid.

6. See Ibid., and Hibbert, *Great Mutiny*, p. 69.

7. Quoted in Mehrotra, *Emergence*, p. 96.

8. Ibid., p. 97.

9. George Bruce Malleson, *The Indian Mutiny of 1857* (New York: Scribner and Welford, 1891), p. 146.

10. Frost, 'Complete Narrative', pp. 534–70.

11. Ibid.

12. Andrew Major, *Return to Empire: Punjab Under the Sikhs and the British in the Mid-Nineteenth Century* (New Delhi: Sterling, 1996), p. 188.

13. Montgomery quoted in Major, *Return to Empire*, p. 183.

14. George Dodd, *The History of the Indian Revolt and of the Expeditions to Persia, China, and Japan, 1856–7–8* (London: W. and R. Chambers, 1859), p. 199.

15. Kevin Hobson, 'The British Press and the Indian Mutiny', posted at http://www.britishempire.co.uk/article/mutinypress.htm

16. Pemberton, *Palmerston*, pp. 249–50.

17. Ibid., pp. 249–50.

18. Ibid., p. 251.

19. Russell, *Diary in India*, Vol. 1, p. 66.

20. Quote by Metcalfe's friend Charles Saunders, cited in Dalrymple, *Last Mughal*, p. 234.

21. Dodd, *Indian Revolt*, p. 243.

22. Dalrymple, *Last Mughal*, pp. 228–29.

23. Sayyid Ahmed Khan, 'Chapter 4: Bijnor' in http://www.columbia.edu/itc/mealac/pritchett/00litlinks/lit_colonial.html

24. Ibid.

25. Ibid.

26. Ibid.

27. Wedderburn, *Hume*, p. 9.

28. Ibid., p. 73.

29. Malleson, *Indian Mutiny*, p. 145.

30. Quoted in Dodd, *Indian Revolt*, p. 294.

31. Gupta, *Nana Sahib*, p. 123.

32. Ibid., p. 6.

33. Report of a Mr Court, a Kanpur magistrate before the mutiny, cited in Gupta, *Nana Sahib*, p. 7.
34. Russell, *Diary in India*, Vol. 1, pp.193–94.
35. Ibid., p. 168.
36. Malleson, *Indian Mutiny*, p. 131.
37. Ibid., p. 129.
38. Gupta, *Nana Sahib*, p. 53.
39. Hibbert, *Great Mutiny*, p. 176; Gupta, *Nana Sahib*, pp. 68–72.
40. Gupta, *Nana Sahib*, p. 81.
41. Hibbert, *Great Mutiny*, p. 177.
42. Gupta, *Nana Sahib*, p. 70.
43. Britons quoted in Ibid., p. 69.
44. Malleson, *Indian Mutiny*, p. 129.
45. Hibbert, *Great Mutiny*, p. 180.
46. Ibid., p. 180.
47. Gupta, *Nana Sahib*, p. 101.
48. Ibid., p. 102.
49. Gupta, largely quoting Mowbray Thomson, *Nana Sahib*, pp. 108–11.
50. Malleson, *Indian Mutiny*, p. 174.
51. Gupta, *Nana Sahib*, p. 140.
52. Ibid., pp.118–19.
53. Order to Subedar Bandu Singh, quoted in Ibid., p. 119.
54. 'Synopsis of the Evidence of the Cawnpore Mutiny' in 'Depositions at Cawnpore' (Calcutta, n.d.), cited in Rudrangshu Mukherjee, 'Satan Let Loose', *Past and Present*, 128 (1990), p. 107.
55. Mukherjee, 'Satan Let Loose', p. 107, citing, Shepherd, 'Personal Narrative of the Outbreak and Massacre at Cawnpore, Lucknow, 1879, p. 42.
56. Mukherjee, 'Satan Let Loose', p. 128, citing Trevelyan, *Cawnpore*, London, 1865, p. 141.
57. Gupta, *Nana Sahib*, p. 129.
58. Asoka Mehta, *1857: The Great Rebellion* (Bombay: Hind Kitabs, 1945), pp. 48–49.
59. Canning, 19 June, 1857, quoted in Darshan Perusek, 'Subaltern Consciousness and the Historiography of the Indian Rebellion of 1857', *Novel* (Spring 1992), pp. 289–90, citing T.R. Metcalfe, *The Aftermath of Revolt: India 1857–80* (Princeton, NJ, 1965), p. 49.
60. Mukherjee, 'Satan Let Loose', p. 111, citing Kaye, *History of the Sepoy War*, ii, pp. 269–70.
61. Ibid., p. 112.
62. Gupta, *Nana Sahib*, p. 138.

63. Ibid., pp. 85–87.
64. Hibbert, *Great Mutiny*, p. 210.
65. Ibid., pp. 210–12.
66. Gupta, *Nana Sahib*, p. 149.
67. Hibbert, *Great Mutiny*, pp. 210–12.
68. Ibid., p. 212.
69. *New Englander*, New Haven, Vol. XVIII, May 1859, p. 363.
70. Rudrangshu Mukerhjee, *Awadh in Revolt: 1857–58* (New Delhi: Oxford University Press, 1984), p. 67, citing statement in secret British files by Ranjit Singh Bissein, intelligence agent.
71. Dodd, *Indian Revolt*, p. 244.
72. Ibid., p. 259.
73. Hibbert, *Great Mutiny*, 366.
74. Dodd, *Indian Revolt*, p. 317.
75. Hibbert, *Great Mutiny*, p. 237.
76. Dodd, *Indian Revolt*, p. 322.
77. Ibid.
78. Ibid.
79. Ibid.
80. Ibid., p. 323.
81. Ibid., p. 324.
82. Hibbert, *Great Mutiny*, p. 252.
83. Ibid.
84. Dodd, *Indian Revolt*, p. 333.
85. Blair B. Kling, *The Blue Mutiny* (Calcutta: Firma KLM, 1977), p. 61.
86. Gupta, *Nana Sahib*, p. 121.
87. Ibid.
88. Dodd, *Indian Revolt*, p. 289.
89. Ibid., pp. 264–65.
90. Russell, *Diary in India*, Vol. 1, p. 155.
91. Dodd, *Indian Revolt*, pp. 264–65.
92. Gupta, *Nana Sahib*, p. 121.
93. Dodd, *Indian Revolt*, p. 265.
94. Ibid., p. 217.
95. Ibid., p. 214.
96. Hibbert, *Great Mutiny*, p. 165.
97. Letter of 11 December 1857 quoted in Barbara English, 'The Kanpur Massacres in India and the Revolt of 1857', *Past and Present*, 142 (February 1994), p. 175, citing Public Record Office, London, 30/29/21/4.
98. Sumanta Banerjee, *The Parlour and the Streets: Elite and Popular*

Culture in Nineteenth Century Calcutta (Calcutta: Seagull Books, 1989), p. 229.

99. Banerjee, *The Parlour and the Streets*, pp. 145–46.
100. Smarajit Chakraborti, *The Bengali Press, 1818–1868: A Study in the Growth of Public Opinion* (Calcutta: Firma KLM, 1976), p. 125.
101. Mitra, *Vidyasagar*, pp. 218–19.
102. Bhabatosh Chatterjee (ed.), *Bankimchandra Chatterjee: Essays in Perspective* (New Delhi: Sahitya Akademi, 1994), p. lxviii.
103. Bimanbehari Majumdar, *History of Political Thought From Rammohun to Dayananda, 1821–84*, Vol. 1 (Calcutta: University of Calcutta, 1934), p. 452.
104. Bankimchandra Chatterjee, *Anandamath*, tr. by Aurobindo Ghose and Barindra Ghose (Calcutta: Basumati Sahitya Mandir, before October 1947), p. 33.
105. Quoted in Mehrotra, *Emergence*, p. 101.
106. Dodd, *Indian Revolt*, p. 244.
107. Dalrymple, *Last Mughal*, p. 303.
108. Frederic Cooper, *Crisis in the Punjab from the 10th of May until the Fall of Delhi* (London: Smith, Elder, 1858; Lahore: H. Gregory, 1858. Reprint by Sang-e-Meel Publications, Lahore 2005), p. 100.
109. Hibbert, *Great Mutiny*, pp. 277–79.
110. Dodd, *Indian Revolt*, p. 301.
111. Hibbert, *Great Mutiny*, p. 309.
112. Dodd, *Indian Revolt*, p. 310.
113. Ibid., p. 312.
114. Ibid., p. 313.
115. Quoted in Wayne G. Broehl, *Crisis of the Raj: The Revolt of 1857 through British Lieutenants' Eyes* (Hanover: University Press of New England, 1986), p. 113.
116. Hibbert, *Great Mutiny*, p. 316.
117. Penderel Moon, *British Conquest*, p. 731.
118. Ibid., p. 731.
119. Dodd, *Indian Revolt*, p. 311.
120. Cecil Woodham-Smith, *Queen Victoria: From her Birth to the Death of the Prince Consort* (New York: Knopf, 1972), pp. 384, 467.
121. Dalrymple, *Last Mughal*, pp. 414–15.
122. Dodd, *Indian Revolt*, p. 312.
123. Dalrymple, *Last Mughal*, pp. 220–21.
124. See 'The Battle for Delhi' by Madhu Prasad in *People's Democracy*, New Delhi, 12 August 2007.

125. From Khwaja Hasan Nizami's *The Agony of Delhi*, translated from the Urdu by A. Sattar Kapadia, posted on www.kapadia.com/TheMutinyinDelhi.html
126. Prasad, 'The Battle for Delhi'.
127. Hibbert, *Great Mutiny*, p. 379.
128. Ibid., p. 127.
129. Ibid., p. 127.
130. Ibid., p. 211.
131. Ibid., p. 123.
132. John Pemble, *The Raj, the Indian Mutiny and the Kingdom of Oudh: 1801–1859* (New Delhi: Oxford University Press, 1977), p. 180.
133. Hibbert, *Great Mutiny*, p. 361.
134. Broehl, *Crisis of the Raj*, p. 283.
135. Keer, *Phooley*, p. 77.
136. Phule, *Gulamgiri*, p. 67.
137. Ibid., p. 59.
138. Ibid., p. 67.
139. Hibbert, *Great Mutiny*, p. 341.
140. Outram's statements, quoted in Dodd, *Indian Revolt*, p. 539.
141. From Benoy Ghose (ed.), *Selections from English Periodicals of 19th-Century Bengal*, Vol. 4 (Calcutta: Papyrus, 1979), p. 196.

CHAPTER 3: 'HALF-DEVIL AND HALF-CHILD'

1. Hobson, 'The British Press', p. 3
2. Letter to Miss Burdett Coutts, quoted in Graham Story and Kathleen Tillotson (eds), *The Letters of Charles Dickens*, Volume 8: 1856–58 (Oxford: Clarendon Press, 1995), pp. 458–60.
3. Letter of 23 October 1857 from Dickens to Emile de la Rue in Story and Tillotson (eds), *The Letters of Charles Dickens*, Volume 8: pp. 471–74.
4. Pemberton, *Palmerston*, p. 251.
5. Hobson, 'The British Press', p. 2.
6. Quoted by Karl Marx, *New York Tribune*, 14 August 1857 (Marx-Engels electronic archive).
7. Hobson, 'The British Press', p. 2.
8. Pemberton, *Palmerston*, p. 251.
9. Quoted in Hobson, 'The British Press', p. 7.
10. See Dan Randall, 'Autumn 1857: The Making of the Indian "Mutiny"', *Victorian Literature and Culture* (2003), Cambridge University Press, p. 10.

11. Randall, 'Autumn 1857', p. 3.
12. *The Times*, London, 8 October 1857, quoted in Randall, 'Autumn 1857', p. 14.
13. http://www.spurgeon.org/sermons/0154.htm
14. See Randall, 'Autumn 1857', p. 10.
15. Ibid., p. 11.
16. Ibid., p. 12.
17. Randall's conclusion in 'Autumn 1857', p. 10.
18. *Marx and Engels Collected Works*, Vol. 40, p. 82. www.marxists.org/archive/marx/index.htm
19. All quotes from the Marx-Engels Archive, www.marxists.org/archive/marx/index.htm.
20. Woodham-Smith, *Queen Victoria*, p. 385.
21. See Randall, 'Autumn 1857', p. 9.
22. Letter of 21 November 1857 to the President of the Board of Control, Canning Papers, cited in Peter Hardy, *The Muslims of British India* (London: Cambridge University Press, 1972), pp. 71–72.
23. Hankinson, *Russell*, p. 117.
24. Philadelphia's *Princeton Review* quoted in Gray, 'Whisper to him the word "India"', p. 395.
25. David Mosler, 'American newspaper opinion on the Sepoy Mutiny, 1857–58', *Australian Journalism Review*, 14: 1 (January–June 1992), pp. 78–87.
26. Mosler, 'American newspaper opinion', pp. 78–87.
27. 'British India', *The Atlantic Monthly*, Volume 1, No. 1 (November 1857), pp. 85–93. http://www.theatlantic.com/issues/1857nov/britind.htm
28. Ibid.
29. *The New Englander*, Vol. XVI (February 1858), p. 100.
30. See Gray, 'Whisper to him the word "India"', p. 404; and also C. Vann Woodward (ed.), *Mary Chesnut's Civil War* (New Haven: Yale University Press, 1981), p. 409.
31. Quoted in Gray, 'Whisper to him the word "India"', p. 398.
32. John W. Blassingame (ed.), *Letters of Frederick Douglass*, Series One, Volume 3: 1855–63 (New Haven: Yale, 1985), p. 203.
33. Theodore Calvin Pease and James G. Randall (eds), *The Diary of Orville Hickman Browning*, Vol. 1, 1850–1864 (Springfield, IL: Illinois State Historical Library, 1925), pp. 309–317.
34. Hankinson, *Russell*, pp. 119–20.
35. Ibid., p. 122.
36. Ibid., p. 123.

37. Ibid., p. 125.
38. Ibid., p. 126.
39. Ibid., p. 127.
40. Ibid.
41. Ibid.
42. Hibbert, *Great Mutiny*, p. 361.
43. Hankinson, *Russell*, p. 128.
44. Ibid., p. 128.
45. Ibid., p. 132.
46. Ibid., pp. 132–33.
47. Ibid., p. 134.
48. Dalrymple, *Last Mughal*, p. 443.
49. What a gift Russell has for observation, description, language, imagination, history, irony, sympathy and realism, all at one and the same time!
50. Diary of 15 June, Hankinson, *Russell*, p. 134.
51. Gupta, *Nana Sahib*, pp. 158–59.
52. Hibbert, *Great Mutiny*, p. 385.
53. Dodd, *Indian Revolt*, p. 508.
54. Diary entry for 10 July 1858, in Hankinson, *Russell*, p. 135.
55. Hankinson, *Russell*, p. 135.
56. Ibid., p. 135.
57. Ibid., p. 136.
58. Ibid.
59. Ibid., p. 137.
60. Woodham-Smith, *Queen Victoria*, p. 385.
61. Ibid., pp. 385–86.
62. *The Annual Register, 1859*, edited by Edmund Burke, published by Rivingtons, 1860. Digitized edition by Google, pp. 203–05.
63. Hankinson, *Russell*, pp. 141–42.
64. Hibbert, *Great Mutiny*, pp. 385–86.
65. Gupta, citing official British records, in *Nana Sahib*, pp. 118–19.
66. Hibbert, *Great Mutiny*, p. 386.
67. Gupta, *Nana Sahib*, pp. 172–73.
68. Ibid., pp. 172–76.
69. Proclamation 'Printed at Bareilly, by Shaiek Nisar Ally, under the supervision of Moulvie Mahomed Kootoob Shah', cited in Dodd, *Indian Revolt*, p. 411.
70. Wedderburn, *Hume*, p. 134.
71. Ibid., pp. 14–15.
72. http://etawah.nic.in/history3.htm
73. Wedderburn, *Hume*, pp. 17–19.

74. http://www.columbia.edu/itc/mealac/pritchett/00litlinks/
    lit_colonial.html
75. Ibid.
76. Ibid.
77. Mosler, 'American newspaper opinion', pp. 78–87.
78. *New Englander*, New Haven, Connecticut, Vol. XVI (February
    1858), pp. 100–42.
79. *North American Review*, Boston, Vol. LXXXVI (April 1858),
    pp. 487–515.
80. Mark Twain, *Following the Equator*, (Hartford, CT: American
    Publishing Company, 1897).
81. Quoted in Mehrotra, *Emergence*, p. 103.
82. Hibbert *Great Mutiny*, pp. 389–91.
83. Pemble, *The Raj*, pp. 247–48.
84. Hankinson, *Russell*, pp. 142–43.
85. Charles Wood, Secretary of State for India, to Viceroy Canning, 8
    April 1861, Wood Papers, cited in Mehrotra, *Emergence*, p. 105.
86. Letter of 21 November 1857 to the President of the Board of
    Control, Canning Papers, cited in Hardy, *The Muslims of British
    India*, p. 72.
87. Mitra, *Vidyasagar*, p. 227.
88. Churchill, *A History*, p. 84.
89. *Friend of India*, 30 March 1865, quoted in Benoy Ghose (ed.),
    Selections from English Periodicals, Vol. 4, p. 67.

CHAPTER 4: LINCOLN'S RISE TO POWER

1. Donald, *Lincoln*, p. 209.
2. Burton, *Age of Lincoln*, pp. 82–83.
3. Ibid., pp. 90–91.
4. Donald, *Lincoln*, p. 235.
5. All the preceding debate quotes from http://www.nps.gov/archive/
   liho/debates.htm
6. Donald, *Lincoln*, pp. 228–29.
7. Burton, *Age of Lincoln*, p. 81.
8. Ibid., p. 82.
9. Ibid., pp. 94–96.
10. Ibid.
11. Thoreau, 'A Plea for Captain John Brown,' 30 October 1859,
    Concord, Mass.
12. Donald, *Lincoln*, p. 239.

13. Burton, *Age of Lincoln*, p. 96.
14. Gray, 'Whisper to him the word "India"', p. 399.
15. Burton, *Age of Lincoln*, pp. 140–41.
16. Donald, *Lincoln*, p. 238.
17. Ibid., p. 239.
18. Speech at Hartford, CT, 5 March 1860, included in *Complete Works of Abraham Lincoln*, Vol. 4 (Rutgers, New Jersey: Rutgers University Press, 1953–90), p. 5.
19. James M. McPherson, *Battle Cry of Freedom* (New York: Oxford University Press, 1988), pp. 232–33.
20. Churchill, *A History*, p. 164.
21. Ibid., p. 166.
22. Eddie (Edward), who died before he was four.
23. Donald, *Lincoln*, p. 273; and entry dated 11 Feb 1861 on http://www.thelincolnlog.org/view
24. Donald, *Lincoln*, p. 271.
25. Ibid., pp. 276–77.
26. Burton, *Age of Lincoln*, p. 118.
27. Donald, *Lincoln*, p. 280.
28. Ibid.
29. Ibid., p. 284.
30. Ibid., p. 269.
31. Hankinson, *Russell*, p. 155.
32. Ibid., p. 156.
33. Ibid., p. 155.
34. Morris's written words quoted in Ibid., p. 155.
35. Hankinson, Russell, p. 156.
36. Ibid.
37. Ibid., pp. 151, 157.
38. Ibid., p. 154.
39. Ibid., p. 156.

CHAPTER 5: AMERICA SHEDS ITS BLOOD

1. All quotes so far in this chapter are from Hankinson, *Russell*, p. 157.
2. Hankinson, *Russell*, p. 158.
3. Ibid.
4. Ibid.
5. Ibid., pp. 158–60.
6. Donald, *Lincoln*, p. 287.
7. Ibid., p. 293.

8. Ibid., p. 288.
9. Churchill, *A History*, p. 168.
10. Hankinson, *Russell*, p. 160.
11. Ibid., p. 161.
12. Ibid.
13. Pemberton, *Palmerston*, pp. 301–02.
14. Donald, *Lincoln*, pp. 289–90.
15. Quote inclusive of parenthetical remark in Pemberton, *Palmerston*, p. 302.
16. Minister not named, in Pemberton, *Palmerston*, p. 302.
17. Hankinson, *Russell*, p. 161.
18. Ibid., pp. 161–62.
19. Ibid., p. 162.
20. Ibid., p. 163.
21. Ibid., pp.163–64.
22. Ibid., p. 165.
23. Churchill, *A History*, p. 173.
24. Joel Parker, *The Domestic and Foreign Relations of the United States* (Cambridge, MA: Welch, Bigelow and Company, 1862), pp. 6, 40–41.
25. Churchill, *A History*, p. 182.
26. Donald, *Lincoln*, p. 304.
27. Churchill, *A History*, p. 171.
28. Ibid., p. 172.
29. Russell's report in *The Times* of 6 August 1861, quoted in Hankinson, *Russell*, pp. 167–68.
30. Churchill, *A History*, pp. 179–80.
31. Ibid., p. 179.
32. Pemberton, *Palmerston*, p. 302.
33. Quotes from Russell's account of Bull Run and of reactions to it are from Hankinson, *Russell*, pp. 167–70.
34. Hankinson, *Russell*, p. 171.
35. Churchill, *A History*, p. 180.
36. Donald, *Lincoln*, pp. 319–20.
37. Ibid., p. 317.
38. Ibid., pp. 312–13.
39. Pemberton, *Palmerston*, pp. 300, 306.
40. Palmerston's words, quoted in Pemberton, *Palmerston*, pp. 306–07.
41. Hankinson, *Russell*, p. 175.
42. Pemberton, *Palmerston*, p. 307.
43. Hankinson, *Russell*, p. 175.

44. Ibid., pp. 180–82.
45. Donald, *Lincoln*, p. 336.
46. Burton, *Age of Lincoln*, p. 154.
47. Donald, *Lincoln*, p. 351.
48. See article 'South Asians fought in US Civil War!' by Francis C. Assisi and Elizabeth Pothen, http://www.indolink.com/displayArticleS.php?id=091405073900
49. Donald, *Lincoln*, p. 363.
50. See Ibid., pp. 368–69.
51. Churchill, *A History*, p. 217.
52. Donald, *Lincoln*, pp. 392–93.
53. Ibid., p. 394.
54. Ibid., p. 387.
55. Ibid.
56. Ibid., p. 386.
57. Ibid., p. 383.
58. *Harper's Weekly*, New York, 12 September 1863.
59. Churchill, *A History*, p. 181.
60. Ibid., pp. 181, 217.
61. Ibid., p. 217.
62. Burton, *Age of Lincoln*, p. 163.
63. Donald, *Lincoln*, p. 399.
64. Ibid.
65. Ibid., pp. 403–05.
66. Letter of 26 January 1863, http://www.thelincolnlog.org/view/1863/1/26
67. Burton, *Age of Lincoln*, p. 182.
68. Ibid.
69. Donald, *Lincoln*, p. 471.
70. Quoted in Wayne Broehl, *Crisis of the Raj*, p. 215.
71. Burton, *Age of Lincoln*, p. 183.
72. Ibid.
73. Donald, *Lincoln*, p. 447.
74. Ibid., p. 460.
75. Ibid.
76. Wills, *Gettysburg*, p. 79.
77. Ibid., p. 44.
78. Ibid., pp. 213, 247.
79. Ibid., pp. 50–51.
80. Donald, *Lincoln*, p. 464.
81. Wills, *Gettysburg*, p. 47.
82. Donald, *Lincoln*, pp. 465–66.

83. Ibid., p. 540.
84. Ibid.
85. Ibid., p. 474.
86. Ibid., p. 475.
87. Grant, quoted in Wills, *Gettysburg*, p. 178.
88. Donald, *Lincoln*, p. 500.
89. Remark by Thurlow Weed, quoted in Ibid., p. 528.
90. Donald, *Lincoln*, p. 489.
91. Ibid., pp. 501–02.
92. Ibid., p. 522.
93. Ibid., p. 523.
94. Ibid., pp. 526–27.
95. Ibid., p. 524.
96. Churchill, *A History*, p. 215.
97. Donald, *Lincoln*, p. 514.
98. Ibid., pp. 525–26.
99. Ibid., p. 529.
100. Ibid., p. 530.
101. Ibid., p. 531.
102. Ibid., p. 547.
103. Churchill, *A History*, p. 258.
104. Donald, *Lincoln*, p. 556.
105. Ibid., p. 554.
106. Churchill, *A History*, p. 262.
107. Donald, *Lincoln*, p. 568.
108. Quoted in Elton Trueblood, *Abraham Lincoln: Theologian of American Anguish* (New York: Harper & Row, 1973), p. 126.
109. Wills, *Gettysburg*, p. 183.
110. Donald, *Lincoln*, p. 568.
111. Burton, *Age of Lincoln*, p. 190.
112. Ibid., pp. 190–91.
113. Quoted in Churchill, *A History*, pp. 261–62.
114. Donald, *Lincoln*, p. 586.
115. Ibid., p. 571.
116. Ibid., p. 589.

CHAPTER 6: CONNECTIONS

1. G. Bhagat, *Americans in India, 1784–1860* (New York: NYU Press, 1970), p. 98. Bhagat quotes a dispatch dated 13 January 1865 from the vice consul in Bombay to the Secretary of State; Bombay Despatches II, National Archives, Washington DC.

2. Bean, *Yankee India*, p. 211.
3. Gray, 'Whisper to him the word "India"', p. 403.
4. Henry Mead, *The Sepoy Revolt: Its Causes and Its Consequences* (London: John Murray, 1857), p. 27.
5. Banerjee, *The Parlour and the Streets*, p. 167.
6. M.V.S. Koteswara Rao. *Communist Parties and United Front—Experience in Kerala and West Bengal* (Hyderabad: Prajasakti Book House, 2003), p. 103.
7. Rolland, *Tolstoy*, pp. 71–73.
8. Ibid., p. 76.
9. Ibid., pp. 76–77.
10. Ibid., p. 75.
11. Ibid., p. 84.
12. Pietro Citati, *Tolstoy*, translated by Raymond Rosenthal (New York: Schocken, 1986), p. 193.
13. Rolland, *Tolstoy*, p. 114.
14. Ibid., p. 135.
15. Ibid., p. 149.
16. Ibid., p. 259.
17. Edward Baker Greenwood, *Tolstoy: The Comprehensive Vision* (New York: St Martin's Press, 1975), p. 29.
18. Leo Tolstoy, *Bethink Yourselves!*, translated by V.G. Chertkov (Boston: Ginn and Company, 1904), posted on http://www.gutenberg.org/etext/27189
19. Doris Kearns Goodwin, *Team of Rivals: The Political Genius of Abraham Lincoln* (New York: Simon & Schuster, 2005), pp. 747–48, citing the *New York World* of 7 February 1908.
20. *Indian Opinion*, Phoenix, Natal, South Africa, 25 December 1909, reproduced in *Collected Works of Mahatma Gandhi*, Vol. 10 (New Delhi: Publications Division, n.d.), p. 244.
21. *Indian Opinion*, 26 August 1905, reproduced in *Collected Works of Mahatma Gandhi*, Vol. 4 (New Delhi: Publications Division, n.d.), pp. 393–95.
22. Bhabatosh Chatterjee (ed.), *Bankimchandra Chatterjee*, p. 13.
23. Ibid., pp. 579–87.
24. Ibid., p. lii.
25. Quoted in Ranajit Guha, *An Indian Historiography* (Calcutta: Bagchi, 1988), pp. 65–66.
26. Quoted in Chakraborti, *The Bengal Press*, p. 179.
27. Chatterjee (ed.), *Bankimchandra Chatterjee*, p. lii.
28. Unsigned article in *Encyclopaedia Britannica*, 1910, reproduced in Ibid., pp. 607–08.

29. Sibnarayan Ray, quoted in Chatterjee (ed), *Bankimchandra Chatterjee*, p. 212.
30. Chatterjee (ed.), *Bankimchandra Chatterjee*, p. 163.
31. Sibnarayan Ray, quoted in ibid., p. 212.
32. Chatterjee (ed.), *Bankimchandra Chatterjee*, p. xxix.
33. Quoted from 'The Bengali Peasant', first published in *Bangadarsan* and later included in part in *Samya*, published in 1879. Quoted in ibid., p. 216.
34. Translation by Bhabatosh Chatterjee, in Chatterjee (ed), *Bankimchandra Chatterjee*, p. lii.
35. Chatterjee (ed.), *Bankimchandra Chatterjee*, pp. lv–lvii.
36. Gray, 'Whisper to him the word "India"', p. 389.
37. Kling, *The Blue Mutiny*, p. 110.
38. Ibid., pp. 121–22.
39. See comment by *Somprakas* in Chakraborti, *The Bengal Press*, p. 146.
40. Afterword by Meenakshi Mukherjee in Bankimchandra Chatterjee, *Rajmohan's Wife* (New Delhi: Ravi Dayal, 1996), p. 145.
41. Chatterjee (ed.), *Bankimchandra Chatterjee*, p. lxv.
42. Quoted in Mitra, *Vidyasagar*, pp. 180–81.
43. Chatterjee (ed.), *Bankimchandra Chatterjee*, p. liv.
44. Sukhamoy Mukherjee, quoted in Chatterjee (ed.), *Bankimchandra Chatterjee*, p. 237.
45. Earlier we had seen a conversation in Simla between Russell and an Indian where the Indian referred to Britons as monkeys. We do not know if Bankim was aware of Russell's account, which would have been available in Calcutta in the 1860s and 1870s.
46. Rezaul Karim quoted in Sabyasachi Bhattacharya, *Vande Mataram: The Biography of a Song* (New Delhi: Penguin Books, 2003), p. 15.
47. Sibnarayan Ray, quoted in Chatterjee (ed.), *Bankimchandra Chatterjee*, p. 217.
48. Ibid.
49. Ibid., p. 219.
50. Bhabatosh Chatterjee, in Chatterjee (ed.), *Bankimchandra*, p. xlii.
51. George F.I. Graham, *The Life and Work of Sir Syed Ahmed Khan* (London, 1885, Reprinted), p. 53.
52. Ibid., pp. 56–57.
53. Ibid., pp. 59–62.
54. Sheikh Mohamad Ikram, *Modern Muslim India and the Birth of Pakistan* (Lahore: Institute of Islamic Culture, 1970), p. 32.
55. Ramesh Rawat, quoted in Shireen Moosvi (ed.), *1857: Facets of the Great Revolt* (New Delhi: Tulika Books, 2008), pp. 128–30.

56. Ibid., pp. 128–30.
57. Pran Nevile (compiler), *The Tribune, 125 years: An Anthology, 1881–2006* (New Delhi: Hay House, 2008).
58. Introduction by Zaituna Umer in Graham, *Sir Syed*, p. xvii.
59. Graham, *Sir Syed*, p. 41.
60. Ibid., p. 79.
61. Letter of 15 October 1869, quoted in Graham, *Sir Syed*, p. 132.
62. Mehrotra, *The Emergence*, p. 109.
63. Mohammed Mujeeb, *The Indian Muslims* (London: George Allen and Unwin, 1967), p. 451.
64. *Sir Syed Ahmed on the Present State of Indian Politics, Consisting of Speeches and Letters Reprinted from the 'Pioneer'* (Allahabad: The Pioneer Press, 1888), pp. 1–24. The modern facsimile version of this work has been published by Sang-e-Meel Publications, Lahore in 1982, translator unknown. 'Nation' has been corrected to 'qaum' (community), the word actually used by Sayyid Ahmed. Both quotations from http://www.columbia.edu/itc/mealac/pritchett/00fwp/
65. *Sir Syed Ahmed on the Present State of Indian Politics*, pp. 29–53. 'Nation' has been corrected to 'qaum' (community), the word actually used by Sayyid Ahmed. Quotation from http://www.columbia.edu/itc/mealac/pritchett/00fwp/
66. Quoted in Shan Muhammad, *Sir Syed* (Meerut: Meenakshi, 1969), pp. 147–48.
67. Ibid., p. 151.
68. Ibid., p. 162.
69. Christian Troll, *Sayyid Ahmed Khan: Reinterpretation of Muslim Theology* (New Delhi: Vikas, 1978), p. 332.
70. Mujeeb, *Indian Muslims*, p. 449.
71. Troll, *Sayyid Ahmed*, p. 221.
72. Hafeez Malik, *Moslem Nationalism in India and Pakistan* (Washington DC: Public Affairs Press, 1963), p. 196.
73. Wedderburn, *Hume*, p. 42.
74. Ibid.
75. Mehrotra, *Emergence*, p. 321.
76. Ibid., p. 311.
77. Ibid., pp. 311–12.
78. Wedderburn, *Hume*, p. 48.
79. Ibid., p. 48.
80. Ibid., p. 47.
81. Mehrotra, *Emergence*, p. 310.
82. Wedderburn, *Hume*, p. 46.

83. Ibid., pp. 46–47.
84. Ibid., p. 81.
85. Mehrotra, *Emergence*, p. 381.
86. *Bengalee*, 27 May 1882, quoted in Ibid., p. 318.
87. Letter of 9 January 1883, quoted in Mehrotra, *Emergence*, p. 306.
88. Mehrotra, *Emergence*, p. 315.
89. Ibid., p. 342.
90. Comment in *Indian Spectator*, 11 March 1883, quoted in Mehrotra, *Emergence*, p. 350.
91. Quoted in Mehrotra, *Emergence*, pp. 354–55.
92. Letter of 23 May 1883, quoted in Mehrotra, *Emergence*, p. 381.
93. Mehrotra, *Emergence*, pp. 355–56.
94. Ibid., p. 344.
95. Letter of 26 March 1883 to W.E. Forster, quoted in Ibid., p. 345.
96. Mehrotra, *Emergence*, p. 376.
97. Ibid., p. 389.
98. Ibid., pp. 381–82.
99. Ibid., p. 385.
100. Ibid., p. 382.
101. *Pioneer*, 12 and 22 June 1885, in Ibid., p. 396.
102. Mehrotra, *Emergence*, pp. 400–01.
103. Ibid., p. 402.
104. Ibid., pp. 411, 415.
105. Ibid., pp. 413, 417.
106. Ibid., p. 417.
107. Ibid., pp. 419–20.
108. Wedderburn, *Hume*, p. 66.
109. Ibid., pp. 72–73.
110. Ibid., p. 76.
111. Ibid., p. 67.
112. John R. McLane, *Indian Nationalism and the Early Congress* (Princeton, N.J.: Princeton University Press, 1977), p. 121.
113. McLane, *Indian Nationalism*, p. 121.
114. Mehrotra, *Emergence*, p. 312.
115. Keer, *Jotirao Phooley*, p. 111.
116. From facsimile of Dedication reprinted in *Slavery*, translated by P.G. Patil and included in *Collected Works of Mahatma Jotirao Phule*, Vol. 1 (Bombay: Education Department, Govt. of Maharashtra, 1991), p. xv.
117. Patil (tr.), *Slavery*, p. xlv.
118. Ibid., pp. 70–72.
119. Ibid., p. xlv.

120. Keer, *Phooley*, p. 120.
121. Ibid., p. 85.
122. Ibid., p. 86.
123. Ibid., p. 95.
124. Ibid., p. 144.
125. Ibid., p. 139.
126. Patil (tr.), *Slavery*, p. xxxv.
127. Keer, *Phooley*, p. 187.
128. Ibid., p. 191.
129. Ibid., p. 215.
130. Ibid., pp. 219–21.
131. Ibid., p. 226.
132. Ibid., p. 194.
133. Mitra, *Vidyasagar*, p. 220.
134. Ibid., pp. 227, 234.
135. Chakraborti, *The Bengali Press*, p. 139.
136. Tagore, quoted by Hiren Mukherjee in Manik Mukhopadhyay (ed.), *The Golden Book of Vidyasagar*, p. 165.
137. Adhikari, *Vidyasagar*, p. 23.
138. Mitra, *Vidyasagar*, pp. 394, 442.
139. Quoted in Tapati Gupta (ed.), *Bankimchandra's Bangadarshan: Selected Essays in Translation* (Kolkata: Das Gupta & Co., 2007), p. 107.
140. Mukhopadhyay (ed.), *The Golden Book of Vidyasagar*, p. 234.
141. Mitra, *Vidyasagar*, p. 346.
142. Ibid., p. 359.
143. Letter of 2 September 1864 in Ibid., p. 223.
144. Mukhopadhyay (ed.), *The Golden Book of Vidyasagar*, p. 254.
145. Mitra, *Vidyasagar*, p. 354.
146. Amales Tripathi, *Vidyasagar: The Traditional Modernizer* (Calcutta: Orient Longman, 1974), pp. 93–94.
147. Ibid.
148. Foreword to Mitra, *Vidyasagar*, p. xxiv.
149. Chatterjee (ed.), *Bankimchandra Chatterjee*, p. 591 ff.
150. Hiren Mukerjee in Mukhopadhyay (ed.), *The Golden Book of Vidyasagar*, p. 163.
151. Vachel Lindsay, 'A Vision called "Lincoln in India"', *The English Journal* (September 1927), pp. 508–09.
152. Remark by Mohandas Gandhi on 16 February 1916, quoted in *Collected Works of Mahatma Gandhi*, Vol. 13 (New Delhi: Publications Division, n.d.), pp. 232–33.
153. Hankinson, *Russell*, p. 185.

154. Ibid., p. 188.
155. Ibid., p. 189.
156. Ibid., p. 236.
157. Ibid., p. 203.
158. Ibid., p. 235.
159. Russell's diary entry for 26 September 1879, quoted in Ibid., p. 247.
160. Hankinson, *Russell*, p. 186.
161. Ibid., p. 266.

BIBLIOGRAPHY

Adhikari, Santosh Kumar, *Vidyasagar and the Regeneration of Bengal* (Calcutta: Subarnarekha, 1980).

Bagal, Jogesh Chandra (ed.), *Bankim Rachnavali* (Calcutta: Sahitya Samsad, 1969).

Bandopadhyay, Pranab, *Pandit Ishwar Chandra Vidyasagar: The Compassionate Educationist* (Calcutta: Anglia Paperbacks, 1988).

Banerjee, Sumanta, *The Parlour and the Streets: Elite and Popular Culture in Nineteenth Century Calcutta* (Calcutta: Seagull Books, 1989).

Bean, Susan, *Yankee India: American Commercial and Cultural Encounters with India in the Age of Sail, 1784–1860* (Salem, MA: Peabody Essex Museum and Ahmedabad: Mapin, 2001).

Bhagat, G., *Americans in India, 1784–1860* (New York: NYU Press, 1970).

Bhattacharya, Sabyasachi, *Vande Mataram: The Biography of a Song* (New Delhi: Penguin, 2003).

Blassingame, John W. (ed.), *Letters of Frederick Douglass*, Series One, Vol. III: 1855–63 (New Haven: Yale, 1985).

Broehl, Wayne G., *Crisis of the Raj: The Revolt of 1857 through British Lieutenants' Eyes* (Hanover: University Press of New England, 1986).

Burton, Orville Vernon, *The Age of Lincoln* (New York: Hill and Wang, 2007).

Chakraborti, Smarajit, *The Bengal Press, 1818–1868: A Study in the Growth of Public Opinion* (Calcutta: Firma KLM, 1976).

Chandra, Bipan, *India's Struggle for Independence* (New Delhi: Penguin, 2001).

Chatterjee, Bankimchandra, *Anandamath*, translated by Aurobindo Ghose and Barindra Ghose (Calcutta: Basumati Sahitya Mandir, published before October 1947).

——, *Rajmohan's Wife: A Novel* (Delhi: Ravi Dayal Publisher, 1996).

Chatterjee, Bhabatosh (ed.), *Bankimchandra Chatterjee: Essays in Perspective* (New Delhi: Sahitya Akademi, 1994).

Churchill, Winston S., *A History of the English-Speaking Peoples*, Vol. IV: *The Great Democracies* (New York: Dodd, Mead and Company, 1954).

Citati, Pietro, *Tolstoy*, translated by Raymond Rosenthal (New York: Schocken Books, 1986).

Complete Works of Abraham Lincoln, Vol. 4 (Rutgers, New Jersey: Rutgers University Press, 1953–90).

Cooper, Frederic, *The Crisis in the Punjab, from the 10ᵗʰ of May until the Fall of Delhi* (London: Smith, Elder, 1858; Lahore: H. Gregory, 1858. Reprint by Sang-e-Meel Publications, Lahore, 2005).

Dalrymple, William, *The Last Mughal: The Fall of a Dynasty, Delhi, 1857* (New Delhi: Penguin, 2007).

Darrow, Clarence and Arthur Morrow Lewis, *Marx versus Tolstoy* (Chicago: Charles H. Kerr & Company, 1911).

Dodd, George, *The History of the Indian Revolt and of the Expeditions to Persia, China, and Japan, 1856–7–8* (London: W and R. Chambers, 1859).

Donald, David Herbert, Lincoln (New York: Jonathan Cape, 1995).

Elton Trueblood, *Abraham Lincoln: Theologian of American Anguish* (New York: Harper & Row, 1973).

English, Barbara, 'The Kanpur Massacres in India and the Revolt of 1857', *Past and Present*, No. 142 (February 1994).

Frost, Thomas, 'Complete Narrative of the Mutiny in India,' *Quarterly Review*, No. 102 (October 1857); http://www.victorianweb.org/history/empire/1857/qr1.html

Gandhi, Rajmohan, *Revenge & Reconciliation: Understanding South Asian History* (New Delhi: Penguin, 1999).

——, *Understanding the Muslim Mind* (New Delhi: Penguin, 1987).

Ghose, Aurobindo, *Bankim Chandra Chatterjee* (Pondicherry: Sri Aurobindo Ashram, 1965).

——, *Bankim—Tilak—Dayananda* (Calcutta: Arya Publishing House, 1947).

Ghose, Benoy, *Studies in the Bengal Renaissance* (Calcutta: National Council of Education, Year of Publication Unknown).

—— (ed.), *Selections from English Periodicals in 19ᵗʰ-Century Bengal*, Vols. 4 and 6 (Calcutta: Papyrus, 1979 and 1981).

Goodwin, Doris Kearns, *Team of Rivals: The Political Genius of Abraham Lincoln* (New York: Simon & Schuster, 2005).

Graham, George F.I., *The Life and Work of Sir Syed Ahmed Khan*, reprint (London: Publisher Unknown, 1885).

Gray, Elizabeth Kelly, '"Whisper to him the word 'India'"': Trans-Atlantic Critics and American Slavery, 1830–1860', *Journal of the Early Republic* (Fall 2008).

Greenwood, Edward Baker, *Tolstoy: The Comprehensive Vision* (New York: St Martin's Press, 1975).

Guha, Arabinda (ed.), *Unpublished Letters of Vidyasagar* (Calcutta: Published by Reba Guha, Year of Publication Unknown).

Guha, Ranajit, *An Indian Historiography* (Calcutta: K.P. Bagchi & Company, 1988).

——, *An Indian Historiography* (Calcutta: K.P. Bagchi & Company, 1988).

Gupta, Pratul Chandra, *Nana Sahib and the Rising at Cawnpore* (Oxford: Clarendon Press, 1963).

Gupta, Tapati (ed.), *Bankimchandra's Bangadarshan: Selected Essays in Translation* (Kolkata: Das Gupta & Co. Pvt. Ltd, 2007).

Hankinson, Alan, *Man of Wars: William Howard Russell of* The Times (London: Heinemann, 1982).

Hardy, Peter, *The Muslims of British India* (London: Cambridge University Press, 1972).

Hatcher, Brian A., *Idioms of Improvement: Vidyasagar and Cultural Encounter in Bengal* (New Delhi: Oxford University Press, 1996).

Herder, Hans, *Bankimchandra Chattopadhyay's Srimadbhagavadgita* (New Delhi: Manohar, 2001).

Hibbert, Christopher, *The Great Mutiny: India 1857* (London: Penguin, 1980).

Hobson, Kevin, 'The British Press and the Indian Mutiny', http://www.edunltd.com/empire/article/mutinypress.htm

Ikram, Sheikh Mohamad, *Modern Muslim India and the Birth of Pakistan* (Lahore: Institute of Islamic Culture, 1970).

Keer, Dhananjay, *Mahatma Jotirao Phooley: Father of Our Social Revolution* (Bombay: Popular Prakashan, 1964).

Kling, Blair B., *The Blue Mutiny* (Calcutta: Firma KLM, 1977).

Lindsay, Vachel, 'A Vision called "Lincoln in India"', *The English Journal* (September 1927).

Lipner, Julius J., 'Re-translating Bankim Chatterji's *Ananda Math*,' *IIC Quarterly* (Summer 2003).

Maitreya, Akshaykumar, *Sirajuddowla* (Calcutta: Publisher Unknown, 1898)

Major, Andrew, *Return to Empire: Punjab under the Sikhs and the British in the Mid-Nineteenth Century* (New Delhi: Sterling, 1996).

Majumdar, Bimanbehari, *History of Political Thought From Rammohun to Dayananda, 1821–84*, Vol. 1 (Calcutta: University of Calcutta, 1934).

Malik, Hafeez, *Moslem Nationalism in India and Pakistan* (Washington DC: Public Affairs Press, 1963).

Malleson, George Bruce, *The Indian Mutiny of 1857* (New York: Scribner and Welford, 1891).

Marx, Karl and Friedrich Engels, *Collected Works*, http://www.marxists.org/archive/marx/works/cw/index.htm

McLane, John R., *Indian Nationalism and the Early Congress* (Princeton, N.J.: Princeton University Press, 1977).

McPherson, James M., *Battle Cry of Freedom* (New York: Oxford University Press, 1988).

Mead, Henry, *The Sepoy Revolt: Its Causes and Its Consequences* (London: John Murray, 1857).

Mehrotra, S.R., *The Emergence of the Indian National Congress* (New Delhi: Vikas, 1971).

Mehta, Asoka, *1857: The Great Rebellion* (Bombay: Hind Kitabs, 1946).

Mitra, Subal Chandra, *Isvar Chandra Vidyasagar: The Story of his Life and Work* (Reprint, Kolkata: Parul Prakashani, 2008, with introduction by R.C. Dutt; first published in 1902).

Moon, Penderel, *The British Conquest and Dominion of India* (London: Duckworth, 1989).

Moosvi, Shireen (ed.), *1857: Facets of the Great Revolt* (New Delhi: Tulika, 2008).

Mosler, David, 'American newspaper opinion on the Sepoy Mutiny, 1857–58', *Australian Journalism Review*, Vol. 14, No. 1 (January–June 1992).

Muhammad, Shan, *Sir Syed* (Meerut: Meenakshi, 1969).

Mujeeb, Mohammed, *The Indian Muslims* (London: George Allen and Unwin, 1967).

Mukerhjee, Rudrangshu, *Awadh in Revolt: 1857–58* (New Delhi: Oxford University Press, 1984).

——, 'Satan Let Loose', *Past and Present*, No. 128 (1990).

——, *Mangal Pandey: Brave Martyr or Accidental Hero?* (New Delhi: Penguin, 2005).

Mukherjee, Meenakshi, 'Afterword' in Bankimchandra Chatterjee, *Rajmohan's Wife* (New Delhi: Ravi Dayal, 1996).

Mukhopadhyay, Manik (ed.), *The Golden Book of Vidyasagar* (Calcutta: All Bengal Vidyasagar Death Centenary Committee, 1993).

Nevile, Pran (compiler), *The Tribune, 125 Years: An Anthology, 1881–2006* (New Delhi: Hayhouse, 2008).

Parker, Joel, *The Domestic and Foreign Relations of the United States* (Cambridge, MA: Welch, Bigelow and Company, 1862).

Pease, Theodore Calvin and James G. Randall (eds), *The Diary of Orville*

Hickman Browning, Vol. I: 1850–1864 (Springfield, IL: Illinois State Historical Library, 1925).

Pemberton, W. Baring, *Lord Palmerston* (London: The Batchworth Press, 1954).

Pemble, John, *The Raj, the Indian Mutiny and the Kingdom of Oudh: 1801–1859* (New Delhi: Oxford University Press, 1977).

Perusek, Darshan, 'Subaltern Consciousness and the Historiography of the Indian Rebellion of 1857', *Novel* (Spring 1992).

Phule, Jotirao Govindrao, *Slavery*, translated by P.G. Patil, in *Collected Works of Mahatma Jotirao Phule*, Vol. 1, (Bombay: Education Department, Government of Maharashtra, 1991).

Prasad, Madhu, 'The Battle for Delhi', *People's Democracy* (12 August 2007).

Randall, Dan, 'Autumn 1857: The Making of the Indian "Mutiny"', *Victorian Literature and Culture* (2003), Cambridge University Press.

Rao, M.V.S. Koteswara, *Communist Parties and United Front—Experience in Kerala and West Bengal* (Hyderabad: Prajasakti Book House, 2003).

Rolland, Romain, Tolstoy, translated by Bernard Miall (New York: E.P. Dutton, 1910).

Russell, William Howard, *My Diary in India, in the year 1858–9*, Vols. I and II (London: Routledge, Warne, and Routledge, 1860).

Said, Edward, *Orientalism* (New York: Vintage Books, 1979).

Sarkar, Indira, *Social Thought in Bengal, 1757–1947* (Calcutta: Oriental Book Agency, 1949).

Sarkar, Tanika, *Bankim Chandra and the Impossibility of a Political Agenda: a Predicament for Nineteenth Century Bengal* (New Delhi: Centre for Contemporary Studies, Nehru Memorial Museum and Library, 1993).

Sir Syed Ahmed on the Present State of Indian Politics, Consisting of Speeches and Letters Reprinted from the 'Pioneer' (Allahabad: The Pioneer Press, 1888).

Story, Graham and Kathleen Tillotson (eds), *The Letters of Charles Dickens*, Vol. 8, 1856–58 (Oxford: Clarendon Press, 1995).

Thoreau, Henry David, *Journal*, General editor, John Broderick, several volumes (Princeton: Princeton University Press, 1981).

Tolstoy, Leo, *War and Peace*, translated by Aylmer Maude (New York: W.W. Norton, 1996).

——, *Bethink Yourselves!*, translated by V.G. Chertkov (Boston: Ginn and Company, 1904), posted on http://www.gutenburg.org/etext/27189

Tripathi, Amales, *Vidyasagar: The Traditional Modernizer* (Calcutta: Orient Longman, 1974).

Troll, Christian, *Sayyid Ahmed Khan: Reinterpretation of Muslim Theology* (New Delhi: Vikas, 1978).

Vann Woodward, C. (ed.), *Mary Chesnut's Civil War* (New Haven: Yale University Press, 1981).

Wedderburn, William, *Allan Octavian Hume: Father of the Indian National Congress, 1829–1912* (London: T. Fisher Unwin, 1913).

Wills, Garry, *Lincoln at Gettysburg: The Words that Remade America* (New York: Touchstone, 1992).

Woodham-Smith, Cecil, *Queen Victoria: From her Birth to the Death of the Prince Consort* (New York: Knopf, 1972).

Zinn, Howard, *A People's History of the United States: 1492–Present* (New York: Harper, 1995).

INDEX